Napoleon and His Marshals

Napoleon and His Marshals
The Men of the First Empire

J. T. Headley

Napoleon and His Marshals: the Men of the First Empire
by J. T. Headley

Published by Leonaur Ltd

Text in this form copyright © 2007 Leonaur Ltd

ISBN: 978-1-84677-367-9 (hardcover)
ISBN: 978-1-84677-368-6 (softcover)

http://www.leonaur.com

Publisher's Note
The opinions expressed in this book are those of the author and are not necessarily those of the publisher.

Contents

Preface	7
Napoleon Bonaparte	13
Marshal Berthier	53
Marshal Augereau	69
Marshal Davoust	91
Marshal St. Cyr	113
Marshal Lannes	139
Marshal Moncey	167
Marshal Macdonald	183
Marshal Mortier	209
Marshal Soult	229
Marshal Murat	259
Marshal Lefebvre	287
Marshal Massena	301
Marshal Marmont	331
Marshal Victor	349
Marshal Brune	365
Marshal Oudinot	375
Marshal Bessieres	393
Marshal Jourdan	409
Marshal Bernadotte	421
Marshal Suchet	437
Marshal Poniatowski	459
Marshal Grouchy	469
Marshal Ney	483

Preface

My chief design in the following work has been to group together and illustrate the distinguished men Bonaparte gathered around him, and with whom he obtained and held the vast power he wielded. The mighty genius of Napoleon has so overshadowed all those beneath him that they have not received their due praise, nor their proper place in history. Their merits have been considered mere reflections of his; and to one intellect and one arm is attributed the vast results they accomplished. But with weak men Napoleon never could have unsettled Europe, and founded and maintained his Empire. The Marshals who led his armies, and governed his conquered provinces, were men of native strength and genius; and as they stand grouped around their mighty chief, they form a circle of military leaders, the like of whom the world has never at one time beheld. To show what these men were unfold their true characters and illustrate their great qualities, it was necessary to describe the battles in which they were engaged. A man is illustrated by his works; if an author, by his books if a politician, by his civil acts and speeches of a ruler, by his administration of public affairs, and if a military man, by his campaigns and battles. To mention merely the actions in which a military man has been engaged, and the victories he won, without describing the manner in which they were conducted, and the genius which gained them, is like illustrating an author by giving a list of his works, or a ruler by naming over the measures he suggested or carried out.

In different circumstances the same talent develops itself differently, and the intellect of France during Bonaparte's career found its proper sphere on the battle-field. The Revolution broke down all the ancient barriers of privilege and left an open field to intellect and genius; but that field, just then, was a military one. Crowds rushed upon it; the strong to win renown, and the weak to sink. The Marshals of France were the first fruits of that freedom. It was not animal courage, nor mere brute force, that measured itself against the intellect of the world, and came off victorious. Our opinions respecting these men have been as erroneous and unjust as they well could be, for they have been regarded merely as ambitious warriors, storming over battle-fields for glory. We forget that they were stern republicans adopting the cause of the people in the darkest hour of France, and knew well for what they were fighting. True, they were not religious men, nor the best representation of patriots in their moral character. But we do not hesitate to honour those rough and severe characters who fought so bravely for freedom in our own revolutionary struggle. Our naval commanders in the last war were not patterns of moral men, but they were of heroes and patriots. Ethan Allen is honoured none the less as a patriot because be was an infidel, while the charge of French infidelity destroys all our sympathy for French republicans. The protracted struggle which those men carried on so triumphantly, they knew perfectly well to be that of liberty against despotism equal rights against privileges. They knew also they were waging a defensive war, and on every great battle-field on which they met their foes, they felt that France was the mighty stake at issue. Instead of being reckless men, wading through blood to power, there are but few juster struggles than those in which they won their laurels; and yet Americans, who never weary of hanging wreaths around the tombs of their successful military leaders, look with an unsympathizing eye on those brave men who fought for the same rights, and to resist the same aggressions.

I have endeavoured also in this work to correct, as far as possible, the erroneous impressions that prevail respecting Napoleon, and the wars he carried on; and to clear his character from the aspersions of English historians, and the slanders of his enemies.

Another design has been to group together some of the most striking events of that dramatic period when Napoleon was marching his victorious armies over Europe. Many of the battle-fields I have described I have visited in person, and hence been able to recall the scenes enacted upon them more vividly than I otherwise could have done.

I am aware that some may object to books of this kind, as fostering the spirit of war, by stimulating the love of glory. But in the first place, if history is to be abjured whenever it treats of battles, it will be reduced to a very small compass, and our revolutionary struggle will pass into utter forgetfulness. I know of no war, of ancient or modern times, more calculated to stimulate the heart of youth to warlike deeds than the history of the two struggles through which we have passed. Besides, the same objection would repudiate most of the Old Testament, and make the heroes which the pen of inspiration delineated with such graphic power, curses of their race. The truth is, war waged for principle is the same as that carried on by the direct command of Heaven, and the woe and suffering that attend it present no more objection to it, than the unmeasured suffering occasioned by sickness and death throughout the world, reflect on the justice or mercy of God. Wars may be prosecuted in a better spirit than those in which the Marshals of France were first engaged; yet they were not only waged against tyranny, as was our own revolutionary war; but, unlike the latter, could not be helped for they were purely defensive.

In the second place, we need not fear the effect of stimulating too much the love of glory in this age of dollars and cents. It is amusing to even sensible men discoursing, in laudatory terms, of the reign of commerce, as bringing about a universal peace, when the only danger of war among the great civilized nations of the earth is found in the rivalry and jealousy of this very spirit of commerce and trade. England deluges India in blood for the sake of commerce, while our last war grew out of her invasions of the rights of commerce. Colonial possessions are sought and obtained for this very purpose; and it is only a few years since we were on the verge of a war with Great Britain, for a narrow strip of territory, which was valuable to her only as a channel of communication with her provinces, which she holds for their commercial importance. And even now the country is alarmed with the prospect of a collision for a wild and desolate tract on the Pacific Ocean, which England wishes to retain solely as a channel of trade. Men of peace are straining every nerve to destroy the love of glory in our youth, while every war among civilized nations, probably for the next century, will be waged to secure the privileges of commerce. Cupidity, not love of glory or personal ambition, is to be the source of future collisions. The grasping spirit is to be dreaded most, and for one I should prefer much, a little more of the chivalric sentiment blended in with our thirst for gold. To me there is cause for alarm rather than congratulation, in the intensity with which the human mind is directed in the peaceful channels of wealth. The earth is alive, and shaking from zone to zone, under the fierce action of the human mind, as it strives after gain and the moment an obstacle is thrown in its way, it starts up in a blaze of indignation. The lovers of peace, in chasing before them the chivalric and heroic spirit which lay at the bottom of ancient wars, are pursuing an enemy that left the field long ago, leaving its place occupied by a more querulous, excitable, and dangerous spirit.

In the third place, the struggles and triumphs of genius should be recorded, even though they took place on a field which, in our days may not be deemed by some the most praiseworthy.

To those who have read my "Alps and the Rhine," and some articles published by me in the American Review, there will seem an utter contradiction in my views there expressed, respecting Napoleon, and those found in this work. In reply, I can only say that my former impressions were obtained, just as I doubt not those of the majority of American readers are from English history and English literature. I had no doubt of their correctness, and designed, in writing of Napoleon, to give him a character corresponding to them. But in reading history solely to understand more fully his character and career, I have been forced, by the most incontrovertible facts, to change my opinions entirely, and I can only regret that I should have given currency to impressions so unjust to a great man, and so false to history. Who would esteem a man that should draw his conclusions respecting our revolutionary struggle, from English historians? and yet he would be more correct than he who forms his opinions of the French Revolution, and after-wars, from the same source.

In the following volumes will be found much that will strike the reader as needless repetition; but when it is remembered that the separate characters described moved frequently amid the same scenes, and even exhibited some of their noblest qualities at the same battles, it will be seen that frequent references to the same event, accompanied perhaps by a similar remark, is necessary to prevent confusion in dates. One is compelled in such a work to go backward and forward constantly in history, and hence often pass over the same points.

The description of the Pass of the Splugen by Macdonald, and the partial description of the battle of Waterloo, in my "Alps and the Rhine," written before the present work was planned, are necessarily repeated here when speaking of those events.

I need not add that I pretend to no originality in this work, except in the way I have arranged and grouped facts already given to the world. I have used, without any hesitation, any author that could help me, and to save the trouble of constant references through the book, I here add the list of those works to which I have been most indebted:

Thiers's French Revolution, Thiers's Consulate and Empire, Napier's Peninsular War, Jomini's Works, Napoleon's Bulletins, Memories of Bourienne, Caulincourt, Las Casas, Voice from St. Helena, Dumas, Segur, Alison, Memoirs of Ney and Murat, Pelet, Stuttenheim, St. Cyr, Camp and Court of Napoleon, Rapp, Southey, etc., etc.

The plates accompanying these volumes have been selected with great care, and from the most authentic sources.

Napoleon Bonaparte

Chapter 1
Napoleon Bonaparte

    Perhaps there is no greater example of the control English literature and English criticism exert over public opinion in this country, than the views they have impressed upon it respecting Bonaparte. With Wordsworth, Southey and Byron in poetry, and Scott, and Alison, and the English Reviews, in prose, all making him a monster in cruelty and selfishness even though he might be an angel in genius; we have, without scruple, adopted the same sentiments, and get him down as a scourge of his race.
    The few American writers that have ever attempted to give an analysis of his character, and a fair criticism on his actions, have failed, by judging him as if he had grown up on the Puritan soil of New England, instead of amid the chaos and anarchy of France, and the exciting sounds of war as Europe moved to battle. Their criticisms have in reality usually been mere essays on the horrors of war, in which Bonaparte figures as the chief illustration. There is no recognition of the peculiar trials that surrounded him, of the genius that mastered them, of the temptations to which he was exposed, and the necessity that frequently compelled him to courses that warred with his wishes.
    English historians make no scruple of belying him; and while some of our American writers, by placing on him the guilt of those desolating wars that loaded Europe with the dead, have done him gross injustice; they have also committed an unpardonable error in history. That English historians should attempt to cover their most successful enemy with unmerited guilt, especially when it is necessary to do so, in order to screen their own nation against the accusations which France lays at her door, is to be expected. Still Scott

has done himself more injury in his Life of Napoleon than he has the great man he slandered; and Mr Mitchell, who has lately written three volumes to convince men that Napoleon was a fool, has succeeded only in proving himself one. Mr. Alison is almost the only one who has at all comprehended his true character; but, while he is forced to bear noble testimony to his genius, he is afraid of offending the prejudices and vanity of his countrymen, and so attempts, as an offset to his praise, to prove him destitute of conscience, and capable of great meannesses. To do this he not only falsifies history, but drags forth, with the most ludicrous gravity, all the petulant speeches he ever made in sudden ebullitions of passion, or in the first chagrin of disappointment. The unjust and passionate remarks a man of Napoleon's temperament, however noble his character, will always make in moments of irritation, are arrayed against his greatest acts with studied exaggeration, and declared sufficient to neutralize them all. This is like going into a man's bed-chamber to report his unguarded speeches, or make a peevish remark to a servant in a moment of irritability offset the noblest acts of his life.

Napoleon Bonaparte, whether we think of his amazing genius his unparalleled power of embracing vast combinations, while he lost sight of none of the details necessary to insure success his rapidity of thought, and equally sudden execution his tireless energy his ceaseless activity his ability to direct the movements of half a million of soldiers in different parts of the world, and at the same time reform the laws restore the finances and administer the government of his country; or whether we trace his dazzling career from the time he was a poor proud charity boy at the Military School of Brienne, to the hour when he sat down on the most brilliant throne of Europe, he is the same wonderful man the same grand theme for human contemplation.

But before entering on his character, it is necessary that whatever unjust prejudices we entertain should be removed, and our errors in history corrected. The first great barrier in the way of rendering him justice is the conviction everywhere entertained, that he alone, or chiefly, is chargeable with those desolating wars that covered the Continent with slain armies. His mounting ambition is placed at the foundation of them all, and no greatness of mind can of course compensate for the guilt of such wholesale murder.

It is impossible for one who has not travelled amid the monarchies of Europe, and witnessed their nervous fear of republican principles, and their fixed determination at whatever sacrifice of justice, human rights, and human life, to maintain their oppressive forms of government, to appreciate at all the position of France at the time of the revolution. The balance of political power had been the great object of anxiety, and all the watchfulness directed against the encroachment of one state on another; and no one can imagine the utter consternation with which Europe saw a mighty republic rise in her midst. The balance of power was forgotten in the anxiety for self-preservation. The sound of the falling throne of the Bourbons rolled like a sudden earthquake under the iron and century-bound framework of despotism, till everything heaved and rocked on its ancient foundations. Our Declaration of Independence, the everlasting and immutable principles of human rights, were uttered in the ears of the astonished world, and unless that voice could be hushed, that alarming movement checked, every monarchy of Europe would soon have a revolution of its own to struggle with. That the Revolution of France is justifiable, if a revolution is ever so, no one acquainted with the history of that time can for a moment doubt. The violence that marked its progress shows only, as Macaulay says, the greater need of it. At all events, France confused, chaotic, bleeding, and affrighted, stood up and declared herself, in the face of the world, a republic. She made no encroachments on other states, sought no war, for she needed all her strength and energy to save herself from internal foes. But the power of Europe determined to crush her at once before she bad acquired strength and consistency. First, Austria and Prussia took up arms, with the avowed purpose of aiding Louis. After his death, Holland, Spain, and England came into the alliance, and moved down on that bewildered republic. Here was the commencement and origin of all the after-wars that devastated Europe. Not on France, but on the allied powers, rests the guilt of setting in motion that terrible train of evils which they would fain transfer to other shoulders. It was a war of principle and a war of aggression. It was despotism invading liberty oppression summoning human rights to lay down its arms, and because it would not, banding the world together to crush the republic that nourished them. Bonaparte was yet a boy when this infamous war was strewing the banks of the Rhine with slain armies.

After struggling bravely for years for self-defence France at length found her saviour in the young Corsican. Quelling the revolt of the sections in Paris, he was appointed to the command of the Army of Italy. He found it badly provisioned, worse paid, ragged and murmuring, yet, by his energy, skill, and, more than all, by his example, restored order and confidence; and, though numbering less than forty thousand men, replenished, as it wasted away, by slender reinforcements, he with it attached and cut to pieces several armies, the most magnificent Austria could furnish, finishing one of the most brilliant campaigns the world has ever witnessed, amid the tumultuous joy of the French. The next year he subjugated Lombardy, and forced the Austrian plenipotentiary, by his daring threats, to sign the treaty of Campo Farmio, which was most favourable to the French Republic. In the bloody battles of Millesimo, Montenotte, Lodi, Arcola, and Castiglione, and Rivoli, he certainly acted as became a general fighting under the orders of his government, carrying on a defensive war with a boldness, skill, and success, considering the superiority of the force opposed to him, deserving of the highest praise.

Returning to Paris in triumph, hailed everywhere as the saviour of France, he notwithstanding became tired of his inactive life, and still more weary of the miserable Directory to whose folly he was compelled to submit, and proposed the expedition to Egypt. This furnishes another charge against Bonaparte, and this war is denounced as aggressive and cruel, growing out of a mad ambition. That it was unjust, no one can deny; but instead of being a thing worthy of censure by the cabinets of Europe, it was simply carrying out their own systems of policy. His designs on the East were just such as England had for years been prosecuting. The East was always to Bonaparte the scene of great enterprises, and Egypt furnished a basis to his operations, and at the same time would serve as a check to English encroachment in the Indies.

While Russia, Austria, and Prussia were stripping Poland, and England was extending her conquests in the Indies cumbering its burning plains with tens of thousands of its own children, and carrying out the most iniquitous system of oppression toward Ireland ever tolerated by a civilized people it does seem ludicrous to hear her historians complimenting the Deity on his even-handed justice, in finally arresting the cruel ambition of Bonaparte and of France.

While the expedition to Egypt was experiencing the vicissitudes that characterized it, Austria, seeing that France had got the lion's share in Italy, joined with Naples, and again commenced hostilities. The French were driven back across the Apennines, and all the advantages gained there over Austria were being lost, when Bonaparte returned in haste from Egypt overthrew the imbecile Directory was proclaimed First Consul and immediately set about the restoration of France. The consolidation of the government the restoration of the disordered finances the pacification of La Vendée the formation and adoption of a constitution, engrossed his mind, and he most ardently desired peace. He, therefore, the moment he was elected First Consul, wrote with his own hands two letters, one to the King of England, and the other to the Emperor of Germany; hoping by this frank and friendly course to appease the two governments, and bring about a general peace. He had acquired sufficient glory as a military leader, and he now wished to resuscitate France, and become great as a civil ruler. In his letter to England, he uses the following language: "Must the war, Sire, which for the last eight years has devastated the four quarters of the world, be eternal? Are there no means of coming to an understanding? How can two of the most enlightened nations of Europe, stronger already and more powerful than their safety or their independence requires, sacrifice to ideas of vain-glory the well-being of commerce, internal prosperity, and the peace of families? How is it they do not feel peace to be the first of necessities as the first of glories?" Similar noble, frank, and manly sentiments, he addressed to the Emperor of Germany. There were no accusations in these letters, no recriminations, and no demands. They asked simply for negotiations to commence, for the spirit of peace to be exhibited, leaving it to after-efforts to settle the terms. Austria was inclined to listen to this appeal from the First Consul, and replied courteously to his letter. But she was trammelled by her alliance with England, and refused to enter into negotiations in which the British Empire was not represented. Pitt, on the contrary, returned an insulting letter to the French Minister heaped every accusation on Bonaparte recapitulated individual acts of violence, and laid them at the door of the French Republic and charged it with designing to overthrow both religion and monarchy throughout the Continent. He declared that the English government must see some fruits of repentance and amendment, before it could trust the proffers of peace; and that the restoration of the Bourbon throne was the only guarantee she should deem sufficient of the good behaviour of the

French government. Bonaparte, in reply, fixed the first aggressive acts clearly on the enemies of France, and then asked what was the use of these irritating reminiscences if the war was to be eternal, because one or the other party had been the aggressor; and then adverting to the proposal that the Bourbons should be restored, asked, "What would be thought of France, if in her propositions she insisted on the restoration of the dethroned Stuarts, before she would make peace?" This home-thrust disconcerted the English Minister; and in reply he frankly acknowledged that his government did not wage war for the re-establishment of the Bourbon throne, but for the security of all governments, and that she would listen to no terms of peace until this security was obtained. This settled the question. England would have no peace while France continued to be a republic. Bonaparte had foreseen all this, and finding he could not separate Austria from her English alliance, immediately set on foot immense preparations for war. Moreau was sent with a magnificent army into Swabia, to drive back the Austrians toward their capital; Massena was appointed over the miserably provided Army of Italy, while he himself fell from the heights of San Bernard, on the plains of Lombardy.

At the fierce-fought battle of Marengo, he reconquered Italy, while Moreau chased the vanquished Austrians over the Danube. Victory everywhere perched on the French standards, and Austria was ready to agree to an armistice, in order to recover from the disasters she had suffered. The slain at Montibello, around Genoa, on the plains of Marengo, in the Black Forest, and along the Danube, are to be charged over to the British government, which refused peace in order to fight for the philanthropic purpose of giving security to governments.

Austria, though crippled, lets the armistice wear away, refusing to make a treaty because she is bound for seven months longer to England. Bonaparte, in the mean time, is preparing to recommence hostilities. Finding himself unable to conclude a peace, he opened the campaign of Hohenlinden, and sent Macdonald across the Splugen. Moreau's victorious march through Austria, and the success of the operations in Italy, soon brings Austria to terms, and the celebrated peace of Luneville, of 1801, is signed.

The energy and ability, and above all the success, of the First Consul, had now forced the continental powers to regard him with respect, and in some cases with sympathy; while England, by her imperious demands, had embroiled herself with all the northern powers of Europe.

But this universal and wasting war began at length to be tiresome to all parties, and, after much negotiation and delay, a general peace was concluded at Amiens, and the world was at rest. Universal joy was spread through France and England, and the transports of the people knew no bounds.

Peace, which Bonaparte needed and wished for, being restored, he applied his vast energies to the development of the resources of France, and to the building of stupendous public works. Commerce was revived the laws administered with energy order restored, and the blessings of peace were fast healing up the wounds of war. Men were amazed at the untiring energy and the amazing plans of Bonaparte. His genius gave a new birth to the nation developed new elements of strength, and imparted all impulse to her growth that threatened to outstrip the greatness of England. His ambition was to obtain colonial possessions, like those of England; and if allowed to direct his vast energies in that direction, there was no doubt France would soon rival the British Empire in its provinces. England was at first fearful of the influence of the French Republic, but now a new cause of alarm seized her. It was evident that France was fast tending toward a monarchy. Bonaparte had been made First Consul for life, with the power to appoint his successor; and it required no seer to predict that his gigantic mind and dictatorial spirit would not long brook any check from f inferior authority. From the very superiority of his intellect, he must merge everything into his majestic plans, and gradually acquire more and more control, till the placing of a crown on his head would be only the symbol of that supreme power which had long before passed into his hands. England, therefore, had no longer to fear the influence of a Republic, and hence fight for the security of government in general. She had, however, another cause of anxiety the too rapid growth of her ancient rival. She became alarmed at the strides with which France advanced under the guiding genius of Napoleon, and refused to carry out the terms of the solemn treaty she had herself signed. In that treaty it was expressly stipulated that England should evacuate Egypt and Malta; while France, on her part, was to evacuate Naples, Tarento, and the Roman States. His part of the treaty, Napoleon had fulfilled within two months after its completion; but ten months had now elapsed, and the English were still in Alexandria and Malta. But Napoleon, anxious to preserve peace, did not see fit to urge matters, and made no complaint till it was suddenly announced that the English government had proclaimed her determination not to fulfil the stipulations she had herself made. The only pretext offered for this violation of a solemn contract was her suspicions that France had designs on these places. The truth was, England with her accustomed jealousy of other nations acquiring colonial possessions, and remembering what a struggle it had just cost her to wrest Egypt and Malta from France resolved, though in violation of her own treaty, not to give them up. Talleyrand was perfectly amazed at this decision of the British ministry, while Napoleon was thrown into a transport of rage. His keen penetration discerned at a glance the policy of England, and the dreadful conflict that must ensue. He saw that she was resolved to resist the advancement of France, and to band, while she could, the powers of Europe against her. He knew that if she would remain at peace, he could by force of arms, and diplomatic skill, compel Russia, Austria, Prussia, and Spain to let him alone to carry out his plans for the aggrandizement of France. But with England constantly counteracting him, and throwing firebrands in the cabinets of the continent, he would be engaged in perpetual conflicts and wranglings. It had, therefore, come to this: England must be chastised into quietness and respect for treaties, or there was to be continual war till France should yield to the strength of superior numbers. England knew that in a protracted war France must fall: for her very victories would in the end melt away her armies, before the endless thousands all Europe could pour upon her; and this she determined to accomplish. But war at this time was the last thing Napoleon wished it interfered with his plans, and cut short his vast projects. Besides, he had won all the military renown he wished in fighting with the rotten monarchies that surrounded him, and his genius sought a wider field in which to display itself. It was, therefore, with the greatest reluctance he would entertain the idea of a rupture. He sent for Lord Whitworth, the English minister at Paris, and had a long personal conversation with him. He recapitulated the constant and unprovoked aggressions of his government on France, ever since the Revolution spoke of his ardent wish to live on terms of amity "But," said he, "Malta must be evacuated: for although it is of no great value in a maritime point of view, it is of immense importance as connected with a sacred treaty and with the honour of France." "For," he continued, "what would the world say, if we should allow a solemn treaty to be violated?" He asked the nation to act frankly and honestly toward him, and h would act equally so toward it. "If you doubt my sincerity," said he, "look at the power and renown to which I have attained. Do you suppose I wish to hazard it all in a desperate conflict?" The English government then endeavoured to negotiate with him to let it retain Malta. "The treaty of Amiens," he replied, "and nothing but the treaty!" Placed in this dilemma, England was compelled to do two things at once: first, violate a treaty of her own making; and second, to take upon herself, in doing it, the responsibility of convulsing Europe, and bringing back all the horrors of the war that had just closed. Napoleon was right, and England was wrong, totally wrong; and if the violation of a solemn treaty is a just cause for war, then is he justifiable. From the objects of peace which had filled his mind, Bonaparte immediately strung his vast energies for the fearful encounter that was approaching. Hostilities commenced, and Napoleon resolved at once to invade England, and strike a deadly blow at the head of his perfidious enemy, or perish in the attempt. He collected an enormous flotilla at Boulogne; and the French coast, that looks toward the English isle, was alive with armies and boats, and rang with the artisan's hammer and the roar of cannon. Nothing but unforeseen circumstances prevented his carrying out this project, which would have shaken the British throne to its foundations.

England drew Russia first into this new alliance, the basis of which was, first, to reduce France to her limits before the Revolution; and second, to secure the peace and stability of the European states. Look for a moment at this perfidious policy this mockery of virtue this philanthropic villainy. Russia, sundered so far from France, was in peaceable possession of all her territory bad not a right to maintain, nor a wrong to redress. England, on the other hand, had no province to wrest back from the enemy no violated treaty to defend no encroachment to resist. Their removal from the theatre of war rendered them secure; and whose peace and stability were they to maintain? They anticipated no danger to themselves. Italy preferred the French domination to the Austrian, for it gave greater liberty and prosperity. Austria did not ask to be propped up, for she had had enough of those alliances which made her own plains the field of combat; and it was with the greatest difficulty she could be brought into the confederacy, and not till her possessions in Italy, which she had ceded to France, were offered as a bribe for her co-operation. Prussia resolutely refused to enter the alliance, and at length sided with France. Russia, Austria, England, and Sweden finally coalesced, and convulsed Europe, and deluged it in blood, to furnish security to those who had not asked their interference. From this moment Napoleon saw that either Russia or England must be humbled or there could be no peace to Europe, no security to France. This accounts for his projected descent on England, and after desperate invasion of Russia.

In the opening of the campaign of 1805 that followed, so glorious to the French arms, the real desires of Napoleon are made apparent. Mack had surrendered Ulm, and with it thirty thousand soldiers, and as the captive army defiled before Bonaparte he addressed them in the following remarkable language: "Gentlemen, war has its chances. Often victorious, you must expect sometimes to be vanquished. Your master wages against me an unjust war. I say it candidly, I know not for what I am fighting. I know not what he desires of me. He has wished to remind me that I was a soldier. I trust he will find that I have not forgotten my original avocation. I will, however, give one piece of advice to my brother, the Emperor of Germany. Let him hasten to make peace. This is the moment to remember that there are limits to all empires, however powerful. I want nothing on the Continent. It is ships, colonies that I desire." This is the language of him who is called the desolator of Europe, in the moment of victory. It was true, he did not know for what he was fighting; he was forced into it. It was equally true, that he wished for nothing on the Continent. He emulated England in her course of greatness, and he was perfectly willing the despots of Europe should sit in quietness on their crazy thrones. For the slain left on the plains of Italy, as Massena swept the enemy from its borders for the tens of thousands strewn on the bloody field of Austerlitz who is chargeable? Not Napoleon not France. Here is a third sanguinary war waged, filling Europe with consternation and the clangour of arms her hospitals with wounded, and her villages with mourning, and her valleys and hills with her slain children and the guilt of the whole is charged over to Napoleon's ambition, while he never went into a war more reluctantly, or with justice more clearly on his side. Mr. Alison, who certainly will not be accused of favouring too much the French view of the matter, nor too eager to load England with crime, is nevertheless compelled to hold the following remarkable language respecting this war: "In coolly reviewing the circumstances under which this contest was renewed, it is impossible to deny that the British government manifested a feverish anxiety to come to a rupture, and that, so far as the two countries were concerned, they were the aggressors." And yet at the opening of the campaign of Austerlitz he indulges in a long homily on the ambition of Napoleon his thirst of glory, and the love of conquest which has seized the French nation. And these are the works we place in our libraries as histories.

I do not design to follow out the subsequent treaties to show who were the aggressors. Russia and England determined never to depart from the basis of their alliance till they had effected the overthrow of Napoleon; while he saw that the humiliation of one or the other of these great Powers was indispensable to the preservation of his possessions and his throne. Conquests alone could produce peace; and the war became one of extermination on the one side, and of vengeance and fierce retaliation on the other. Napoleon felt that he was to be treated without mercy or faith, unless he surrendered France into the hands of the despots of Europe, to be disposed of as they should think necessary for their own security, and the stability of the feudal system, on which their thrones were based. That after this he should wage war with a desperation and violence that made Europe tremble, cannot be wondered at. But up to the peace of Tilsit, he and France are free from the guilt of the carnage that made the plains of Europe one vast Golgotha.

Some time after this assertion was written down, I had occasion to refer to Napier's Peninsular War for some historical fact, and fell upon the following statement which, coming as it does from an Englishman, and one of such high authority in military matters, I am induced to quote: "Up to the peace of Tilsit," says Napier, "the wars of France were essentially defensive; for the bloody contest that wasted the Continent so many years was not a struggle for pre-eminence between ambitious powers not a dispute for some accession of territory nor for the political ascendancy of one or other nation but a deadly conflict to determine whether aristocracy or democracy should predominate whether equality or *privilege* should henceforth be the principle of European governments."

But how much does this "up to the peace of Tilsit" embrace? First, all the first wars of the French Republic the campaigns of 1792,

'93, '94, and '95 and the carnage and woe that made up their history. Second, eleven out of the eighteen years of Bonaparte's career the campaigns of 1796, in Italy and Germany the battles of Montenotte, Millesimo, Dego, Lodi, Arcola, Castiglione, and Rivoli the campaigns of 1797, and the bloody battle-fields that marked their progress. It embraces the wars in Italy and Switzerland, while Bonaparte was in Egypt; the campaign of Marengo and its carnage; the havoc around and in Genoa; the slain thousands that strewed the Black Forest and the banks of the Danube where Moreau struggled so heroically; the campaign of Hohenlinden and its losses. And yet this is but a fraction to what remains. This period takes in also, the campaign of Austerlitz and its bloody battle, and the havoc the band of war was making in Italy, the campaign of Jena, and the fierce conflicts that accompanied it; the campaign of Eylau, and the battles of Pultusk, Golymin, Heilsberg, crowned by the dreadful slaughter of Eylau; the campaigns of Friedland and Tilsit, and the multitudes they left on the plains of Europe. All these terrible campaigns, with their immense slaughter, does an English historian declare to be the result of a defensive war on the part of France not merely a defence of territory, but of human rights against tyranny. Let republicans ponder this before they adopt the sentiments of prejudiced historians, and condemn as a monster the man who was toiling over battle fields to save his country from banded oppressors.

That Bonaparte loved dominion, no one ever doubted; but that it led him to battle constantly the allied Continental powers, is untrue. On the contrary, Mr. Napier declares that he was not only defending France against aggression, but democracy against aristocracy equal rights against privileged oppression.

Nothing can be more ludicrous than the assertion that Napoleon sought to conquer Europe., and fell in carrying out his insane project. In youth, as all young soldiers are, he was desirous of military glory. His profession was that of arms, and he bent all his young energies to the task of excelling in it, and succeeded. But when he became Emperor of France, he stood on the summit of military renown, and needed and sought no more fame as a warrior. He was ambitious to excel as a monarch. He designed to follow in the steps of England, and finally outstrip her in her mighty progress, by extending commerce, and establishing colonies. The secret of the whole opposition he received from her after the Republic had ceased to exist, sprung from her knowledge of his policy. The East was regarded by him as the appropriate theatre for his ambition; but the East, England determined nobody should plunder of its enormous wealth but herself, and so she banded Europe together to overthrow him. The encroachments of France in the South of Europe during a time of peace are the only pretext offered by the English government for her interference and aggression. It was not that her territory was invaded, her rights assailed, or treaties with her violated, It was simply a philanthropic motive if we may believe her statements, that caused her to whelm Europe in blood. The encroachments of France could not be allowed the extension of her empire must be arrested; and yet, since she violated the treaty of Amiens broke up a universal peace and brought on universal war she has, solely, for the sake of self-aggrandizement, added more to her territory in the Mysore, than France ever did to hers, put all her conquests together. Now let France insist that England shall give up these possessions; and form an alliance with Russia, Austria, and Prussia, the basis of which shall be war with England, till she shall retire to her original boundaries before her aggressions in the East commenced; and the conflict in which England would be plunged, and the slaughters that would follow, would be charged on her as justly as those which followed the rupture of the peace of Amiens can be laid at the door of France. There is this difference, however. France gained her possessions in resisting aggressive power, and had them secured to her by treaty, while her domination was preferred to that which the conquered provinces must fall under should she abandon them. But England commenced an unprovoked war on a peaceful people, and reduced them to slavery from no nobler motive than the love of gold. It is time that Americans, who have suffered so much from the imperious policy of England, and seen so much, on our own shores, of her grasping spirit after colonial possessions, should look on her conduct subsequent to the French Revolution through other medium than her own literature.

I have not designed, in this defence of Napoleon, and of France, to prove that the former always acted justly, or from the most worthy motives; or that the Republic never did wrong; but to reveal the principles which lay at the bottom of that protracted war which commenced with the Revolution, and ended only with the overthrow of Napoleon. It was first a war of despotism and monarchy against republicanism, and then a war of suspicion and jealousy and rivalry.

Having thus cleared Napoleon of the crime of desolating Europe with his victorious armies, it will not be so difficult to look with justice on his character and life.

His boyish actions while a poor scholar at Brienne have been adduced as pre-shadowings of his future career. But the truth is, with more talent than his playmates with more pride and passion I find nothing in him different from other boys of his age. His solitary walks, and gorgeous dreams, and brilliant hopes, at this early period, belong to every boy of ardent temperament and a lively imagination. In ordinary times, these golden visions would have faded away with years and experience; and Napoleon Bonaparte would have figured in the world's history only as a powerful writer, or a brilliant orator. The field which the Revolution left open to adventurers enabled him to realize his extravagant hopes. His ambition was a necessary result of his military education, while the means so unexpectedly furnished for gratifying it fed it with a consuming flame. His abrupt, laconic style of speaking corresponded well with his impetuous temper, and evinced, at an early age, the iron-like nature with which he was endowed.

His career fairly commenced with his quelling the revolt of the sections. True, his conduct at the siege of Toulon had caused him to be spoken of favourably as an under officer, but it was with unfeigned surprise that the Abbé Sieyès, Rewbel, Letourneur, Roger Ducos, and General Moulins saw him introduced to them by Barras, as the commander he bad chosen for the troops that were to defend the Convention. Said General Moulins to him, "You are aware that it is only by the powerful recommendation of citizen Barras, that we confide to you so important a Post?" "I have not asked for it," dryly replied the young lieutenant, "and if I accept it, it will be because, after a close examination, I am confident of success. I am different from other men; I never undertake anything I can not carry through." This sally caused the members of the Convention to bite their lips, for the implied sarcasm stung each in his turn. "But do you know," said Rewbel, "that this may be a very serious affair that the sections " "Very well," fiercely interrupted the young Bonaparte, "I will make a serious affair of it, and the sections shall become tranquil." He had seen Louis XVI. put on the red cap, and show himself from the palace of the Tuileries to the mob, and unable to restrain his indignation at the sight exclaimed to his companion Bourienne,

"What madness! he should have blown four or five hundred of them into the air, and the rest would have taken to their heels." Deprived of his command, he had wandered around Paris during the terrible scenes of the Revolution, learning every day lessons which he would yet have occasion to improve. He had gone so far as to dictate a long and written proposal to Monsieur, for the defence of the tottering throne, offering himself as commander of the troops, to be organized for the quelling of the insurgents. To the proposal of this unknown individual, no reply was deigned; and the author of it soon after saw the royal head roll on the scaffold; and retired to his bed sick from the excitement and horror of the spectacle. But the experience furnished by these scenes rendered him a fit leader to the troops of the Convention; and when on the mighty populace, and the headlong advance of the National Guard, his artillery loaded to the muzzle with grape-shot thundered, he announced the manner in which he would treat with a mob. After this, Barras became his patron, and introduced him to Josephine, and persuaded him to marry her, by offering as a dowry the command of the Army of Italy.

It was not without misgivings that such generals as Massena, Rampon, Augereau, and others, saw a young man of slender frame, but twenty-seven years old, assume the command of the army. But his independent manner, firm tone, and above all the sudden activity he infused into every department by his example, soon gave them to understand that it was no ordinary leader whose orders they were to obey. From this brilliant campaign, he went up by rapid strides to First Consul, and finally Emperor of France.

One great secret of his success is to be found in the union of two striking qualities of mind, which are usually opposed to each other. He possessed an imagination as ardent, and a mind as impetuous, as the most rash and chivalric warrior, and yet a judgment as cool and correct as the ablest tactician. His mind moved with the rapidity of lightning, and with the precision and steadiness of naked reason. He rushed to his final decision as if he overleaped all the intermediate space, and yet he embraced the entire ground, and every detail in his passage. In short, he could decide quick and correctly too. He did not possess these antagonist qualities in a moderate degree, but he was at the same time the most rapid and the most correct of men, in the formation of his plans. He united two remarkable natures in his single person. It usually happens that the man of sage counsel and far-reaching mind, who embraces every detail and weighs every probability, is slow in coming to a decision. On the other hand, a mind of rapid decision and sudden execution commonly lacks the power of combination, and, seeing but one thing at a time, finds itself involved in plans it can neither thwart nor break through. It was the union of these two qualities that gave Bonaparte such immense power over his adversaries. His plans were more skilfully and deeply laid than theirs, and yet perfected before theirs were begun. He broke up the counsels of other men, by the execution of his own. This power of thinking quick, and of thinking right, is the rarest exhibited in history. It gives the possessor of it all the advantage that thought ever has over impulse, and all the advantage, too, that impulse frequently has over thought by the suddenness and unexpectedness of its movements.

His power of combination was unrivalled. The most extensive plans, involving the most complicated movements, were laid down with the clearness of a map in his mind; while the certainty and precision, with which they were all brought to bear on one great point, took the ablest generals in Europe by surprise. His mind seemed vast enough for the management of the globe, and not so much encircled everything, as contained everything. It was hard to tell whether he exhibited more skill in conducting a campaign or in managing a single battle. With a power of generalization seldom equalled, his perceptive faculties, that let no detail escape him, were equally rare.

As a military leader, he has no superior in ancient or modern times. He marched his victorious troops successively into almost every capital of Europe. Meeting and overwhelming in turn the armies of Prussia, Austria, Russia, and England, he for a long time waged a successful war against them all combined; and exhausted at last by his very victories, rather than by their conquests, he fell before superior numbers, which in a protracted contest must always prevail. His first campaign in Italy, and the campaign of Austerlitz, are, perhaps, the most glorious he ever conducted. The first astonished the world, and fixed his fortune. In less than a year, he overthrew four of the finest armies of Europe. With fifty-five thousand men, he had beaten more than two hundred thousand Austrians taken prisoners nearly double the number of his whole army, and killed half as many as the entire force he had at any one time in the field. The tactics he adopted in this campaign, and which he never after departed from, correspond singularly with the character of his mind. Instead of following up what was considered the scientific mode of conducting a campaign and a battle, he fell back on his own genius, and made a system of his own, adapted to the circumstance in which he was placed. Instead of opposing wing to wing, centre to centre, and column to column, he rapidly concentrated his entire strength on separate portions in quick succession. Hurling his combined force now on one wing, and now another, and now throwing it with the weight and terror of an avalanche on the centre, he crushed each in its turn; or cutting the army in two, destroyed its communication and broke it in pieces. And this was the way his mind worked. He concentrated all his gigantic powers on one project at a time, until it stood complete before him, and then turned them unexhausted on another. He grappled with and mastered each in turn penetrated and dismissed it with a rapidity that astonished his most intimate friends.

He was brave as courage itself, and never scrupled to expose his life when necessary to success. The daring he exhibited in the revolt of the sections, when, with five thousand soldiers, he boldly withstood forty thousand of the National Guard and mob of Paris, he carried with him to his fall. At the terrible passage of Lodi, where, though General-in-Chief, he was the second man across the bridge; at Arcola, where he stood, with the standard in his hand, in the midst of a perfect tempest of balls and grape-shot; and at Wagram, where he rode on his white steed, backward and forward, for a whole hour, before his shivering lines, to keep them steady in the dreadful fire that thinned their ranks, and swept the ground they stood upon, he evinced the heroic courage that he possessed, and which was a part of his very nature. This, with his stirring eloquence, early gave him great command over his soldiers. They loved him to the last, and stood by the republican General, and the proud Emperor, with equal affection. Bonaparte was eloquence itself. His proclamations to his soldiers evince not only his knowledge of the human heart, but his power to move it at his will. Whether causing one of the articles in Sieyès's constitution to be rejected, by his withering sarcasm; or rousing his soldiers to the loftiest pitch of enthusiasm by his irresistible appeals; or carrying away those conversing with him by his brilliant thoughts and forcible elocution, he exhibits the highest capacities of an orator. His appeals to the courage of his soldiers, and his distribution of honours, with so much pomp and display, perfectly bewildered and dazzled them, so that in battle it seemed to be their only thought how they should exhibit the greatest daring, and perform the most desperate deeds. Thus, soon after the battle of Castiglione, and just before the battle of Rivoli, he made an example of the 39th and 85th regiments of Vaubois Division, for having given way to a panic, and nearly lost him the battle. Arranging these two regiments in a circle, he addressed them in the following language: "Soldiers, I am displeased with you you have shown neither discipline, nor valour, nor firmness. You have allowed yourselves to be chased from positions where a handful of brave men would have stopped an army. Soldiers of the 39th and 85th, you are no longer French soldiers. Chief of the Staff, let it be written on their standards, 'They are no longer of the Army of Italy.'"

Nothing could exceed the stunning effect with which these words fell on those brave men. They forgot their discipline, and the order of their ranks, and bursting into grief, filled the air with their cries, and rushing from their ranks, crowded with most beseeching looks and voices around their general, and begged to be saved from such a disgrace, saying, "Lead us once more into battle, and see if we are not of the Army of Italy." Bonaparte, wishing only to implant feelings of honour in his troops, appeared to relent, and, addressing them some kind words, promised to wait to see how they should behave. In a few days he did see the brave fellows go into battle, and rush on death as if going to a banquet, and prove themselves, even in his estimation, worthy to be in the Army of Italy. It was by such reproaches for ungallant behaviour, and by rewards for bravery, that he instilled a love of glory that made them irresistible in combat. Thus we see the Old Guard, dwindled to a mere handful in that fearful retreat from Russia, close round him as they marched past a battery, and amid the storm of lead that played on their exhausted rank sing the favourite air, "Where can a father be so well, as in the bosom of his family." So, also, just before the battle of Austerlitz, in his address to the soldiers, he promised them he would keep out of danger if they behaved bravely, and burst through the enemy's ranks; but if they did not, he should himself rush into the thickest of the fight. There could not be a stronger evidence of love and confidence between soldier and general, than was evinced by this speech, made on the commencement of one of the greatest battles of his life.

Another cause of his wonderful success was his untiring activity of both mind and body. No victory lulled him into a moment's repose no luxuries tempted him to ease and no successes bounded his impetuous desires. Labouring with an intensity and rapidity that accomplished the work of days in hours, he nevertheless seemed crowded to the very limit of human capacity by the vast plans and endless projects that asked and received his attention. In the cabinet he astonished every one by his striking thoughts and indefatigable industry. The forms and ceremonies of court could keep his mind hardly for an hour from the labour which he seemed to covet. He allowed himself usually but four or five hours' rest, and during his campaigns exhibited the same almost miraculous activity of mind. He would dictate to one set of secretaries all day, and after he had tired them out call for a second and keep them on the stretch all night, snatching but a brief repose during the whole time. His common practice was to rise at two in the morning, and dictate to his secretaries for two hours, then devote two hours more to thought alone, when he would take a warm bath and dress for the day. But in a pressure of business this division of labour and rest was scattered to the winds, and he would work all night. With his nightgown wrapped around him, and a silk handkerchief tied about his head, he would walk backward and forward in his apartment from dark till daylight, dictating to Caulincourt, or Duroc, or D'Albe his chief secretary, in his impetuous manner, which required the highest exertion to keep pace with; while Rustan, his faithful Mameluke, which he brought from Egypt, was up also, bringing him, from time to time, a strong cup of coffee to refresh him. Sometimes at midnight, when all was still, this restless spirit would call out, "Call D'Albe: let every I one arise:" and then commence working, allowing himself no intermission or repose till sunrise. He has been known to dictate to three secretaries at the same time, so rapid were the movements of his mind, and yet so perfectly under his control. He never deferred business for an hour, but did on the spot what then claimed his attention. Nothing but the most iron-like constitution could have withstood these tremendous strains upon it. And, as if Nature had determined that nothing should be wanting to the full development of this wonderful man, as well as no resources withheld from his gigantic plans, she had endowed him with a power of endurance seldom equalled. It was not till after the most intense and protracted mental and physical effort combined, that he gave intimations of being sensible to fatigue. In his first campaign in Italy, though slender and apparently weak, he rode five horses to death in a few days, and for six days and nights never took off his boots, or retired to his couch. He toiled over the burning sands of Egypt, and through the snowdrifts of Russia, with equal impunity spurring his panting steed through the scorching sunbeams of Africa, and forcing his way on foot, with birchen stick in his band, over the icy path as he fled from Moscow with the same firm presence. He would sleep in the palace of the Tuileries, or on the shore of the swollen Danube, with naught but his cloak about him, while the groans of the dying loaded the midnight air with equal soundness. He was often on horseback eighteen hours a day, and yet wrought up to the intensest mental excitement all the while. Marching till midnight, he would array his troops by moonlight; and, fighting all day, he hailed victor at night; and then, without rest, travel all the following night and day, and the next morning fight another battle, and be a second time victorious. He is often spoken of as a mere child of fortune; but whoever in this world will possess such powers of mind, and use them with such skill and industry, and has a frame that will stand it, will always be a child of fortune. He allowed nothing to escape his ubiquitous spirit; and whether two or five campaigns were going on in different kingdoms at the same time, they were equally under his control, and results calculated with wonderful precision.

Another striking characteristic of Napoleon, and which contributed much to his success, was self-confidence. He fell back on himself in every emergency, with a faith that was sublime. Where other men sought counsel, he communed with himself alone; and where kings and emperors called anxiously on the statesmen and chieftains around their thrones for help, he summoned to his aid his own mighty genius. This did not result from vanity and conceit, but from the consciousness of power. He not only took the measure and capabilities of every man that approached him, but he knew he saw beyond their farthest vision, and hence could not but rely on himself, instead of others.

This self-confidence, which in other men would have been downright madness, in him was wisdom. It was the first striking trait in his character he exhibited. At the siege of Toulon, a mere boy, he curled his lip at the science of the oldest generals in the army, and offered his own plan for the reduction of the town, with an assurance that astonished them. In quelling the revolt of the sections, this sublime self-reliance utterly confounded the heads of the Convention. If it had ended here, it might have been called the rashness and ardour of youth crowned with unexpected success. But throughout his after-career; in those long-protracted efforts in which intellect and genius always triumph, we ever find him standing alone, calling none but himself to his aid. Inexperienced and young, he took command of the weak and ill-conditioned Army of Italy, and instead of seeking the advice of his government and his generals, so that he might be screened in case of defeat, where defeat seemed inevitable, he seemed to exult that he was at last alone, and almost to forget the danger that surrounded him, in his joy at having a free and open field for his daring spirit. His fame and after-fortune all rested on his success and conduct in this outset of his career; yet he voluntarily placed himself in a position where the result, however disastrous it might be, would be chargeable on him alone. He flung the military tactics of Europe to the winds, and, with his little band around him, spurned both the science and the numbers arrayed against him.

With the same easy confidence he vaulted to the throne of France, and felt an empire rest on his shoulders, apparently unconscious of the weight. He looked on the revolutionary agitation, the prostration and confusion of his kingdom, without alarm; and his eagle glance pierced at once the length and breadth and depth and height of the chaos that surrounded him. Yet, so natural does he seem in this position that, instead of trembling for his safety, we find ourselves inspired by the same confidence that sustained him, and expecting great and glorious results. He seems equal to anything, and acts as if he himself was conscious he was a match for the world. Stern, decided, plain, he speaks to the King of England, the Emperor of Russia, of Austria, and to all Europe, in the language of a superior rather than of an equal. Angry, yet alarmed at the haughty tone of this plebeian king, the crowned heads of Europe gathered hastily together, to consult what they should do. With the same quiet confidence with which he saw the mob advancing on his batteries in the garden of the

Tuileries, he beheld their banded armies move down on his throne. This single man this plebeian, stood up amid the monarchies of Europe, and, bending his imperial frown on the faithless kings that surrounded him, smote their royal foreheads with blow after blow, till the world stood aghast at his resumption and audacity. Their scorn of his plebeian blood gave way to consternation, as they saw him dictating terms to them in their own capitals; while the freedom with which he put his haughty foot on their sacred majesties filled the bosoms of their courtiers with horror. He wheeled his cannon around their thrones with a coolness and inflexibility of purpose that made "the dignity which doth hedge a king" a most pitiful thing to behold. He swept, with his fierce chariot, through their ancient dynasties, crushing them out as if they had been bubbles in his path; then, proudly pausing, let them gather up their crowns again. While, astonished at the boldness of his irruption into Egypt, they were listening to hear again the thunder of his guns around the Pyramids, they suddenly saw his mighty army hanging along the crest of the Alps; and before the astonishing vision had fairly disappeared, the sound of his cannon was beard shaking the shores of the Danube, and his victorious eagles were waving their wings over the capital of the Austrian Empire. One moment his terrible standards would be seen along the shores of the Rhine; the next, by the banks of the Borysthenes, and then again fluttering amid the flames of Moscow. Europe never had such a wild waking-up before, and the name of Napoleon Bonaparte became a spell-word, with which to conjure up horrible shapes of evil. Victory deserted the standards of the enemy the moment that the presence of Napoleon among his legions was announced in their camp, and when it was whispered through the ranks that his eye was sweeping the battle-field, the arm of the foeman waxed weak; and he conquered as much by his name as by his armies. This boldness of movement, giving him such immense moral power, arose from his confidence in himself. Even where his plans seemed madness and folly, so confidently did he carry them on that men believed he saw resources of which they were ignorant, and hence their course became cautious and wavering, and defeat certain.

    Nothing can be more sublime than this self-reliance of Napoleon in the midst of a world in arms against him. It is the confidence of genius and intellect arrayed against imbecility and fear. That no hesitation should mark his course amid the complicated affairs he was compelled to move, no vacillation of that iron will be seen when everything else shook about him, is indeed a marvel. The energy of a single soul, poised on its own great centre, gathering around it, as by sympathy, the mightiest spirits of the age, and crushing under it obstacles that before seemed insurmountable, has had no such exhibitions since the time of Cæsar.

But with all Napoleon's cool judgment and self-confidence, there was not a marshal in the army of so impetuous and impatient a temper as he. He settled every plan in his own mind with the precision of a mathematical problem; and if any unforeseen obstacle interposed, threatening to change the result, he became perfectly furious with excitement, acting and talking as if he thought it to be a violation of reason and justice. He planned with so much skill, and calculated results with so much precision, that if he did not succeed, he felt there must be blame, shameful neglect, somewhere. From his youth up he could never brook contradiction, and drove with such headlong speed toward the object he was after, that he frequently secured it through the surprise and consternation occasioned by the desperation that marked his progress. In the cabinet and in the field he exhibited the same restless fever of mind, and seemed really to suffer from the strong restraints his despotic judgment placed over his actions. It was impossible for him to keep still; and the most headlong speed in travelling did not seem rapid enough for his eager spirit. Bad rider as he was, he delighted in spurring over fences and chasms, where his boldest riders had gone down; but even when sweeping over a field on a tearing gallop, he could not be quiet, but constantly jerked the reins, which he always held in his right hand. When delayed in writing despatches, behind the time appointed for his departure for the army, the moment he had finished, the cry "To horse" acted like an electric shock on his attendants, and in a moment every man was at the top of his speed, and the next moment the entire suite were driving like a whirlwind along the road. In this way he would go all day without stopping; and if despatches met him on the way, he would read them as he rode, throwing envelopes and unimportant letters, one after another, from the carriage window, with a rapidity that showed how quickly he devoured the contents of each. He usually opened these despatches himself but if his secretary did it for him, he would sit and work at the window-sash with his fingers, so necessary was some outlet to the fierce action of his mind. He would drive through the army at the same furious rate; and when the outriders called out "Room for the Emperor!" every one felt he could not be too quick in obeying; and before the utter confusion of clearing the way had passed, the cortège was seen flying like a cloud across the plain, beyond hearing, and almost out of sight. But through the Guards he always moved with becoming pomp and solemnity, saluting the officers as he passed.

Maps were his invariable companions in a campaign, and be always had one spread out at night in his apartment, or a tent which was always pitched amid the squares of the Old Guards, surrounded with candles, so that he might rise at any moment and consult it; and when on the road or in the field he wanted one, so impatient was he known to be that the two officers who carried them rode down everything between them and his horse or carriage. On such occasions he would frequently order the map he desired to be unrolled on the ground, and, stretching himself full length upon it, in a moment be lost to everything but the campaign before him. A remarkable instance of his impatience and impetuosity is exhibited in the manner he received Marie Louise on her way to meet him. As she drove up to the post town where he expected her, he jumped into the carriage all wet with rain as he was, and embraced this daughter of the Cæsars with the familiarity of an old relative; and, ordering the postilions to drive at full gallop to Compiègne, insisted on having the conjugal rites before marriage, and obtained them. But perhaps there is not a more striking instance of the impetuosity of his feelings than his mad ride to Paris when it was enveloped by the allied armies. Being himself deceived by the enemy, they had got full three days' start of him toward the capital, with a force that bore down everything in their passage. It was then Napoleon strained every nerve to reach the city before its capitulation. He urged his exhausted army to the top of its speed, and on the 29th of March, the day before he left it, he marched with the Imperial Guard forty miles. Wearied out, the brave cuirassiers could no longer keep pace with his haste, and he set out alone for Paris. Despatching courier after courier to announce his approach, he drove on with furious speed; but as the disastrous news was brought him that the enemy were struggling on the heights of Montmartre, his impatience knew no bounds. He abandoned his carriage as being too slow, though it came and went with frightful velocity on the astonished peasantry, and changing it for a light *calèche*, he sprang into it, and ordered the postilions to whip the horses to the top of their speed. He dashed away as if life and death hung on every step. "Faster, faster!" he cried to the postilions, though the whip fell incessantly on the flanks of the panting steeds. "Faster, faster!" he cried " as houses and fields swept past him like a vision. His throne, his crown, his empire, shook in the balance, and the flying chariot seemed to creep over the lengthened way. Nothing could satisfy him, and the cry of "Faster, faster," still rang in the ears of the astonished postilions, though the carriage-wheels were already on fire from their rapid revolutions. Vain speed! Paris had fallen.

This impetuosity of temper and hatred of restraint made him frequently overbearing and unjust to his officers, when they had failed in executing his plans. In the first transport of passion he would hear no defence and no apology; but after-reflection made him more reasonable and just, and a generous act would repay a sudden wrong. It was this trait of character, which grew stronger as he drew toward the close of his career, that made many around him declare that he hated the truth. It was not the truth which aroused him, but the declaration that his plans would be or had been baffled. He was so confident that he usually knew more than all around him, that he in time became so self-opinionated that he could not brook advice which clashed with his views. With weight and velocity both, his mind had terrible momentum, and even in a wrong way often conquered by its irresistible power.

Napoleon was a great statesman as well as a military leader. His conversations in his exile evince the most profound knowledge of political science, while the order he brought out of chaos, and indeed the glorious resurrection he gave to France, show that he was not great in theory alone. He was equal to Cæsar as a warrior, to Bacon in political sagacity, and above all other kings in genius.

Perhaps Napoleon exhibits nowhere in his life his amazing grasp of thought and power of accomplishment more than in the year and a half after his arrival from Egypt. Hearing that the Republic was everywhere defeated, and Italy wrested from its grasp, he immediately set sail for France, and escaping the English fleet in a most miraculous manner, protected by "his star," reached France in October. By November he had overthrown the inefficient Directory, and been proclaimed First Consul with all the attributes, but none of the titles, of king. He immediately commenced negotiations with the allied powers, while at the same time he brought his vast energies to bear on the internal state of France. Credit was to be restored, money raised, the army supplied, war in Vendèe suppressed, and a constitution given to France. By his superhuman exertions and all-pervading genius, he accomplished all this and by next spring was ready to offer Europe peace or war. Order sprang from chaos at his touch the tottering government stopped rocking on its base the moment his mighty hand fell upon it wealth flowed from the lap of poverty, and vast resources were drawn from apparent nothingness. France, rising from her prone position, stood ready to give battle to the world. Europe chose war. The gigantic mind that had wrought such prodigies in seven months in France now turned its concentrated strength and wrath on the enemy. Massena he sent to Genoa to furnish an example of heroism to latest posterity; Moreau he despatched to Swabia to render the Black Forest immortal by the victories of Engen, Moeskirch, and Biberach, and sent the Austrians in consternation to their capital, while he himself, amid the confusion and wonderment of Europe at his complicated movements, precipitated his enthusiastic troops down the Alps, and by one bold and successful stroke wrested Italy from the enemy, and forced the astonished and discomfited sovereigns to an armistice of six months. Unexhausted by his unparalleled efforts, no sooner was the truce proclaimed than he plunged with the same suddenness yet profound forethought with which he rushed into battle, into the distracted politics of Europe. By a skilful policy of offering Malta to Russia at the moment it was certain to fall into the hands of England, he embroiled these two countries in a quarrel, while by promising Hanover to Prussia he bribed her to reject the coalition with England and consent to an alliance with himself. At the same time he planned the league of the neutral powers against England armed Denmark and Sweden, and closed all the ports of the Continent against her, and prepared succours for Egypt. While his deep sagacity was thus baffling the cabinet of England, involving her in a general war with Europe, and pressing to her lips the chalice she had just forced him to drink, he apparently devoted his entire energies to the internal state of France and the building of public works. He created the Bank of France put, the credit of government on a firm basis began the Codes, spanned the Alps with roads sufficient monuments in themselves of his genius and restored the complete supremacy of the laws throughout the kingdom. All this he accomplished in six months, and at the close of the armistice was ready for war. The glorious campaign of Hohenlinden followed, and Austria, frightened for her throne, negotiated the peace of Luneville, giving the world time to recover its amazement and gaze more steadily on this mighty sphere that had shot so suddenly across the orbits of kings.

That Napoleon in all this was ambitious no one doubts, but his ambition was indissolubly connected with the welfare and glory of France. Power was the ruling star in his heaven, but he sought it in order to make France powerful. His energies developed hers, and the victories he won were for her safety and defence. He is accused of having aimed at supreme power, and nothing short of it would have satisfied him. A second Alexander, he waded through seas of blood, and strode over mountains of corpses, solely to accomplish this object, and his fall was the fall of one who aimed at Universal Empire. Mr. Alison takes up this piece of nonsense, and gives us pages of the merest cant about the dangers of ambition and love of power, and the Providence that arrests it declaring, in so many words, that Napoleon sought the subjugation of Europe. If this were true he might have spared the tribute he pays to Napoleon's genius, for it would prove him the sublimest fool that ever held a sceptre. To assert that he ever dreamed of being able to subjugate England, Russia, Prussia, Austria, and the northern powers of Europe, and combine them in one vast empire, of which he would be the head, is too ridiculous to receive a serious refutation. That he ever expected to make England a dependent province on France, there is not an intelligent man in the British Empire believes; yet English historians will never have done their cant about this modern Alexander, who fell because he sought to conquer the world. Napoleon, as I have said, would have been glad to have adopted the let-alone policy both with England and Russia, as well as Austria and Prussia, if they would have allowed it. He was ambitious, but he knew too well that with Europe banded against him he must sooner or later fall; and the utmost limit of his hopes was to break this coalition by crippling either Russia or England. Could he have done this, he would soon have extorted a peace from the rest of Europe that would have allowed him to prosecute his ambitious schemes in the East, where they would have been successful. England wished this road to wealth and to empire left open to her, so she uttered a vast deal of nonsense about unlimited power and the danger of Europe, till she induced Europe to crush Napoleon. The East, as I before remarked, with its boundless wealth and imbecile population, he always regarded as the true field where fame and empire were to be laid, and he would have been glad any moment if Europe would have left him to pursue the career he commenced in Egypt. That he would have been as unprincipled in his aggressions on peaceable states as heartless in the means he employed as reckless of the law of nations as perfidious in his policy as cruel in his slaughters and as grasping after territory, as the British Empire has since shown herself to be, his life, character, and plans leave but little room to doubt. Perhaps it is better that he wasted his immense energies as he did, in breaking to pieces the despotisms of Europe. As it was, he rolled the Revolution over the French borders, and sent it with its earthquake throes the length and breadth of the Continent.

I have thus spoken of Bonaparte comparatively, and not as an individual judged by the law of right. I wished to place him beside the monarchs, and governments that surrounded him, and see where the balance of virtue lay. He was ambitious so was Pitt; while the ambition of the former was far less selfish, heartless, and cruel than that of the latter. One insisted on the treaty of Amiens, by which the world was bound to peace; the other broke it, and involved Europe in war solely for selfish ends. Napoleon has been blamed for robbing France of her republican form of government, and reinstating monarchy; and men are prone to compare him with Washington, and wonder why he could not have imitated his example, and, content with the peace and prosperity of his country, returned to the rank of citizen, and left a name unspotted by blood and violence. In the first place, the thing was absolutely impossible. A pure republic France could not have been with the population the Revolution left upon her bosom. As ignorant of liberty and undisciplined as the South American states and Mexico, she would have been rocked like them with endless revolutions, until European powers had overcome her and replaced a Bourbon on the throne. And if her population had been prepared for complete freedom, the monarchs of Europe would not have allowed her to establish a republic in peace. Imagine the United States in the midst of the Revolution, surrounded by despotic thrones Canada, the West, Mexico, and Florida all so many old monarchies, thoroughly alarmed by the sudden appearance of a free state in their midst, and in their affright banding themselves together to crush the infant republic, and you will have some conception of the situation of France during the Revolution. Let Washington have commanded our forces, and in resisting this war of aggression have wrested from one of the powers dominions to which it had no claim, as France took Italy from Austria. Suppose this despotic feudal alliance was kept up, and no permanent peace would be made till Washington was overthrown; his career and ours would have been very different. Our plains would have all been battle-fields until we had broken up the infamous coalition, or been ourselves overborne. In such a position were Bonaparte and France placed, and such a war was waged till they fell. Placing ourselves in a similar position, we shall not find it difficult to determine where the chief guilt lay, or be wanting in charity to Napoleon for the recklessness with which he carried on a war against powers so destitute of faith and of virtue and whose aggressive policy had well-nigh crushed the hopes of freedom on the Continent. But had these circumstances not existed, he never would have been a Washington, for he possessed few of his moral qualities. Washington appears in grander proportions as a moral than as an intellectual man, while Bonaparte was a moral dwarf; and I do not well see how he could be otherwise. Dedicated from childhood to the profession of arms, all his thoughts and associations were of a military character. Without moral or religious instruction, he was thrown while a youth into the vortex of the Revolution; and in the triumph of infidelity, and the overthrow of all religion, and the utter chaos of principles and sentiments, it was not to be expected he would lay the foundation of a religious character. He emerged from this into the life of the camp and the battle-field, and hence became morally what most men would be in similar circumstances. Besides, his very nature was despotic. He could not brook restraint, and, conscious of knowing more than those around him, he constantly sought for power that he might carry out those stupendous plans which otherwise would have been interrupted. I have no doubt Napoleon's highest ambition was to reign as a just and equitable monarch amid the thrones of Europe, expending his vast energies elsewhere; and that much of his violence and recklessness arose from the consciousness that he was to expect no faith or honesty or justice or truth from the perfidious nations that had bound themselves together to crush him. One thing is certain, had he been less a monarch, France would not have withstood, as long as she did, the united strength of Europe.

Bonaparte is charged with being cruel, but it is unjust. He was capable of great generosity, and exhibited pity in circumstances not to be expected from a man trained on the battle-field. Hearing once of a poor English sailor, who, having escaped from confinement, had constructed a frail boat of cork and branches of trees, with which he designed to put to sea, in the hopes of meeting an English vessel, and thus reaching England; he sent for him, and on learning from his lips that this bold undertaking was to get back to his aged mother, he immediately despatched him with a flag of truce on board an English ship, with a sum of money for his aged parent, saying that she must be an uncommon mother to have so affectionate a son. The guide who conducted him over the San Bernard, and who, ignorant of the mighty man that bestrode the miserable animal by his side, gave him a full account of his life and plans of his betrothal and inability to marry for want of a piece of land, was not forgotten by him afterward. The land was bought and presented to the young man by order of Napoleon. Repeated acts of kindness to poor wounded soldiers was one of the cords of iron which bound them to him. The awful spectacle which a battlefield presents after the carnage is done frequently moved him deeply, and he wept like a child over his dying friend Lannes. His sympathies, it is true, never interfered with his plans. What his judgment approved, his heart never countermanded; and what he thought necessary to be done, he did, reckless of the suffering it occasioned. He was inflexible as law itself in the course he had decided upon as the most expedient. The murder of the Duke of Enghien is perhaps the greatest blot on his character, but he was goaded into this by the madness and folly and villainy of the race to which this unfortunate prince belonged. In the midst of his vast preparations for a descent upon England, he was informed of a plot to assassinate him and place a Bourbon on the throne. The two ends of this conspiracy were Paris and London, between which there was an unbroken line of communication across the Channel. The secret route was discovered, and several of the conspirators arrested. The Bourbons in England were at the bottom of it, and English gold paid the expense. Pichegru had arrived in Paris, with the infamous Georges, who had so nearly succeeded in taking the life of the First Consul by the explosion of the infernal machine. Moreau had been sounded, and was found ready to aid in the assassination of his former general, but would not listen to the proposal of re-establishing the Bourbon dynasty. His envy had made him the enemy of Napoleon, and he wished to occupy his place. This jar between the conspirators caused delay and uncertainty, which enabled Napoleon to ferret it out. Georges himself, after much trouble, was taken, and he, with other inferior conspirators, confessed the plot, and acknowledged that "the Prince" was expected from England to head the conspiracy. Napoleon despatched soldiers to the sea-coast to arrest whoever might land at the point designated by the conspirators. They watched by the shore for days; and though a small vessel kept hovering near, as if waiting for signals to land, it was suspicious all was not right, and finally moved off altogether. Moreau was tried, found guilty, and exiled the mildest punishment he could possibly expect. Pichegru was thrown into prison, but "the Prince," whom Napoleon was feverishly anxious to get hold of, was not to be found. This whole plot, interrupting as it did his vast plans, and exciting the feelings of the people to a state bordering on revolution, filled him with uncontrollable rage. He felt that he was not regarded as a respectable enemy; for even princes of the blood, and nobles, were endeavouring to assassinate him like a common ruffian. With his usual watchfulness he began to inquire about the exiled princes; and being told that one was at Ettenheim, near Strasbourg, he immediately despatched a spy to watch his movements, for he had not the least doubt that every Bourbon was in the conspiracy.

This spy reported that General Dumourier, another old but exiled general, was with the Prince. This mistake decided Napoleon to arrest him, sacred as his person ought to have been on neutral territory. Whether he afterward became convinced of the young Duke's innocence or not, matters very little as to his guilt. He wished to destroy some Bourbon prince, and he had determined to execute the first one that fell into his hands. To be waylaid and shot like a dog by Bourbon princes enraged him so, that the voice of justice could not be heard. Seated on his proud eminence, bending his vast energies to the most stupendous plans that ever filled a human mind, he was reminded that royal blood regarded him as only a fit victim for the assassin's knife; and he determined to teach kings that he would deal by them openly as they had done by him secretly. Some idea of his feelings may be got from the language he frequently indulged in when speaking of the princes and nobles that were engaged in this conspiracy. Said he, "These Bourbons fancy that they may shed my blood like some wild animal, and yet my blood is quite as precious as theirs. I will repay them the alarm with which they seek to inspire me; I pardon Moreau the weakness and errors to which he is urged by stupid jealousy, but I will pitilessly shoot the very first of these princes who shall fall into my hands; I will teach them with what sort of a man they have to deal." * He classed the Bourbons together, knew them to be inspired with the same feelings toward him, and, whether bound by contract or not, sympathizing with each other in this conspiracy. In a spirit of fierce retaliation and rage, and to stop forever the plotting of these royal assassins, he determined to make a terrible example of one, and the young Duke d'Enghien fell. The news of his death filled the courts of Europe with horror, and was one of the causes of the general alliance against Napoleon that followed. This high-handed act of injustice can not be condemned too emphatically, but it was not the cold-blooded act of a cruel man. It was a crime committed in passion, by a spirit inflamed with the consciousness of having been outraged by those from whom better things were to be expected. England lifted up her hands in pious horror at the act, yet bad not one word to say about the premeditated murder of Napoleon by the Bourbons. If he, instead of one of their number, had fallen, we should have beard no such outcry from the crowned heads of Europe. He had only made a Bourbon drink the cup they had prepared for his lips. The horror of the crime consisted not in its injustice, but that he had dared to lay his hands on the sacred head of royalty. And yet this act, as unjust and wicked as it is conceded to have been, was no more so than that of England in banishing Napoleon, when he had thrown himself on her generosity, to a lonely and barren isle, where she could safely vent her august spleen in those petty annoyances she should have disdained to inflict; or that of the allies, in allowing Marshal Ney to be shot, in direct violation of a treaty they had themselves made.

The sum of the matter is, Napoleon's moral character was indifferent enough; yet as a friend of human liberty, and eager to promote the advancement of the race, by opening the field to talent and genius, however low their birth, he was infinitely superior to all the sovereigns who endeavoured to crush him. He loved not only France as a nation, and sought her glory; but he secured the liberty of the meanest of her subjects. There was something noble in his very ambition, for it sought to establish great public works, found useful institutions, and send the principles of liberty over the world.

As a just and noble monarch, he was superior to nine-tenths of all the kings that ever reigned in Europe, and as an intellectual man, head and shoulders above them all.

The attempt has also been made to fix the charge of cruelty and oppression on him, from the joy manifested in France at his overthrow, and the cursings and obloquy that followed his exile. But the first exultation that follows a new peace is not to be considered the sober feeling of the People. His return from Elba is overwhelming evidence against such accusations. Without any plotting beforehand, any conspiracy to make a diversion in his favour, he boldly cast himself on the affections of the people. An established throne, a strong government, and a powerful army, were on one side the love of the people on the other, and yet, soldier as he was, he believed the latter stronger than all the former put together. What a sublime trust in the strength of affection does his stepping ashore with his handful of followers exhibit. Where is the Bourbon, or European monarch, that would have dared to do this, or felt he had, by his efforts for the common welfare, laid the people under sufficient obligations to expect a universal rush to his arms? It was not the soldiers, but the common people, who first surrounded him. As he pitched his tent without Cannes, the inhabitants flocked to him with their complaints, and gathered around him as the redresser of their wrongs. As he advanced toward Grenoble, the fields were alive with peasants, as they came leaping like deer from every hill, crying *"Vive l'Empereur!"* Thronging around him, they followed him with shouts to the very gates of the town. The commandant refused him admittance, yet the soldiers within stretched their arms through the wickets, and shook hands with his followers without. At length a confused murmur arose over the walls, and Napoleon did not know but it was the gathering for a fierce assault on his little band. The tumult grew wilder every moment; six-thousand inhabitants from one of the *faubourgs* had risen *en masse*, and with timbers and beams came pouring against the gates. They tremble before the resistless shocks reel and fall with a crash to the ground, and the excited multitude stream forth. Rushing on Napoleon, they drag him from his horse, kiss his hands and garments, and bear him with deafening shouts, on their shoulders, into the town. He next advances on Lyons, the gates of which are also closed against him, and bayonets gleam along the walls. Trusting to the power of affection, rather than to arms, he gallops boldly up to the city. The soldiers within, instead of firing on him, breaking over all discipline burst open the gates, and rush in frantic joy around him, shouting *"Vive l'Empereur!"* He is not compelled to plant his cannon against a single town: power returns to him not through terror, but through love. He is not received with the cringing of slaves, but with the open arms of friends, and thus his course toward the capital becomes one triumphal march. The power of the Bourbons disappears before the returning tide of affection, like towers of sand before the waves; and, without firing a gun, Napoleon again sits down on his recovered throne, amid the acclamations of the people. Who ever saw a tyrant and an oppressor received thus? Where is the monarch in Europe that dare fling himself in such faith on the affections of his subjects? Where was ever the Bourbon that could show such a title to the throne he occupied? Ah! the people do not thus receive the man who forges fetters for their limbs; and Napoleon at this day holds a firmer place in the affections of the inhabitants of France, than any monarch that ever filled its throne.

The two greatest errors of Napoleon were the conquest of Spain and the invasion of Russia. The former was not only an impolitic act, but one of great injustice and cruelty. In order to strike English commerce, he was willing to invade an independent kingdom, and finally seize its throne and cover its plains with the slain of its own subjects. The invasion of Russia might have terminated differently, and been recorded by historians as the crowning monument of his genius, but for the burning of Moscow by the inhabitants; an event certainly not to be anticipated. He lost the flower of his army there, and instead of striking the heart of his enemy he pierced his own.

It is useless, however, to speak of the mistakes that Napoleon made, and show how he should have acted here, and planned there, to have succeeded; or attempt to trace the separate steps, in the latter part of his career, to his downfall, and pretend to say how they might have been avoided. After taking into the calculation all the chances and changes that did or would come all the losses that might have been prevented, and all the successes that might have been gained, and pointing out great errors here and there in his movements, it is plain that nothing less than a miracle could have saved the tottering throne of the Empire. After the disaster of Leipzig, and the losses sustained by different divisions of the army in that campaign, and the mortality which thinned so dreadfully the French armies on the Rhine, France felt herself exhausted and weak. In this depressed state, the civilized world was preparing its last united onset upon her. From the Baltic to the Bosphorus from the Archangel to the Mediterranean, Europe had banded itself against Napoleon. Denmark and Sweden struck hands with Austria, and Russia, and Prussia, and England; while, to crown all, the Princes of the confederation of the Rhine put their signature to the league, and one million and twenty-eight thousand men stood up in battle array on the plains of Europe, to overthrow this mighty spirit that had shaken so terribly their thrones.

France, which had before been drained to meet the losses of the Russian campaign, could not, with her utmost efforts, raise more than a third of the number of this immense host.

Her provinces were invaded, and this resistless array were pointing their bayonets toward Paris. In this dreadful emergency, though none saw better than he the awful abyss that was opening before him, Napoleon evinced no discouragement and no hesitation. Assembling the conscripts from every quarter of France, and hurrying them on to headquarters, he at length, after presenting his fair-haired boy to the National Guards as their future sovereign, amid tears and exclamations of enthusiasm, and embracing his wife for the last time, set out for the army. His energy, his wisdom, and incessant activity soon changed the face of affairs. He had struggled against as great odds in his first Italian campaign; and if nothing else could be done, he at least could fall with honour on the soil of his country. Never did his genius shine forth with greater splendour than in the almost superhuman exertions he put forth in this his last great struggle for his empire. No danger could daunt him no reverses subdue him no toil exhaust him and no difficulties shake his iron will. In the dead of winter, struggling with new and untried troops, he fought an army outnumbering his own two to one beat them back at every point, and sent dismay into the hearts of the allied sovereigns, as they again saw the shadow of his mighty spirit over their thrones. He was everywhere cheering and steadying his men, and on one occasion worked a cannon himself as he did when a youth in the artillery; and though the balls whistled around him till the soldiers besought him to retire, he exclaimed, "Courage! the bullet that is to kill me is not yet cast." At length the whole allied army was forced to retreat, and offered peace if he would consent to have his empire dismembered and France restored to its limits before the Revolution. This he indignantly refused; preferring rather to bury himself amid the ruins of his empire. But with his comparative handful of raw recruits, what could be do against the world in arms? His rapid victories began to grow less decisive; the glory with which he had anew covered the army waxed dim; and his star, that had once more blazed forth in its ancient splendour in the heavens, was seen sinking to the horizon.

The allies entered the capital, and Napoleon was compelled to abdicate. On the day after the signature of the treaty by which he was divested of power and sent an exile from the country he had saved deserted by all his soldiers, his marshals, his army even by his wife and family, he said to Caulincourt at night, after a long and sad reverie, "My resolution is taken; we must end: I feel it." At midnight the fallen Emperor was in convulsions; he had swallowed poison. As his faithful Caulincourt came in, he opened his eyes, and said, "Caulincourt, I am about to die. I recommend to you my wife and son; defend my memory. I could no longer endure life. The desertion of my old companions in arms had broken my heart." Violent vomiting, however, gave him relief; and his life was saved.

His farewell to his faithful Old Guard, before he departed from Fontainebleau for Elba, was noble and touching. He passed into their midst as he had been wont to do when he pitched his tent for the night in their protecting squares, and addressed them in words of great tenderness. "For twenty years," said lie, "I have ever found you in the Path of honour and glory. Adieu, my children; I would I were able to press you all to my heart, but I will at least press your eagle." With overpowering emotion, he clasped the general in his arms, and kissed the eagle. Again bidding his old companions adieu, he drove away, while cries and sobs of sorrow burst from those brave hearts that had turned for him the tide of so many battles. They besought the privilege of following him in his fallen fortunes; but were refused their prayer.

But Elba could not long hold that daring, restless spirit. The next year he again unrolled his standard in the capital of France, and the army opened its arms to receive him. After an exhibition of his wonted energy and genius during the hundred days' preparation, he at length staked all on the field of Waterloo. There the star of his destiny again rose over the horizon, and struggled with its ancient strength to mount the heavens of fame. The battle-cloud rolled over it; and when it again was swept away, that star had gone down sunk in blood and carnage, to rise no more forever.

Volumes have been written on this campaign and last battle; but every impartial mind must come to the same conclusion, that Napoleon's plans never promised more complete success than at this last effort. Wellington was entrapped; and with the same co-operation on both sides, he was lost beyond redemption. Had Blucher stayed away as Grouchy did, or had Grouchy come up as did Blucher, victory would once more have soared with the French eagles. It is vain to talk of Grouchy's having obeyed orders. It was plainly his duty, and his only duty, to detain Blucher, or follow him.

Bonaparte has also been blamed for risking all on the last desperate charge of the Old Guard; but he well knew that nothing but a decided victory could save him. He wanted the moral effect of one; and without it he was lost and he wisely risked all to win it. He is also blamed, both in poetry and prose, for not throwing away his life when the battle was lost. If personal daring and personal exposure had been called for in the disorder, and success could have been possible, by flinging himself into the very jaws of death, he would not have hesitated a moment. But the rout was utter; and though he did wish to die, and would have done so but for his friends, had he succeeded in his purpose, it would have been simply an act of suicide, for which his enemies would have been devoutly thankful.

His last hope was gone, and he threw himself into the hands of England, expecting generous, but receiving the basest, treatment. She banished him to an inhospitable rock in the midst of the ocean; and, having caged the lion, performed the honourable task of watching at the door of the prison, while her parasites kept a faithful record of the complaints and irritations of the noble sufferer, whose misfortunes they had not the magnanimity to respect. But not all this could dim the splendour of that genius whose great work was done. The thoughts that here emanated from him, and the maxims he laid down, both in political and military life, show that he could have written one of the most extraordinary books of his age, as easily as he had become one of its greatest military leaders and rulers.

But at length that wonderful mind was to be quenched in the night of the grave; and Nature, as if determined to assert the greatness of her work to the last, trumpeted him out of the world with one of her fiercest storms. Amid the roar of the blast, and the shock of the billows, as they broke where a wave had not struck for twenty years and amid the darkness, and gloom, and uproar of one of the most tempestuous nights that ever rocked that lonely isle, Napoleon's troubled spirit was passing to that unseen world where the sound of battle never comes, and the tread of armies is never beard. Yet even in this solemn hour his delirious soul, caught perhaps by the battle-like roar of the storm without, was once more in the midst of the fight, struggling by the Pyramids, or Danube, or on the plains of Italy. It was the thunder of cannon that smote his ear; and amid the wavering light, and covering smoke, and tumult of the scene, his glazing eye caught the heads of his mighty columns, as, torn yet steady, they bore his victorious eagles on, and *"Tête d'armée"* broke from his dying lips. Awestruck and still, his few remaining friends stood in tears about his couch, gazing steadfastly on that awful kingly brow; but it gave no further token, and the haughty lips moved no more. Napoleon lay silent and motionless in his last sleep.

When the prejudice and falsehood and hatred of his enemies shall disappear, and the world can gaze impartially on this plebeian soldier rising to the throne of an empire measuring his single intellect with the proudest kings of Europe, and coming off victorious from the encounter rising above the prejudices and follies of his age, "making kings of plebeians and plebeians of kings" grasping, as by intuition, all military and political science expending with equal facility his vast energies on war or peace turning with the same profound thought from fierce battles to commerce, and trade, and finances; I say when the world can calmly thus contemplate him, his amazing genius will receive that homage which envy, and ignorance, and hatred now withhold.

And when the intelligent philanthropist shall understand the political and civil history of Europe, and see how Napoleon broke up its systems of oppression and feudalism proclaiming human rights in the ears of the world, till the Continent shook with the rising murmurs of oppressed man study well the changes he introduced, without which human progress must have ceased see the great public works he established the institutions he founded the laws he proclaimed, and the civil liberty he restored and then, remembering that the bloody wars that offset all these were waged by him in self-defence, and were equal rights struggling against exclusive despotism he will regret that he has adopted the slanders of his foemen and the falsehoods of monarchists.

Marshal Berthier

Chapter 2
Marshal Berthier

Nothing is more unfortunate for a great man than to be born beside a greater, and walk during lifetime in his shadow. It is equally unfortunate to be great only in one department that is still better filled by another. Had Shakespeare not lived, Massinger might have stood at the head of English dramatists; and had Alfieri kept silent, a host of writers, now almost unknown, would have occupied the Italian stage. Had it not been for Cæsar, Brutus might have ruled the world; and were it not for Bonaparte, many a French general would occupy a separate place in that history of which they are now only transient figures. Great men, like birds, seem to come in flocks; and yet but one stands as the representative of his age. The peak which first catches the sunlight is crowned monarch of the hills, and the rest, however lofty, are but his body-guard. Much injustice has been done to Bonaparte's generals by not allowing for the influence of this principle. There is scarcely a historian that will concede to such men as Lannes, Davoust, Murat, and Ney, any dominant quality, except bravery. Under the guiding intellect of Napoleon, they fought nobly; but, when left to their own resources, miserably failed. Yet the simple truth is: being compelled, by their relative position, to let another plan for them, they could do little else than execute orders. A mind dependent is cramped and confined, and can exhibit its power only by the force and vigour with which it executes rather than forms plans.

But if it be a misfortune for a great man to live and move in the shadow of a still greater, it is directly the reverse with a weak man. The shadow of the genius in which he walks mantles his stupidity, and, by the dim glory it casts over him, magnifies his proportions.

Such was the position of Boswell to Johnson, and this is the secret of Berthier's fame. Being selected by Napoleon as the chief of his staff, and his most intimate companion, he has linked himself indissolubly with immortality.

The times in which Bonaparte lived were well calculated to produce such men as he gathered around him. A revolution, by its upturnings, brings to the surface materials of the existence of which no man ever dreamed before. Circumstances make men, who then usually return the compliment, and make circumstances. In ordinary times, as a general rule, the souls of men exhibit what force and fire they may contain, in those channels where birth has placed them. This is more especially true in all monarchical and aristocratical governments. The iron framework they stretch over the human race effectually presses down every throb that would otherwise send an undulation over the mass. No head can lift itself except in the legitimate way, while very small heads, that happen to hit the aperture aristocracy has kindly left open, may reach a high elevation. Revolution rends this framework as if it were a cobweb, and lets the struggling, panting mass beneath suddenly erect themselves to their full height and fling abroad their arms in their full strength. The surface, which before kept its even plane, except where a star or decoration told the right of the wearer to overlook his fellow, becomes all at once a wild waste of rolling billows. Then man is known by the force within him, and not by the pomp about him. There is also a prejudice and bigotry always attached to rank, which prevents it from seeing the worth below it, while it will not measure by a just standard, because that would appreciate its own excellence. Those, on the contrary, who obtain influences through the soul and force they carry within them, appreciate these things alone in others, and hence judge them by a true criterion.

Thus Bonaparte himself sprung from the middle class of society selected men to lead his armies from their personal qualities alone. This is one great secret of his astonishing victories. Dukes and princes led the allied armies, while men headed the battalions of France. Bonaparte judged men by what they could do, and not by their genealogy. He looked not at the decorations that adorned the breast, but at the deeds that stamped the warrior not at the learning that made the perfect tactician, but the real practical force that wrought out great achievements. Victorious battlefields were to him the birthplace of titles, and the commencement of genealogies; and stars were hung on scarred and war-battered, rather than on noble, breasts. He had learned the truth taught in every physical or moral revolution, that the great effective moulding characters of our race always spring from the middle and lower classes. All reformers also start there, and they always must, for not only is their sight clearer and their judgment more just, but their earnest language is adapted to the thoughts and sympathies of the many. Those men also who rise to power through themselves alone feel it is by themselves alone they must stand; hence the impelling motive is not so much greatness to be won, as the choice between it and their original nothingness. Bonaparte was aware of this, and of all his generals who have gone down to immortality with him, how few were taken from the upper classes! Augereau was the son of a grocer, Bernadotte of an attorney, and both commenced their career as private soldiers. Bessières, St. Cyr, Jourdan, and the fiery Junot all entered the army as privates. Kleber was an architect; the impetuous Lannes the son of a poor mechanic; Lefevre, Loison, and the bold Scotchman Macdonald were all of humble parentage. The victorious Massena was an orphan sailor boy, and the reckless, chivalric Murat the son of a country landlord. Victor, Suchet, Oudinot, and the stern and steady Soult were each and all of humble origin, and commenced their ascent from the lowest step of Fame's ladder. And last of all, Ney, the "bravest of the brave," was the son of a poor tradesman of Sarre Louis.

Immediately on the assumption of supreme power, Napoleon created eighteen marshals, leaving two vacancies to be filled afterward. Four of these were honorary appointments, given to those who had distinguished themselves in previous battles, and were now reposing on their laurels as members of the Senate. The other fourteen were conferred on generals destined for active service, but in reward of their former deeds. The first four were Kellerman, Lefevre, Periguin, and Serruier. The fourteen active marshals were Jourdan, Berthier, Massena, Lannes, Ney, Augereau, Brune, Murat, Bessières, Moncey, Mortier, Soult, Davoust, and Bernadotte. Kleber and Desaix were dead, both killed on the same day, one in Egypt and the other at Marengo, or they would have been first on this immortal list.

All these had been active generals, and had distinguished themselves by great deeds, and won their renown by hard fighting, except Berthier. Their honours were the reward of prodigies of valour and exhibitions of heroism seldom surpassed. Berthier alone obtained his appointment for his services in the staff, and partly, I am inclined to believe, for his personal attachment for Napoleon. Without any merit as a military leader, he still deserves a place among the distinguished Marshals of the Empire, for is intimate relationship with Napoleon.

Alexander Berthier was born at Versailles, on the 20th of November, 1753. His father was the coast surveyor to Louis XVI., and acquired great reputation for his skill in this department. Young Berthier naturally became proficient in mathematical studies was a capital surveyor, and excelled in drawing. Though filling the situation in his father's office with a faithfulness and ability that promised complete success in his profession, he nevertheless preferred the army. By his father's connection with government, he was enabled to obtain a commission at the outset in the dragoons, and as lieutenant in Rochambeau's staff came to the United States, and served during the war of the American Revolution. I know of no act of his, during this time, worthy of note. He had none of the daring and intrepidity so necessary to form a good commander. At the time of the French Revolution, he was officer in the National Guards, and stood firm to the royal cause till the Guards themselves went over, when he himself became a fiery republican. He was chief of the staff in the first campaigns of the Republic, on the Rhine and northern frontier, and though faithful and efficient in the discharge of his duties, received no promotion. Not having sufficient energy and force to distinguish himself by any brilliant exploit, he obtained merely the reputation of being a faithful officer. In the first campaign in Italy, he was quartermaster to Kellerman; but when Bonaparte took command of the army, he made him chief of his staff, and promoted him to the rank of major-general.

From that time on, for eighteen years, he scarce ever left the side of Bonaparte. We find him with him on the sands of Egypt, and amid the snows of Russia; by the Po, the Rhine, the Danube, and the Niemen, and admitted to an intimacy that few were allowed to enjoy. It seems natural for a strong, powerful mind to attach itself to a weak one; for its desire is not so much for sympathy and support, as for the privilege of relaxing and unbending itself, without impairing its dignity, or exposing its weaknesses. Berthier seemed to place no restraint on him. He had such a thorough contempt for his intellect, and knew in what awe and reverence he held him, that his presence relieved his solitude without destroying it. It is true, Berthier's topographical knowledge, and his skill in drawing maps and charts, and in explaining them, made him indispensable to Bonaparte, who relied so much on these things in projecting his campaigns. Especially as the channel through which all his orders passed, he became more necessary to him than any other single officer in the army. Yet, Berthier was admitted into privacies to which none of these relations gave him a claim. When it was necessary for Bonaparte to be in the open air for a long time, early in the morning, or late at evening, a huge fire was always built by the Chasseurs, to which he allowed no one to approach, unless to feed it with fuel, except Berthier. Backward and forward, with his hands behind his back, he would walk his grave and thoughtful face bent on the ground until the signals were made of which he was in expectation, when he would throw off his reserve, and call out to Berthier, "To horse."

Bonaparte's travelling carriage, a curiosity in itself, was arranged as much for Berthier as for himself. Notwithstanding the drawers for his despatches, and his portable library, he had a part of it partitioned off for the latter. True, he did not give him half, nor allow him the *dormeuse*, on which he himself could recline and refresh himself. But Berthier was content, even with the privilege allowed him, though it furnished him anything but repose, for Bonaparte made use of the time in which his cortège was sweeping like a whirlwind along the road, to examine despatches, and the reports of the positions, etc. As he read he dictated his directions, which Berthier jotted down, and, at the next stopping-place, filled out with a precision that satisfied even his rigorous master. Methodical in all he did doing nothing in confusion the rapid hints thrown out by Napoleon assumed a symmetry and order under his pen that required no explanation, and scarce ever needed an alteration. In this department he was almost as tireless as Napoleon himself. He would write all night, with a clearness of comprehension and an accuracy of detail, that was perfectly surprising. Apparently without the mental grasp and vigour necessary to comprehend the gigantic plans he filled out with such admirable precision, he nevertheless mapped them down as if they had been his own. A hint from Napoleon was sufficient for him; for so accustomed had he become to the action of his mind, that he could almost anticipate his orders. He had lived and moved, and breathed so long in the atmosphere of that intellect, that he became a perfect reflector to it. He knew the meaning of every look and gesture of the Emperor, and a single glance would arrest him, as if it had the power to blast. At the battle of Eylau, when Augereau's shattered ranks came flying past him, pursued by the enemy, Napoleon suddenly found himself, with only his staff about him, in presence of a column of four thousand Russians. His capture seemed inevitable, for he was on foot, and almost breast to breast with the column. Berthier immediately, in great trepidation, called out for the horses. Napoleon gave him a single look, which pinned him as silent in his place as if he had been turned to stone. Instead of mounting his horse, he ordered a battalion of his guard to charge. The audacious column paused, and, before it could recover from its surprise, six battalions of the Old Guard, and Murat's Cavalry, were upon it, rending it to pieces. So perfectly mechanical was his mind, that it was impossible to confuse him by the rapid accumulation of business on his hands. He was, among papers, what Bonaparte was on a battlefield always himself; clearheaded and correct, bringing order out of confusion, in a manner that delighted his exacting master. Bonaparte appreciated this quality in his major-general, and tasked it to the utmost. He once said that this was the great merit of Berthier, and of "inestimable importance" to him. "No other could possibly have replaced him." The services he performed were amply rewarded by making him Marshal of the Empire, grand huntsman, Prince of Neufchatel, and Prince of Wagram. Yet, such a low opinion did Napoleon have of this Prince and Marshal's character, that he once said: "Nature has evidently designated many for a subordinate situation; and among them is Berthier. As chief of the staff, he had no superior; but he was not fit to command five hundred men." From this intimate relationship with Napoleon, however, and all the orders coming through his hands, many began to think he was the light of Napoleon's genius. "Napoleon and Berthier" were coupled so constantly in men's months, that they began to be joined in praise by those who knew neither personally, and there might, to this day, have been a great difference of opinion respecting his merit, if he had never attempted anything more than to obey orders.

Still Berthier showed at times ability which brought on him the commendations of the Commander-in-chief. At Lodi, Arcola, and indeed throughout the first campaign of the young Bonaparte, he behaved with so much bravery, and brought such aid to the army, that he was most honourably mentioned in the reports to the Directory.

On Bonaparte's return to Paris, after his victorious campaign in Italy, Berthier was left in command of the army. Not long after, in an *émeute* in Rome, the French Legation was assailed, and the young General Duphet killed, which brought an order from the Directory to Berthier to march on the city. Arrived at the gates of the home of the Cæsars, the soldiers were transported with enthusiasm; and they, with the republican citizens, conducted Berthier through the Porta di Popolo in triumph to the Capitol, as the victorious generals of old were wont to be borne. The intoxicated multitude, thinking the days of ancient glory, when Rome was a republic, had returned, sang the following memorable hymn as they carried him toward the

Capitol

Romain, leve les yeux: là fut le Capitole;
Ce pont est le pont du Coclès,
Ces chardons sont converts des cendres de Scévole,
Lucrèce dort sous ces cyprès
Là Brutus là immola la râce;
Ici c'engloutit Curtius;
Et Cesar à cette autre place
Fut poignardé par Cassius.
Rome, là liberté t'appelle!
Romp tes fers, ose t'affranchir;
Un Romain dort libre pour elle,
Pour elle un Romain dort mourir.

Te Deum was chanted in St. Peter's by fourteen cardinals, and the old Roman form of government proclaimed in the ancient Forum.

But he was no sooner installed in his place, than he began to practice such extortion and pillage, that even his own officers broke out in open complaints against him; and he had to leave the army and set out for Paris.

He was one of those selected by Bonaparte to accompany him to Egypt. Berthier could not bear to leave his "beloved General's" side; but, though forty-three years of age, he had conceived such a violent passion for one Madame Visconti, that it quite upset his weak intellect, and, drove him into paroxysms of grief when he thought also of leaving the object of his passion. He hastened to Toulon, and told Bonaparte that he was sick, and could not go; and requested to be left behind. But his prayers and tears fell on a heart that had no sympathy with such nonsense, and he was forced to set sail. The long, tedious voyage the separation of so many thousand miles the new an glorious field to honour and fame which Egypt spread out before him, could not drive the image of his dear Visconti from his mind. He had a tent placed beside his own fitted up in the most elegant style, in which was suspended the portrait of this lady. Here "the chief of the staff of the army of Egypt" would retire alone, and, prostrating himself before it, indulge in the most passionate expressions of love and grief, and went so far at times even as to burn incense to it, as if it were a goddess, and he an ignorant devotee. At Alexandria, his grief became so intense, that he besought Bonaparte to allow him to return. Finding it impossible to drive this absurd passion from the turned head of his major-general, he at length granted his request. Poor Berthier bade his commander a solemn farewell, and departed. In a few hours, however, he returned, his eyes swimming in tears, saying, after all, he could not leave his "beloved General."

He accompanied Bonaparte in his return to France, and with Lannes and Murat was his chief reliance and confidant in his plans to overturn the Directory. After the establishment of the Consular system, and his own appointment as First Consul, Napoleon did not forget the services of Berthier, but gave to him the portfolio of War. He bestowed on him also, at different times, large sums of money, which might as well have been thrown in the Seine, as to all good they did this imbecile spendthrift. On one occasion he presented him with a magnificent diamond worth nearly twenty thousand dollars, saying: "Take this; we frequently play high: lay it up against a time of need." In a few hours it was sparkling on the head of his lady-love.

This mad passion, outliving separation, change, and all the excitements of the camp and battlefield, was doomed

to a most bitter disappointment. At the urgent request of Napoleon, he finally married a princess of Bavaria. But scarcely was the marriage consummated when, as if on purpose to complete his despair, the husband of Madame Visconti died. This was too much for Berthier. Cursing his miserable fate, he hastened to Napoleon overcome with grief, exclaiming: "What a miserable man I am! Had I been only a little more constant, Madame Visconti would have been my wife."

I remarked before that Berthier might possibly have passed for a good general, had he not gratuitously revealed is own weakness to the eyes of Europe. At the opening of the campaigns of Abensberg, Landshut, and Eckmuhl, Napoleon dispatched him to the headquarters of the army, with definite directions the sum of which was, to concentrate all the forces around Ratisbon, unless the enemy made an attack before the 15th, in which case he was to concentrate them on the Lech, around Donauwerth. Berthier, seized with some wonderful idea of his own, instead of carrying out the Emperor's orders to the very letter, as he had ever before done, acted directly contrary to them. Instead of concentrating the army, he scattered it. The Austrians were advancing, and the notion instantly seized him of executing a prodigious feat, and of stopping the enemy at all points.

Massena and Davoust, commanding the two principal corps of the army, he separated a hundred miles from each other, while at the same time he placed Lefebvre, Wrede, and Oudinot in so absurd a position that these experienced generals were utterly amazed. Davoust became perfectly furious at the folly of Berthier told him he was dooming the army to utter destruction, while Massena urged his strong remonstrance against this suicidal measure. As he was acting under Napoleon's orders, however, they were compelled to obey him, though some of the marshals declared that he was a traitor, and had been bribed to deliver up the army. Nothing but the slowness of the Archduke's advance saved them. His army of a hundred and twenty thousand men could, at this juncture, have crushed them almost at a blow, if it had possessed one-quarter the activity Napoleon soon after evinced. While matters were in this deplorable state, and Berthier was in an agony at his own folly, and utterly at loss what to do, Napoleon arrived at headquarters. He was perfectly amazed at the perilous position in which his army was placed.

His hasty interrogations of every one around him soon placed the condition of the two armies clearly before him; and his thoughts and actions, rapid as lightning, quickly showed that another spirit was at the head of affairs. Officers were dispatched hither and thither on the fleetest horses Berthier's orders were all countermanded, and the concentration of the army was effected barely in time to save it. Immediately on his arrival at Donauwerth he dispatched a note to

Berthier, saying: "What you have done appears so strange, that if I was not aware of your friendship, I should think you were betraying me. Davoust is at this moment more completely at the Archduke's disposal than my own." Davoust was also perfectly aware of this, but thought only of fulfilling his orders like a brave man. In speaking of this afterward, Napoleon said: "You can not imagine in what a condition I found the army on my arrival, and to what dreadful reverses it was exposed if we had to deal with an enterprising enemy. I shall take care that I am not surprised again in such a manner." The chief of the staff was never after suspected of being anything more than a mere instrument in the hands of the Emperor.

The change that passed over the French army was instantaneous, and the power of intellect and genius, working with lightning-like rapidity, was never more clearly seen than in the different aspect Napoleon put on affairs in a single day. Under his all-pervading, all-embracing spirit, order rose out of confusion, and strength out of weakness. Had an Austrian general committed such a blunder in his presence as Berthier did in the face of the Archduke Charles, he would have utterly annihilated him.

It is useless to follow Berthier through the long campaigns, in which he never quitted the Emperor's side, as he only now and then appears above the surface, and then merely as a good chief of the staff, and a valuable aid in the cabinet with his topographical knowledge. He was with him in his last efforts to save Paris and his throne. He, with Caulincourt, was by his side in that gloomy night when, in his haste to get to his capital, he could not wait for his carriage, but walked on foot for a mile, chafing like a fettered lion. They were the only auditors of that terrible soliloquy that broke from his lips as he strode on through the darkness. Just before, when news was brought that Paris bad capitulated, the expression of his face as he turned to Caulincourt and exclaimed, "Do you hear that?" was enough to freeze one with horror; but now his sufferings melted the heart with pity. Paris was illuminated by the innumerable watch-fires that covered the heights, and around it the allied troops were shouting in unbounded exultation over the glorious victory that compensated them for all their former losses; while but fifteen miles distant, on foot, walked its king and emperor through the deep midnight his mighty spirit wrung with such agony that the sweat stood in large drops on his forehead, and his lips worked in the most painful excitement. Neither Berthier nor Caulincourt dared to interrupt the rapid soliloquy of the fallen Emperor, as he muttered in fierce accents: "I burned the pavement my horses were swift as the wind, but still I felt oppressed with an intolerable weight; some thing extraordinary was passing within me. I asked them to hold out only twenty-four hours. Miserable wretches that they are! Marmont, too, who had sworn that he would be hewn in pieces rather than surrender! And Joseph ran off, too my very brother! To surrender the capital to the enemy what poltroons! They had my orders; they knew that, on the 2d of April, I would be here at the head of seventy thousand men! My brave scholars, my National Guard, who had promised to defend my son; all men with a heart in their bosoms, would have joined to combat at my side! And so they have capitulated, betrayed their brother, their country, their sovereign degraded France in the sight of Europe! Entered into a capital of eight hundred thousand souls, without firing a shot! It is too dreadful! That comes of trusting cowards and fools. When I am not there, they do nothing but heap blunder on blunder. What has been done with the artillery? They should have had two hundred pieces, and ammunition for a month. Everyone has lost his head; and yet Joseph imagines that he can lead an army, and Clarke is vain enough to think himself a minister; but I begin to think Savary is right, and that he is a traitor;" then suddenly rousing himself, as if from a troubled dream, and as if unable to believe so great a disaster, he turned fiercely on Caulincourt and Berthier and exclaimed: "Set off, Caulincourt; fly to the allied lines; penetrate to headquarters; you have full powers; fly! fly!" It was with difficulty that Berthier and Caulincourt could persuade him that the capitulation had been concluded. Yielding at length to the irreversible stroke of fate, he turned back, joined his carriages, and hastened to Fontainebleau, where he arrived a little after sunrise.

That was a gloomy day for him; and while he was pondering on his perilous position, endeavouring to pierce the night of misfortune that now enveloped him, Paris was shaking to the acclamation of the multitude, as the allied armies defiled through the streets. Caulincourt had been sent off to make terms with the victors, but nothing would do but Napoleon's abdication and he was forced to resign. Then commenced the shameful desertion of his followers, which broke his great heart, and drove him in his anguish to attempt the destruction of his life. Among these feeble and false-hearted men was Berthier. Napoleon was a crownless, throneless man, without an army without favour, or the gifts they bring and Berthier had no longer any motive for attaching himself to him, except that of honour and noble affection both of which he was entirely destitute of. Afraid to turn traitor before his benefactor's face, he asked permission to go to Paris on business, promising to return the next day. When he had left, Napoleon turned to the Duke of Bassano, and said "He will not return." "What!" replied the Duke, "can Berthier take such a farewell?" "He will not return," calmly replied Napoleon. "He was born a courtier. In a few days you will see my Vice Constable begging an appointment from the Bourbons. It mortifies me to see men I have raised so high in the eyes of Europe, sink so low. What have they done with that halo of glory, through which men have been wont to contemplate them?" He was right; Berthier returned no more. Too mean to entertain or even act a noble sentiment and yet with sufficient conscience to feel the glaring ingratitude and baseness of his treachery, and fearing to confront the man who had elevated him to honour, and heaped countless benefits on his head; he shrunk away like a thief, to kiss the foot of a Bourbon. A few days after, he presented himself at the head of the Marshals before Louis XVIII., saying "France having groaned for the last twenty-five years under the weight of the misfortunes which oppressed her, had looked forward to the happy day which now shines upon her." This infamous falsehood, crowning his base treason, ingratitude, and blasphemy was uttered within one week after he had sworn to Bonaparte he would never desert him, whatever adversity might befall him. When the Bourbon King made his public entry into Paris, Berthier was seen riding in front of the carriage in all the pomp of his new situation. But even the common people could not witness the disgrace this companion and private friend of Napoleon put on human nature, in silence. As he rode along, reproachful voices met his ear, saying, "Go to the island of Elba, Berthier! go to Elba!" There was his place. Honour, gratitude, affection, manhood all called him there, but called in vain. A seat in the Chamber of Peers, and a command in the King's body-guard, were the price he received for covering himself with infamy in the sight of the world.

But his baseness was doomed to receive another reward, for the next year Napoleon was again in France. As Louis withdrew to Ghent, Berthier wished to accompany him; but the King bad sufficient penetration to see that one who had deserted his greatest friend and benefactor in the hour of adversity, would not be slow to betray him; and hence intimated that he could dispense with his company. Trusted by no one, he retired to Bomberg, in his father-in-law's dominions. Here, on the 19th of May, 1816, he was seen leaning out of the window of his hotel, as the allies were defiling past, in their retreat from France. A moment after, his mangled body was lifted from the pavement, where it lay crushed and lifeless at the very feet of the Russian soldiers. Some say he was thrown out by the soldiers themselves; others, that he leaped purposely from the window to destroy himself. His death is surrounded in mystery; but the common belief is, that, Judas-like, stung with remorse and shame for his treachery, and finding himself deserted by his new master, and fearing the vengeance of his old one, he took this method of ending a life which had become burdensome, and added to all his other crimes that of suicide.

But he need not have feared Bonaparte he held him in too great contempt to make him an object of vengeance, and was beard to say, on his march to Paris "The only revenge I wish on this poor Berthier, would be to see him in his costume of captain of the body-guard of Louis." He knew that he would writhe under his smile of contempt, more than under the stroke of a lance.

Berthier wrote a history of the expedition into Egypt, and, if he had survived Napoleon, would probably have given an account of his private life, which would have added much to the facts already collected.

Marshal Augereau

CHAPTER 3

Marshal Augereau

There is very little pleasure in contemplating a character like that of Augereau, especially when one is led, from his rank and titles, to expect great qualities. Augereau had simple bravery, nothing more, to render him worthy of a place amid the Marshals of the Empire. He was not even a second-rate man in anything but courage; and there he had no superior. As a fierce fighter one whose charge was like a thunderbolt, and whose tenacity in the midst of carnage and ruin nothing seemed able to shake he was worthy to command beside Massena, Ney, Lannes, Davoust, and Murat but there the equality ended. He owed his Marshal's baton not so much to his generalship, as to his having served in Bonaparte's first campaigns in Italy, and helped, by his bravery, to lay the foundation-stone of the young Corsican's fame. Napoleon, in the height of his power, did not forget the young Chiefs, with whom he won his first laurels, and to whose unsurpassed valour he owed the wondrous success of his first campaigns. It was with such men as Murat, Massena, Lannes, Victor, and Augereau that he conquered four armies, each large as his own. With all his genius, he could have accomplished so much with no other men. In those rapid and forced marches those resistless onsets, and in that tireless activity, without which he was ruined these men were equal to his wishes and his wants. Massena and Augereau were among the first of these fiery leaders, and astonished Europe by the brilliancy of their exploits. Bonaparte, in his letter to the Directory, calls him "the brave Augereau." At Lodi, Castiglione, and Arcola, he won his ducal title, and his Marshal's staff.

Born November 14, 1757, in the Faubourg St. Marceau, of Paris, the son of a grocer, Pierre-François Charles Augereau always retained the marks of his origin. Living in a democratic quarter of the city, and sprung from a democratic stock, he was as thorough a Jacobin as ever outraged humanity.

Of an adventurous, ardent spirit, he left Paris when a mere youth, and entered the army of the King of Naples as a common soldier. Finding nothing to do, and apparently nothing to gain in the service, he left it in mingled disappointment and disgust. Poor and without friends, he taught fencing in Naples, as a means of support, and remained there till he was thirty-five years of age. But the all-powerful Revolution, which dragged into its vortex every stern and fierce spirit France possessed, soon hurried him into scenes more congenial to his tastes. Being compelled to leave Naples, in 1792, by the edict of the King, which forced all Frenchmen of Revolutionary principles out of the kingdom, he returned to Paris, and enlisted as a volunteer in the army of the Pyrenees. Here he had a clear field for his daring, and soon won himself a reputation that secured his rapid promotion. When he entered the army as a volunteer, he was thirty-five years of age at thirty-eight he found himself brigadier-general, and in two years more general of division. Foremost in the place of danger resistless in the onset, he had acquired a reputation for daring, that made him a fit companion for Napoleon in his Italian campaigns. Though so much older than the Commander-in-chief, he soon learned to bow to his superior genius, and followed him with a courage and fidelity that did not go unrewarded.

I have often imagined the first interview between the young Bonaparte and the veteran generals of the Army of Italy. There were Rampon, Massena, and Augereau, crowned with laurels they had won on many a hard-fought field. Here was a young man, sent to them as their Commander-in-chief, only twenty-seven years of age. Pale, thin, with a stoop in his shoulders, his personal appearance indicated anything but the warrior. And what else had he to recommend him? He had directed some artillery successfully against Toulon, and quelled a mob in Paris, and that was all. He had no rank in civil matters indeed, had scarcely been heard of and now, a mere stripling, without experience, never having conducted an army in his life, he appears before the two scarred generals, Massena and Augereau, both nearly forty years of age, as their Commander-in-chief. When called to pay their first visit to him, on his arrival, they were utterly amazed at the folly of the Directory. The war promised to be a mere farce. Young Bonaparte, whose quick eye detected the impression he had made on them, soon by the firmness of his manner and his vigour of thought, modified their feelings. At the Council of War, called to discuss the proper mode of commencing hostilities, Rampon volunteered a great deal of sage advice recommended circumspection and prudence, and spoke of the experienced generals that were opposed to them. Bonaparte listened, full of impatience, till he was through; and then replied, in his impetuous manner: "Permit me, gentlemen, with all due deference to your excellent observations, to suggest some new ideas. The art of war, rest assured, is yet in its infancy. For many ages men have made war in a theatrical and effeminate manner. Now is not the time for enemies mutually, to appoint a place of combat, and advancing, with their hats in hand, say, '*Gentlemen, will you have the goodness to fire.*' We must cut the enemy in pieces precipitate ourselves like a torrent on their battalions, and grind them to powder; that is, bring back war to its primitive state fight as Alexander and Cæsar did. Experienced generals conduct the troops opposite to us! So much the better, so much the better! It is not their experience that will avail them against me. Mark my words, they will soon burn their books on tactics, and know not what to do. ... The system I adopt is favourable to the profession of arms; every soldier becomes a hero; for when men are launched forward with impetuosity, there is no time for reflection, and they will do wonders. Yes, gentlemen, the first onset of the Italian army will give birth to a new epoch in military affairs. *As for us, we must hurl ourselves on the foe like a thunderbolt, and smite like it. Disconcerted by our tactics, and not daring to put them in execution, they will fly before us as the shades of night before the uprising sun.*" The manner and tone in which this was said, and that eloquence, too, which afterward so frequently electrified the soldiers, took the old generals by surprise, and Augereau and Massena turned to each other with significant looks; and Rampon, after he had gone out, remarked, "Here is a man that will yet cut out work for government."

Such feelings and bold projects suited well the impetuous and daring Augereau, and Bonaparte could not have had a better general in the kind of war he was to wage. Where it was to be marching all night, and fighting all day, for days in succession and one must be equal to three, by the rapidity of his movements and the force of his onsets Augereau was just the man. There was little room for the exhibition of military tactics on the part of the several commanders. The whole theatre of war was under the immediate inspection of Bonaparte. He planned and directed everything, without going through even the form of calling a council of war. His officers had simply to obey orders and to a man like Augereau, who could never reason, but was great in action this was the very field for him to win fame in. There was little room for mistakes, except on the field of battle, and he made few there. Tell him to storm such a battery, cross such a river, in the midst of a murderous fire, or force such a wing of the army, and he would do it, if it was to be done. His soldiers loved him with devotion, and would follow him into any danger. His activity and rapidity of motion, together with his tireless energy also rendered him a powerful ally to Bonaparte. In campaigns where such velocity of movement was necessary, in order to compensate for numbers, that the army seemed endowed with wings, flying from point to point, to the utter astonishment of the enemy, and an endurance was demanded that could cope with that of Bonaparte, who seemed made of iron, Augereau was at home. Thus, in the first battle of Montenotte, we find him fighting beside the young Corsican, and, at the close of the battle, left in command, with instructions to renew the attack in the night. But not yet fully understanding the spirit that headed the army, he neglected to obey the order, and hence lost a great advantage. A few days after, he assailed the Piedmontese, at Millesimo, and won that bloody battle. With such fury did he charge them, and so terrible was the shock, that every pass leading into Piedmont was forced; and in the hurry and tumult of the overthrow, their general was driven, for self-preservation, with ten thousand men, into an old and impregnable castle. Around this structure Augereau formed his columns, and marched boldly up to carry it by assault. Then commenced one of those struggles of knightly days. The assailants rained down Stones and rocks, and missiles of every description, which bore away whole companies at a time. Amid the cries and shouts of the assailants, and the falling of stones, the combat raged, till night closed the scene. In the morning, Provera, the Piedmontese commander, was compelled to surrender.

Piedmont was humbled, and entered into a treaty with Bonaparte. In the two engagements at Castiglione, he fought one alone, and one with Bonaparte; and earned the title of Duke of Castiglione, which the Emperor afterward bestowed on him. Bonaparte advanced with Massena on Conato, and sent Augereau to drive the Austrians from the heights of Castiglione. The latter had driven General Valette from them the day before; and Augereau was sent to retake them. Valette, though he fought with an obstinacy that would have honoured an Austrian, had not resisted with the courage that must animate the Army of Italy, if it would not be lost. It was no common firmness that could resist the successive shocks to which it was exposed. While one was compelled to fight two, and as he beat them, ever fight other two a courage and tenacity were needed that no ordinary assault could overcome. Bonaparte, in his fierce rides to and fro to different parts of the army, had killed five horses in a few days. He himself had planned the campaigns fought at the head of the columns marched all night, and battled all next day bivouacked with the common soldier, and eaten his coarse bread passed sleepless nights and anxious days and to have an important post yielded because assailed by superior force was an example which, if followed, would insure his overthrow and he made an example of Valette to the whole army. He broke him in presence of his own troops and all the officers; 'thus stamping him with everlasting disgrace. He wished to impress on his officers and men, that he expected desperate deeds of them, and nothing else would satisfy him. No sooner was this done, than he sent Augereau to retake the lost heights. Burning with rage at the disgrace Valette had brought on the French arms, he departed with exultation on his dangerous mission. Never would *he* be broke in the presence of his soldiers for want of courage. Bonaparte might break his sword above his grave but never fix the stain of cowardice on his name. He reached Castiglione as Bonaparte arrived at Lonato. Burning with impatience, he formed his men into columns, and rushed to the assault. Then commenced one of the most terrible days of Augereau's life. Placing himself at the head of his troops, he moved up the slope, and entered the storm of grapeshot that swept the hill-side. His smitten columns staggered before it then closed up the rent ranks, and marched, with a shout of defiance, forward. But when they came within range of the musketry also, the double storm was too severe to withstand; and they recoiled before it. Augereau rallied them again to the attack, and the brave fellows joyfully entered the destructive fire over the dead bodies of their companions; but the overwhelming force of such superior numbers, and such commanding and powerful batteries was too much for human energy and again the army slowly and reluctantly swung back its bleeding, mangled form down the hill. Augereau, begrimed with powder and smoke, and enraged at the defeats he endured, seemed to court death. Where the balls fell thickest, there was he fighting in front of his men; and where the storm raged fiercest he was seen sternly breasting it. Again and again did he lead his exhausted and diminished army to the perilous assault; and there, in the midst of whole companies that fell at every discharge, cheer on the soldiers. Amid the dead and the dying, he moved that day like a spirit of the infernal world. He seemed impervious to bullets; while the fierce purpose of his heart, to carry those heights or leave his crushed army and his own body upon them, imparted to his aspect and his movements a desperation that told his men that victory or annihilation was before them. For the last time did he lead them to the assault the heights were carried, amid deafening cheers and the French standards waved from the summit. Augereau's brow cleared up; and, as he looked off from the spot of victory, he saw Bonaparte hastening to his relief. The heart of this veteran swelled with pride as he received the commendations of the young commander-in-chief. Bonaparte never forgot this battle; and years after, when a captive on the isle of St. Helena, he said, "Ah! *that was the most brilliant day of Augereau's life.*"

Battle of Castiglione

A few days after the second battle of Castiglione was fought, and Italy again put up as the mighty stake. The two armies stood perpendicular to a range of hills that crossed the plain on Bonaparte's left. On these heights the left wing of the French and the right of the Austrians rested, while the two armies stretched in parallel lines out into the plain. All night long had Bonaparte been riding among his troops to arrange them for the coming conflict, and when daylight first broke over the eastern hills, he saw Serruerier's division approaching the field of battle. The action then commenced on the heights where Massena commanded. The two armies, inactive on the plain below, turned their eyes upon the hillside where volumes of smoke were rising in the morning air; and the incessant roll of musketry amid strains of martial music, told where their companions were struggling in the encounter of death. Augereau commanded the centre in the plain, and as he watched the firing along the heights, his impatient spirit could scarcely brook the inaction to which he was doomed. At length he received the welcome orders to charge. The onset was tremendous, and though the Austrians being superior in numbers by one-third resisted bravely, they were at length forced to yield to the shock. The whole line along the heights and through the plain bent backward in the struggle, and finally turned in full retreat. The victory was in the hands of the French, but the soldiers were too weary to urge the pursuit. The sun was stooping to the western horizon when the combat was done, and the exhausted army slept on the field of battle. For days they had marched and combated without cessation, and humble endurance could go no further. Even Bonaparte was worn out, for his slender frame had been tasked to the utmost, and his thin features looked laggard and wan. He had galloped from division to division over the country, superintending every movement and directing every advance; for he would trust no one with his orders; since the slightest mistake would ruin him. Nothing but lofty genius, combined with ceaseless energy and the most tireless activity, could have saved his army. It is said that during these six days he never took off his boots, or even lay down. A week of such mental and physical excitement, without one moment's interval of repose, was enough to shatter the most iron constitution; and it is no wonder he is found writing to the Directory that his strength is gone, and all is gone but his courage. With thirty thousand men he had, these six days, defeated sixty thousand killed and taken prisoners two-thirds the number of his own army, and astonished the world by his achievements.

The next day Augereau was pressing after the flying enemy, and entered Verona in triumph. A few weeks after he and Massena fought their way into Bassano together through the fire of the enemy, leaving the ground without covered with the dead. Bonaparte arrived at night on the field of battle, and as he was spurring his horse through the corpses that strewed the ground, a dog leaped out from under the cloak of his dead master, and barked furiously at him. He would now lick his unconscious master, then stop to bark at Napoleon, and again return to his caresses. The silence of the mournful scene broken so abruptly by this faithful dog the strength of his attachment outliving that of all other friends, and showing itself here on the field of the dead and the picture of that affectionate creature lavishing its unheeded caresses on the hand that should feed it no more produced an impression on his heart that he never forgot, and affected him more than that of any other battle scene of his life. But perhaps Augereau never appeared to greater advantage than at the——

Battle of Arcola

Bonaparte, wearied by continual fighting exhausted by his very victories was with his army of fifteen thousand men at Verona, when a fresh army of more than thirty thousand suddenly appeared before the town. His position was desperate, and his ruin apparently inevitable. The soldiers murmured, saying, "After destroying two armies, we are expected to destroy also those from the Rhine." Complaints and discouragements were on every side; but in this crisis, Napoleon, without consulting any one, took one of those sudden resolutions that seem the result of inspiration. In the rear of the Austrians was a large marsh, crossed by two long causeways, and on these he determined to place his army. Crossing the Adige twice during the night, the morning saw his army in two divisions, one under Massena, and the other under Augereau, stretched in two massive columns on these two dykes, while on every side of them was a deep marsh. This daring and consummate stroke, none but the genius of Bonaparte would ever have conceived, or dared to have adopted, if proposed. Along these narrow causeways numbers gave no advantage; everything depended on the courage and firmness of the heads of the columns. With Augereau and Massena to lead on his own, he had no doubt of success. Augereau, leading his column along the causeway on which he was posted, came up to the Adige and bridge of Arcola on the opposite side of which was the town of Arcola and attempted to force it; but the tremendous fire that swept it almost annihilated the head of the column, and it fell back. It was then he performed the daring deed, which Bonaparte on his arrival imitated. Seeing his men recoil before the fire, he seized a pair of colours, and bidding his men follow after, rushed on the bridge and planted them in the midst of the iron storm. With a loud and cheering shout, the brave troops rushed to the charge; but nothing could withstand that murderous fire. The head of the column sank on the bridge, and Augereau himself, overthrown, was borne back in the refluent tide of his followers.

Soon after, the Austrians, under Mitrouski, attacked him in turn upon the dyke; but after a fierce struggle he repulsed them, and chasing them over the bridge, again attempted to pass it. But though the column advanced with the utmost intrepidity into the volcano that blazed at the farther extremity, the fire was too severe to withstand, and it again recoiled, and the soldiers threw themselves down behind the dyke to escape the bullets. At this critical juncture, Bonaparte, who deemed the possession of Arcola of vital importance, came up on a furious gallop. Springing from his horse, he hastened to the soldiers lying along the dyke, and asking them if they were the conquerors of Lodi, seized a standard, as Augereau had done, and exclaiming, "Follow your General!" advanced through a perfect hurricane of grape-shot to the centre of the bridge, and planted it there. The brave grenadiers pressed with level bayonets close after their intrepid leader; but, unable to endure the tempest of fire and of lead which the hotly worked battery hurled in their faces, they seized Bonaparte in their arms, and trampling over the dead and dying, came rushing back through the smoke of battle. But the Austrians pressed close after the disordered column, and drove it into the marsh in the rear, where Bonaparte was left up to his arms in water. But the next moment, finding their beloved chief was gone, the soldiers cried out, over the roar of battle, "Forward, to save your General!" Pausing in their flight, they wheeled and charged the advancing enemy, and driving them back over the morass, bore off in triumph the helpless Napoleon. In this deadly encounter of the heads of columns, and successive advances and repulses, the day wore away, and the shades of a November night parted the combatants. The Austrians occupied Arcola, the French retired to Ronco, or sank to rest in the middle of the causeways they bad held with such firmness during the day. The smoke of the guns spread itself like a mist over the marsh, amid which the dead and dying lay together. In the morning the strife again commenced on this strange field of battle two causeways in the midst of a marsh. The Austrians advanced in two columns along them, till they reached the centre, when the French charged with the bayonet, and routed them with prodigious slaughter hurling them in the shock by crowds, from the dyke into the marsh. The second day passed as the first, and when night returned the roar of artillery ceased, and Bonaparte slept again on the field of battle. The third morning broke over this dreadful scene, and the diminished, wearied armies roused themselves for a last great effort. Massena, charging on the run, cleared his dyke; while the left-hand one, after a desperate encounter, was also swept of the enemy, and Arcola evacuated. Bonaparte, now thinking the enemy sufficiently disheartened and reduced to allow him to hazard an engagement in the open field, deployed his army into the plain across the Alpon, where the two armies drew up in order of battle. Before the signal for the onset, he resorted to a stratagem, in order to give force to his attack. He sent twenty-five trumpeters through a marsh of reeds that reached to the left wing of the Austrians, with orders to sound the charge the moment the combat became general. He then ordered Massena and Augereau to advance. With an intrepid step they moved to the attack, but were met with a firm resistance, when all at once the Austrians heard a loud blast of trumpets on their flank, as if a whole division of cavalry was rushing to the charge. Terror-stricken at the sudden appearance of this new foe, they gave way and fled. At the same time the French garrison of Legnagno, in the rear, issuing forth, by order of Napoleon, and opening their fire upon the retiring ranks, completed the disorder, and the bloody battle of Arcola was won. Augereau and Massena were the two heroes of this hard-fought field.

This was in November the next January the battle of Rivoli took place, and while Napoleon and Massena were struggling on the heights, Augereau was pressing, the rear guard of the Austrians, who had come between him and the blockading force of Mantua. He had taken 1500 prisoners, and fourteen cannon, and was still straining every effort to arrest the danger that was threatening the troops around the town, when Bonaparte arrived from the field of victory with reinforcements; and Mantua fell.

In these astounding victories, Augereau appears as one of the chief actors. When all the other generals were wounded, he and Massena stood, the two pillars of Napoleon's fortune. To carry out successfully his system of tactics requiring such great activity, firmness, and heroism Augereau was all he could wish. Beloved by his soldiers, he could hurl them into any danger, and hold them firm against the most overwhelming numbers.

After the fall of Mantua he was sent to Paris to present to the Directory sixty stands of colours, the fruits of the recent victories. His heroic conduct had paved the way for a cordial reception; and the Directory had already honoured him, by presenting to him and

Bonaparte the colours each had carried at Arcola, at the head of his grenadiers, and planted on the centre of the bridge in the midst of the fire.

The presentation of the colours was a magnificent sight. They were carried by sixty old veterans, who bore them along with the pride and martial bearing of youthful heroes. Augereau placed his father and mother beside him, notwithstanding their low origin; while one of his brothers acted as his aide-de-camp. The son had returned covered with glory, and they were called in to share it.

The next June he was again sent to Paris for a double purpose: first, and chiefly, to get him out of the army, where his violent republican principles were fomenting disorder. With peace and idleness, came the discussion of political subjects among the soldiers, and Augereau showed himself a thorough Jacobin. The second object was, to sustain the Directory, which was threatened with overthrow. Augereau was delighted with this mission; for he loved the strife of factions as much as he did the combat of the field, though much less fitted for it. He made himself ridiculous at once. To be in Paris, which he first left a poor boy, as a victorious general flattered on every side by eulogies and public entertainments turned his head and he went about bragging of his exploits, and boasting that he had taught Bonaparte the art of war indeed originated those brilliant plans to which the latter owed his victories. He frightened his best friends, all but Barras, who liked to see him among the Jacobins, uttering his ultra-revolutionary principles. There was no taming him by reason, for Augereau was incapable of serious thought, and so they approached him through his vanity. At length he became a little more circumspect, and was appointed to the command of the 17th Military Division, of Paris. As Commander-in-chief, he soon played an important part in the political affairs of the capital. The Revolution of the 18th Fructidor was effected by him. All had been prepared on the evening of the 17th, and at midnight the inhabitants of Paris were alarmed by seeing twelve thousand soldiers, with Augereau at their head, marching toward the palace of the Tuileries. There was no commotion, no apparent cause for this extraordinary military display; yet all night long was heard the steady tramp of soldiers, and the heavy rumbling of artillery over the pavements. At length a solitary cannon, the signal gun, sent its roar over the breathless city, calling to mind the nights when the loud peal of the tocsin, and the beat of the alarm-drum, roused up the multitude to scenes of violence and blood. Immediately the troops approached the gates of the palace of the Tuileries, and ordered them to be opened. The guards refused, and there was preparation for resistance, when Augereau appeared with his staff.

Ramel, the commandant, notwithstanding the defection among his troops, still showed a disposition to resist, when Augereau thus addressed him, "Commandant Ramel, do you recognize me Chief of the 17th Military Division?"

"Yes," replied Ramel.

"Well, then, as your superior officer, I command you to place yourself under arrest." He immediately obeyed. At six o'clock in the morning, the Deputies were prisoners, and the Revolution effected.

For the management of this affair, which Augereau attributed to his own cleverness, he expected and sought a seat in the Directory. He expostulated and threatened, but the Directors had used him all they wished, and they would not call him to sit among them. He had no other resource left, but to get a majority of the vote of the Councils in his favour. Failing in this, also, he became turbulent and violent; and finally, as a last resort, the Directory, to get rid of him, appointed him to the command of the army of Germany, a post left vacant by the death of General Hoche. Enacting the fool here, in his style of living, and the outward pretensions he exhibited, he finally alarmed the Directory by the Jacobinical principles he was disseminating in the army, and the discontent he spread among the inhabitants; and was deprived of his command, under the pretext of sending him to Perpignan, to collect an army that was destined for Portugal. This appointment was a mere farce, and Augereau was to all intents disgraced. In 1799, he was elected, by the department of the Upper Garonne, as a member of the Council of Five Hundred.

When Bonaparte returned from Italy, Augereau withdrew from him, and during the revolution of the 18th of Brumaire, by which the Directory was overthrown, and the power of France passed into the hands of the First Consul, he stood ready to take advantage of any favourable movement to place himself at the head of the troops, and overwhelm the hero of Egypt and his friends. As things began to grow dark around Napoleon, in that most critical day of his life, he determined to go to the two councils with his staff. He met Augereau on the way. The latter said to him sarcastically, "There, you have got yourself into a pretty plight."

"It was worse at Arcola," was the brief reply of Bonaparte. The establishment of the Consular government, and the subsequent brilliant campaign of Marengo, wrought a wonderful change in Augereau's republican principles, and he was glad to pay court to Napoleon; and, for his timely conversion, was restored to favour. In 1805—6, in Austria and Prussia, he exhibited his old valour. At Jena, especially, he showed himself worthy to combat beside his former comrades in Italy. Afterward at Golymin, Lechocqzin, and Landsberg, though fifty years of age, he evinced the impetuosity and firmness of his early days. His political ambition bad been given to the winds, as he once more found himself on the field where glory was to be won.

The next year, at the battle of Eylau, he commenced the action, and exhibited there one of those heroic deeds which belong to the age of chivalry, rather than to our more practical times.

Charge at Eylau

The night previous to the battle, he had lain tossing on his uneasy couch burned with fever, and tortured by rheumatic pains that deprived him almost of consciousness. But at daylight, the thunder of cannon shook the field on which he lay. The tremendous batteries on both sides had commenced their fire, making the earth tremble under their explosions as if a volcano had opened on the plain. Augereau lay and listened for a while to the stern music his soul had so often beaten time to then hastily springing from his feverish bed called for his horse. His attendants, amazed at this sudden energy, stood stupefied at the strange order; but the fierce glance of the chieftain told them that he was not to be disobeyed. His battle-steed was brought, and the sick and staggering warrior with difficulty vaulted to the saddle. Feeling his strength giving way, and that he was unable to keep his seat, he ordered his servants to bring straps and bind him on. They obeyed and strapped him firmly in his place, when, plunging his spurs into his steed, he flew, in a headlong gallop, to the head of his corps. His sudden appearance among his soldiers animated every heart. The two armies were in battle array the trumpets sounded, and amid the furious beat of drums and roar of cannon, Soult poured his mighty columns on the centre, while Augereau, at the head of his sixteen thousand men, charged, like fire, on the left. Whole ranks went down at every discharge; for the heavy shots tore through Augereau's dense masses with frightful effect. Still the columns closed over the huge gaps made in them and pressed forward to the assault. But suddenly, while Augereau was cheering on his men, and straining every nerve to make headway against the desolating batteries, a snow squall darkened the air, and swept with the rush of a whirlwind over the two armies, blotting out the very heavens. So thick and fierce was the driving storm, that Augereau could not see two rods ahead of him. Both armies were snatched from his sight in an instant, and even of his own men none but those directly about him could be seen. In a moment the ground was white with snow; while it sifted over the columns as if silently weaving their funeral shroud. Baffled and confused, not knowing which way to move, they staggered blindly over the field. Still the Russian cannon, previously trained on the spot, played furiously through the storm. Unable to see even the blaze of the discharge, these brave soldiers would hear the muffled explosions in the impenetrable gloom, and then behold their ranks mowed through, and mangled, as if a falling rock had crushed among them. In the midst of this awful carnage-enveloped by the blinding, driving snow, they were suddenly assailed on both sides by infantry and cavalry. In the midst of the uproar of nearly a thousand cannon, Augereau could not hear the tread of the infantry, or the tramp of the cavalry, and was wholly unaware of their approach. The Russians had marked the course of the columns before the snow squall wrapped them from sight, and now advanced on both sides to crush them to pieces. Without warning or preparation, the French soldiers saw the long lances of the Cossacks emerge from the thick storm, in a serried line, in their very faces; and in the twinkling of an eye, those wild horsemen were trampling through their ranks. Before this terrible tide of cavalry and infantry the columns sank as if engulfed in the earth. The hurried commands and shouts of Augereau, were never heard, or heard in vain. Still bound to his steed, he spurred among the disordered troops striving by his voice and gestures, and more than all by his daring example, to restore the battle. But wounded and bleeding, he only galloped over a field of fugitives flying in every direction, while the Cossacks and Russian cavalry sabred them down without mercy. *Of the sixteen thousand, only fifteen hundred found their ranks again.* Trampling down the dead and the dying, the victorious enemy burst with loud hurrahs into Eylau, and even into the presence of Napoleon himself, and nearly made him prisoner. It was to arrest this sudden disorder, that Murat, with his fourteen thousand cavalry, backed by the Imperial Guard, was ordered to charge.

The wounded Augereau was left without a corps to command, and sent back to Paris, in order to recover his health the author of the "Camp and Court of Napoleon" says "in disgrace to gratify a fit of spleen." Says that author, "Enraged at the indecisive result of the day, Napoleon wreaked his spleen on the marshal, and sent him home in disgrace." Whatever might be the disgrace, the cause here assigned is a gratuitous falsehood. In Napoleon's bulletin home giving an account of the battle of Eylau he speaks of Augereau three times:–first, to describe the sudden snow-squall that blinded his army, causing it to lose its direction, and grope about for half an hour in uncertainty; second, to make mention of his wound; and, finally, to say, "The wound of Marshal Augereau was a very unfavourable accident, as it left his corps, in the very heat of the battle, without a leader to direct it." In a bulletin dated nineteen days after, Augereau is again mentioned in the following terms:

> À la bataille d'Eylau le Maréchal Augereau, couvert de rhumatismes, était malade et avait à peine connaissance; mais le canon réveille les braves: il vole au galop à la tête de son corps, âpres s'être fait attaches sur son cheval. Il a été constamment exposé au plus grand feu, et a même été légèrement blessé. L'Empereur vient de l'autoriser à rentrer en France pour y soigner sa santé.

This is an unique mode of venting one's spleen on a man.

Two years after he was appointed to supersede St. Cyr in Spain, then besieging Gerona. Taken sick in his route, it was some time before he assumed the command of the army, and he even delayed it after he was recovered. He saw that the service was to be a harassing one, requiring great efforts, without yielding much glory. At length, however, he took the command of the siege, and humanely offered an armistice of a month, provided the inhabitants would surrender at the termination of it, should no army come to their relief. They refusing this proposal, he pressed the siege and reduced the town. His whole management, however, in the Peninsula his foolish proclamations, and useless cruelties, and failures show the little real strength of character he possessed. He was soon recalled. While Napoleon was engaged in the Russian expedition, Augereau remained stationed at Berlin. Although an admirable leader of a division, and brave in the hour of battle, Napoleon found him unfit to direct an army or to be entrusted with weighty matters in a great campaign. The truth is, Augereau's rank as marshal entitled him to a command he was not able to fill; a good general, he made a bad marshal. Nevertheless, in the last struggle to save the tottering empire of France, he fought with his accustomed valour. Especially at Leipzig he appears in his former strength and daring. Hastening by forced marches to the city, scattering the enemy from his path as he came, he arrived in time to strike once more for Napoleon and his throne. The next year the Emperor entrusted him with the defence of Lyons, with the order to hold it to the last extremity. Arriving at the city, he found there only seven hundred regular troops and a thousand National Guards, while twenty thousand Austrians were marching toward it. Knowing he could not defend the city with this feeble force, he hastened to Valence in the south, to bring up reinforcements. For a while, though fifty-seven years old, he exhibited the vigour of his early campaigns. He wrote to Napoleon, demanding help, while at the same time he strained every nerve to strengthen himself. He sent a thousand men in post carriages from Valence in a single day. This was the last spark, however, of the old fire; for though reinforced by Napoleon till his army numbered twenty thousand men, he did not follow up his successes as he ought, and contributed nothing in the desperate struggle the Emperor was making for his throne. The latter wished Augereau to hover on the rear of the allied army, while he dashed against it in front; but all his orders to that effect were powerless to remove the torpor that had seized his energies. He said he was afraid to trust his troops, as they were inexperienced soldiers, etc. Napoleon, in reply, told him to forget his age, and think of the days of glory when he fought at Castiglione. He urged him to move his troops together into one column, and march into Switzerland. Said Clarke, writing in the name of the Emperor, in reply to his complaint of the meagre equipments of his soldiers:

> He desires me to tell you that the corps of Gerard, which his done such great things under his eyes, is composed entirely of conscripts half naked. He has at this moment four thousand National Guards in his army with round hats, with peasants' coats and waistcoats, and without knapsacks, armed with all sorts of muskets, on whom he puts the greatest value; he only wishes he had thirty thousand of them.

But the appeal was all in vain; and while the knell of the empire was tolling Augereau remained inactive and useless. At length, however, he seemed to rouse himself for a moment, and obeying Napoleon's orders, marched on Geneva, and defeated the Austrians before the town. Compelled, however, to retire, he retreated toward Lyons, and at Limonet fought his last battle. It was brave and worthy of his character; but though he left nearly three thousand of the enemy dead on the field, while he lost but two thousand, he was compelled to retire, and evacuate Lyons, retreating toward Valence.

At the latter place, a proclamation was issued by the inhabitants on Napoleon's abdication, loading the fallen Emperor with the most opprobrious epithets, and extolling Louis XVIII. as the idol of his country. To this atrocious proclamation Augereau's signature was affixed. On his way to Elba, Napoleon met Augereau unexpectedly near Valence, and an interview took place which, from the different versions given of it, furnishes a curious illustration of the historical contradictions connected with this period.

Says the *Court and Camp of Napoleon*:

> Soon after this the 'Fructidor General' and the ex-Emperor met at a short distance from Valence, as the latter was on his way to Elba. 'I have thy proclamation,' said Napoleon, 'thou hast betrayed me.'
>
> 'Sire,' replied the marshal, 'it is you who have betrayed France and the army, by sacrificing both to a frantic spirit of ambition.'
>
> 'Thou hast chosen thyself a new master,' said Napoleon.
>
> 'I have no account to render thee on that score,' replied the general.
>
> 'Thou hast no courage,' replied Bonaparte.
>
> ''Tis thou hast none,' responded the general, and turned his back without any respect on his late master.

This precious bit of dialogue is detailed with so much minuteness that one would incline to believe it, even against counter-statements, were it not for the falsehood it bears on its own face. The whole scene is unnatural, and to wind up with a charge of cowardice on the part of each is supremely ridiculous. For two men who had fought side by side at Lodi, Arcola, and Castiglione, and stormed together over so many battlefields, to accuse each other of cowardice at that late hour would be a child's play that Augereau might stoop to but Napoleon never.

Here is another account of this interview by Mr. Allison:

> At noon on the following day, he accidentally met Augereau on the road, near Valence; both alighted from their carriages, and, *ignorant of the atrocious* proclamation, in which that marshal had so recently announced his conversion to the Bourbons, the Emperor embraced him, and they walked together on the road for a quarter of an hour in the most *amicable manner.* It was observed, however, that Augereau kept his helmet on his head as he walked along. A few minutes after, the Emperor entered Valence, and beheld the proclamation placarded on the walls.

It need not be remarked that the latter is the more reliable account of the two. A great many of the incidents of Napoleon's life which have been gathered up by English writers are as fabulous as the first account of this interview between him and Augereau.

Louis XVIII. rewarded him by making him Peer of France, and bestowing on him the Cross of St. Louis, and the command of the 14th Division in Normandy.

On Napoleon's landing from Elba, Augereau was struck with astonishment to find himself proclaimed by the Emperor as a traitor. He, however, made no reply, hoping by a seasonable conversion to extricate himself from the difficulties that surrounded him. Republican as he was, he never allowed his principles to interfere with his self-interest nor his conscience with his safety. No sooner had Napoleon entered Paris in triumph than Augereau issued a proclamation to his soldiers, urging them once more to "march under the victorious wings of those immortal eagles which had so often conducted them to glory." Napoleon, who had never respected him, and after his infamous proclamation at Valence thoroughly despised him, paid no attention to this delicate compliment of his flexible marshal. Knowing him too thoroughly to trust him, and disdaining to molest him, he let the betrayer of two masters pass into silent neglect. Poor Augereau, robbed of all his plumes, retired to his country estate, where he remained till the second restoration, when he again sent in his protestations of devotion to the King. But there is a limit, even to a Bourbon's vanity; and, Louis turning a deaf ear on his solicitations and flattery, he again retired to his estate, where he died in June, 1816, of a dropsy in the chest.

Augereau was essentially a mean man, though a brave one. He was a weak-headed, avaricious, selfish, boasting soldier, yet possessing courage that would not have disgraced the days of chivalry. His soldiers loved him, for he kept strict order and discipline among them, and exposed himself like the meanest of their number in the hour of danger. Without sufficient grasp of thought to form a plan requiring any depth of combination, or even intellect enough to comprehend one already furnished to his hand, he nevertheless surveyed a field of battle with imperturbable coolness, and his charge was like a falling thunderbolt.

His want of education, and the early habits and associations he formed, were enough to spoil a man of even more strength of character than he possessed. He came under the influence of Napoleon's genius at too late an age to receive those impressions which so effectually remoulded some of the younger lieutenants.

Marshal Davoust

CHAPTER 4

Marshal Davoust

It is hard to form a correct opinion of such a man as Davoust. The obloquy that is thrown upon him, especially by English historians, has a tendency to destroy our sympathy for him at the outset and distort the medium through which we ever after contemplate him. Positive in all his acts, and naturally of a stern and fierce temperament, he did things in a way, and with a directness, and an abruptness, that indicated a harsh and unfeeling nature. But if we judge of men by their actions, and not also by the motive which prompted them, we shall be compelled to regard the Duke of Wellington as one of the most cruel of men. His whole political course in England his steady opposition to all reform his harsh treatment of the petitions of the poor and helpless, and heartless indifference to the cries of famishing thousands, argue the most callous and unpitying nature. But his actions though causing so much suffering, and awakening so much indignation, that even his house was mobbed by his own countrymen, and his grey hairs narrowly escaped being trampled in the dust by an indignant populace have all sprung from his education as a military man. Everything must bend to the established order of things, and the suffering of individuals is not to be taken into the account. The same is true of Davoust. Trained from his youth to the profession of arms, accustomed, even in his boyhood, to scenes of revolutionary violence, with all his moral feelings educated amid the uproar of battle or the corruptions of a camp, the life of the warrior was to him the true life of man. Success, victory, were the only objects he contemplated, making up his mind beforehand that suffering and death would attend the means employed. Hence his fearful ferocity in battle the headlong fury with which he tore through the ranks of the enemy, and the unscrupulous manner in which he made war support war. These were the natural results of his firm resolution to conquer, and of his military creed that "to the victors belong the spoils." He did nothing by halves, nor had he anything of the *suaviter in modo*, which glosses over so many rough deeds and conveys the impression they were done from necessity rather than desire.

Louis-Nicholas Davoust was born at Annaux, in Burgundy, 10th of May, 1770, one year after Bonaparte. His family could lay claim to the title of noble, though, like many Italian *cavaliers*, who are too poor to own a horse, it was destitute of lands or houses. Young Davoust, being destined for the army, was sent to the military school of Brienne, where was also the charity boy, Bonaparte. At the age of fifteen he obtained a commission; but his fiery, impetuous nature soon involved him in difficulty with his superior officers, and it was taken from him. In the Revolution he became a fierce republican, and after the death of Louis was appointed over a battalion of volunteers, and was sent to join Doumourier, then commanding the army of the Republic on the Rhine. When Doumourier, disgusted with the increasing horrors of the Revolution endeavoured to win the army over, to march against the Terrorists, the young Davoust used his utmost endeavours to steady the shaking fidelity of the troops. Doumourier was finally compelled to flee to the Austrians, almost alone; and Davoust, for his efforts and faithfulness, was promoted to the rank of brigadier-general, and during five years fought bravely on the banks of the Rhine and Moselle. When Bonaparte returned from Italy, where he had covered himself and the army with glory, Davoust sought to unite his fortunes with those of the young Corsican. He was consequently joined to the expedition to Egypt, and under the walls of Samanhout and Aboukir fought with a bravery that showed he was worthy of the place he had sought. He was not included with those selected by Bonaparte to accompany him to France, and did not return till the latter was proclaimed First Consul.

Attaching himself still more closely to one whose fortunes were rising so rapidly, he was placed at the head of the grenadiers of the Consular Guard, and soon after, through the influence of Bonaparte, obtained the hand of the sister of General Le Clerc, a lady of captivating manners and rare beauty.

The road to fame was now fairly open to the young soldier, and he pursued it with a boldness and energy that deserved success. In 1801 he was made Marshal of the Empire, and the next year found him at the head of a corps of the Grand Army. Around Ulm, at Austerlitz, chief of all at Auerstadt, he performed prodigies of valour, and fixed forever his great reputation. At Eylau and Friedland he proved that honours were never more worthily bestowed than when placed on his head. For his bravery and success at Eckmuhl he received the title of Prince of Eckmuhl, and soon after, at Wagram, showed that Bonaparte never relied on him in vain.

The three following years he spent in Poland, as governor of the country and commander of the French army there, and gave great offence to the inhabitants by the heavy contributions he laid upon them, and the unfeeling manner in which they were collected.

In 1812 we find him at the head of the first corps of the Grand Army the first to cross the Niemen and commence the splendid pageant of that memorable day. He crossed at one o'clock in the morning, and took possession of Kowno. Napoleon had his tent pitched on an eminence, a few rods from the bank, and there watched the movements of his magnificent legions. Two hundred thousand men, on that day, and forty thousand horses, in splendid array and full equipment, and most perfect order, slowly descended to the bridges, and to the stirring strains of martial music, and under the folds of a thousand fluttering banners, moved past the imperial station, rending the heavens with their shouts, while the saluting trumpets breathed forth their most triumphant strains. Throughout this disastrous campaign he fought with the heroism and firmness of Ney himself.

The next year, after the Russian campaign, he made his headquarters in Hamburg, and defended the city heroically against the Russians, Prussians, and Swedes combined. He held out long after Napoleon's abdication, resolutely refusing to surrender the place, until General Gerard arrived on the part of Louis XVIII. He then gave in his adhesion to the Bourbons, but was among the first to declare for the Emperor, on his return from Elba. After the overthrow at Waterloo, he took command of that portion of the army which still remained faithful to Napoleon, and retreated to Orleans, and did not give in his adhesion to the Bourbons until the Russians were marching against him.

This brief outline of Davoust's career embraces the whole active life of Napoleon, and was filled up with the most stirring scenes, and marked by changes that amazed and shook the world. The role that he played in this mighty Napoleonic drama shows him to have been an extraordinary man, and furnishes another evidence of the penetration that characterized Bonaparte in the selection of his generals.

The three striking characteristics of Davoust were great personal intrepidity and daring, perfect self-possession and coolness in the hour of peril, and almost invincible tenacity. With all these rare gifts, he was also a great general. In the skill with which he chose his ground, arranged his army, and determined on the point and moment of attack, he had few superiors in Europe. Rash in an onset, he was perfectly cool in repelling one. This combination of two such opposite qualities, so prominent in Napoleon, seemed to be characteristic of most of his generals, and was one great cause of their success.

His personal daring became proverbial in the army, and whenever he was seen to direct a blow it was known that it would be the fiercest, heaviest one that could be given. His susceptibility of intense excitement carried him, in the hour of battle, above the thought of danger or death.

Battle of Auerstadt

One of the most successful battles he ever fought was that of Auerstadt, where he earned his title of duke. The year before, at Austerlitz, he had exhibited that coolness in sudden peril, and that unconquerable tenacity, which made him so strong an ally on a battle-field. The night before the battle of Jena, Napoleon slept on the heights of Landgrafenberg, whither he had led his army with incredible toil, and at four in the morning it was an October morning rode along the lines and addressed his soldiers in that stirring eloquence which he knew so well how to use. The dense fog that curtained in the dark and chilly morning lifted, and rent before the fierce acclamations that answered him, and with the first dawn his columns were upon the enemy. When the unclouded sun, at nine o'clock, broke through, and scattered the fog, it shone down on a wild battle-field, on which were heard the incessant thunder of artillery and rattle of musketry, interrupted, now and then, by the heavy shocks of cavalry and the shouts of maddened men. Napoleon was again victorious, and at six o'clock in the evening rode over the cumbered ground, while the setting sun shone on a different scene from that which its rising beams had gilded. But not at Jena was the great battle of the 14th of October fought, nor was Napoleon the hero of the day. Less than thirty miles distant within hearing of his canon, could he have paused to listen Davoust was winning the victory for him, by prodigies of valour, to which the hard-fought battle of Jena was an easy affair. Napoleon imagined he had the King of Prussia, with his whole army, on the heights of Landgrafenberg and they *were* behind them two days previous. With ninety thousand men, he supposed he was marching on over a hundred thousand, instead of on forty thousand, as the result proved. After several hours of hard fighting, the Prussians, it is true, were reinforced by twenty thousand under Ruchel, making sixty thousand against ninety thousand, with Napoleon at their head and Murat's splendid cavalry in reserve. At Auerstadt, matters were reversed. The King of Prussia, with nearly two-thirds of his army, had marched thither, and with sixty thousand men threatened to crush Davoust, with only thirty thousand. Napoleon, ignorant of this, sent a despatch to him, which he received at six o'clock in the morning, to march rapidly on, Apolda, in the rear of the army he was about to engage and defeat. If Bernadotte was with him, they were to march together; but as the former had received his orders before, and this seemed a permission rather than an order, he refused to accede to Davoust's request to join their armies. He took his own route, and but for the heroism and unconquerable firmness of the latter this act would have cost him his head.

Davoust, with his thirty thousand troops, of which only four thousand were cavalry, pushed forward, not expecting to meet the enemy till toward evening. But a short distance in front of him, on the plateau of Auerstadt, that spread away from the steep ascent up which his army, fresh from their bivouacs, was toiling, lay the King of Prussia, with fifty thousand infantry, and ten thousand splendid cavalry, the whole commanded by the Duke of Brunswick. The fog that enveloped Napoleon on the heights, of Landgrafenberg, and covered the battle-field of Jena with darkness, curtained in, also, the heights of the Sonnenberg and the army of the King of Prussia. At eight in the morning the vanguard of Davoust came unexpectedly upon the enemy, also advancing. The dense and motionless fog so concealed everything that their bayonets almost crossed before they discovered each other. Even then, both supposing they had come on a single detachment only, sent forward a small force to clear the way, the Prussians to open the defile up which Davoust was struggling, and the French to do the same thing, so that they could continue their march.

The upper end of this defile opened, as I remarked, on to the elevated plain of Auerstadt, far up the Sonnenberg mountains. Davoust sent on the brave and heroic Gudin, with his division, to clear it, and occupy the level space on the top, at all hazards. In a few minutes Gudin stood, in battle array, on the plateau, though entirely shut out from the enemy by the dense fog. Blucher, with nearly three thousand hussars, was ordered to ride over the plateau and sweep it of the enemy. The former part of the order he obeyed, and came dashing through the mist with his body of cavalry, when suddenly they found themselves on the bayonets' point, and the next moment shattered and rolled back by a murderous fire that seemed to open from the bowels of the earth. Rallying his men, however, to the charge, Blucher came galloping up to the French, now thrown into squares, and dashed, with his reckless valour, on their steady ranks. Finding, from the incessant roll of musketry, that Blucher was meeting with an obstinate resistance, the King of Prussia sent forward three divisions to sustain him. These, with Blucher's hussars, now came sweeping down on Gudin's single division, threatening to crush it with a single blow. One division against three, supported by twenty-five hundred cavalry, was fearful odds; but Gudin knew his defeat would ruin the army, now packed in the defile below, and, making desperate efforts to reach the plateau, presented a firm front to the enemy, and proved, by his heroic resistance, worthy to be under the illustrious chief that commanded him. Hitherto the combat had been carried on amid the thick fog that stubbornly clung to the heights, involving everything in obscurity, and only now and then lifted, like the folds of a curtain, as the artillery and musketry exploded in its bosom. At this dreadful crisis, however, it suddenly rolled over the mountain, and, parting in fragments, rode away on the morning breeze, while the unclouded sun flashed down on the immense Prussian host, drawn up in battle array. It was at this same hour the fog parted on the plains of Jena, and revealed to the astonished Prussians their overwhelming enemy rushing to the charge. *There* the sun shone on ninety thousand Frenchmen, moving down, with resistless power, on forty thousand Prussians, but *here* on sixty thousand Prussians, enveloping thirty thousand Frenchmen. Nothing could be more startling than the sudden revelation which that morning sun made to Davoust; he expected to find only a few detachments before him, and lo! there stood a mighty army with the imposing front of battle. As his eye fell on the glittering ranks of infantry, and flashing helmets of the superb cavalry, it embraced at once the full peril of his position. It was enough to daunt the boldest heart, but fear and Davoust were utter strangers. He was not to reach Apolda that day, that was certain, and fortunate he might consider himself if he reached it at all in any other way than as a prisoner of war. The struggle before him was to be against desperate odds, one against two, while ten thousand cavalry stood in battle array their formidable masses alone sufficient, apparently, to sweep his army from the field. Of Gudin's brave division of seven thousand men, which had fought, one against three, to maintain the plateau till his arrival, half had already fallen. The tremendous onsets of cavalry and infantry together on him could not be much longer withstood; but at this juncture the other divisions of the army appeared on the field, and with rapid step and in admirable order moved into the line of battle. The two armies were now fairly engaged. The mist had rolled away, as if hasting in affright from the scene of carnage, and under the unclouded sun there was no longer any room for deception. Davoust was fairly taken by surprise, and had on his hands an army double that of his own, while a retreat without a rout was impossible. With that coolness and self-possession which rendered him so remarkable in the midst of the conflict, he gave all his orders, and performed his evolutions, and conducted the charges, thus inspiring, by his very voice and bearing, the soldiers with confidence and courage. He rode through the lines, his brow knit with his stern resolve and with the weight that lay on his brave heart, and his clear, stern voice expressing by its very calmness the intensity of the excitement that mastered him. The next moment the plain fairly rocked and trembled under the headlong charge of the Prussian cavalry as they came pouring on the French infantry. The shock was terrific; but that splendid body of horse recoiled from the blow as if it had fallen against the face of a rock instead of living men. The French threw themselves into squares, and the front rank, kneeling, fringed with their glittering bayonets the entire formations, while the ranks behind poured an incessant volley on the charging squadrons. These would recoil, turn, and charge again, with unparalleled but vain bravery. Prince William, who led them on, disdaining to abandon the contest, again and again hurried them forward with an impetuosity and strength that threatened to bear down everything before them. Sometimes a square would bend and waver a moment like a line of fire when it meets the blast, but the next moment would spring to its place again, presenting the same girdle of steel in front and the same line of fire behind. Goaded to desperation and madness by the resistance he met with, and confident still of the power of his cavalry to break the infantry, he rallied his diminished troops for the last time and led them to the charge. These brave men rode steadily forward through the storm of grapeshot and bullets that swept their path, till they came to the very muzzles of the guns; but not a square broke, not a battalion yielded. Furious with disappointment they then rode round the squares, firing their pistols in the soldiers' faces, and spurring their steeds in wherever a man fell. But all this time a most murderous fire wasted them; for while they swept in rapid circles round each square a girdle of light followed them, and the fire of the musketry rolled around the living wall, enveloping it in smoke and strewing its base with the dead. At length Prince William himself was stretched on the field, where half his followers already lay bleeding, and the remainder withdrew.

Davoust, feeling how everything wavered in the balance, multiplied himself with the perils that environed him. With no cavalry able to contend with that of the enemy, he was compelled to rely entirely on his infantry. The rapidity, coolness, and precision with which they performed their evolutions saved him from a ruinous defeat. Now he would suddenly throw a division into squares, as the splendid Prussian cavalry came thundering upon it, and, repelling the shock, unroll them into line to receive a charge of infantry, or throw them into close columns to charge in turn. The battle rested on his life; yet his personal presence at the points of danger was equally necessary to victory, and he seemed to forget he had a life to lose. He never appeared better than on this day. The intense action of his mind neutralized the strong excitement of his feelings which usually bore him into battle; and he rode through the driving storm with the stern purpose never to yield written on his calm, marble-like countenance in lines that could not be mistaken. He had imparted the same feelings to his followers, and the tenacity with which they disputed every inch of ground; and held firm their position against the united onsets of cavalry and infantry, astonished even their enemies.

The heights of Sonnenberg never witnessed such a scene before, and the morning sun never looked down on a braver-fought battle. The mist of the morning had given place to the smoke of canon and musketry that curtained in the armies; and the whole plateau was one blaze of light streaming through clouds of dust, with which the fierce cavalry had filled the air. Old Sonnenberg quivered on its base under the shock, and its rugged sides were streaked with wreaths of smoke that seemed rent by violence from the tortured war-cloud below. Amid this wild storm Davoust moved unscathed, his uniform riddled with balls and his guard incessantly falling around him. At length a shot struck his chapeau and bore it from his head among his followers. Prince William was down; the Duke of Brunswick had been borne mortally wounded from the fight, while scores of his own brave officers lay stretched on the field of their fame, yet still Davoust towered unhurt amid his ranks. At length Morand was ordered to carry the heights of Sonnenberg and plant the artillery there, so as to sweep the plateau below. This brave general put himself at the head of his columns, and with a firm step began to ascend the slope. The King of Prussia, perceiving at a glance how disastrous to him the conquest of this position would be, charged in person at the head of his troops. For a moment the battle wavered; but the next moment the heroic Morand was seen to move upward, and in a few minutes his artillery opened on the plain, carrying death and havoc through the Prussian ranks.

The plateau was won, and Davoust master of the field. But, not satisfied with his success, he determined to complete the victory by carrying the heights of Eckartsberg, which protected the retreat of the enemy. The trumpets immediately sounded the charge, and the wearied Gudin pressed forward. But the King had already rallied his shattered troops behind a reserve of fifteen thousand men which had not yet been engaged. There, too, in security, the iron-souled Blucher rallied the remnants of his splendid cavalry. It was in this crisis Davoust showed himself the great commander, and fixed forever his military fame. This reserve, only a third less than his entire force, would have wrung the victory from almost any other hand than his. I do not believe there were three generals in the French army that would not have been defeated at this point, there was not *one* in the allied armies. Here was an army of some twenty-four thousand men, wearied with a morning's march and a half-day's severe fighting, dragging its bleeding columns up to a perilous assault; while fifteen thousand troops, sustained by the new reformed cavalry and infantry, fell with the energy of despair upon it. Blucher stood eyeing the ranks, ready, the moment a column shook, to dash on it with his cavalry. The day so nobly battled for and won seemed at last about to be lost. Wearied troops against fresh ones, a division against a corps, such was the relative strength of the armies. But Davoust gathered his energies for a last effort, and poured his wearied but resolute troops in such strength and terror on the enemy that they swept down everything in their passage, charged the artillerymen at their pieces, and wrenched their guns from their grasp, turned the cavalry in affright over the field, and carried the heights with shouts of victory that were echoed back from old Sonnenberg, as Morand, driving back the enemy that had just attacked him in his position, came driving down the slope, scattering like a wild wind everything before him. The Prussians were utterly defeated, and the tired Davoust paused amid the wreck of his army, and surveyed the bloody field that should stand as an everlasting monument of his deeds.

That was a gloomy night for the Prussian King. Fleeing from the disastrous field, with his disheartened troops, he was soon crossed in his track by the fugitives from the equally disastrous plains of Jena. The wreck of Jena came driving on the wreck of Auerstadt, and the news of one overthrow was added to that of another, sending indescribable confusion and terror through the already broken ranks. Whole divisions disbanded at once. The artillerymen left their guns, the infantry their ammunition and baggage wagons; all order was lost, and nothing but a cloud of fugitives, of all that magnificent army that moved in such pomp to battle, was seen driven through the darkness. The King, himself well-nigh captured, struggled no longer for his army, but for his life.

Such was the battle of Auerstadt, fought on the same day with that of Jena. For his heroic conduct Davoust was created Duke of Auerstadt, and, to honour him still more, Napoleon appointed him to enter first the Prussian capital thus showing to the whole army his right to the precedence. Not satisfied with having done this, and also with mentioning him in terms of unqualified praise in his bulletin home, he, two weeks after, in reviewing his corps on the road to Frankfort, extolled the valour of the soldiers, and, calling the officers in a circle around him, addressed them in terms of respect and admiration, and expressed his sympathy for the losses they had sustained. Davoust stepped forward and replied, "Sire, the soldiers of the Third Corps will always be to you what the Tenth Legion was to Cæsar."* Brave words, which his after-conduct, and that of his corps, on many a hard-fought field, verified. This battle cost Davoust about eight thousand killed and wounded, among which were two hundred and seventy officers. The brave Gudin lost more than half of his whole division.

In the campaign of Eylau, the same year, Davoust sustained the high reputation he had gained at Auerstadt. He commanded the advance guard on the route to Warsaw, and at the passage of the Ukra, at Pultusk and Golymin, fought with his accustomed bravery. But it was at the bloody combat of Eylau, he performed the greatest service for Napoleon, for he saved him from utter defeat. Twice

---

* Mr. Alison, in giving an account of this battle, with his accustomed readiness to accuse Napoleon of falsehood and meanness, and equal readiness himself to falsify, says: "Napoleon's official account of the battle of Jena, in the fourth bulletin of the campaign (it was the *fifth* bulletin), is characterized by that extraordinary intermixture of truth and falsehood, and unceasing jealousy of any general who appeared to interfere with his reputation, which, in one who could so well afford to be generous in that particular, is a meanness in an especial manner reprehensible." And further on he quotes the bulletin itself, commencing thus: "On our right the corps of Marshal Davoust performed prodigies. Not only *did he keep in check, but maintain a running fight for three leagues with* the bulk of the enemy's troops, etc., etc." Now, if Napoleon said this, he uttered a downright falsehood, as great as the one Mr. Alison has himself uttered. But by what authority he presumes to translates [sic] "*Mais mena battant pendant plus de trois lieues,*" "Maintained a running fight," one would be puzzled to determine; and the French scholar will transfer to him the charges he prefers against Napoleon. And instead of treating him with neglect, he, in this hasty, short bulletin, places Davoust far above all his other marshals in the praise he bestows, while he *practically* goes still further, making him Duke of Auerstadt conferring on him the honour of leading his brave corps first into Berlin, and afterwards selecting him and his officers out to receive his special approbation in sight of the army. Davoust did not complain, and this heaping of honour upon honour did not look like "jealousy and meanness."

that day was Napoleon rescued from ruin, first, in the morning, by Murat's splendid charge of cavalry on the Russian centre, after the destruction of Augereau's corps, and the repulse of Soult; and last, by the victory Davoust won over the left wing of the army, just before night closed over the scene of slaughter. The French left and centre had been driven back the Russians were far in advance of their position in the morning, and they only waited the approach of Lestocq on the right, to complete the victory. But the heroic corps that had won the battle of Auerstadt was there. Davoust had struggled since morning with invincible bravery; and Friant and Morand, who had covered themselves with glory at Auerstadt, here enacted over again their great deeds. The victory swung to and fro, from side to side, till at length the two lines approached within pistol-shot of each other, when the Russians gave way. The artillerymen were bayoneted at their guns, and, though reinforced and partially successful in turn, the mighty columns of Davoust poured over that part of the field like a resistless torrent. Huge columns of smoke rising from burning Serpallen, which he had set on fire in his passage, came riding the gale that swept along the Russian lines heralded by the triumphal shouts of his conquering legions as they thundered over the field and carried dismay to the astonished Russians. The left wing was forced back till it stood at right angles with the centre; when the reserve was brought up, and the victorious Davoust, who had so suddenly brightened the threatening sky of Napoleon, was arrested in his career. At this critical moment Lestocq arrived on the field. He had but one hour before dark in which to recover these heavy losses. Instantly forming his men into three columns, he advanced on the nearest hamlet, Kuschnitten, which St. Hilaire had just carried, and where he had established himself, threatening seriously the Russian lines. Under a tremendous cannonade Lestocq stormed and retook it, and immediately forming his men into line advanced on Anklappen, where Davoust, with the other divisions of his corps, lay, right in rear of the Russian centre, and which formed the limit of his onward movement. He had fought for eight dreadful hours, and at last wrung victory almost from defeat itself; and now, wearied and exhausted, could poorly withstand the assault of these fresh troops. He roused himself, however, for the last time, and that little hamlet and the wood adjoining became the theatre of a most deadly combat. It was fighting over again the Prussian reserve at Auerstadt, save that now he was exhausted by eight instead of four hours' fighting. Still he put forth almost superhuman efforts to keep the advantage he had gained. He rushed into the thickest of the fight in person, cheered and rallied on his wearied troops for the twentieth time, calling on them by their former renown to brave resistance. "Here," said he, "is the spot where the brave should find a glorious death; the coward will perish in the deserts of Siberia." The brave fellows needed no fiery words to stimulate their courage. They joyfully followed their leaders to the charge, but in vain. Napoleon, in the distance, through the dim twilight, saw this little hamlet enveloped in a blaze of light as the army rushed upon it, and for a whole hour watched his brave marshal, wrapped in the fire of the enemy, struggling to win for him the victory. With grief he saw him at length forced out of the blazing ruins, and slowly retire with his bleeding army over the field. And now the night drew her curtain round the scene, darkness fell on the mighty hosts, the flash of musketry grew less and less frequent, the sullen canon ceased their roar, and the bloody battle of Eylau was over. At midnight the Russians begin to retreat, and Bonaparte remained master of the field thanks to the brave and fiery-hearted Davoust.

Cavalry Action at Eckmuhl

The battle of Eckmuhl, where he carried the title of Prince, was distinguished by one of the fiercest cavalry actions on record; and as described by Stuttenheim, Pelet, and others, must have been a magnificent spectacle.

Lannes, who had recently arrived from Spain, took command of two of his divisions, and with two such leaders that renowned corps could not well fail of victory. Coming from Landshut, where he had been victorious the day before, Davoust and his brave troops ascended the slope whose summit looked down on the villages of Eckmuhl and Laichling. It was a spring noon, and that green valley lay smiling before them, as if fresh from the hand of its Creator. Embosomed in trees and gardens arid winding streams, it seemed too sacred to be trampled by the hoof of war. But though no clangour of trumpets broke its repose, and the trees shook their green tops in the passing breeze, and the meadows spread away like carpets from the banks of the streams, and here and there the quiet herds were cropping the fresh herbage or reclining under the cool shade, yet there was an ominous stillness in the fields. No husbandman was driving his plough, and no groups of peasants were seen going to their toil; but that bright valley seemed holding its breath in expectation of some fearful catastrophe. Banners were silently fluttering in the breeze, and in the openings of the woods glittered bayonets and helmets, for the Archduke Charles was there with his army, waiting the approach of the enemy. Napoleon gazed long and anxiously on the scene, and then issued his orders for the attack. Davoust came fiercely down on the left, while Lannes, with two divisions of the corps, assailed the village in front. In a moment all was uproar and confusion. The roar of artillery, the rolling fire of the infantry, and the heavy shock of cavalry, made that village tremble as if on the breast of a volcano. In a few minutes the shouts of Davoust's columns were heard over the noise of battle as they drove the enemy before them. His success and that of Lannes together had so completely turned the Archduke's left that he was compelled to order a retreat. The streets of Eckmuhl were piled with the dead, and the green meadows, ploughed up by the artillery, were red with flowing blood.

Napoleon then directed an advance of the whole line. The Archduke retired behind Eglofsheim, where he planted powerful batteries, curtained in front by twelve squadrons of heavy armed cuirassiers and a cloud of hussars. The French infantry, in hot pursuit, paused as they saw this living wall rise before them. Napoleon then ordered up his own cavalry to fall upon them. The hussars on both sides charged first, while the cuirassiers looked on. After witnessing charge after charge, leaving the victory in the hands of neither party, the Austrian cuirassiers put themselves in motion. The trumpets sounded the charge, thousands of helmets rose and fell at the blast; the plain shook with the muffled tread of the advancing host, and the next moment they burst with the sound of thunder on the French hussars, scattering them like pebbles from their feet, and, sweeping in one broad, resistless wave over the field, bore down with their terrible front on the French infantry. But there was a counterblast of trumpets, and before the startling echoes had died away Napoleon's resistless cuirassiers emerged into view. Spurring their steeds into a trot, and then into a headlong gallop, with their plumes and banners floating back in the breeze, they swept forward to the shock. The spectacle was sublime, and each army held its breath in awe as these warlike hosts went rushing on each other. Their dark masses looked like two thunder-clouds riding opposite hurricanes and meeting in mid-heaven. The clouds of dust rolling around their horses' feet the long lines of flashing helmets above and the forest of shaking sabres over all, gave them a most terrible aspect as they swept onward. The shock in the centre shook the field; and the two armies ceased their firing to witness the issue. The cannoneer leaned on his gun, and the soldier stooped over his musket, absorbed in the spectacle; while in the first rude meeting horses and riders, by scores and hundreds, rolled on the plain. Then commenced one of those fierce hand-to-hand fights so seldom witnessed between cavalry. In the first heavy shock one body or the other gives way, and a few minutes decide which is the successful charge. But here it was like two waves of equal strength and volume and velocity meeting in full career, and cresting and foaming over each other as they struggle for the mastery. The sudden silence that fell over the field as the two armies ceased firing added to the terror of the scene. The sight was new, even to those veteran troops. They were accustomed to the tumult and uproar of battle, where the thunder of canon and rattle of musketry and shock of cavalry are mingled in wild confusion. But here there was nothing heard but the clear ringing of steel, save when the trumpets gave their blast.

It was not the noise of a battle-field, but that of ten thousand anvils ringing under the fierce strokes of the hammer. The sun went down on the struggle, and his farewell rays glanced over swaying helmets and countless sabres crossing each other like lightning in the air. Twilight deepened over the field, and then it was one broad gleam of light above the struggling hosts, as the fire flew beneath their rapid strokes. The stars came out upon the sky, but their rays were dimmed by the dazzling sparks as sword crossed sword or glanced from steel armour and at length the quiet moon came sailing in beauty up the heavens and shed her reproving light on the strife. But nothing could arrest the enraged combatants. Fighting in the light of their own flashing steel, they saw neither moon nor stars.

At length the ringing strokes grew fainter and fainter, and that dark mass, canopied with fire of its own making, seemed to waver to and fro in the gloom; and then the heavy tramp of rushing steeds was heard. The Austrians, after leaving two-thirds of their entire number stretched on the plain, broke and fled, and horses and riders lay piled together in heaps on the rent and trodden plain.

The next day the victorious army was at the gates of Ratisbon.

The three following years Davoust spent in Poland as commander-in-chief of the forces and governor of the country. His conduct here, and, after the campaign of Russia, at Hamburg, has given rise to severe accusations against him. It has been characterized as "ruthless and oppressive." The Abbé de Pradt declared that he "filled all Poland with dread, and brought much disgrace on the French name." To acquire such a reputation from an ally like Poland goes far to prove that his character as a general was sullied by his conduct as a governor. But the character an enemy may give of their conqueror, especially if he is forced to levy heavy contributions, and create distress among the inhabitants in order to support his army, must be taken with many grains of allowance. Thus, the title of the "Hamburg Robespierre," which the citizens of Hamburg gave him while he held the city against the combined attacks of the allies, may or may not be just. Their assertion is of no consequence one way or the other. If many poor families were turned out to starve, and the hospitals seized for his own sick und wounded, and women were forced to work at the fortifications, and ruinous contributions were levied, and much distress produced, as is asserted, they do not prove the epithet given him to be merited. The whole question turns on the fact whether these things were necessary for the defence of the place and the salvation of the army. The famine and pestilence and death which a besieged army usually brings on the inhabitants would, by this mode of reasoning, stamp every commander of a city as a monster unless he surrendered without resistance. There is no proof that Davoust did anything that his perilous position did not render necessary. He defended himself against a united army, and exhibited that tenacity of purpose and power of will over the most discouraging obstacles which rendered him illustrious.

His exactions in Poland were not for his personal benefit, but for the maintenance of his troops, and it is unjust to stamp a commander as cruel because his situation calls for severe measures. Contributions levied for personal aggrandizement, and suffering inflicted from personal revenge or hatred, leave the author of them without excuse; but the same results caused by an effort to save the army may be justifiable on the strictest rules of war. Napoleon, both in is memoirs and at St. Helena, does not corroborate the statements of English historians respecting Davoust. In speaking of the defence of Hamburg he says that Davoust was a name abhorred by the inhabitants, but adds, "When a general receives the defence of the city, with orders to maintain it at all hazards, it is not easy for him to receive the approbation of the inhabitants"; and at St. Helena, where he had no motive to disguise the truth, he said: "I do not think him a bad character. He never plundered for himself. He certainly levied contributions, but they were for the army. It is necessary for an army, especially when besieged, to provide for itself."

In the campaign of Russia Davoust distinguished himself and his corps in almost every great battle. He fought bravely at Valentina, and his corps suffered severely. But, alas! Gudin at the head of his immortal division, with which he commenced the battle of Auerstadt, was here, while heading a charge, struck by a canon-ball and borne dead from the field. The next morning this division showed the marks of the fierce encounter they had sustained. As Napoleon rode past it, he saw nothing but skeletons of regiments left in it. The wearied soldiers, black with the smoke of battle, stood leaning on their bent bayonets, twisted in the fierce shock of the day before, while the field around them exhibited a perfect wreck of overthrown trees, shattered wagons, dead horses, and mangled men. He was so deeply impressed with the scene that he remarked "*With such men you could conquer the world.*"

Davoust opened the "battle of the giants" at Borodino. As he moved over the field with his dense masses toward the flame of the batteries, his horse, mortally wounded, fell under him, and he himself received a blow which for a while rendered him unable to command his troops. Recovering, however, he rushed in the thickest of the fight just as Ney hurled his corps on the centre. These two illustrious chiefs united their armies and fought side by side in that desperate, unparalleled struggle for the heights of Semonowskie.

Previous to this, Davoust and Murat had a quarrel which well-nigh ended in a fight. Commanding the advance guard together, they could not agree on the measures to be adopted. The headlong rashness of Murat seemed downright madness to the methodical mind of Davoust, and the latter became insubordinate under the command of the former. Thus, in approaching Wiasma, the cavalry of the two armies became engaged, and Murat, wishing to support his own with the infantry, put himself at the head of one of Davoust's divisions, and was about to make a charge when the latter stepped forth and forbade his men to march, declaring that the movement was rash and perilous. Murat appealed to the gallantry of the soldiers, and endeavoured to lead them on, but the authority of Davoust prevailed. After the battle was over, the "*preux chevalier*" shut himself up in his tent and gave way to a violent fit of rage, declaring that Davoust had insulted him, and he would wipe out the affront with his sword. He was just starting to go and attack him when Belliard prevented him by pointing out the consequence to his friends and the army. He was persuaded to pocket the insult, though in the effort to do it tears started to his eyes, and the fearless warrior wept that he could not avenge himself.

But through all this campaign Davoust was a host in himself. When the retreat from Moscow commenced he was appointed to command the rear-guard, which post he held till his corps was almost annihilated, and then he joined the Emperor.

In the battle of Krasnoi, which Napoleon fought in order to save Davoust, whom the Russians threatened to cut off, the marshal was so hard pressed that he lost his baton and a great part of his corps. Napoleon was at Krasnoi, and Davoust, struggling up from Smolensko, enveloped in the enemy. Hearing of his marshal's peril, he drew his sword, saying, "I have long enough acted the emperor; now is the moment to become the general again," and marched on foot toward Smolensko. He soon descried Davoust coming up, but it was a sight enough to appal the stoutest heart. He was moving slowly forward, perfectly enveloped in Cossacks, that formed a dense moving mass of which he and his devoted followers were the centre. Added to this, the French marshal, in his great efforts to join Napoleon, was marching straight on a superior force of the Russians. He saved but the skeleton of his corps.

But, though no longer commanding the rear-guard, he still kept halting resolutely in every defile and giving battle to the enemy, disputing, with his accustomed bravery, every spot of ground on which a defence could be made. It was there he showed the advantage of that stern military discipline which had so often brought on him the charge of cruelty. He and Ney alone, of all the marshals, were able to preserve order among their troops. Through the dreary wilderness, plunging on amid the untrodden snow, without provision or fuel, stumbling over the fallen ranks of their comrades, and pressed by a victorious enemy, the French soldiers gave way to despair, and flung away their arms and lay down to die. Amid these trying circumstances Davoust exhibited his great qualities. Giving way to no discouragement, disheartened by no reverses, he moved amid the wreck around him like one above the strokes of misfortune. To arrest this disorder among his troops, he caused every soldier that flung away his arms to be stripped by his companions and insulted, and thus made despair fight despair. He arrived at Orcha with only four thousand out of the seventy thousand with which he started. He had lost everything belonging to himself, endured cold, hunger, and fatigue without a murmur, and entered Orcha with the fragments of his army, on foot, pale, haggard, and wasted with famine. He had not even a shirt to put on his back, and a handkerchief was given him to wipe his face, which was covered with frost. A loaf of bread was offered him, which he devoured with the eagerness of a starving man, and then sat down exclaiming, "None but men of iron frames can support such hardships; it is physically impossible to resist them; and there are limits to human strength, the farthest of which have been endured."

Segur relates an anecdote of him, when called from the wreck of the army to Paris, which was worthy of Murat. Passing through a small town with only two others, where the Russians were daily expected, their appearance enraged the already exasperated populace, and they began to press with murmurs and execrations around his carriage. At length some of the most violent attempted to unharness the horses, when Davoust rushed among them, seized the ringleader, and, dragging him along, bade his servants fasten him behind his carriage. The boldness of the action perfectly stunned the mob, and without a show of resistance they immediately opened a passage for the carriage and let it move untouched through their midst, with its prisoner lashed on behind.

Of his after-career I have already spoken. When Bonaparte returned from Elba, Davoust, among the first to welcome him, was made Minister of War. He is accused of having treated the fallen Napoleon, after his second overthrow, like a man destitute alike of honour and shame. But there is no proof he ever uttered the language put into his mouth, and he held on firmly to the last. He finally gave in his adherence, though not in the most manly or heroic style, and returned to his country-seat. The next year, however, he obtained permission to reside in Paris, and three years after, 1819, he was given a seat in the Chamber of Peers. He lived but four years after this, and died in June, 1823, of a pulmonary affection. His son succeeded to his wealth and his peerage.

Marshal St. Cyr

CHAPTER 5

Marshal St. Cyr

Louis Gouvion St. Cyr was a different man from many of the other marshals. His character was more firm and complete settled on a broader basis and capable of greater development. Though he seems not to have run his career with the same uninterrupted success as the others, and he is sometimes called unfortunate, yet the cause is to be found in himself. Less impulsive and more methodical than those daring spirits which cast light around the mighty genius they followed his devotion less warm and his admiration less enthusiastic his complaints and recriminations meant more in the ears of Bonaparte than those of such men as Murat and Junot and Lannes. The penetrating mind of the Emperor, which fathomed at a glance every character that came under his observation, saw less to love and more to fear in St. Cyr than in them. The anger of the latter was not a sudden spark that kindled and went out; and when once estranged he was not easily won over. Even his hatred was not impulsive, but rooted itself in his judgment and thoughts rather than in his passing feelings. Power was not likely to be conferred on a man whose stern independence diminished the value of the gift. Still he had no cause to complain of fortune, nor of the neglect of Napoleon, if we except the long delay of his marshal's baton.

He was born at Toul, of humble parentage, in April, 1764. His parents designed him for a painter, and in his youth he went to Rome to study the great masters before entering on his career. There his mind became filled with those wonderful creations of art, and his youthful ambition pointed to a field as unlike the one he was to tread as it well could be. In ordinary times he might have been a respectable painter, perhaps a distinguished one. But his life was to be one of action rather than of imagination his hand was to wield a sword instead of a pencil, and to enact great scenes on a battle-field rather than trace them on canvas. The breaking out of the Revolution summoned him, with thousands of others, to a field of great exploits, and, overturning all at once his schemes as an artist, sent him forth into the world a soldier of fortune. He enlisted as a private in a company of volunteers and marched to the Rhine, where the Republic was making its first struggle for existence. He rose rapidly from one grade to another till, at the age of thirty-one, he found himself general of division. His promotion was not owing so much to his personal bravery and deeds of daring as to his knowledge of military tactics.

In 1798 he combated under Massena in Italy; and after that commander was compelled to withdraw from Rome, on account of the insurrection of his troops, was appointed in his place, and by his reputation as a just man and his wise management restored subordination and discipline. When Bonaparte returned from Egypt St. Cyr was sent to the Rhine to take part in that victorious campaign.

The theatre on which Moreau was to act was the angle made by the Rhine where it bends at Basle from its western direction and flows north along the shores of Germany and France. The famous Black Forest is enclosed in this bend of the river. Here the Austrian general, M. de Kray, was posted, with his lines reaching almost from Constance to Strasburg ready to dispute the passage of the Rhine with the French. St. Cyr had served under Moreau a long time, and on this very ground, and the latter placed great confidence in his judgment. The third corps, composed of twenty-five thousand men, was placed under his command, and formed the centre of the army. But at the outset an unhappy cause of division arose between the two generals, which never healed, and ended finally in an open rupture. Not satisfied with dividing the army into four corps, each complete in itself, with cavalry, artillery, etc., thus leaving much discretionary power to each general, Moreau insisted on taking the separate command of one corps himself. This St. Cyr opposed on the ground that his attention would be too much taken up with the affairs of this single corps and the general movements of the army neglected. The end proved that he was right, but Moreau persisting in his arrangements, as he most certainly had a right to do, the co-operation of the former was not so hearty and generous as it ought to have been. Thus, at the battle of Engen, and afterwards at Maeskirch, where Moreau was hard pushed and came near losing the day, St Cyr did not arrive on the field till the fight was over. The officers around Moreau accused St. Cyr of treachery, and of keeping back on purpose, to allow the army to be cut to pieces. But the truth is, the latter, offended at Moreau's procedure, ceased to concern himself about his movements and confined himself to his own corps. He would not stir without orders, and seemed determined to make Moreau feel the necessity of changing his conduct by acting the part of a mere machine, moving or stopping as he was bidden, and doing nothing more. Such independent dilatoriness would have cost him his place at once under Bonaparte. His tardiness during the battle of Maeskirch saved the Austrians from a total rout. His excuse for not coming up was that he had received no orders, though Moreau insisted he had sent them. It made no difference, however; he was in hearing of the heavy cannonading in front, and knew that a tremendous struggle was going on, and the fate of the army, perhaps, sealing. Had Desaix acted thus at Marengo Bonaparte would have lost Italy. Not only did *he* have no orders to march on Marengo, but counter ones to proceed to Novi, yet no sooner did he hear the distant roll of cannon toward the former place than he put his army in motion, and, marching it at the top of its speed, arrived just in time to turn a ruinous defeat into a victory.

The next day, however, St. Cyr would have wiped out the remembrance of this negligence by crushing the Austrian army to pieces had Moreau not been full of suspicions and averse to everything but the most mathematical regularity. The Austrians, in their retreat, were crowded on the shores of the Danube, in a sort of half-circle made by the bend of the river; so that there was no room to manoeuvre, while consternation was visible in their ranks. St. Cyr, though cool and steady, saw at once that by a firing and impetuous charge he could roll the whole unwieldy mass into the river, and waited anxiously the order to advance. In the mean time he brought forward some of his guns and trained them on the close-packed troops of the enemy. Finding, however, that his cannonading failed to draw the attention of Moreau to the spot, he sent an officer to him requesting permission to charge. But the former refused, either from too great prudence, or, as it is more probable, from want of confidence in the good faith of his general. The opportunity slipped by, and the Austrians made good their passage over the Danube.

COMBAT AT BIBERACH

    A few days after, however, St. Cyr performed one of those brilliant actions which stamp the man of genius. The Austrians had retreated, and Moreau did not expect to overtake them for another day. In the mean time, St. Cyr had received orders to push on beyond Biberach, a little town which lay on the line of the enemy's retreat. But to his surprise, on coming up to this village he found that the Austrians had recrossed the Danube and marched back to Biberach to defend it on account of the magazines it contained. The entrance to it by the road St. Cyr was marching was through a narrow defile which opened right in front of the village. The Austrian general, thinking it would be unsafe to put the defile in his rear, left ten thousand men to guard it while he posted his army behind the town on an eminence forming an excellent position. As St. Cyr came up he saw at once the advantage it gave the enemy. But, thinking the rout of the ten thousand guarding the pass would shake the courage of the whole army in rear, he wished to order an attack immediately, and would have done so had his whole corps of twenty-five thousand men been with him. But his best division under Ney had been sent to observe the Danube, and though orders were immediately dispatched to hasten him up he could nowhere be found. At this lucky moment, however, he heard the firing of Richenpanse's division, which had come up by a cross road. Thus strengthened, he no longer hesitated, and without waiting for the whole to form in order he hurled his own battalions on the enemy. The order to charge was given, and his brave troops advanced at double-quick time to the onset. Overthrown and routed, the enemy swept in a confused mass through the defile and through the village, hurrying onward to the heights on which the army was posted. Following close on their heels, St. Cyr entered Biberach in hot pursuit.

    Here, however, he arrested and re-formed his men, and began to reconnoitre the enemy's position. The river Riess crossed by a single bridge and a marsh lay between the village and those heights on which nearly sixty thousand men were drawn up in order of battle. It was a bold attempt to attack with a little over twenty thousand men sixty thousand occupying so formidable a position; and for a moment he hesitated in his course. Pushing forward his men, however, he crossed the Riess and the marsh, and drew up in front of the enemy. At this moment he saw the Austrians he had routed at the defile approach the army on the heights. The ranks opened to let them pass to the rear, and in this movement his clear and practised eye saw evidences of alarm and irresolution which convinced him at once that the firmness of the enemy's troops was shaken. He immediately sent forward some skirmishers to fire on them. The general discharge which this mere insult drew forth made it still clearer that the whole moral power, which is ever greater than physical strength, was on his side; and though the enemy outnumbered him three to one, and occupied a splendid position, his resolution was immediately taken. Forming his three divisions into three solid columns, he began to ascend with a firm step the slopes of the Wittemberg.

Nothing can be more sublime than this faith in the moral over the physical. This was not the headlong rashness of Murat, reckless alike of numbers or position, but the clear calculations Of reason. St. Cyr, who was one of the ablest tacticians in the French army, perceived at a glance that on one side were numbers and irresolution, on the other confidence and courage. When the Austrians saw those columns scaling the mountain-side with such an intrepid step and bold presence, they were seized with a panic, and turned and fled, leaving thousands of prisoners in the hands of St. Cyr. He carried out here successfully the very plan he proposed to Moreau when the enemy lay packed in a curve of the Danube.

The Austrians retreated to Ulm, which was strongly fortified, and St. Cyr, who had tried the metal of their soldiers, and who, from a convent that overlooked the enemy, saw and comprehended their position, begged permission to carry it by assault. In this he was joined by Ney and Richenpanse, who offered to answer for the success of it on their own heads. But Moreau did everything by manoeuvres, and, preferring a less certain good to a probable greater one, refused his consent. A man never storms through mathematics, and to Moreau war was a mathematical science. A short time after, however, one of his grand manoeuvres came very near destroying his left wing. Pretending he was about to march on Munich, he extended his line over the space of sixty miles, leaving St. Suzanne with 15,000 men alone on the left bank of the Danube.

If the Austrian general had possessed any genius, or even common sense, he would have crushed this division at a blow by falling with his entire force upon it. As it was, however, he sent a large body of cavalry to assail it, which enveloped it like a cloud, threatening to sweep it from the field. In the mean time masses of Austrian infantry came pouring out of Ulm to second the attack, until these fifteen thousand brave French were compelled to resist the onset of twenty-four thousand Austrian infantry and twelve thousand cavalry. Retreating in squares, they mowed down their assailants with their rolling fire, steadily pursuing their way over the field. Hour after hour did the combat rage, and though the ground was strewed with the dead not a square broke, not a battalion fled. St. Cyr, posted on the other side of the river, at some distance from the scene where the Iller joins the Danube hearing the cannonading, hastened forward to the spot. It was not Moreau in danger, but St. Suzanne, and he waited for no orders. Coming up opposite the field of battle, he found all the bridges broken down, and immediately planting his artillery so as to cover a ford across which he was beginning to pour his intrepid columns he opened a fierce fire on the enemy. Hearing this cannonading, and fearing for their retreat, the Austrians immediately began to retire toward Ulm.

After this engagement, from the movements of Moreau, the whole army expected an assault on the city, but after various manoeuvres this cautious leader established his army and determined to remain inactive till he heard from Bonaparte, who was descending into Italy. The generals complained, St. Cyr openly remonstrated, and had many fierce altercations with him. The unequal distribution of provisions was another cause of dissensions and bitter recriminations. General Grenier arriving at this time, St. Cyr wished to resign his command to him, but Moreau refusing his consent he retired altogether from the army under the plea of ill health.

In October of the same year he is seen fighting bravely in Italy. The next year he was called by Bonaparte to the Council of State, and the year following (1801) took the place of Lucien Bonaparte as Ambassador to the Court of Madrid. He was soon after appointed to the command of the Neapolitan army, where he remained inactive till 1805, when he was made Colonel-General of the Cuirassiers, and received the Grand Eagle of the Legion of Honour. In the following campaigns of Prussia and Poland he distinguished himself, and in 1807 was appointed Governor of Warsaw. After the peace of Tilsit he was sent to Spain, where he won but few laurels; and indulging in unjust, unmanly complaints, was finally superseded by Augereau. Two years of disgrace and exile followed. But in 1812, in the Russian campaign, he appears again, and exhibits the same great qualities of a commander, and, fighting bravely at Polotsk, receives the long withheld, though long deserved, marshal's baton.

The next year he commanded at Dresden, when it was assailed by the allies; and after their repulse held possession of it till the disasters that overtook the French army left him once more at the mercy of the allies, and he was compelled to capitulate. He returned to France after the Restoration, and was given by Louis a seat in the Chamber of Peers.

On the landing of Napoleon from Elba he retired into the country and remained there inactive till the second overthrow of the empire at Waterloo. On the King's return he was honoured with the Order of St. Louis and presented with the portfolio of the War ministry. In the autumn of the same year, however, he retired because he could not give his consent to the treaty of Paris. But two years after he was made Minister of the Marine, from whence he passed to the War Office. While in this department he succeeded in getting a law passed by which no man was to receive a commission in the army till he had served two years as a soldier. This thoroughly democratic measure sprung from his experience of the superior efficiency of those officers who had arisen from the ranks, and also, perhaps, from a desire to pay a compliment to his own career. In 1819, being strongly opposed to the proposed change in the law of elections, he resigned his office, and never after appeared in public life.

The great characteristics of St. Cyr were clear-sightedness on the field of battle, perfect method in all his plans, and a cold, deep spirit. However he might fail in a great campaign, on the field where an engagement was to take place he was regarded one of the ablest tacticians in the army. His eye took in the enemy's position and his own at a glance, and he saw at once the best course to be taken. In forming his plans he seemed to omit no detail necessary to success, while the moral feeling of the two armies was not forgotten. The latter he Calculated with the same nicety he did numbers; and it is interesting to observe what reliance he always placed upon it. He possessed, to a certain extent, that combination which distinguished Napoleon, and belonged more or less to all his great generals, viz.: clearness and rapidity of thought. But this power in him arose from a different cause than with them. Napoleon and Ney and Massena and Kleber possessed strong minds and strong imaginations also, yet they were so well balanced as only to strengthen each other. The imagination never became so excited as to confuse the operations of reason, while the judgment never acquired such a mastery, as in Moreau, that inspiration and impulse could have no control. Cool, clear-headed, and self-collected, they planned with the sobriety of reason, and yet kept it in such abeyance that in moments of excitement they could be carried away by the impulse of genius. Their imaginations acted as a powerful stimulant to the mental powers, giving them greater rapidity without forcing them into confusion; but St. Cyr possessed none of this impulsiveness. He frequently *acted* as if he did, but his most headlong movements were as much the result of calculation as his soberest plans. Consummate art took the place of a vivid imagination with him. He could *calculate* the inspirations of genius, and knew when he *ought* to be moved by impulse; his mind had great rapidity of movement, but it was the rapidity of mere logic. There was a certainty in his operations on which one could depend, and he himself placed the most implicit confidence in his own judgment. He had all the qualities of a great commander, and but for his unsocial disposition and cold, repulsive nature would doubtless early have attained to the highest honours of the empire. Napoleon rewarded the brave, but lavished his choicest favour on the brave that *loved him.* Never governed by attachment himself, how could St. Cyr expect others to be swayed by it in their treatment of him. Nevertheless, Napoleon always treated him with justice, and frequently rewarded him with places of trust. The neglect to make him marshal, when, on assuming the imperial crown, he made out that immortal list, was apparently undeserved, and gave rise, perhaps justly, to some charges of favouritism.

St. Cyr was an obstinate man in the prosecution of his own plans, and equally so in his opposition to those which differed from them; and though ready to condemn others, when thwarted or condemned himself he flew into a passion and his head became filled with all forms of suspicion. Thus, when he and Moreau could not agree, and he found there was a clique around the commander-in-chief arrayed against him instead of performing his duty bravely, and winning back that confidence which others had unjustly deprived him of, he first became remiss and inactive, then fierce and condemnatory, and finally threw up his command. He ought to have known that was no way either to screen himself front unjust charges or win his way to power. He did not seem to know the meaning of the device, "I bide my time." Thus also in Spain, when placed over the army destined to act in Catalonia, he became peevish, complaining and foolish. It was true the army was not an effective one; but, on the other hand, the enemy he had to contend with was not a dangerous one. Besides, it was the greatest compliment Napoleon could pay him to appoint him over a poor army from which he expected victory. The Emperor knew it was badly conditioned, but he could not help it and the only remedy of the evil in his power was to place an able and skilful commander over it. A poor general would have insured its ruin. Yet St. Cyr, instead of winning confidence and renown by executing great things with small means, began to grumble. Ney, when conducting the retreat from Russia, created means where an ordinary man would have declared it impossible, and out of his very defeats and disasters wove for himself the brightest wreath that hangs on his tomb. But St. Cyr not only complained, though successful in all his engagements winning every battle but accused Napoleon of placing him there on purpose to ruin him because he had belonged to the army of the Rhine under Moreau; and this splenetic and ridiculous statement of his has been taken up and incorporated in English histories as an evidence of the Emperor's meanness.* How such an accusation could have received a sober thought is passing strange.

Napoleon, at the head of the French empire, nourished such a hostility to Moreau for winning the Battle of Hohenlinden, which he, as First Consul, sent him there on purpose to gain, and on whose success depended his own that years after he transferred it to one

---

* This silly accusation has found its way into one of our school books, "Camp and Court of Napoleon," which contains many errors in fact as, for instance, it states that Moncey was at the battle of Marengo, when he was on the Tessino, and knew nothing of the engagement till it was over. It says, also, that he was in the Russian expedition, when he was not. Mr. Alison reiterates the same nonsense.

of Moreau's generals, by placing him over a poor army in Spain, at a time he was straining every nerve to subdue the kingdom. The simple statement of the charge, and the circumstances connected with it, show it to be the absurdest thing, that ever entered a diseased brain. Besides, Napoleon did not take this roundabout way to disgrace those who were displeasing to him. St. Cyr ought to have seen this after he was superseded by Augereau, and not have incorporated such a silly charge into his work.

Offended and proud, he left his command to hurry Augereau to assume his place, thus evincing openly his contempt for the rebuke the Emperor had given him for his folly. Two years of disgrace and exile showed that Napoleon knew a shorter way to ruin the generals that had offended him.

The truth is, St. Cyr was placed where he was compelled to put forth great efforts without winning much renown. It was hard work without corresponding reward, but he should have waited patiently for the latter on some more fortunate field, remembering that a good general is known by his sacrifices as much as by his victories. Once resigning his command in anger, and once disgraced for the same reason, argues very poorly for the amiability of the man.

Previous to this, in 1807, he fought bravely in the campaign of Prussia and Poland, and especially at Heilsberg, though there was no opportunity offered for great actions, as he commanded only a division under Soult. But in 1812, as before remarked, in the great Russian expedition, he had an opportunity to distinguish himself, and won that place among the renowned leaders that followed Napoleon which his services richly merited.

BATTLE OF POLOTSK

In the first battle of Polotsk, in the advance to Moscow, Oudinot, with his corps, was assaulted by Wittgenstein, and the French marshal was wounded. St. Cyr immediately succeeded him as commander-in-chief of the army, composes of thirty thousand men. This was what he had long desired. Disliking to serve under any other officer, the moment his actions were unfettered he exhibited his great qualities as a military leader. He immediately adopted his own plan of operations, and with that clearness of perception and grasp of knowledge which distinguished him proceeded to put it in execution. For a whole day after the engagement in which Oudinot was wounded, he kept the Russian general quiet by sending proposals respecting the removal of the wounded, and by making demonstrations of a retreat. But as soon as darkness closed over the armies he began in silence to rally his men, and, arranging them in three columns, by five in the morning was ready for battle. The signal was given the artillery opened its destructive fire, rousing up the Russian bear ere the morning broke, and his three columns poured in resistless strength on the enemy, carrying everything before them. But, even in the moment of victory, St. Cyr came very near being killed. A French battery, suddenly charged by a company of Russian horse, was carried, and the brigade sent to support it being overthrown and borne back over the cannon, that dared not open lest they should sweep down their own troops, spread disorder in their flight. The cannoneers were sabred at their pieces, and the French horse, overwhelmed in the general confusion, also fled, overturning the commander-in-chief and his staff, and sending terror and dismay through the ranks. St. Cyr was compelled to flee on foot, and finally threw himself into a ravine to prevent being trampled under the hoofs of the charging horse. The French cuirassiers, however, soon put an end to this sudden irruption, and drove the daring dragoons into the woods. The victory was complete, and a thousand prisoners remained in the hands of St. Cyr, and the marshal's baton was given him as a reward for his bravery.

Here he remained for two months, while Wittgenstein kept at a respectful distance. In the mean time Moscow had blazed over the army of the empire, and the disheartened and diminished host was about to turn its back on the smouldering capital and flee from the fury of a northern winter. Wittgenstein, who had not been idle, though he dared not to attack St. Cyr, had by constant reinforcements more than doubled his army. The French commander, on the other hand, had carried on a partisan warfare for two months, which, together with sickness and suffering, had reduced his army one-half; so that in the middle of October he had but seventeen thousand men, while the Russian army amounted to fifty-two thousand. To add to the peril of his position, another Russian army, under Steingell, was rapidly moving down to hem him in while Napoleon, three hundred miles in the rear, was sealing his fate by tarrying around Moscow. Macdonald was the only person from whom he could hope for succour, and he sent pressing requests to him for reinforcements. But that brave commander had already discovered signs of defection in his Prussian allies and dared not weaken his force. St. Cyr, therefore, was left to meet his fate alone. As of on purpose to insure his ruin, he was without entrenchments, not having received orders from the Emperor to erect them. Secure of his prey, the Russian general, on the 18th of October, bore down with his overwhelming force on the French lines.

The battle at once became furious. St. Cyr was one of the first struck. Smitten by a musket-ball, he could neither ride his horse nor keep his feet still he would not retire. Everything depended on his presence and personal supervision; for the struggle against such fearful odds was to be a stern one. Pale and feeble, yet self-collected and clear-minded as ever, he was borne about by his officers amid the storm of battle, cheering on his men again and again to the desperate charge. Seven times did the Russian thousands sweep like a resistless flood over the partial redoubts, and seven times did St. Cyr steadily hurl them back, till night closed the scene, and fourteen thousand men slept on the field of victory they had wrung from the grasp of fifth thousand. When the morning dawned, the Russian general seemed in no hurry to renew the attack. St Cyr arose from his feverish couch, where the pain from his wound and his intense anxiety had kept him tossing the long night, and was borne again to the field of battle. He perceived at once that the hesitation of the enemy did not arise from fear of a repulse, but from some expected manoeuvre which was to be the signal of assault; and so he stood in suspense, hour after hour, firmly awaiting the approach of the dense masses that darkened the woods before him, till, at ten o'clock, an aid-de-camp was seen spurring at a furious gallop over the bridge, the hoofs of his horse striking fire on the pavements as he dashed through the village toward the commander-in-chief, Steingell, with thirteen thousand Russians, had come, and was rapidly marching along the other side of the river to assail him in rear. Hemmed in between these two armies, St. Cyr must inevitably be crushed. Imagine for a moment, his desperate condition. Polotsk stands on the left side of the Dwina, as you ascend it, with only one bridge crossing the river to the right bank. Behind this wooden town St. Cyr had drawn up his forces in order of battle, with the formidable masses of the Russian army in front, threatening every moment to overwhelm him. In the mean time, word was brought that thirteen thousand fresh troops were approaching the bridge on the other side, cutting off all hopes of retreat. Here were two armies, numbering together more than sixty thousand men, drawing every moment nearer together to crush between them fourteen thousand French soldiers commanded by a wounded general. But St. Cyr, forgetting his wound, summoned all his energies to meet the crisis that was approaching. He gave his orders in that quiet, determined tone which indicates the settled purpose of a stern and powerful mind. Unseen by Wittgenstein he despatched three regiments across the river to check the progress of Steingell, while he, with his weakened forces, should withstand the shock of the Russian army before him as best he could. Thus the two armies stood watching each other, while the roar of artillery on the farther side approached nearer and nearer every moment, showing that the enemy was sweeping before him the few regiments that had been sent to retard him. At length the French batteries which had been planted on the farther bank of the Dwina to protect the camp were wheeled round, ready to fire on the new enemy, which was expected every moment to emerge into view. At this sight a loud shout of joy rolled along the Russian lines, for they now deemed their prey secure. But the Russian general still delayed the signal of attack till he should see the head of Steingell's columns.

In consternation the French generals gathered around St. Cyr, urging him to retreat; but he steadily refused all their counsel and urgent appeals, declaring that with his first retrograde movement the Russian army would descend upon him, and that his only hope was in delay. If Steingell did not make his appearance before dark, he could retreat under the cover of night; but to fall back now was to precipitate an attack that was most unaccountably delayed. For three mortal hours he stood and listened to the roar of the enemy's cannon, shaking the banks of the river as it mowed its way toward the bridge; now gazing on the opposite shore, now on the fifty thousand Russians before him in order of battle, and now on his own band of heroes, till his agitation became agony. Minutes seemed lengthened into hours, and he kept incessantly pulling out his watch, looking at it, and then at the tardy sun, which his eager gaze seemed almost to push down the sky.

The blazing fire-ball, as it stooped to the western horizon, sending its flashing beams over the battle array on the shores of the Dwina, never before seemed so slow in its motions. St. Cyr afterward declared that he never in his life was so agitated as in the three hours of suspense he then endured. The shock and the overthrow can be borne by a brave heart; but, in a state of utter uncertainty, to stand and watch the dial's face, on whose slow-moving shadow rests everything, is too much for the calmest heart. At length, when within a half-hour's march of the bridge, Steingell halted. Had he kept on a few minutes longer, the head of his columns would have appeared in sight, which would have been the signal of a general attack. Nothing could have been more favourable to St. Cyr than this unexpected halt; and a dense fog soon after spreading over the river, wrapping the three armies in its folds, hastened on the night and relieved his anxious heart. The artillery was immediately sent over the bridge, and his divisions were pressing noiselessly as possible after it, when Legrand foolishly set fire to his camp, so as not to let it fall into the hands of the enemy. The other divisions followed his example, and in a moment the whole line was in a blaze. This rash act immediately revealed to the enemy the whole movements. Its batteries opened at once, the roused columns came hurrying onward, while blazing bombs, hissing through the fog in every direction, fell on the town, which blazed up in the darkness, making a red and lurid light, by which the two armies fought the one for existence, the other for victory. Amid the burning dwellings the wounded marshal stood, and contested every inch of ground with the energy of despair; and slowly retiring over the blazing timbers, by the light of the conflagration, brought off his army in perfect order, though bleeding at every step. It was three o'clock in the morning before the Russians got possession of the town. In the mean time St. Cyr had gained the farther bank, and destroyed the bridge in the face of the enemy, and stood ready for Steingell, who had soundly slept amid all the uproar and strife of that wild night. The latter seemed under the influence of some unaccountable spell, and could not have acted worse had he been bribed by the French. In the morning, when he aroused himself for battle, St. Cyr was upon him, and, after relieving him of one-sixth of his army, drove him into the wood several miles from the place of action. Ten thousand Russians had fallen in these three days of glory to St. Cyr.

This brave marshal, though wounded, was compelled, on account of dissensions among the generals, to keep command of his troops and commence his retreat. Reversing Napoleon's mode of retreat from Moscow, he, with ten thousand men, kept nearly fifty thousand at bay; so that they did not make more than three marches in eight days. After eleven days of toil and combat and suffering, in which he, though wounded, had exhibited a skill, courage, and tenacity seldom surpassed, he at length effected a junction with Victor, who had marched from Smolensko to meet him.

After the termination of that disastrous campaign he is seen next year at Dresden, struggling to uphold the tottering throne of Napoleon. With twenty thousand men he was operating round the city, and, fearing that the allies would make a demonstration upon it, wrote to that effect to Napoleon, who was combating Blucher in Silesia. But the latter did not agree with him, and kept pushing his projects in the quarter where he then was, when the astounding intelligence was brought him that the allied forces were marching on Dresden. St. Cyr saw at once his danger, and prepared, as well as his means permitted, to meet it. But after some fierce fighting with Wittgenstein's advanced guard his old foe of Polotsk, in Russia he retired within the redoubts of Dresden and patiently waited the result.

Battle of Dresden

A hundred and twenty thousand soldiers, with more than five hundred pieces of cannon, covered the heights that overlooked his entrenchments. It was the latter part of August, and everything was smiling in summer vegetation, when this mighty host pitched their tents on the green hills that encircled the city.

On the evening of their approach St. Cyr wrote to Napoleon the following letter:

Dresden
23rd Aug., 1813; ten at night.
At five this afternoon the enemy approached Dresden, after having driven in our cavalry. We expected an attack this evening; but probably it will take place to-morrow. Your Majesty knows better than I do what time it requires for heavy artillery to beat down enclosure walls and palisades.

The next night at midnight he despatched another letter to him, announcing an immediate attack, and closing up with, "We are determined to do all in our power; but can answer for nothing more with such young soldiers." Immediately on the reception of the first letter, Napoleon surrendered his command to Macdonald, and turned his face toward Dresden. Murat was despatched in hot haste to announce his arrival and reassure the besieged. In the middle of his guards, which had marched nearly thirty miles a day since the commencement of the war, he took the road to the city.

To revive his sinking troops he ordered twenty thousand bottles of wine to be distributed among them, but not three thousand could be procured. He, however, marched all next day, having despatched a messenger to the besieged to ascertain the exact amount of danger. Said Napoleon to the messenger, Gourgaud: "Set out immediately for Dresden, ride as hard as you can, and be there this evening see St. Cyr, the King of Naples, and the King of Saxony encourage every one. Tell them I can be in Dresden to-morrow with forty thousand men, and the day following with my whole army. At daybreak visit the outposts and redoubts consult the commander of engineers as to whether they can hold out. Hurry back to me to-morrow at Stolpen, and bring a full report of St. Cyr's and Murat's opinion as to the real state of things."

Away dashed Gourgaud in hot haste, while the Emperor hurried on his exhausted army. Gourgaud did not wait till daybreak before he returned. He found everything on the verge of ruin; the allied army was slowly enveloping the devoted city, and when, at dark, he issued forth from the gates, the whole summer heavens were glowing with the light of their bivouac fires, while a burning village near by threw a still more baleful light over the scene. Spurring his panting steed through the gloom, he at midnight burst in a fierce gallop into the squares of the Old Guard, and was immediately ushered into the presence of the anxious Emperor. The report confirmed his worst fears. At daylight the weary soldiers were roused from their repose, and, though they had marched a hundred and twenty miles in four days, pressed cheerfully forward; for already the distant sound of heavy cannonading was borne by on the morning breeze. At eight in the morning, Napoleon and the advanced guard reached an elevation that overlooked the whole plain in which the city lay embosomed; and lo, what a sublime yet terrific sight met their gaze! The whole valley was filled with marching columns, preparing for an assault; while the beams of the morning sun were sent back from countless helmets and bayonets that moved and shook in their light. Here and there volumes of smoke told where the batteries were firing, while the heavy cannonading rolled like thunder over the hills. There, too, was the French army, twenty thousand strong, packed behind the redoubts, yet appearing like a single regiment in the midst of the host that enveloped them. Courier after courier, riding as for life, kept dashing into the presence of the Emperor, bidding him make haste if he would save the city. A few hours would settle its fate. Napoleon, leaving his guards to follow on, drove away in a furious gallop, while a cloud of dust along the road alone told where his carriage was whirled onward. As he approached the gates, the Russian batteries swept the road with such a deadly fire that he was compelled to leave his carriage and crawl along on his hands and knees over the ground, while the cannon-balls whistled in an incessant shower above him.

Suddenly and unannounced, as if he had fallen from the clouds, he appeared at the royal palace, where the King of Saxony was deliberating on the terms of capitulation. Waiting for no rest, he took a single page, so as not to attract the enemy's fire, and went forth to visit the outer works. So near had the enemy approached that the youth by his side was struck down by a spent musket-ball. Having finished his inspection and settled his plans, he returned to the palace, and hurried off couriers to the different portions of the army that were advancing by forced marches toward the city. First, the indomitable guards and the brave cuirassiers, eager for the onset, came pouring in furious haste over the bridge. The overjoyed inhabitants stood by the streets, and offered them food and drink; but though weary, hungry, and thirsty, the brave fellows refused to take either, and hurried onward toward the storm that was ready to burst on their companions. At ten o'clock the troops commenced entering the city infantry, cavalry, and artillery pouring forward with impetuous speed till there appeared to be no end to the rushing thousands. Thus without cessation did the steady columns arrive all day long, and were still hurrying in, when at four o'clock the attack commenced. The batteries that covered the heights around the city opened their terrible fire, and in a moment Dresden became the target of three hundred cannon, all trained upon her devoted building. Then commenced one of war's wildest scenes. St. Cyr replied with his artillery, and thunder answered thunder, as if the hot August afternoon was ending in a real storm of heaven. Balls fell in an incessant shower in the city, while the blazing bombs, traversing the sky, hung for a moment like messengers of death over the streets, and then dropped, with an explosion that shook the ground, among the frightened inhabitants. Amid the shrieks of the wounded and the stern language of command was heard the heavy rumbling of the artillery and ammunition-wagons through the streets, and in the intervals the steady tramp, tramp of the marching columns, still hastening in to the work of death, while over all, like successive thunder-claps where the lightning falls nearest, spoke the fierce batteries that were exploding on each other. But the confusion and death and terror that reigned through the city as the burning buildings shot their flames heavenward were not yet complete. The inhabitants had fled to their cellars, to escape the balls and shells that came crashing every moment through their dwellings; and amid the hurry and bustle of the arriving armies, and their hasty tread along the streets, and the roll of drums, and rattling of armour and clangour of trumpets, and thunder of artillery, the signal was given for the assault *three cannon-shots from the heights of Raecknitz*. The next moment six massive columns, with fifty cannon at their head, began to move down the slopes, pressing straight for the city. The muffled sound of their heavy, measured tread was heard within the walls, as in dead silence and awful majesty they moved steadily forward upon the batteries.

It was a sight to strike terror into the heart of the boldest, but St. Cyr marked their advance with the calmness of a fearless soul, and firmly awaited the onset that even Napoleon trembled to behold. No sooner did they come within the range of artillery than the ominous silence was broken by its deafening roar. In a moment the heights about the city were in a blaze, the fifty cannon at the head of those columns belched forth fire and smoke; and amid the charging infantry, the bursting of shells, the rolling fire of musketry, and the explosion of hundreds of cannon, St. Cyr received the shock. For two hours did the battle rage with sanguinary ferocity. The plain was covered with dead; the suburbs were overwhelmed with assailants, and ready to yield every moment; the enemy's batteries were playing within fifteen rods of the ramparts; the axes of the pioneers were heard on the gates; and shouts, and yells, and execrations rose over the walls of the city. The last of St. Cyr's reserves were in the battle, and had been for half an hour, and Napoleon began to tremble for his army. But at half-past six, in the hottest of the fight, the Young Guard arrived, shouting as they came, and were received in return with shouts by the army, that for a moment drowned the roar of battle. Then Napoleon's brow cleared up, and St. Cyr for the first time drew a sigh of relief.

The gates were thrown open, and the impetuous Ney, with the invincible Guard, poured through one like a resistless torrent on the foe, followed soon after by Murat with his headlong cavalry. Mortier sallied forth from another; and the Young Guard, though weary and travel-worn, burst with loud cheers on the chief redoubt which, after flowing in blood, had been wrested from the French and swept it like a tornado.

Those six massive columns, thinned and riddled through, recoiled before this fierce onset like the waves when they meet a rock and slowly surged back from the walls. In the mean time dark and heavy clouds began to roll up the scorching heavens, and the distant roll of thunder mingled with the roar of artillery. Men had turned this hot August afternoon into a battle-storm, and now the elements were to end it with a fight of their own. In the midst of the deepening gloom, the allies, now for the first time aware that the Emperor was in the city, drew off their troops for the night. The rain came down as if the clouds were falling, drenching the living and the dead armies; yet Napoleon, heedless of the storm, and knowing what great results rested upon the next day's action, was seen hurrying on foot through the streets to the bridge, over which he expected the corps of Marmont and Victor to arrive. With anxious heart he stood and listened, till the heavy tread of their advancing columns through the darkness relieved his suspense; and then, as they began to pour over the bridge, he hastened back, and, traversing the city, passed out at the other side and visited the entire lines that were now formed without the walls. The bivouac fires shed a lurid light over the field, and he came at every step upon heaps of corpses, while groans and lamentations issued from the gloom in every direction; for thousands of wounded, uncovered and unburied, lay exposed to the storm, dragging out the weary night in pain. Early in the morning Napoleon was on horseback and rode out to the army. Taking his place beside a huge fire that was blazing and crackling in the centre of the squares of the Old Guard, he issued his orders for the day, Victor was on the right; the resistless Ney on the left, over the Young Guard while St. Cyr and Marmont were in the centre, which Napoleon commanded in person.

The rain still fell in torrents, and the thick mist shrouded the field as if to shut out the ghastly spectacle its bosom exhibited. The cannonading soon commenced, but with little effect, as the mist concealed the armies from each other. A hundred and sixty thousand of the allies stretched in a huge semicircle along the heights, while Napoleon, with a hundred and thirty thousand in the plain below, was waiting the favourable moment in which to commence the attack. At length the battle opened on the right, where a fierce firing was heard as Victor pressed firmly against an Austrian battery. Suddenly Napoleon heard a shock like a falling mountain. While Victor was engaging the enemy in front, Murat, unperceived in the thick mist, had stolen around to the rear, and without a note of warning burst with twelve thousand cavalry on the enemy. He rode straight through their broken lines, trampling under foot the dead and dying. Ney was equally successful on the left, and as the mist lifted it showed the allied wings both driven back. The day wore away in blood; carts, loaded with the wounded, moved in a constant stream into the city; but the French were victorious at all points; and when night again closed over the scene the allied armies had decided to retreat.

It was in this battle Moreau fell. He had just returned from the United States, at the urgent solicitation of the Emperor Alexander, to take up arms against his country.

This was his first battle, and Napoleon killed him. About noon on the last day of the fight he noticed a group of persons on an eminence a half a mile distant. Supposing they were watching his manoeuvres, he called a captain of artillery, who commanded a battery of eighteen or twenty pieces, and, pointing to them said: "*Throw a dozen bullets into that group, at one fire; perhaps there are some little generals in it.*" He obeyed, and it was immediately seen to be agitated. One of the balls had struck Moreau's leg just below the knee, and cutting it off, passed through his horse, carrying away the other leg also. The next day a peasant picked up one of the boots, with the leg in, which the surgeon had left on the field, and brought it to the King of Saxony, saying it belonged to a superior officer. The boot, on examination, was found to be neither of English nor French manufacture, and they were still in doubt. The same day the advance guards, while in pursuit of the enemy, came upon a little spaniel that was roaming over the field, moaning piteously for its master. Around its neck was a collar, on which was written, "*I belong to General Moreau.*"

Both legs of the unfortunate general had to be amputated, which he bore with stoical firmness, calmly smoking a cigar during the painful operation. It is a little singular that by this same battery and same captain another French traitor who occupied a high rank in the Russian army General St. Priest was afterward killed under similar circumstances. Napoleon gave the order in that case as in this.

The death of Moreau cast a gloom over the kingly group that assembled to hold a council of war, and on the 28th, the morning after the battle, the allied army was in full retreat, and the bloodstained field was left in the hands of the French.

But what a field it was! For two days a thousand cannon had swept it, and three hundred thousand men had struggled upon it in the midst of their fire. The grassy plain was trodden into mire, on which nearly twenty thousand men, mangled, torn, and bleeding, had been strewn. Many had been carried into the city during the night; but some stark and stiff in death; some reclining on their elbows, pale and ghastly, and calling for help; others writhing in mortal agony amid heaps of the slain still covered the ground. Others, which had been hastily buried the day before, lay in their half-covered graves here a leg and there an arm sticking out of the ground; while, to crown the horror of the scene, multitudes of women were seen roaming the field, not to bind up the wounded, but to plunder the dead. They went from heap to heap of the slain, turning over the mangled bodies and stripping them of their clothing; and, loaded down with their booty, gathered it in piles beside the corpses. Unmolested in their work, they made the shuddering field still more ghastly by strewing it with half-naked forms. White arms and bodies stretched across each other, or, dragged away from the heaps they had helped to swell, made the heart of even Napoleon turn faint as he rode over the scene of slaughter. Oh, what a comment on war, and what a cure for ambition and the love of glory, was this field! The terrified and horror-stricken inhabitants came out from the cellars of their burnt dwellings and strove to relieve this woe by burying the dead and succouring the wounded.

After the disasters that soon befell other portions of the French army under Vandamme, Macdonald, and Oudinot,

St. Cyr was ordered back to Dresden, with thirty thousand men, under the expectation of soon evacuating it again after he had destroyed the fortifications around it; but Napoleon, changing his plan, sent him word to keep it to the last extremity. The disastrous battle of Leipzig rendered his situation desperate, for it shut him off from all reinforcements. Previously the allies had placed twenty thousand men before the city to observe it. Against these St. Cyr advanced, and routed them, and thus opened the country about to the foragers. But when Leipzig fell, the allies again directed their attention to the place, and St. Cyr saw their victorious armies once more hem him in. Insufficient supplies had already weakened his men, so that he had the mere shadow of an army, while the multitudes of the sick and wounded added to the burdens that oppressed him. The maimed and wounded which he had been ordered to send by boats to Torgau could not be got off. Only three thousand were sent, though multitudes, hearing they were to leave their fetid hospitals, crawled out to the banks of the river, and when they found all the boats were filled and they were to be left behind, refused to return to the city, and lay down in rows along the shore. Wasted with sickness and wounds, these ranks of spectres lay all night in the cold to be ready for the next boat that should appear. In the mean time the famine and suffering increased in the city. St. Cyr could not hear a word from Napoleon, and was left, without orders, to save his army as he could. But the soldiers were depressed and spiritless, the German auxiliaries deserted him, and, the ammunition becoming exhausted, he was driven to desperation. In this hopeless condition he resolved to sally forth and cut his way through the fifty thousand that environed him, and, joining the garrison at Torgau and Wittenberg, fight his way back to the Rhine.

Carrying out this bold determination he sallied forth with his fifteen thousand men. Vain and last effort! His weary, half-famished soldiers staggered back from the shock and were compelled to flee into the city. All hope was gone. The bread-shops were closed and the mills silent, though the miserable crowds pressed around them, threatening and beseeching by turns. Famine stalked through the streets, followed by pestilence and woe and death. The meat was exhausted, and the starving soldiers fell on their horses and devoured them. Thirty were slain every day; and at length, around the carcasses in the streets, poor wretches were seen quarrelling for the loathsome food; even the tendons were chewed to assuage the pangs of hunger. Two hundred bodies were carried every day from the hospitals to the churchyard, where they accumulated so fast that none were found to bury them; and they were "laid naked in ghastly rows along the place of sepulchre." The dead tumbled from the overloaded carts, and over the corpses that thus strewed the streets the wheels passed, crushing the bones with a sound that made even the drivers shudder. Some were hurried away before they were dead, and shrieked out as they fell on the hard pavement. Multitudes were thrown into the river, some of whom, revived by the cold water, were seen flinging about their arms and legs in a vain struggle for life. Silent terror and faintness and despair filled every heart. Amid this accumulation of woe St. Cyr moved with his wonted calmness, though the paleness on his cheek told how this suffering around him wrung his heart. He endured and suffered all as became his brave spirit; and then, finding there was no hope (for he no longer had men that could fight), he consented to capitulate. He offered to surrender the city on condition he should be allowed to return with his soldiers to France, not to fight again till regularly exchanged. The terms were agreed to, and he marched out of the city; but so wan and worn were the soldiers that he himself said that probably not more than one-fourth would ever reach the Rhine. He was spared the trial of conducting this ghost of an army back to France. The allies, with the faithlessness of barbarians, had no sooner got him in their power than they marched him and his army into Bohemia as prisoners of war. Had Napoleon perjured himself in this manner the world would have rung with the villainous deed. The brave St. Cyr firmly protested against this violation of the laws of civilized nations, and hurled scorn and contempt on the sovereigns who thus stamped themselves with infamy in sight of the world, threatening them with future vengeance for the deed. It was all in vain, for he had fallen into the hands of victors who were moved neither by sentiments of honour nor sympathy for the brave.

The course of St. Cyr, on the abdication of Napoleon, and his return and final overthrow, has been already spoken of. He died in March, 1830, and sleeps in the cemetery of Pere-la-Chaise. A noble monument crowns his grave, and he rests in peace amid the heroes by whose side he fought.

St. Cyr was a human man, and abstained from those excesses which stained the reputation of so many of the military leaders of his time. He was possessed of great talents, and deserved all the honours he received. His *Journal des Operations de l'Armee de Catalogue, en 1808-9, sur le commandment du Général Gouvion St. Cyr*, is an able work, though tinged with acrimony against Napoleon, which is as unjust as his conduct was foolish.

Marshal Lannes

CHAPTER 6

Marshal Lannes

Bonaparte always chose his marshals on the eclectic principle. Wherever he found *one great* quality, he laid it under contribution. The great error, even with sensible men, is, they bring every one to a single standard and judge him by a single rule. Forgetting the variety everywhere visible in nature, and that the beauty and harmony of the whole depend on the difference of each part, they wish to find in every man that proportion and balance of all his qualities which would make him perfect. Disappointed in this, they seek the nearest approximation to it; and hence prefer an ordinary intellect, if well balanced, to a great one, if great only in some particular direction. Forgetting that such a character is unbalanced only because it has at least *one* striking quality, they reject its aid or content themselves with more prudent, mediocre minds. This may do for a merchant, but not for a government or military leader. The collection of twenty thousand common minds furnishes no additional strength, while the union of one-twentieth of that number, each of which possesses force in only one direction, gives immense power. It is true, one well-balanced intellect is needed to control these conflicting energies and force them to act in harmony on one great plan, or they will only waste themselves on each other. Bonaparte was such a controlling mind, and he cared not how one-sided the spirits were he gathered about him, if they only had force; he was after *power*, acting in whatever direction. A combination of men, each of whom could do one thing well, must do all things well. Acting on this principle, he never allowed a man of any striking quality to escape him. Whether it was the cool and intrepid Ney or the chivalric Murat, the rock-fast Macdonald or the tempestuous Junot, the bold and careful Soult or the impetuous Lannes, it mattered not. He needed them all, and he thus concentrated around him the greatest elements of strength that man can wield. It is fearful to see the spirits Napoleon moulded into his plans and the combined energy he let loose on the armies of Europe. Knowing the moral power of great and striking qualities, he would have no leader without them. In this he showed his consummate knowledge of human nature, especially of Frenchmen. Enthusiasm, and the reliance on one they never trusted in vain in battle, will carry an army farther than the severest discipline. A company of conscripts would follow Ney as far as a body of veterans a common leader. So would a column charge with Lannes at their head when with a less daring and resolute man they would break and fly. Moral power is as great as physical, even where everything depends on hard blows. Mind and will give to the body all its force; so do they also to an army. The truth of this was witnessed and proved in our struggle with the parent country.

Jean Lannes was born in Lectoure, a small town in Normandy, in April, 1769. His father was a humble mechanic, and, designing his son for a similar occupation, he bound him out at an early age as an apprentice. In ordinary times young Lannes would probably have remained in the humble station in which his birth had placed him, and become in time, perhaps, a passable shoemaker or carpenter. But the call which the Revolution sent forth for the military talent of France could not be resisted, and young Lannes ran away from his master and enlisted as a common soldier in the army. Soon after he was sent with the army that operated on the Pyrenean frontier. Here he soon exhibited the two striking traits of his character traits which eminently fitted him for the scenes in which his life was to pass viz., reckless daring and unconquerable resolution. These qualities, shining out in the beat of battle and in the most desperate straits, soon won for him the regard of his officers, and he was made chief of brigade. In this rank he fought under Lefebvre, but soon after, for some cause known only to the Convention, which yet scarcely knew the cause of anything it did, he was deprived of his commission, and returned to Paris. Amid the conflicting elements that surrounded the young soldier in the French capital, he soon found work to do. An ardent republican, his bold politics and bolder manner could not long escape the notice of government, and he was sent to the army in Italy. As chief of a battalion at Milesimo, he conducted himself so gallantly, and fought with such desperate impetuosity, that he arrested Napoleon's attention in the hottest of the engagement, and he made him colonel on the spot. Crossing the Po soon after, under the enemy's fire, he was the first to reach the opposite bank; and finally crowned his brilliant exploits at Lodi, where he was made general of brigade, and soon after of division.

After the successive victories of Montenotte, Milesimo, and Dego, Napoleon resolved to push on to Milan. In his progress he was forced to cross the Adda at Lodi. Twelve thousand Austrian infantry and four thousand cavalry, with a battery of thirty cannon, stood at the farther extremity of the bridge he was to cross to dispute its passage. On the 1st of May he arrived at Lodi with his army. The Austrian cannon and musketry began immediately to play on the bridge, so that it seemed impossible to reconnoitre the ground. But Napoleon, sheltering his men behind the houses of the town, sallied out into the midst of the deadly storm, and immediately arranged his plan. Forming a column of seven thousand picked men, he placed himself at their head and rushed on the bridge; but the cannon-balls and grapeshot and the bullets of the infantry swept every inch of the narrow defile and rattled like an incessant shower of hailstones against its stony sides. So incessant and furious was the discharge that a cloud of smoke lay like a dense fog around it yet into its very bosom moved the intrepid column. The sudden volley that smote their breasts made those bold men reel and stagger back as if smitten by a bolt from heaven. For a moment the column wavered and balanced on the pass; for a thousand had already fallen, and it was marching straight into a volcano of fire; but the next moment, seeing themselves supported by the tirailleurs that were fording the stream beneath the arches, the soldiers shouted, "*Vive la République!*" and, receiving the storm of cannon-balls and grapeshot on their unshrinking bosoms, rushed forward and bayoneted the artillerymen at their guns. Lannes was the *first man across, and Bonaparte the second*. Spurring his excited steed on the Austrian ranks, he snatched a banner from the enemy, and just as he was about to seize another his horse sank under him. In a moment the swords of half a dozen cuirassiers glittered above him, and his destruction seemed inevitable. But, extricating himself with incredible exertion from his dying steed, he arose amid the sabre strokes that fell like lightning around him, and, leaping on the horse of an Austrian officer behind him, slew him with a single stroke, and, hurling him from his saddle, seated himself in his place, and then, wheeling on the enemy, charged the cuirassiers like a thunderbolt, and fought his way through them single-handed, back to his followers. It is said that Napoleon never forgot the bearing of Lannes on that occasion. The fury of a demon seemed to possess him, and the strength of ten men appeared to be concentrated in his single arm. No wonder Bonaparte promoted him on the spot. His own daring was reckless enough, but Lannes's was still more so, and it seems almost a miracle that he escaped death.

Napoleon, whom his soldiers here for the first time gave the title of "the little corporal," in honour of his courage, was ever after accustomed to speak of this sanguinary struggle as "the terrible passage of the bridge of Lodi." It was by such acts of heroic valour that Lannes acquired the sobriquet in the army of "Orlando" and "Ajax." A few months after he exhibited the same fearlessness of character and headlong courage at the passage of the bridge of Arcola. During all this bloody struggle Lannes never left him; but, advancing when he advanced, charging like fire by his side, and covering his person with his own body from the bullets that mowed everything down around them, he received three wounds, which well-nigh relieved him of his life. He was suffering from a wound when he entered the battle, but it did not prevent him from doing deeds of incredible daring. Nothing shows the personal exposure and personal daring of the generals who one after another rose to be marshals and dukes more than the frequency with which they were wounded in their earlier career. Here, after three pitched battles, Murat, Ney, Macdonald, Berthier, and Lannes were all wounded.

One cannot follow him through all his after-career, but must select out those particulars in which he exhibited his most striking qualities. Lannes was frank, even to bluntness, and so impatient of restraint that he sometimes became insubordinate, but was always brave and firm as a rock in the hour of battle. Indeed, his very impatience of control and frequent outbursts of passion when crossed in his purpose made him rise in excitement and increase in daring the greater the obstacles that opposed him. Always heading his columns in the desperate onset and exposing his person where death reaped down the brave fastest, he so fastened himself in the affections of his soldiers that they would follow him into any extremity. By the openness of his character and brilliancy of his exploits he fixed himself deeply also in the heart of Napoleon, who always wished him by his side and leaned on him in battle as he did on Ney. But the impetuosity of his character demanded constant action, and he grew irritable and unmanly when compelled to suffer without resistance. He could encounter any obstacle against which he was allowed to dash and would enter any danger where he could swing the arm of defiance; but he had none of the martyr-spirit in him. Pinion him and he would become frantic under suffering. He needed self-control and the discipline of calm and collected thought. Trained in the camp and educated in the roar of battle, he was all action and excitement. Yet his excitement made him steady. In the midst of falling thousands and the shock of armies his mind worked with singular clearness and power. It needed the roar of cannon and the tumult of a battle-field to balance the inward excitement which drove him on. Hence in his earlier career he could not be trusted alone with an army, and Bonaparte knew it. But he learned the duties of a great leader fast, and Napoleon says himself of him, "I found him a dwarf, I lost him a giant."

In the campaign of Egypt he appears the same great general, and fought at Aboukir and Acre as he had done before at Lodi and Arcola. At Acre he nearly lost his life, and was carried from the field of battle severely wounded. But in the march from Alexandria to Cairo, across the desert, he exhibited that impatience and irritability before mentioned. In the midst of a boundless plain of sand, without water, parched by the sun, and surrounded by troops of Bedouins, the army gave way to despair, and Murat and Lannes among the rest. Wherever there was a battery to be stormed, or an army of eighty thousand men to be annihilated, none spurred more joyously into the battle than they. But to bear up against the solitude and silence of the desert against hunger and thirst and a burning sun foes that could not be routed or even assailed, required more self-control than either possessed. They became dispirited and desperate, and dashed their plumed hats to the ground and trampled them in the sand, and it is said even conspired to return to Alexandria with the army. Ney and Macdonald never would have acted thus.

Selected by Bonaparte as one of the eight officers to return with him to France, he played an important part in that conspiracy by which the government of France was overthrown and the commander-in-chief of the army became the First Consul of the Empire.

Bonaparte, having resolved to overthrow the imbecile Directory and take the power into his own hands, assembled around him the most determined spirits the army could furnish. On the morning that he mounted his steed and rode toward the Tuileries, resolved to stake everything on one bold move and pass the power of France into his own hands, seven men, as yet only partially known to fame, were assembled in the palace, sworn to his interests and bound to his destiny. Those seven names afterward made Europe tremble. They were Moreau, Murat, Marmont, Macdonald, Berthier, Lefebvre, and Lannes. Only one was wanting the intrepid Ney. Napoleon felt the loss of him, and when about to present himself before the bar of the Ancients said: "*I would give at this moment two hundred millions to have Ney by my side.*"

Being employed a while in France, Lannes afterward joined the army destined to Italy, and shared largely in the glory of that brilliant campaign. He accompanied Napoleon over the St. Bernard, or rather he went over five days before him. The vanguard, composed of six regiments, was placed under his command, and he set out at midnight for the top of the pass. While Bonaparte was still at Martigny, Lannes was rushing down into Italy, and had already opened his musketry on the Austrians. When the whole army was stopped by the fort of Bard, he was still sent on with the advance guard by another path to take possession of the valley of Ivrea.

Battle of Montebello

But one of the most remarkable actions of his life, illustrating best the iron will and unsurpassed bravery of the man, was his battle with the Austrians at Montebello, which gave him the title of duke. Still leading the vanguard he had carried over the St. Bernard, he came upon the Po, and upon nearly eighteen thousand Austrians, admirably posted, with their right wing resting on the Apennines and their left reaching off into the plain; while the whole field was swept by batteries that lined the hillsides. When he beheld this strong array and discovered their position, he saw at once that he must retreat, or fight with no hope, except to maintain his ground till Victor, five or six miles in the rear, could come up. Independent of the superior position of the Austrian, they had between seventeen and eighteen thousand, while Lannes could muster only about eight thousand men, or less than half the number of his enemy. But his rear rested on the Po, and, fearing the effect of a retreat in such a disastrous position, he immediately resolved to hazard an attack. The cheerfulness with which his soldiers advanced to this unequal combat shows the wonderful power he wielded over them. They were not only ready to march on the enemy, but advanced to the charge with shouts of enthusiasm. There can scarcely be a more striking instance of valour than the behaviour of Lannes on this occasion. There was no concealment of the danger, no chance of sudden surprise, and no waiting the effect of some other movement on which his own would depend. It was to be downright hard fighting, and he knew it fighting, too, against hopeless odds for the first few hours. But all the heroic in him was aroused, and his chivalric bearing before his army inspired them with the highest ardour. Especially after the battle was fairly set, and it was necessary to make one man equal to three, he seemed endowed with the spirit of ten men. He was everywhere present, now heading a column in a charge, now rallying a shattered division, and now fighting desperately, hand to hand, with the enemy. Without waiting the attack of the Austrians, he formed his troops *en echelon* and advanced to the charge. Two battalions marched straight on the murderous artillery, which, stationed in the road, swept it as the cannon did the bridge of Lodi. The third battalion endeavoured to carry the heights, while Watrin, with the remainder, marched full on the centre. The battle at once became terrific. Before the furious onset of the French, the Austrians were driven back, and seemed about to break and fly, when a reserve of the Imperialists came up, and six fresh regiments were hurled on their exhausted ranks. The heights of Revetta had been carried, but the fresh onset was too heavy for the victorious troops, and they were driven in confusion down the hill. The centre staggered back before the superior numbers and the heavy fire of the artillery; but still Lannes rallied them to another and another effort. Under one of the most destructive fires to which a division was perhaps ever exposed, he supported his men by almost superhuman efforts. Standing himself where the shot ploughed up the ground in furrows about him, he not only coolly surveyed the danger, but by his commands and presence held his men for a long time in the very face of death. But it was impossible for any column, unless all composed of such men as Lannes, long to withstand such a fire; and they were on the point of turning and fleeing, when one of the divisions of Victor's corps arrived on the field and rushed with a shout into the combat. This restored for a time the fight. The Austrians were again repulsed, when, bringing up a fresh reserve, the French were forced to retire. Now advancing and now retreating, the two armies wavered to and fro, like mist when it first meets the rising blast. As division after division of Victor's corps came up, the French rallied, till at length, when they had all arrived, and the two armies stood twelve to eighteen thousand the whole French force and the whole Austrian reserve in the field the combat became dreadful. Though pressed by such superior numbers, and wasted by such commanding and hotly worked batteries, Lannes refused to yield one inch of the ensanguined field. It is said that his appearance in this battle was absolutely terrific. Besmeared with powder and blood and smoke, he rode from division to division, inspiring courage and daring in the exhausted ranks, rallying again and again the wasted columns to the charge, and holding them by his personal daring and reckless exposure of his life hour after hour to the murderous fire. General Rivaud, battling for the heights, and the brave Watrin, charging like fire on the centre, cheered at every repulse by the calm, stern voice of Lannes, fought as Frenchmen had not fought before during the war. The moral power which one man may wield was never more visible than on this occasion. Lannes stood the rock of that battle-field, around which his men clung with a tenacity that nothing could shake. Had he fallen, in five minutes that battle would have been a rout. On his life hung victory, and yet it seemed not worth a hope in the steady fire through which he constantly galloped. From eleven in the morning till eight at night, for nine long hours, did he press with an army, first of six, then of twelve thousand, on one of eighteen thousand, without intermission or relief. It was one succession of onsets and repulses, till darkness began to gather over the scene. One-fourth of his army had sunk on the field where they fought. At length Rivaud, having carried the heights, came down like an avalanche on the centre, while Watrin led his intrepid column for the last time on the artillery. Both were carried, and the Austrians were compelled to retreat. Bonaparte arrived just in time to see the battle won. He rode up to Lannes, surrounded by the remnants of his guard, and found him drenched with blood, his sword dripping in his exhausted hand, his face blackened with powder and smoke-and his uniform looking more as if it had been dragged under the wheels of the artillery during the day than worn by a living man. But a smile of exultation passed over his features as he saw his commander gazing with pride and affection upon him, while the soldiers, weary and exhausted as they were, could not restrain their joy at the victory they had won.

Such was the terrible battle of Montebello; and Lannes in speaking of it afterward said in referring to the deadly fire of artillery before which he held his men with such unflinching firmness, "*I could hear the bones crash in my division like hail-stones against the windows.*" A more terrific description of the effect of cannon-shot on a close column of men could not be given. I have heard of single-handed sea-fights of frigate with frigate, where the firing was so close and hot that the combatants could hear the splitting of the timbers in the enemy's ship at every broadside, but never before heard of a battle where the bones could be heard breaking in the human body as cannon-balls smote through them. Yet no one would ever have thought of that expression had it not been suggested to him by what he actually heard. At all events, Lannes never fought a more desperate battle than this, and as evidence that Napoleon took the same view of it he gave him the title of Duke of Montebello, which his family bear with just pride to this day.

Battle of Marengo

Bonaparte did not forget the great qualities of a commander he exhibited on this occasion, and ever afterward placed him in the post of danger. In the battle of Marengo, which took place a few days after, he performed prodigies of valour. Wandering over this renowned battle-field, Lannes was recalled to my mind at almost every step. The river Bormida crosses the plain between the little hamlet of Marengo, of some half a dozen houses, and Alessandria, where the Austrians lay encamped. Coming out from the city in the morning, and crossing the Bormida under a severe fire of the French, they deployed into the open field, and marched straight on Victor, posted just before Marengo. He had stationed himself behind a deep and muddy stream, resembling, indeed, in its banks and channel a narrow canal rather than a rivulet, and sustained the shock of the enemy with veteran firmness for two hours; but, overpowered by superior numbers, he was fast losing his strength when Lannes came up and restored the combat. There, divided only by this narrow ditch, across which the front ranks could almost touch bayonets, did the tirailleurs stand for two hours and fire into each other's bosoms, while the cannon, brought to within pistol-shot, opened horrible gaps in the dense ranks at every discharge, which were immediately filled with fresh victims. It did not seem possible, as I stood beside this narrow stream over which I could almost leap, that two armies had stood and fired into each other's faces hour after hour across it.

But I do not design to go into the particulars of this battle. Austrian numbers and the two hundred Austrian cannon were too much for Victor and Lannes both together. The little stream of Fontanone was carried, and these two heroes were compelled to fall back on the second line. This, after a desperate resistance, was also forced back. Victor's corps, exhausted by four hours' fighting, finally gave way, and broke and fled toward Lannes' division which alone was left to stay the reversed tide of battle. Seeing that all now rested on him, he put forth one of those prodigious efforts for which he was remarkable in the hour of extreme danger. Forming his men into squares, he began slowly to retreat. The Austrian army moved en masse upon him, while eighty pieces of cannon sent an incessant shower of round and grape shot through his dense ranks, mowing them down at every discharge like grass. Still he held the brave squares firm. Against the charge of cavalry, the onset of infantry, and the thunder of eighty cannon, he opposed the same adamantine front. When pressed too hard by the infantry, he would stop and charge bayonet, then commence again his slow and heroic retreat. Thus he fought for two hours, retreating only two miles in the whole time, leaving entire ranks of men on almost every foot of ground he traversed. But between the steady onset of the Hungarian infantry, which halted every ten rods and poured a deadly volley on his steady squares, and the headlong charge of the Imperial cavalry, sweeping in a fierce gallop around them, and the awful havoc of those eighty cannon, incessantly playing on the retreating masses, no human endurance could longer withstand the trial. Square after square broke and fled, and the field was covered with fugitives crying, "*Tout est perdu, sauve qui peut.*" Still Lannes, unconquered to the last, kept those immediately about him unshaken amid the storm and devastation. Scorning to fly, unable to stand, he allowed his men to melt away before the destructive fire of the enemy, while the blowing up of his own caissons, which he could not bring away, added tenfold terror to the thunder of cannon that shook the field. He and the Consular Guard, also in square, moved like "living citadels" over the plain, and furnished a wall of iron behind which Bonaparte was yet to rally his scattered army and turn a defeat into a victory.

From early in the morning till three o'clock in the afternoon the battle had raged with ceaseless fury, and now the head of Desaix's column, with banners flying and trumpets sounding, was seen advancing with rapid step over the plain. Immediately at the commencement of the battle Bonaparte despatched his aids-de-camp with urgent haste for Desaix. But as the report of the first cannon fired on Marengo rose dull and heavy on the morning air the hero of Egypt stood and listened; and as he heard the distant and heavy cannonading like the roll of far-off thunder come booming over the plain he suspected the enemy he was after at Novi was on the plains of Marengo, and despatched Savary in haste to the former place to see. Finding his suspicions true, he immediately put his army in motion, and was miles on his way, when the dust of fierce riders in the distance told him he was wanted. Sending forward his aids-de-camp on the fleetest horses to announce his approach, he urged his excited army to the top of its speed. At length, as he approached the field and saw the French army in a broken mass rolling back, he could restrain his impatience no longer, and, dashing away from the head of his column, spurred his steed over the plain and burst in a fierce gallop into the presence of Napoleon. A short council of the generals was immediately held, when most advised a retreat. "What think you of it?" said Napoleon to Desaix. Pulling out his watch, he replied, "The battle is lost, but it is only three o'clock; there is time to gain another." Delighted with an answer corresponding so well with his own feelings, he ordered him to advance and with his 6,000 men hold the whole Austrian force in check, while he rallied the scattered army behind him. Riding among them he exclaimed, "Soldiers, you have retreated far enough; you know it is always my custom to sleep on the field of battle." The charge was immediately beat and the trumpets sounded along the lines. A masked battery of twelve cannon opened on the advancing column of the Austrians, and before they could recover their surprise Desaix was upon them in a desperate charge. "Go," said he to his aid-de-camp, "tell the First Consul I am charging and must be supported by the cavalry." A volley of musketry was poured in his advancing column, and Desaix fell pierced through the heart by a bullet. His fall, instead of disheartening his men, inspired them with redoubled fury, and they rushed on to avenge his death. Napoleon, spurring by where the hero lay in death, exclaimed, "It is not permitted me to weep now." No, every thought and feeling was needed to wring victory from that defeat. The battle again raged with its wonted fury. But the tide was turned by a sudden charge of Kellerman at the head of his cavalry, which, cutting down a column of two thousand men in two, made fearful havoc on the right and left. Soon the whole Austrian army were in full retreat, and, being without a commanding officer, broke and fled in wild confusion over the plain. "To the bridge! to the bridge!" rose in terrified shouts, as the turbulent mass rolled back toward the Bormida. Their own cavalry, also in full retreat, came thundering through the broken ranks and, trampling down the fugitives, added to the destruction that already desolated the field. All were hurrying to the bridge, which was soon choked by the crowds that sought a passage; and horses and riders and artillery and infantry were rolled together into the Bormida, that grew purple with the slain. Melas, the Austrian general, who at three o'clock, supposing the battle won, had retired to his tent, now rallied the remnants of his few hours before victorious but now overthrown army on the further shores of the river. Twelve thousand had disappeared from his ranks since the morning sun shone upon them, flushed with hope and confident of victory. The combat had lasted for twelve hours, and now the sun went down on the field of blood. Over the heaps of the slain and across the trampled field Savary, the aid-de-camp and friend of Desaix, was seen wandering in search of the fallen chief. He soon discovered him by his long, flowing hair (he had already been stripped naked by those after the spoils) and, carefully covering his body with the mantle of a hussar, had him brought to the headquarters of the army. Desaix saved Bonaparte from a ruinous defeat at Marengo, and saved him, too, by not waiting for orders, but moving immediately toward where the cannonading told him the fate of the army and Italy was sealing. Had Grouchy acted thus, or had Desaix been in his place at Waterloo, the fate of that battle and the world would have been different.

 Lannes wrought wonders on this day, and was selected by Napoleon, in consideration of his service, to present to government the colours taken from the enemy. This calls to mind a scene which took place in Paris just before Bonaparte set out on the expedition. The news of Washington's death had just been received, and Bonaparte thus announced it to his army: "Washington is dead! That great man fought against tyranny; he consummated the independence of his country. His memory will be ever dear to the French people, as to all freemen of both worlds, and most of all to French soldiers, who, like him and the soldiers of America, are fighting for equality and freedom." Ten days' mourning were appointed and a solemn ceremony performed in the Church of the Invalides. Under the solemn dome Bonaparte assembled all the authorities of France and the officers of the army, and there, in their presence, Lannes presented to the government ninety-six colours, taken in Egypt. Berthier, then Minister of War, sitting between two soldiers, both a hundred years old, shaded by a thousand standards, the fruits of Bonaparte's victories, received them from the hand of Lannes, who pronounced a warlike speech as he presented them. The young Republic of France went into mourning for the Father of the American Republic, and this was the funeral ceremony.

Soon after this, Lannes was sent as an ambassador to Portugal, and, feeling too much the power Bonaparte and France wielded, treated with that independent nation as if its king and ministers had been subordinates in the army. He was better at the head of a column than in the cabinet, and got no honour to himself from his office as ambassador. This very bluntness and coarseness, which rendered him fit only for the camp and the battle-field, and which indeed was the cause of his receiving this appointment, were sufficient reasons for his not having it. Being commander the Consular Guard, he administered its chest and disbursed the money entrusted to him with such prodigality and recklessness that there was a general complaint. It was done with the full knowledge and authority of Napoleon, yet he reproved him for it when the excitement became too great to be any longer disregarded. This exasperated Lannes so much that he indulged in the most abrupt language toward the First Consul, and resolved to replace the money that had been expended. But from all his victories he had little left, and Augereau was compelled to loan him the sum he needed, saying: "There, take this money; go to that ungrateful fellow for whom we have spilt our blood; give him back what is due to the chest, and let neither of us be any longer under obligations to him." But Napoleon could not afford to lose two of his best generals, and, thinking it was better to keep such turbulent spirits apart, sent Augereau to the army and Lannes as ambassador to Portugal.

Recalled to the army, he fought at Austerlitz, Jena, Eylau, and Friedland with his accustomed valour. In the campaign of Eylau, at the battle of Pultusk, he advanced with his corps of 35,000 men in the midst of driving snow squalls and knee-deep in mud, up to the very muzzles of a hundred and twenty cannon.

In 1808 he was sent to join the army in Spain. In crossing the mountains near Mondragon he came very near losing his life. His horse stumbled and in the effort to rally fell back on him, crushing his body dreadfully by his weight. He who had stormed over so many battle-fields, and been hurled again and again from his seat amid trampling squadrons as his horse sunk under him, and yet escaped death, was here on a quiet march well-nigh deprived of his life.

The surgeon, who had seen a similar operation performed by the Indians in Newfoundland, ordered a sheep to be skinned immediately, and the warm pelt sewed around the wounded marshal's body. His extremities in the mean time were wrapped in hot flannels and warm drinks were given him. In ten minutes he was asleep, and shortly after broke into a profuse perspiration, when the dangerous symptoms passed away. Five days after he led his columns into the battle at Tudela, and completely routed an army of forty thousand men.

Siege of Saragossa

The next year he was appointed to take charge of the siege at Saragossa, which had been successively under the command of Moncey and Junot. The camp was filled with murmurs and complaints. For nearly a month they had environed the town in vain. Assault after assault had been made; and from the 2nd of January, when Junot took the command, till the arrival of Lannes in the latter part of the month, every night had been distinguished by some bloody fights, and yet the city remained unconquered. Lannes paid no heed to the complaints and murmurs around him, but immediately, by the promptitude and energy of his actions, infused courage into the hearts of the desponding soldiery. The decision he was always wont to carry into battle was soon visible in the siege. The soldiers poured to the assault with firmer purpose and fought with more resolute courage. The apathy which had settled down on the army was dispelled. New life was given to every movement; and on the 27th, amid the tolling of the tower-bell, warning the people to the defence, a grand assault was made, and after a most sanguinary conflict the walls of the town were carried, and the French soldiers fortified themselves in the convent at St. Joseph.

Unyielding to the last, the brave Saragossans fought on; and, amid the pealing of the tocsin, rushed up to the very mouths of the cannon, and perished by hundreds and thousands in the streets of the city. Every house was a fortress, and around its walls were separate battle-fields where deeds of frantic valour were done. Day after day did these single-handed fights continue, while famine and pestilence walked the city at noonday and slew faster than the swords of the enemy. The dead lay piled up in every street, and on the thick heaps of the slain the living mounted and fought with the energy of despair for their homes and their liberty. In the midst of this incessant firing by night and by day, and hand-to-hand fights on the bodies of the slain, ever and anon a mine would explode, blowing the living and dead, friend and foe, together in the air. An awful silence would succeed for a moment, and then over the groans of the dying would ring again the rallying cry of the brave inhabitants. The streets ran torrents of blood, and the stench of putrefied bodies loaded the air. Thus for three weeks did the fight and butchery go on within the city walls, till the soldiers grew dispirited and ready to give up the hope of spoils if they could escape the ruin that encompassed them. Yet theirs was a comfortable lot to that of the besieged. Shut up in the cellars with the dead, pinched with famine, while the pestilence rioted without mercy and without resistance, they heard around them the incessant bursting of bombs and thunder of artillery and explosions of mines and crash of falling houses, till the city shook night and day as if within the grasp of an earthquake. Thousands fell daily, and the town was a mass of ruins. Yet unconquered, and apparently unconquerable, the inhabitants struggled on. Out of the dens they had made for themselves amid the ruins, and from the cellars where there were more dead than living, men would crawl to fight who looked more like spectres than warriors. Women would man the guns, and, musket in hand, advance fearlessly to the charge; and hundreds thus fell, fighting for their homes and their firesides. Amid this of devastation, against this prolonged and almost hopeless struggle of weeks, against the pestilence that had appeared in his own army, and was mowing down his own troops, and, above all, against the increased murmurs and now open clamours of the soldiers, declaring that the siege must be abandoned till reinforcements could come up Lannes remained unshaken arid untiring. The incessant roar and crash around him, the fetid air, the exhausting toil, the carnage, and the pestilence, could not change his iron will. He had decreed that Saragossa, which had heretofore baffled every attempt to take it, should fall. At length, by a vigorous attempt, he took the convent of St. Lazan in the suburbs of the town, and planted his artillery there, which soon levelled the city around it with the ground. To finish this work of destruction by one grand blow, he caused six mines to be run under the main street of the city, each of which was charged with three thousand pounds of powder. But before the time appointed for their explosion the town capitulated. The historians of this siege describe the appearance of the city and its inhabitants after the surrender as inconceivably horrible. With only a single wall between them and the enemy's trenches, they had endured a siege of nearly two months by 40,000 men, and continued to resist after famine and pestilence began to slay faster than the enemy. Thirty thousand cannon-balls and sixty thousand bombs had fallen in the city and fifty-four thousand of the inhabitants had perished. Six thousand only had fallen in combat, while forty-eight thousand had been the prey of the pestilence. After the town had capitulated but twelve thousand were found able to bear arms, and they looked more like spectres issuing from the tombs than living warriors.

Saragossa was taken; but what a capture! As Lannes rode through the streets at the head of his victorious army he looked only on a heap of ruins, while six thousand bodies still lay unburied in his path. Sixteen thousand lay sick, while on the living famine had written more dreadful characters than death had traced on the fallen. Infants lay on the breasts of their dead mothers, striving in vain to draw life from the bosoms that never would throb again. Attenuated forms, with haggard faces and sunken eyes and cheeks, wandered around among the dead to search for their friends; corpses bloated with famine lay stretched across the threshold of their dwellings, and strong-limbed men went staggering over the pavements, weak from want of food or struck with the pestilence. Woe was in every street, and the silence in the dwellings was more eloquent than the loudest cries and groans. Death and famine and the pestilence had been there in every variety of form and suffering. But the divine form of Liberty had been there too, walking amid those mountains of corpses and ruins of homes, shedding her light through the subterranean apartments of the wretched and with her cheering voice animating the thrice-conquered, yet still unconquered, to another effort, and blessing the dying as they prayed for their beloved city.

But she was at last compelled to take her departure, and the bravest city of modern Europe sunk in bondage. Still her example lives, and shall live to the end of time, nerving the patriot to strike and suffer for his home and freedom, and teaching man everywhere how to die in defending the right. A wreath of glory surrounds the brow of Saragossa, fadeless as the memory of her brave defenders. Before their achievements the moral grandeur of their firm struggle, and the depth and intensity of their sufferings the bravery and perseverance of the French and Lannes sink into forgetfulness. Yet it was no ordinary task the latter had given him [sic], and it was by no ordinary means that he executed it. It required all the iron in his nature to overcome the obstacles that encompassed him on every side.

The renown which belongs to him from the manner in which he conducted this siege to its issue has been somewhat dimmed by the accusations English historians have brought against him. He is charged with having, three days after the siege, dragged the tutor and friend of Palafox from his bed-side, where he was relieving his wants and administering to him the consolations of religion, and bayoneting him and another innocent chaplain on the banks of the Ebro. He is charged, also, with levying a contribution of 50,000 pairs of shoes and 8,000 pairs of boots and medicines, etc., necessary for a hospital, on the beggared population. He is accused of rifling a church of jewels to the amount of 4,687,000 francs, and appropriating them all to himself; and, worst of all, of having ordered monks to be enveloped in sacks and thrown into the river, so that when their bodies were thrown ashore in the morning they would strike terror into others. He is also accused of violating the terms of capitulation by sending the sick Palafox, the commander-in-chief, a close prisoner to France, when he had promised to let him retire wherever he chose. These are Mr. Alison's allegations; but as Madame d'Abrantes is the only authority he gives, they are all to be doubted, at least in the *way* they are stated, while some of them carry their falsehood in their very inconsistency; and one hardly knows which to wonder at most, the short-sighted pique of Madame Junot (alias d'Abrantes) which could originate them, or the credulity or national prejudice of Mr. Alison which could endorse them.

Junot had been unsuccessful in conducting the siege, and had been superseded in the command by Lannes, who had won the admiration of Europe by his success. That Junot's wife should feel this was natural, and that her envy should cause her to believe any story that might meet her ear tending to disparage her husband's rival was womanlike. Besides, Junot received less of the spoils than he would have done had he been commander-in-chief. This also warped the fair historian's judgment especially the loss of the jewels of our Lady of the Pillar, which she declares Lannes appropriated to himself. All this was natural in her, but how Mr. Alison could suppose any one would believe that Lannes wreaked his entire vengeance against the city of Saragossa and its brave inhabitants by spearing two harmless priests on the banks of the Ebro is passing strange. He must find some other reason for the act before any one will believe it. But the accusation that he drowned a few monks to frighten the rest is still more laughable. One would think that Lannes considered himself in danger from monkish conspiracies to resort to this desperate method of inspiring terror. If this story was to be believed at all, one would incline to think he did it for mere amusement, to while away the tedious hours in a deserted, ruined, famine-struck, and pestilence-struck city. To inspire a sepulchre and hospital with terror by drowning few monks was certainly a very original idea of his.

In the storming of Ratisbon Lannes exhibited one of those impulsive deeds which characterized him. Seeing a house leaning against the ramparts, he immediately ordered the artillery against it, which soon broke down the walls, and left them a sort of stepping-stones to the tops of the walls of the city. But such a destructive fire was kept up by the Austrians on the space between the French and it that they could not be induced to cross it. At length Lannes seized a scaling-ladder, and, rushing into and through the tempest of balls that swept every foot of the ground, planted it firmly against the ruined house and summoned his men to follow. Rushing through the fire, they rallied around him, scaled the walls, and poured into the city, and opened the gates to the army.

But now we come to the close of Lannes' career. He had passed through three hundred combats, and proved himself a hero in fifty-three pitched battles. Sometimes the storm swept over him, leaving him unscathed; sometimes, desperately wounded, he was borne from the field of his fame, but always rallied again to lead his host to victory. But his last battle-field was at hand, and one of the strongest pillars of Napoleon's throne was to fall amid clouds and darkness.

Battle of Aspern

In the summer of 1809, after Vienna had fallen into his hands, Napoleon determined to pass the Danube and give the Archduke Charles battle on the farther shore. The Danube near Vienna flows in a wide stream, embracing many islands in its slow and majestic movement over the plain. Bonaparte resolved to pass it at two points at the same time, at Nussdorf, about a mile above Vienna, and against the island of Lobau, farther down the river. Lannes took charge of the upper pass and Massena of the lower the two heroes of the coming battle of Aspern. Lannes failing in his attempt, the whole army was concentrated at Lobau. On the evening of the 19th of May Bonaparte surprised the Austrians on the island, and, taking possession of it and the other islands around it, had nothing to do but throw bridges from Lobau to the northern bank of the Danube in order to march his army over to the extended plains of Marchfield, that stretched away from the bank to the heights of Bisomberg, where lay the Archduke with a hundred thousand men. Through unwearied efforts Bonaparte was able to assemble on the farther shore, on the of the 21st, forty thousand soldiers. The Archduke saw, from the height he occupied, every movement of the French army, which seemed by its rashness and folly to be rushing into the very jaws of destruction.

It was a cloudless summer morning, and as the glorious sun came flashing over the hill-tops a forest of glittering bayonets sent back its beams. The grass and the flowers looked up smilingly to the blue heavens, unconscious of the carnage that was to end the day. Just as the sun had reached its meridian, the command to advance was heard along the heights, answered by shouts that shook the earth, and the roll of drums and thousands of trumpets, and wild choruses of the soldiers. While Bonaparte was still struggling to get his army over the bridge, and Lannes's corps was on the farther side, and Davoust in Vienna, the Austrian army of eighty thousand men came rolling down the mountain-side and over the plain like a resistless flood. Fourteen thousand cavalry accompanied this magnificent host, while nearly three hundred cannon came trundling with the sound of thunder over the ground. The army advanced in five massive columns, with a curtain of cavalry in front to conceal their movements and direction. Bonaparte looked with an unquiet eye on this advancing host, while his own army was still separated by the Danube. In a moment the field was in an uproar; Lannes, who had crossed, took possession of Essling, a little village that stood half a mile from the Danube, and Massena of Aspern, another village standing, at the same distance from the river, and a mile and a half from Essling. These two villages were the chief points of defence between which the French army was drawn up in line. Around these two villages, in which were entrenched these two renowned leaders, were to be the heat and strength of the battle. Three mighty columns were seen marching with firm and rapid steps toward Aspern, while toward Essling, where the brave Lannes lay, there seemed a countless host moving. Between thundered the two hundred and ninety pieces of cannon as they slowly advanced, enveloping the field in a cloud of smoke, blotting out the noonday sun, and sending death and havoc amid the French ranks. As night drew on the conflict became indescribably awful. Bursting shells, explosions of artillery, and volleys of musketry were mingled with shouts of victory and cries of terror, while over all, as if to drown all, was heard at intervals the braying of trumpets and strains of martial music. The villages in which Massena and Lannes maintained their ground with such unconquerable firmness took fire and burned with a red flame over the nightly battle-field, adding ten-fold horror to the work of death. But I do not intend to describe the first day's battle, as I shall refer to it again when speaking of Massena and Bessières, who fought with a desperation and unconquerable firmness that astonished even Napoleon.

At eleven o'clock at night the uproar of battle ceased, and through the slowly retiring cloud of war that rolled away towards the Danube the stars came out one by one to look on the dead and the dying. Groans and cries loaded the midnight blast, while the sleeping host lay almost in each other's embrace. Bonaparte, wrapped in his military cloak, lay stretched beside the Danube, not half a mile from the enemy's cannon. The sentinels could almost shake hands across the space that separated them; and thus the living and the dead slept together on the hard-fought field, while the silent cannon, loaded with death, were pointing over the slumbering hosts. Lulled by the Danube that rolled its turbulent flood by his side, and canopied by the stars, Napoleon rested his exhausted frame while he revolved the disastrous events of the day and pondered how he might redeem his error. Massena had lost most of Aspern, but Lannes still held Essling, and had held it during one of the most sanguinary struggles of that fiercely fought battle.

Early in the morning, as soon as the light broke over the eastern hills, the two armies were again on their feet, and the cannon opened anew on the walls of living men. The French troops were dispirited, for the previous day had been one of defeat, while the Austrians were full of hope. But the rest of Lannes's corps had crossed the Danube during the night, while Davoust, with nearly thirty thousand more, was marching with flying colours over the bridge. The Archduke had also received reinforcements, so that two armies of about a hundred thousand each stood ready to contest the field on the second day. At the commencement of the onset Lannes was driven for the first time from Essling; but St. Hilaire coming up to his aid, he rallied his defeated troops and led them back to the charge, retook the place, and held it, though artillery, infantry, and cavalry thundered upon it with shocks that threatened to sweep the village itself from the plain.

At length Bonaparte, tired of acting on the defensive, began to prepare for his great and decisive movement on the centre. Massena was to hold Aspern, Davoust to march on Essling, while Lannes the brave Lannes, who had fought with such courage and almost superhuman energy for two days was ordered, with Oudinot, to force the centre and cut the Austrian army in two. Bonaparte called him to his side, and from his station behind the lines which overlooked the field pointed out to him the course he wished him to take. Lannes spurred to his post, and when all was ready Napoleon came riding along the lines to animate the soldiers in the decisive onset that was about to be made. The shouts of "*Vive l'Empereur!*" with which they received him were heard above the roar of battle and fell with an ominous sound upon the Austrian lines. Apprised by the shouts where the Emperor was passing, they immediately turned their cannon in that direction, hoping by a chance shot to strike him down. General Monthier was killed by his side, but he passed unhurt through the fire. In a few minutes Lannes's terrible columns were on the march, and moved with rapid step over the field. Two hundred cannon were placed in front and advanced like a rapidly moving wall of fire over the cumbered ground. Behind was the cavalry the irresistible horsemen that had swept so many battle-fields for Napoleon, and before the onset of which the best infantry of Europe had gone down.

The Imperial Guard formed the reserve. Thus arrayed and sustained, those steady columns entered the close fire of the Austrian batteries and the deadly volleys of the infantry. Lannes knew that the fate of the battle was placed in his hands, and that the eye of Napoleon was fixed with the deepest anxiety upon him. He felt the weight of Europe on his shoulders, and determined to sustain it. In front, clearing a path for his strong legions, went the artillery, rending the serried lines as though they had been threads of gossamer. Around the threatened point the whole interest of the battle gathered, and the most wasting and destructive fire opened on Lannes's steady ranks. But nothing could resist the weight and terror of their shock. Through and through the Austrian lines they went, with the strength of the in-rolling tide of the sea. Into the wild battle-gorge thus made by their advance the cavalry plunged at headlong gallop, shaking their sabres above their heads, and sending their victorious shouts over the roar of the artillery. They dashed on the ranks with such fury that whole battalions broke and fled, crying "All is lost." Amid this confusion and dismay still advanced the firm column of Lannes. On, on it moved with the strength of fate itself, and Bonaparte saw with delight his favourite marshal wringing the crown from Germany and lacing it on his head. At length the enveloped hoist pierced to the reserve grenadiers of the Austrian army, and the last fatal blow seemed about to be given. In this dreadful crisis the Archduke showed the power and heroism of Napoleon himself. Seeing that all was lost without a desperate effort, and apparently not caring for his life if defeat must be endured, he spurred his steed among the shaking ranks, rallying them by his voice and bearing to the charge, and seizing the standard of Zach's corps, which was already yielding to the onset, charged at their head like a storm. His generals, roused by his example, dashed into the thickest of the fight, and at the head of their respective divisions fell like so many rocks upon the head of Lannes's column. Those brave officers, almost to a man, sunk before the fire that received them; but that dreadful column was checked for the first time in its advance, and stood like a living rock amid its foes. The Austrians were thrown into squares, and stood in checkers on the field. Into the very heart of these Lannes had penetrated and stopped. The empire stopped with him, and Napoleon saw at once the peril of his chief. The brave cuirassiers that had broken the best infantry of the world were immediately ordered to the rescue. Shaking the ground over which they galloped their glittering armour rattling as they came they burst into the midst of the enemy and charged the now steady battalions with appalling fury. Round and round the firm squares they rode, spurring their steeds against the very points of the bayonets, but in vain. Not a square broke, not a battalion fled; and, charged in turn by the Austrian cavalry, they were compelled to fall back on their own infantry. Still Lannes stood amid the wreck and carnage of the battle-field around him. Unable to deploy so as to return the terrific fire that wasted him, and disdaining to fly, he let his ranks melt away beside him. Being in squares, the Austrians could fire to advantage, while Lannes could only return it from the edges of his column. Seeing that he dare not deploy his men, the Archduke advanced the cannon within five rods of them, and there played on the dense masses. Every discharge opened huge gaps, and men seemed like mist before the destructive storm. Still that shivering column stood as if rooted to the ground, while Lannes surveyed with a flashing eye the disastrous field from which he saw there was no relief. Amid this destruction, and in this crisis, the ammunition began to fail, and his own cannon were less hotly worked. Just then, too, the news began to fly over the field that the bridges over the Danube had been carried away by the heavy boats that had been floated down against them. Still Lannes disdained to fly, and seemed to resolve to perish in his footsteps. The brave marshal knew he could not win the battle; but he knew also he could die on the spot where he struggled for an empire. Bonaparte, as he looked over the disordered field from his position, saw at once that the battle was lost. Still in this dreadful crisis he showed no agitation or excitement. Calm and collected, as if on a mere review, he surveyed the ruin about him, and by his firm bearing steadied the soldiers and officers amid whom he moved. Seeing that no time was to be lost if he would save the remnant of his army for the bridges were fast yielding to the swollen stream he ordered a general retreat. Lannes and his army then began to retire over the field. In a moment the retreat became general, and the whole army rolled heavily toward the bridge that crossed to the island of Lobau. As they concentrated on the shore it became one mighty mass where not a shot could fall amiss.

The Archduke, wishing to turn this retreat into a total rout, immediately advanced with his whole army upon

them. His entire artillery was brought up and arranged in a semicircle around this dense mass crowding on to the bridges, and poured their concentrated storm into a perfect mountain of flesh. It seemed as if nothing could prevent an utter overthrow; but Lannes, cool and resolute as his Emperor, rallied his best men in the rear and covered the retreating and bleeding army. With Massena by his side, now steadying his troops by his words and actions, now charging like fire on the advancing lines, these two heroes saved the army from burial in the Danube.

Lannes never appeared to better advantage than on this occasion. His impetuosity was tempered by the most serious and thoughtful actions, and he seemed to feel the importance of the great mission with which he had been entrusted. At length, dismounting from his horse to escape the tempest of cannon-balls which swept down everything over the soldiers' heads, he was struck by a shot as he touched the ground, which carried away the whole of the right leg and the foot and ankle of the left. Placed on a litter, he was immediately carried over the bridge into the island, where Bonaparte was superintending some batteries with which to protect the passage. Seeing a litter approach him, Napoleon turned, and, lo! there lay the bleeding and dying Lannes. The fainting marshal seized him by the hand, and in a tremulous voice exclaimed: "Farewell, sire. Live for the world, but bestow a passing thought on one of your best friends, who in two hours will be no more."

The roar of battle was forgotten, and reckless alike of his defeat and the peril of his army, of all, save the dying friend by his side, Napoleon knelt over the rude couch and wept like a child. The lip that had seemed made of iron during the day now quivered with emotion, and the eye that had never blenched in the wildest of the battle now flowed with tears. The voice of affection spoke louder than the thunder of artillery, and the marble-hearted monarch wept. And well he might. For there before him, mangled and torn, lay the friend of his youth and the companion of his early career he who charged by his side at Lodi and Arcola, saved his army at Montebello, and Italy at Marengo, who opened Ratisbon to his victorious army nay, the right hand of his power broken and fallen forever. "Lannes," said he, in his overpowering emotion, "do you not know me? It is the Emperor, it is Bonaparte, your friend; you will yet live." "I would that I might," replied the dying hero, "for you and my country, but in an hour I shall be no more." Soon after he fainted away, and then became delirious. He lingered thus for nine days, now charging in his frantic dreams at the head of his column, now calling wildly on the Emperor to come to him, and now raving about his cruel fate. He would not hear of death, and when told that he must die, that nothing could same him "Not save a Marshal of France!" he exclaimed, "and a Duke of Montebello! Then the Emperor shall hang you." No, death spares neither marshals nor dukes, and the hero of so many combats had fought his last battle.

Lannes was prodigal of money, notwithstanding the attempt of Mr. Alison to make him covetous; frank even to bluntness, and unconscious of fear. In the midst of battle his penetrating eye detected every movement with precision. Napoleon himself says of him: "Lannes was wise, prudent, and withal bold; gifted with imperturbable *sang froid* in presence of the enemy." There was not a general in the French army that could manoeuvre thirty thousand infantry on the field of battle so well as he, and had he lived, he would have become as distinguished for his military skill as he was for his bravery. His intellect was developing rapidly, and Napoleon was astonished at the growth of his understanding. In a few years more he would have been one of the ablest generals of his time. The rashness of youth was rapidly giving way to the reflection of the man, and his character was forming on a solid and permanent basis. He was but forty years of age when he died. His soldiers loved him like children, and a poor officer never was forgotten by him. His wife, whom he married in poverty, and from the lower ranks of life, partook of his generosity and kindness.

The eldest son of Lannes, the present Duke of Montebello, married not many years ago in Paris a daughter of Charles Jenkinson, an English gentleman.

Marshal Moncey

CHAPTER 7

Marshal Moncey

There can be no greater contrast than that between Moncey and most of Napoleon's other marshals. The moral qualities in him predominated over the mental, and while he did everything right he did nothing brilliant. Notwithstanding the injustice of it, the world will insist on judging every man by the same standard without regard to the natural temperament or mental constitution. For the quiet, upright, and charitable life a man naturally of a mild spirit and equable feelings leads, he receives all the praise of one who has combated his fierce propensities and by a long process of self-discipline chastened his spirit and corrected his actions. The world seems to forget he is acting out his natural tendencies, and to be rash, positive, and encroaching would require a painful effort. Being without force of will and the concentration of purpose which loves action and seeks great accomplishments, he is not at home in the violence of political revolutions or the fierce tumult of battle. In following the peaceful and even path he treads, he is consulting his own tastes and inclinations, yet men point to him as a model. He may be a good man, and worthy of all admiration; yet were the world filled with such it would stagnate. Such men never make reformers conceive and execute vast plans, or push the race onward toward its final goal.

Neither will men average character. They will not allow for the peculiar nature with which one is endowed, nor let his good and bad qualities balance each other. A man of strong and vivid imagination and impetuous spirit may not only exhibit more principle, show more self-control, and acquire greater virtue in disciplining himself to the point from which errors are still committed, than he who is without spot or blame, out spot or blame, but his actions if mingled up would take a higher level. One error "covers a multitude" of virtues in this world.

Moncey and Murat were as different as light and darkness; neither one could have been the other by any possible training. The career of the former was like a stream flowing through valleys, steady and equable; that of the latter like a rushing wave, now breaking in grandeur on the shore, and now retiring out of sight into the deep. The former cultivates our sentiments, the latter kindles our imagination and awakens our emotions. Murat was a chivalric knight, Moncey an honest man. One went down like a gallant ship at sea; the other slowly wasted away in the peaceful port where he sought shelter and repose. But, if Moncey was not a brilliant man, he exhibited in the early part of his career the qualities of a good general, and received the reward of his bravery and success in being made Duke of Cornegliano and Marshal of the Empire.

Rose-Adrien de Moncey was born at Bezançon, in July, 1754. His father was lawyer of the town parliament, and designed to fit his son for his own peaceful pursuits. But young Adrian, seized with a love for military life so common to youth, enlisted when but fifteen years old in the infantry. His father, thinking that the rigors of a camp life would soon disgust him, let him remain six months, and then procured his discharge. He, however, soon ran away, and enlisted in another regiment of infantry. His father, seeing the force of his inclinations, left him to pursue his own course, and he served as grenadier for three years. Having been engaged in no battle in that time, and receiving no promotion, he concluded to abandon his musket and return home, where he commenced the study of law. But a garrison being in town, it awakened all his old habits and tastes, and drew him away from his studies. As a natural result, he again became a soldier, and in about four years reached the rank of sub-lieutenant of dragoons. The Revolution breaking out, a new life opened to him, and he entered at once on his successful career. Drafted into a battalion of light-infantry, he went up rapidly to captain, chief of battalion, and general of division. During the first campaigns of the Republic he distinguished himself as a brave and upright officer.

In 1794 he was sent to the Western Pyrenees to defend the frontiers of France against the invasions of Spain. After the success of Dugomier in the East, it was resolved to invade Spain in turn by Catalonia and Navarre. The army advanced in three columns through three different passes Moncey commanded the third. He forced the passage appointed to him, took St. Sebastian, and on the next day fired the gates of Tolosa. Constant successes followed the army, which filled the Convention with joy. The representative Garrau, after enumerating the extraordinary victories that had been gained, closed with saying, "The soldiers of this army are not men they are either demons or gods." The whole state of French affairs was changed in that quarter, and as it was attributed chiefly to the energy and skill of Moncey, he was nominated commander-in-chief. Hearing of his nomination, he wrote to the Convention not to ratify it, as he did not deem himself qualified for the station. But the Convention paid no heed to his remonstrance, and he was proclaimed "Commander-in-chief of the Army of Spain." He soon showed that the government had not misplaced its confidence; for, pursuing his success, he beat the Spaniards at Lecumberry and Villa Nova, passed the Deva, overcame the enemy at Villa Real and Mont Dragon took Bilboa, routed the enemy at Vittoria, and overrun all Biscay. The court at Madrid, alarmed at the rapid advance of the republican general, offered terms of peace, which were accepted, and the victorious Moncey left the field of his fame, and returned to France. In 1796 he was sent to command the army on the side of Brest. Having used all his endeavour to heal the divisions in Vendée, he was appointed at the end of the year to command the first military division at Bayonne. Here he remained idle, while the French army was filling the world with its deeds, along the Nile and around the Pyramids, and winning laurels in the Alps and by the Rhine.

When Bonaparte was appointed First Consul, Moncey, then at Paris, received the command of the fifteenth military division at Lyons. Soon after, when the former commenced operations in Italy, the latter was despatched thither with fifteen thousand men. While the former was descending from the heights of St. Bernard, the latter was leading his army of fifteen thousand men over the pass of St. Gothard. His historians have made him present at the battle of Marengo, but on the day of that great victory to the French he was guarding the Tessino, awaiting orders from Bonaparte.

In 1801 he was made chief inspector of the *gens d'armerie*, and three years after received his marshal's baton. Grand officer of the Legion of Honour, President of the Electoral College of his own department, and Duke of Cornegliano, followed in rapid succession.

In 1808, when Napoleon invaded Spain, Moncey was sent into Valencia at the head of ten thousand men to watch the country between the Lower Ebro and Carthagena, and if he thought advisable to attack Valencia itself. Hearing at Cuenea that an army of thirty thousand men was gathering to attack him, and that the insurrection in the province was rapidly increasing, he resolved to march on the city of Valencia. He immediately, according to his instructions, sent a despatch to General Chabran, whom he supposed to be at Tortosa, to march also toward the city, and effect a junction with his army there on the 27th or 28th of the month. In the mean time he moved forward with his small army toward the place.

Forcing the river Cabriel, he continued his march without serious interruption and took up his position at Otriel. But hearing that the patriots to the number of twelve thousand were entrenching themselves at Cabrillas on his left he turned aside to attack them. As he came up to them his experienced eye saw immediately the advantageous position they had taken. Their centre was behind a deep, narrow defile, lined with precipitous rocks, on which were gathered multitudes of armed peasantry, while the two wings stretched along the side of a steep and rocky mountain. Opening his artillery on the centre, and keeping his cavalry hovering about the defile in order to draw off the attention of the enemy, he despatched General Harispe to turn their flank. The plan was successful, and the enemy was routed at all points. Continuing his march he arrived before Valencia on the 27th, but no General Chabran was there, nor could he get any tidings of him. He, however, disposed his forces to the best advantage, opened his artillery, and summoned the city to surrender. But a walled town, filled with eighty thousand inhabitants and surrounded by trenches flooded by water, so that no approach could be made except through the gates, was not likely to yield to an army of ten thousand men without a struggle. Moncey then undertook to carry it by assault a foolish attempt, unless, as is reported, a smuggler had promised to betray the place.

The assault was unsuccessful; the people were in arms; and a friar traversing the streets, with a cross in one hand and a sword in the other, roused them by his fiery words to the highest pitch of enthusiasm.

In the mean time, no intelligence having been received of Chabran, and the ammunition being nearly expended, and a thousand wounded men encumbering his troops, he concluded to raise the siege, and fell back to Quarte. Hearing at this place that the Spanish general was on the march for Almanza to intercept the communication of the French army, he resolved to advance and attack him before he could leave the kingdom of Murcia, from which lie was hastening. In carrying out this plan Moncey, though now fifty-four years of age, exhibited a vigour of resolution and rapidity of movement that would have honoured the youngest general in the army.

Serbelloni was impeded in his march by the sudden appearance of the French marshal before him, and hastily took position behind the river Xucar.

Moncey, however, forced the passage, and Serbelloni retired to some heights that commanded the high road to Almanza, designing to take possession of the defiles before the town, and there dispute the entrance with the enemy. But Moncey's rapidity of movement again defeated him; for, marching all night, he drew up his army in the principal gorge and saluted the Spaniards as they approached in the morning with a discharge of artillery. Having dispersed them, he entered the town in triumph.

The whole province soon after arising in arms, his position became perilous, and Caulincourt was sent to reinforce him. Thus strengthened, he began to march back on Valencia. But Savary, entrusted with the chief command for a short time in this department, arrested his movements with so little ceremony that he was offended, and returned to Madrid. Soon after he was ordered to besiege Saragossa. Arriving before the city, he summoned the inhabitants to surrender, and prevent the slaughter that must ensue if the siege was carried on. In a few days, however, he was superseded by Junot.

Moncey's operations were not very brilliant, and could not well be with so small a force; still he killed and wounded, in the several battles he fought, a number equal to his entire army, showing that he was anything but an inactive and inefficient leader. Napier, in speaking of his operations in Valencia, gives him great credit, and says: "Marshal Moncey, whose whole force was at first only eight thousand French, and never exceeded ten thousand men, continued marching and fighting without cessation for a month, during which period he forced two of the strongest mountain passes in the world crossed several large and difficult rivers carried the war into the very streets of Valencia, and, being disappointed of assistance from Catalonia, extricated his division from a difficult situation, after having defeated his opponents in five actions, killed and wounded a number of them equal in amount to the whole of his own force, and made a circuit of three hundred miles through a hostile and populous country without having sustained any serious loss, without any desertion from the Spanish battalions incorporated with his own, and, what was of more importance, having those battalions much increased by desertions from the enemy." In another place he says, "Moncey, though an old man, was vigorous, active, and decided."

"Recalled to Paris by Napoleon, he was sent into Flanders to repel the English, who were threatening a descent upon Antwerp. The failure of that expedition leaving him without active employment, he was appointed to the command of the army of reserve in the North. When Napoleon projected his fatal Russian campaign, Moncey, then an old man, threw in his strenuous remonstrance against it. After its disastrous termination, he did but little till the allies invaded France. When Napoleon, in that crisis of his life, roused himself to meet the storm that was darkening over his throne, he saw, with his far-reaching glance, that the enemy might approach to Paris; and among his last dispositions was the reorganization of the National Guard, over which he placed the veteran Moncey.

On the Monday previous to his setting out for the army, to make his last stand for his empire, he assembled the officers of the National Guard in the Palace of the Tuileries, and there, in solemn pomp, committed his son to their charge. The Empress advanced first into the apartment, followed by Madame Montesquieu carrying the infant king already proclaimed King of Rome. The innocent child, but three years old, was dressed in the uniform of the National Guard, and his blue eyes sparkled with delight at the gay ornaments that now for the first time adorned his vestments, while his golden locks clustered in ringlets about his neck. Taking him by the hand, Napoleon stepped into the midst of the circle of officers, and thus addressed them: "Gentlemen, I am now to set out for the army, and I entrust to you that which I hold dearest in the world my wife and son. Let there be no political dissensions; let the respect for property, regard for order, and, above all, the love of France, fill every bosom. I do not conceal from you that in the struggle that is to come the enemy may approach on Paris, but a few days will end the affair. Before they arrive I will be on their flanks and rear, and annihilate those who dare violate our country." After he had closed his address, a silence, like that of the grave, succeeded, and he took the child in his arms and presented him to the aged Moncey. The old man, who had stood so many battle shocks unmoved, was now unnerved; and the quivering lip and swimming eye told of the deep emotions that mastered him, as he received the sacred trust. "This," said Napoleon, "is your future sovereign." He then presented the child to the other officers, and, as with sad and serious countenance he walked uncovered through their ranks, sudden shouts of enthusiasm filled the apartments; amid the cries of "*Vive l'Empereur*," and "*Vive le Roi de Rome*," tears burst from eyes unaccustomed to weep.

On Tuesday morning, at three o'clock, Napoleon left his palace for the army, never to see his wife and son again.

At length the allied armies were approaching to Paris; and soon the heights around the city were covered with their victorious legions. But previous to this the Empress and her son, by order of Napoleon, had left Paris. Still the National Guard combated bravely, and Marshal Moncey, firm and steadfast to the end, struggled on after all hope was gone, and remonstrated against submission until Marmont's defection ruined everything. He then resigned his command to the Duke of Montmorency, and, faithful to the last, retired with a few troops to Fontainebleau, to Napoleon. After the abdication of the Emperor he gave in his adhesion to the new government and was confirmed in his office of Inspector-General of the Horse of the King's household, and in June following made Chevalier of Saint Louis, and two days after Peer of France.

When the news of Napoleon's landing reached Paris he addressed the *gens d'armes*, reminding them of the oath they had taken to be faithful to the King. He himself never swerved from his new allegiance; and after the second overthrow of Napoleon at Waterloo was appointed, as the oldest of the marshals, to preside at the trial of Ney. But the firm and upright old soldier not only refused to sit in the Council of War, but drew up an able and bold remonstrance to the King against the act. This letter came to light a few years after, and was unpublished in this country, and though Moncey, then in favour, saw fit to deny it authenticity, it was in terms that rather confirmed than weakened the common belief of its authorship. The published letter not corresponding in every particular with the written one, allowed him to disavow it for the sake of the King, who did not wish to take the obloquy of having treated so noble an appeal with disregard. He says, "Placed in the cruel alternative to disobey your Majesty or violate my conscience, I am forced to explain myself to your Majesty. I do not enter into the question of the guilt or innocence of Marshal Ney; your justice, and the equity of his judges, must answer for that to posterity, which weighs in the same balance kings and subjects." After speaking of the general peace and security which were established, and that there was no cause for this highhanded act of cruelty, except that the allies wished to take vengeance on one whose very name reminded them of their humiliation, he begs the King to refuse his sanction to it. As for himself, he says, in true nobility of spirit: "My life, my fortune, all that I hold most dear, belong to my King and my country; *but my honour is my own*; and no power can rob me of it. What, shall I pronounce upon the fate of Marshal Ney! Permit me, Sire, to ask your Majesty, where were these accusers when Ney was marching over the field of battle? Ah! if Russia and the allies are not able to pardon the victor of Borodino, can France forget the hero of Beresina? Shall I send to death one to whom France owes her life her families, their children, their husband, and parents? Reflect, Sire; it is, perhaps, the last time that truth shall come near your throne.

"It is very dangerous, very impolitic to push the brave to despair. Ah, if the unhappy Ney had accomplished at Waterloo what he had so often done before, perhaps he would not have been drawn before a military commission. Perhaps those who to-day demand his death would have implored his protection...." "Nobly said, brave Moncey, in this trying hour of France, when each was seeking to preserve his own head or fortune. This single act should make him immortal. Braving the hatred of the King and the vengeance of the allies, he, whose life was no stain, here interposes himself between an old companion in arms and death. His place, his fortune, and his liberty he regarded light as air when put in the balance with his honour and with justice. To any but a Bourbon's heart this appeal would not have been in vain, and that unhappy race would have been saved another stain on its character, and England a dishonour which she never can wipe from her history.

This bold refusal of the oldest marshal to be president of the council of war to try Ney, accompanied with such an noble appeal to the king and deep condemnation of the allies, awakened, as was to be expected, the deepest indignation. The only reply to it was a royal order depriving him of his rank as marshal and condemning him without trial to three months' imprisonment. This order was countersigned by Marshal St. Cyr, to his everlasting disgrace. He had better died on the field of his fame, or been shot like Ney by kingly murderers, than put his signature to such a paper. If all the marshals had entered their solemn protest against the act, as Moncey did, it is doubtful whether Ney would have been slain.

The disgrace and imprisonment of the old marshal, without even the farce of a trial, was in perfect keeping with the despotic injustice that had beforehand resolved on Ney's death. But what a pitiful exhibition of kingly violence was this shutting up an old man over sixty years of age, whose head was whitened in the storm of battle, and on whose name was no stain or even reproach, for daring in the nobleness of his nature to refuse to condemn an old companion in arms, by whose side he had fought so long and bravely for France and for freedom.

When power departed from Napoleon, most of his marshals, in their eagerness to save their hard-earned honours and rank and fortune, showed themselves wanting in some of the noblest qualities of man. But Moncey, unmoved by all his reverses, still kept his honour bright and his integrity unshaken; and the night that he laid his grey hairs on his prisoner's pillow witnessed a nobler deed than the day that looked on his most victorious battle-field.

Louis XVIII. was not long in perceiving the bad policy of this petty tyranny; and when the three months' imprisonment was ended, he reinstated him in his rank, and in 1820 named him commandant of the 9th military division, and soon after chevalier of the order of Saint Esprit.

In the inglorious Spanish war of 1823, Moncey, then nearly seventy years of age, was appointed over the fourth corps. He marched into Spain, fought several battles, and finally sat down in regular siege before Barcelona. The capitulation of this city after some severe fighting ended the war; and Moncey returned to France and received the grand cross of Saint Louis and a seat in the Chamber of Peers.

In the late Revolution of 1830 Moncey took no part. He had long foreseen the storm which Charles X, by determination to keep up the Bourbon reputation for folly, was gathering over his head, and saw without regret the overthrow of his throne. His age and sorrow for the death of his only son, who in leaping a ditch in a hunting excursion accidentally discharged his gun and killed himself, had driven him from public life. But when the Bourbon throne went down again he replaced with joy his old cockade of 1792.

After the death of Marshal Jourdan in 1834 he was appointed governor of the Invalides. Nothing could be more touching than the sight of this old veteran, now eighty years of age, among the mutilated and decrepit soldiers of Napoleon. Sustained by two servants, he would drag himself from hall to hall amid the blessings of those old warriors, many of whom had seen him, in the pride of manly strength and courage, lead his columns into battle. Nearly two hundred officers, and more than three thousand men, the wreck of the grand army, were assembled here and the oldest marshal of the empire placed at their head. How striking the contrast which Moncey and those few thousand men in their faded regimentals presented to the magnificent army which Napoleon had led so often to victory. From the Pyramids, from Lodi, Arcola, Marengo, Austerlitz, Jena, Wagram, and Borodino, where the eye rests on mighty armies moving to battle and to victory, amid the unrolling of standards and pealing of trumpets, the glance returns to the bowed form and grey hairs and trembling voice of Moncey, as he moves on the shoulders of his attendants through the ranks of these few aged soldiers, who have come maimed from almost every battle-field of Europe to die in the bosom of France.

Time had taken what the sword left. Napoleon, the spell-word which had startled Europe, was now spoken in mournful accents, and the fields in which they had seen him triumph were but as dim remembrances. On a far distant isle that mighty spirit had sunk to rest, and the star that had illuminated a hemisphere had left the heaves forever. What ravages time makes! Who would have thought as he gazed on the aged Moncey, borne carefully along, his feeble voice saluting his old companions in arms, that fire had ever flashed from that eye, and amid the uproar of cannon and shock of cavalry he had carried death through the ranks of the enemy, and that those bowed and limping soldiers had shouted on the fierce-fought fields of Austerlitz, Borodino, and Wagram, or sent up their war cry from the foot of the Pyramids?

The old soldiers loved to see the form of Moncey in their midst, and greeted him wherever he went with words of affection and respect. Indeed, all who knew him loved him, for his private life was as spotless as his military career. He was the friend of humanity, the patron of education, and the firm supporter of every benevolent scheme. Upright and kind, he was ever true to himself and merciful to his enemies. No acts of cruelty marred his conquests, and even his captives learned to love him. His face indicated the humane and generous character he exhibited. He was not a brilliant man, but, as Napoleon once said, "*he was an honest man.*" He was not wanting in intellectual qualities, but they predominated too much over his impulsive ones to render him capable of those great and chivalrous actions which characterized so many of Napoleon's generals. Those sudden inspirations which so often visit genius in the hour of danger or excitement he was an utter stranger to. He did all things well and preserved through a long career the respect and confidence of the Emperor; for though he never flattered him in power, he never betrayed him in misfortune. His natural character was better suited to the military tactics of Wellington than Napoleon; who decided, impetuous, and rapid himself wished to have around him men of similar character and temperament.

The closing up of Moncey's life presents perhaps the most affecting scene in it. When the remains of Napoleon, a few years ago, were brought from St. Helena, Moncey, though nearly ninety years of age, was still governor of the Hotel des Invalides, and hence was appointed to receive them in the name of those disabled veterans. All France was agitated as the time drew near when the vessel was expected that bore back the dead Emperor to her shores. The insulted hero had already slept too long amid his foes, and when the vessel that was wafting him home swept down on the coast of France the excitement could scarcely have been greater had he been landing with sword in hand.

On the day of solemn procession in Paris the whole city was abroad, and Napoleon in the height of his power never received more distinguished honour than when dead he was borne through the capital of his former empire. As the procession passed through the streets, the beat of the muffled drum and the prolonged and mournful blast of the trumpet as it rose and fell through the solemn requiem and all the signs of a nation's woe filled every heart with the profoundest grief.

There, beside the coffin, walked the remnants of the Old Guard, once the pride and strength of the Emperor and the terror of Europe; and there, too, was his old war-horse, covered with the drapery of mourning, on whose back he had galloped through the battle; and over all drooped the banner of France, heavy with crepe, all mourning in silence for the mighty dead.

The church that was to receive the body was crowded in every part of it, waiting its arrival, when the multitude was seen to part in front, and an old man bowed with years, his white locks falling over a whiter visage, and seemingly ready himself to be laid in the tomb, was borne through the throng in a large arm-chair, and placed at the left of the main altar beside the throne. Covered with decorations and honours that contrasted strangely with his withered form and almost lifeless features, he sat and listened to the heavy dirge that came sweeping through the church, as if memory was trying in vain to recall the past. *That was Marshal Moncey*, now nearly ninety years of age, brought hither to welcome his old commander back to his few remaining soldiers. As the funeral train slowly entered the court the thunder of cannon shook the solid edifice, blending in their roar with the strains of martial music. They, too, seemed conscious beings, and striving with their olden voices to awaken the chieftain for whom they had swept so many battle-fields. But drum and trumpet tone and the sound of cannon fell alike on the dull ear of the mighty sleeper. His battles were all over, and his fierce spirit gone to a land where the loud trumpet of war is never heard.

As the coffin approached, the old invalid soldiers drew up on each side of the way, in their old uniform, to receive it. The spectacle moved the stoutest heart. The last time these brave men had seen their Emperor was on the field of battle, and now, after long years, his coffin approached their midst. The roar of cannon and the strains of martial music, brought back the days of glory, and as their eyes met the pall that covered the form of their beloved chief they fell on their knees in tears and sobs and reached forth their hands in passionate sorrow. Overwhelmed with grief, and with the emotions that memory had so suddenly wakened, this was the only welcome they could give him. On swept the train till it entered the church; and as the coffin passed through the door, heralded by the Prince de Joinville with his drawn sword in his hand, the immense throng involuntarily rose, and a murmur more expressive than words filled the house. The

King descended from his throne to meet it, and the aged Moncey, who had hitherto sat immovable and dumb, the mere "phantom of a soldier," suddenly struggled to rise. The soul awakened from its torpor, and the dying veteran knew that Napoleon was before him. But his strength failed him; with a feeble effort he sank back in his chair, while a flash of emotion shot over his wan and wasted visage like a sunbeam, and his eye kindled a moment in recollection. It was a striking spectacle that silent coffin and that old marshal together. Nothing could be more appropriate, either, than this reception of Napoleon's body. The old soldiers, and the oldest marshal of the Empire welcoming him back to a resting-place in their midst, to sleep where they could keep guard and visit his tomb.

Soon after this event Moncey died, and, his only son being dead, his title of Duke of Cornegliano was conferred on M. Duchene, who married his only surviving daughter.

Marshal Macdonald

CHAPTER 8

Marshal Macdonald

It is astonishing to see what resolute and iron men Bonaparte gathered around him. Everything that came near him seemed to run in his mould, or rather, perhaps, he would confide in no one who did not partake more or less of his character. Some as much unlike him as men could well be, and worthy of no regard, he had around him because he could use them, but to none such did he trust his armies or commit the fate of a battle. Those whom he trusted with his fate and fortunes he knew by stern experience to be men that never flinched in the hour of peril, and were earth-fast rocks amid the tumult of a battle-field. He *tried* every man before he committed the success of his great plans to him. Rank and fortune bought no places of trust from him. He promoted his officers on the field of the slain, and gave them titles amid the dead that cumbered the ground on which they had proved themselves heroes by great deeds. When Bonaparte rode over one of his bloody yet victorious battle-fields, as was his custom after the conflict, he saw from the spots on which the dead lay piled in largest heaps where the heat and crisis of the battle had been. From his observatory he had watched the whole progress of the strife, and when he rode over the plain it was not difficult to tell what column had fought bravest, or what leader had proved himself worthiest of confidence; and on the spot where they *earned* their reward he *gave* it, and made the place where they struggled bravest and suffered most the birthplace of their renown. This custom of his furnished the greatest of all incitements to desperate valour in battle. Every officer knew that the glass of his Emperor swept the field where he fought, and the quick eye that glanced like lightning over every object was constantly on him, and as his deeds were so would his honours be. This strung the energies of every ambitious man and Bonaparte would have none others to lead his battalions to their utmost tension. What wonder is it, then, that great deeds were wrought, and Europe stood awe-struck before enemies that seemed never to dream of defeat?

Macdonald was one of those stern men Bonaparte loved to have in his army. He knew what Macdonald attempted to do he would never relinquish till he himself fell or his men fled. There was as much iron and steel in this bold Scotchman as in Bonaparte himself. He had all his tenacity and invincibility without his genius.

Macdonald was the son of a Scotchman, of the family of Clanronald, who had fought under the standard of Prince Charles Edward on the fatal field of Culloden, and after its disastrous issue fled to France and settled in Sancerre. There the subject of this sketch was born in November, 1765, and received the name of Etienne Jacques Joseph Alexandre Macdonald. He belonged to the army before the revolution, and during its progress took the republican side. He was an aid-de-camp in the first Republican army that advanced on the Rhine at the declaration of war, and distinguished himself throughout that miserably conducted campaign. At the battle of Jemappe he fought with such bravery that he was promoted to the rank of colonel. Engaged in almost every battle in the Low Counties, he was appointed to lead the van of the army at the North, and in the winter campaign of 1794 performed one of those deeds of daring for which he was afterward so distinguished. The batteries of Nimeguen swept the river Waal, so that it was deemed impossible to cross it with any considerable force, yet Macdonald led his column over the smooth ice and through the storm of lead that devoured his ranks and routed the enemy. For this gallant deed he was made general of brigade. In 1796, at Cologne and Dusseldorf, he commanded the army, and soon after was sent by the Convention into Italy.

After the conquest of the Papal States in 1798, he was made governor of Rome. In his new capacity he exhibited other talents than those of a military leader. He could scarcely have been placed in a more trying position than the one he occupied as governor of the Eternal City. The two factions one of which acted with the revolution and the other against it kept the population in a perpetual ferment. Insurrections and popular outbreaks occurred almost every day, while the indignity that had been offered the Pope, and the indiscriminate pillage of the Vatican palaces, and churches exasperated the upper classes beyond control and it required a strong arm to maintain the French authority in the city. Macdonald did as well, perhaps, as any one could have done in his circumstances.

An insurrection soon after having broken out at Frosinone, which he found himself unable to quell, except with the destruction of a large number of his own men, he ordered the houses to be fired and the insurgents massacred. Mack at length drove him from Rome, but, being in turn compelled to evacuate it, Macdonald re-entered, and finally left it to conquer Naples.

The entrance of the French into the latter city was over mountains of corpses, for the inhabitants of every class down to the miserable *lazzaroni* fought with the desperation of madmen for their homes. And even after the army had entered within the walls it could advance only by blowing up the houses, and finally conquered by obtaining, through the treachery of a Neapolitan, the castle of St. Elmo, from whence the artillery could be brought to bear on the town below. The famous Parthenopeian Republic was immediately established, and Macdonald entrusted with the supreme command. Mack, who had charge of the army opposed to the French, was an inefficient man. His forces outnumbered those of the French three to one, but he lacked the nerve to contend with Bonaparte's generals. When Nelson heard of his appointment as commander-in-chief of the forces in the south of Italy, he remarked. "Mack cannot travel without five carriages. I have formed my opinion of him."

That was the great difficulty with many of the continental generals; they could not submit to the hardships and exposures and constant toil that such men as Ney and Macdonald and Napoleon cheerfully encountered. But another man soon led his armies into southern Italy. The invincible Suwarrow, who had never yet turned his back on a human foe, began to sweep down through the peninsula. Macdonald could not contend with the superior force now brought against him and commenced a masterly retreat toward Tuscany, which tested his skill as a general more than any other act of his life.

Still advancing north, he came upon Suwarrow at the river Trebbia, and there for three days endured the shock of the entire Russian army. After the first day's battle the two armies bivouacked on opposite sides of the river, to wait for the morning light to renew the combat.

At six o'clock the Russians advanced to the attack. Macdonald, finding that he must fight, though anxious to delay till Moreau could come up, poured his battalions across the river, but after a most desperate struggle was compelled to retire again over the Trebbia. The quiet stream swept with a gentle murmur between the foemen, while the watch-fires of both camps were reflected from its placid bosom. All was still as the moonlight sleeping there, when three French battalions, mistaking their orders, advanced into the river and began to fire on the Russian outposts. Both armies, taken by surprise, supposing a grand attack was to be made, rushed to arms. In a moment all was hurry and confusion. The artillery on either bank opened their fire, the cavalry plunged headlong into the water, the infantry followed after; and there, in inextricable confusion, the two armies, up to their middle in water, fought by moonlight, while the closely advanced cannon played on the dark masses of friend and foe with dreadful effect.

This useless slaughter at length being stopped, the two weary hosts again lay down to rest on the shore, so near that each could almost hear the breathing of the other. Early in the morning they prepared for the third and last day's battle, and at ten o'clock Macdonald advanced to the attack. His men, up to their arm-pits in water, steadily crossed the river in the face of a murderous fire. The battle was fiercely contested, but the French were finally driven again over the Trebbia with great loss, and next day were compelled to retreat.

The battle of Trebbia was one of the fiercest that had yet been fought, and though Macdonald was blamed for his tactics, he there evinced that indomitable courage and tenacity which afterward so distinguished him. As it was, had Suwarrow received no reinforcements, or had Macdonald been aided to the same extent, the issue of it would doubtless have been different. Nearly thirty thousand men had fallen during these three terrible days. The courage, the tenacity and firmness of the troops on both sides were worthy of that field on which nineteen hundred years before the Romans and Carthaginians had battled for Italy.

In the revolution of the 18th. Brumaire, which overthrew the Directory and made Bonaparte First Consul, Macdonald was by his side, and with Murat, Lefebvre, Marmont, Lannes, and others passed the power of France over into his hands.

For the service he rendered on this occasion Napoleon appointed him to the command of the army in the Grisons. A letter from him to General Regnier, then with the army in Egypt, shows his exalted views of Napoleon. In an extract he says: "Since you left we have been compelled to lament over the capriciousness of fortune, and have been defeated everywhere, owing to the impotence of the old tyrannical Directory. At last Bonaparte appeared, upset the audacious government, and seizing the reins, now directs with a steady hand the car of the revolution to that goal all good men have long waited to see it reach. Undismayed by the burden laid upon him, this wonderful man reforms the armies, calls back the citizens, flings open the prison in which innocence has pined, abolishes the old revolutionary laws, restores public confidence, protects industry, revives commerce, and, making the republic triumphant by his arms, places it in that high rank assigned it by heaven."

In 1802 he was sent as ambassador to Copenhagen, where he remained a year. On his return he was appointed Grand Officer of the Legion of Honour. But soon after he incurred the displeasure of Bonaparte by his severe condemnation of the trial and sentence of Moreau. Macdonald had fought beside the hero of Hohenlinden; they had planned and counselled together, and he felt keenly the disgrace inflicted on his old companion in arms. Fearless in court as he was in battle, he never condescended to flatter nor refrained from expressing his indignation against meanness and injustice. His words, which were uttered without disguise, and couched in the plain, blunt terms of a soldier, were repeated to Napoleon, who afterward treated him with marked coolness. Too proud to go where he was not received as became his rank, and equally disdaining to make any efforts to produce a reconciliation when he had told what he considered the simple truth, he kept away from court altogether.

Bonaparte seemed to have forgotten him, and let him remain inactive while Europe was resounding with the great deeds of the generals that were leading his victorious armies over the Continent. Macdonald felt this keenly. He who had fought so manfully the bloody battle of the Trebbia, performed such prodigies of valour in Italy, and finally, to the astonishment of the world, led his army in midwinter over the Splugen amid hurricanes of snow and falling avalanches, did not deserve this neglect from one whom he had served so faithfully, and in whose hands he had helped place the supreme power of France. Bonaparte, in his towering and unjust pride, allowed a few expressions, unjust, it is true, but springing from the very excellences of that character which made him the prop of his throne, to outweigh the years of service he had rendered and the glorious victories he had brought to his standard.

The campaign of Austerlitz with its "Sun" of glory, Jena and its victories, Eylau and its carnage and doubtful issue, Friedland with its deeds of renown and richly bestowed honours, passed by and left Macdonald unnoticed and uncalled for. Thus years of glory rolled away. But in 1807 Bonaparte, who either thought that he had sufficiently punished him or felt that he could dispense no longer with his powerful aid, gave him command of a corps under Eugene Beauharnais. He advanced into Styria, fought and captured the Austrian general Meerfeldt, helped to gain the victory of Raab, and soon afterward saved Napoleon and the empire at Wagram by one of the most desperate charges recorded in the annals of war. Created marshal on the field of battle, he was next appointed to the government of Gratz, where he exhibited the nobler qualities of justice and mercy. The bold denouncer of what he deemed injustice in his Emperor was not likely to commit it himself. By the severe discipline he maintained among the troops preventing them from violating the homes and property of the inhabitants and by the equity and moderation with which he administered the government entrusted to him he so gained the love and respect of the people that on his departure they made him a present of 100,000 francs, or nearly $20,000, and a costly box of jewels as a wedding gift for one of his daughters. But he nobly refused them both, replying, "Gentlemen, if you consider yourselves under any obligation to me, repay it by taking care of the three hundred sick soldiers I am compelled to leave with you."

Not long after he was made Duke of Tarentum, and in 1810 was appointed to command the army of Augereau in Catalonia, who had been recalled. Acting in conjunction with Suchet he carried on for a while a species of guerrilla warfare, for which he was by nature little fitted. In 1812 he commanded the tenth corps of the Grand Army in its victorious march into Russia, and was one of the surviving few who, after performing prodigies of valour, and patiently enduring unheard-of sufferings in that calamitous retreat, struggled so nobly at Bautzen and Lutzen and Leipzig to sustain the tottering throne of Napoleon. He never faltered in his attachment nor refused his aid till Bonaparte's abdication and exile to Elba. He was strongly opposed to his mad attempts to relieve Paris, which ended in his immediate overthrow. He declared to Berthier that the Emperor should retire to Lens, and there fall back on Augereau, and, choosing out a field where he could make the best stand, give the enemy battle. "Then", he said, "if Providence has decreed our final hour, we shall at least die with honour." Unwavering in his attachment to the last, when the allies had determined on the Emperor's abdication he used every effort to obtain the most favourable terms for him and his family. This generous conduct, so unlike what Bonaparte might have expected from one whom he had treated so unjustly, affected him deeply. He saw him alone at Fontainebleau, and in their private interview previous to his departure for Elba acknowledged his indebtedness to him, expressed his high regard for his character, and regretted that he had not appreciated his great worth sooner. At parting he wished to give him some memorial of his esteem, and handing him a beautiful Turkish sabre, presented by Ibrahim Bey when in Egypt, said, "It is only the present of a soldier to his comrade."

When the Bourbons re-ascended the throne Macdonald was made a Peer of France, and never after broke his oath of allegiance. Unlike Murat, and Ney, and Soult, and others of Napoleon's generals, he considered his solemn oath sacred, and though, when sent to repel the invader, his soldiers deserted him at the first cry of *"Vive l'Empereur,"* he did not follow their example, but making his escape hastened to Paris to defend Louis. After the final overthrow of Napoleon at Waterloo he was promoted from one post of honour to another, till he was made Governor of the 21st Military Division and Major-General of the Royal Guard. He visited soon after Scotland, and hunting up his poor relatives bestowed presents upon them, and finally, on the overthrow and abdication of Charles X, gave his allegiance to Louis Phillippe.

This brief outline of his history gives us space to speak more fully of the three great acts of his life. When commanding the army in the Grisons Macdonald was ordered by Napoleon to pass the Splugen with his forces in order to form the left wing Of his army in Italy. This was in the campaign of Italy, after Bonaparte's return from Egypt. Though no braver or bolder man than Macdonald ever lived, he felt that the execution of the First Consul's commands was wellnigh impossible, and sent General Dumas to represent to him the hopelessness of such an undertaking. Bonaparte beard him through, and then with his usual recklessness of difficulties replied, "I will make no change in my dispositions. Return quickly and tell Macdonald that an army can always pass in every season where two men can place their feet." Like an obedient officer he immediately set about preparations for the Herculean task before him.

Passage of the Splugen

The present pass over this mountain is a very different thing from the one which Macdonald and his fifteen thousand men traversed. There is now a carriage-way across cut in sixteen zigzags along the breast of the mountain. But the road he was compelled to go was a mere bridle-path going through the gorge of the Cardinel. To understand some of the difficulties that beset him and his army, imagine a gloomy defile leading up to the height of *six thousand five hundred feet* above the level of the sea, while the raging of an Alpine storm and the rapid sweep of avalanches across it add tenfold horror to the wintry scene. First comes the deep, dark defile called the Via Mala, made by the Rhine, here a mere rivulet, and overhung by mountains often three thousand feet high. Along the precipices that stoop over this mad torrent the path is cut in the solid rock now hugging the mountain wall like a mere thread, and now shooting in a single arch over the gorge that sinks three hundred feet below. Strangely silent snow peaks pierce the heavens in every direction, while from the slender ridges that spring from precipice to precipice over the turbulent stream the roar of the vexed waters can scarcely be heard. After leaving this defile the road passes through the valley of Schams, then winding up the pine-covered cliffs of La Raffla strikes on to the bare face of the mountain going sometimes at an angle of forty-five degrees and finally reaches the naked summit, standing bleak and cold in the wintry heavens. This was the Splugen Pass Macdonald was commanded to lead his army of 15,000 men over in midwinter.

It was on the 20th of November he commenced his preparations. A constant succession of snowstorms had filled up the entire path, so that a single man on foot would not have thought of making the attempt. But when Macdonald had made up his mind to do a thing, that was the end of all impossibilities. The cannon were dismounted and placed on sleds, to which oxen were attached; the ammunition divided about on the backs of mules, while every soldier had to carry, besides his usual arms, five packets of cartridges and five days' provisions. The guides went in advance and stuck down long black poles to indicate the course of the path beneath, while behind them came the workmen clearing away the snow, and behind them still the mounted dragoons, with the most powerful horses of the army, to beat down the track. The first company had advanced in this manner nearly half-way to the summit, and were approaching the hospice, when a low moaning was heard among the hills, like the voice of the sea before a storm. The guides understood too well its meaning, and gazed on each other in alarm. The ominous sound grew louder every moment, till suddenly the fierce Alpine blast swept in a cloud of snow over the breast of the mountain, and howled like an unchained demon through the gorge below. In an instant all was confusion and blindness and uncertainty. The very heavens were blotted out, and the frightened column stood and listened to the raving tempest that threatened to lift the rock-rooted pines that shrieked above them from their places, and bring down the very Alps themselves. But suddenly another still more alarming sound was heard amid the storm "An avalanche! An avalanche!" shrieked the guides, and the next moment an awful white form came leaping down the mountain, and, striking the column that was struggling along the path, passed straight through it into the gulf below, carrying thirty dragoons and their horses along with it in its wild plunge. The black forms of steeds and their riders were seen for one moment suspended in mid-heavens, and in the next disappeared among the ice and crags below. The head of the column immediately pushed on and reached the hospice in safety, while the rear, separated from it by the avalanche, and struck dumb by this sudden apparition crossing their path with such lightning-like velocity, and bearing to such a fearful death their brave comrades, refused to proceed, and turned back to the village of Splugen.

For three days the storm raged amid the mountains, filling the heavens with snow and hurling avalanches into the path, till it became so filled up that the guides declared it would take fifteen days to open it again so as to make it at all passable. But fifteen days Macdonald could not spare. Independent of the urgency of his commands, there was no way to provision his army in these savage solitudes, and he must proceed. He ordered four of the strongest oxen that could be found to be led in advance by the best guides. Forty peasants followed behind, clearing away and beating down the snow, and two companies of sappers came after to give still greater consistency to the track, while on their heels marched the remnant of the company of the dragoons, part of which had been borne away by the avalanche three days before. The post of danger was given them at their own request. They presented a strange sight amid those Alpine solitudes. Those oxen with their horns just peering above the snow toiled slowly on, pushing their unwieldy bodies through the drifts, while the soldiers up to their arm-pits struggled behind. Not a drum or bugle note cheered the solitude or awoke the echoes of those silent peaks. The footfall gave back no sound in the soft snow, and the words of command seemed smothered in the very atmosphere. Silently, noiselessly the vast but disordered line stretched itself upward, with naught to break the deep stillness of the wintry noon save the fierce pantings of the horses and animals, as with reeking sides they strained up the ascent.

This day and the next being clear and frosty, the separate columns passed in safety, with the exception of those who sunk in their footsteps overcome by the cold. The successful efforts of the columns these two days induced Macdonald to march all of the remaining troops over the next day; and so, ordering the whole army to advance, commenced, on the 5th of December, the passage. But fresh snow had fallen the night previous, filling up the entire track, so that it had all to be made over again. The guides, expecting a wind and avalanches after this fresh fall of snow, refused to go till they were compelled to by Macdonald. Breast deep the army waded up the difficult and desolate path, making in six hours but six miles, or *one mile an hour*. They had not advanced far however, when they came upon a huge block of ice and a newly fallen avalanche that entirely filled up the way. The guides halted before these new obstacles and refused to proceed, and the head of the column wheeled about and began its march down the mountain. Macdonald immediately hastened forward, and placing himself at the head of his men, walked on foot, with a long pole in his hand, to sound the treacherous mass he was treading upon, while he revived the drooping spirits of the soldiers with words of encouragement. "Soldiers," said he, "your destinies call you into Italy; advance and conquer first the mountain and the snow, then the plains and the armies." Ashamed to see their general hazarding his life at every step where they had refused to go, they returned cheerfully to their toil. But before they could effect the passage the voice of the hurricane was again heard on its march, and the next moment a cloud of driving snow obliterated everything from view. The path was filled up, and all traces of it swept utterly away. Amid the screams of the guides, the confused commands of the officers, and the howling of the storm, was heard the rapid thunder-crash of avalanches.

    Then commenced again the stern struggle of the army for life. The foe they had to contend with was not one of flesh and blood. To sword-cut, bayonet-thrust, and the blaze of artillery, the strong Alpine storm was alike invulnerable. On the serried column and straggling line it thundered with the same reckless power, while over all the drifting snow lay like one vast winding-sheet. No one who has not seen an Alpine storm can imagine the fearful energy with which it rages through the mountains. The light snow, borne aloft on its bosom, is whirled and scattered like an ocean of mist over all things. Such a storm now piled around them the drifts which seemed to form instantaneously, as by the touch of a magician's wand. All was mystery and darkness, gloom and affright. The storm had sounded its trumpet for the charge, but no note of defiance replied. The heroes of so many battle-fields stood in still terror before this new and mightier foe. Crowding together, as though proximity added to their safety, the frightened soldiers crouched and shivered to the blast that seemed to pierce their very bones with its chilling cold. But the piercing cold, and drifting snow, and raging storm, and concealed pitfalls, were not enough to complete this scene of terror. Avalanches fell in rapid succession from the top of the Spulgen. Scaling the breast of the mountain with a single leap, they came with a crash on the shivering column, bearing it away to the destruction that waited beneath. The extreme density of the atmosphere, filled as it was with snow, imparted infinite terror to these mysterious messengers of death as they came down the mountain declivity. A low, rumbling sound would be heard amid the pauses of the storm; and as the next shriek of the blast swept by a rushing as of a counterblast smote the ear; and before the thought had time to change, a rolling, leaping, broken mass of snow burst through the thick atmosphere, and the next moment rushed with the sound of thunder far, far below, bearing away a whole company of soldiers to its deep, dark resting-place. One drummer, carried over the precipice, fell unhurt to the bottom of the bottom of the gulf, and crawling out from the mass of the snow which had broken his fall, began to beat his drum for relief. Deep down, amid the crushed forms of avalanches, the poor fellow stood, and for a whole hour beat the rapid strains which had so often summoned his companions to arms. The muffled sound came ringing up the face of the precipice, the most touching appeal that could be made to a soldier's heart. But no hand could reach him there, and the rapid blows grew fainter and fainter till they ceased altogether, and the poor drummer lay down to die. He had beaten his last reveille, and his companions passed mournfully on, leaving the Alpine storm to sing his dirge.

On the evening of the 6th of December, the greater part of the army had passed the mountains, and the van had pushed on as far as Lake Como. From the 26th of November to the 6th of December, or nearly two weeks, had Macdonald been engaged in this perilous pass. Nearly two hundred men had perished in the undertaking, and as many more mules and horses.

And never can one in imagination see that long straggling line, winding itself like a huge anaconda over the lofty snow-peak of the Splugen with the indomitable Macdonald feeling his way in front covered with snow, while ever and anon huge avalanches sweep by him and the blinding storm covers his men and the path from his sight, and hear his stern, calm, clear voice, directing the way, without feelings of supreme wonder. There is nothing like it in modern history, unless it be Suwarrow's passage of the Glarus in the midst of a superior enemy. Bonaparte's passage over the St. Bernard so world-renowned was mere child's play compared to it. That pass was made in pleasant weather, with nothing but the ruggedness of the ascent to obstruct the progress. Suwarrow, on the contrary led his mighty army over the Praegel, breast-deep, in snow, with the enemy on every side of him, mowing down his ranks without resistance. Macdonald had no enemy to contend with but nature but it was nature alive and wild. The path by which he conducted his army over the Splugen was nearly as bad in summer as the St. Bernard the time Napoleon crossed it. But in midwinter to make a path, and lead an army of fifteen thousand men through hurricanes and avalanches, where the foot of the chamois scarce dared to tread, was an undertaking from which even Bonaparte himself would have shrunk. And Napoleon never uttered a greater untruth than when he said "The passage of the Splugen presented without doubt some difficulties, but winter is by no means the season of the year in which such operations are conducted with most difficulty; the snow is then firm, the weather settled, and there is nothing to fear from the avalanches, which constitute the true and only danger to be apprehended in the Alps." Bonaparte would have suppose that no avalanches fall in December, and that the passage of the Splugen in the midst of hurricanes of snow was executed in "settled weather." What then must we think of his passage of the St. Bernard, in summer time, without a foe to molest him or an avalanche to frighten him!

But Macdonald's difficulties did not end with the passage of the Splugen. To fulfil the orders of Napoleon, to penetrate into the valley of the Adige, he had no sooner arrived at Lake Como than he began the ascent of the Col Apriga, which also was no sooner achieved than the bleak peak of Mount Tonal arose before him. A mere sheep-path led over this steep mountain, and the army was compelled to toil up it in single file through the deep snow. And when he arrived at the summit, which was a small flat about fifty rods across, he found the Austrians there, prepared to dispute the passage with him. This narrow flat lay between two enormous glaciers that no human foot could scale, and across it the enemy had built three entrenchments forming a triple line, and composed chiefly of huge blocks of ice cut into regular shapes and fitted to each other. Behind these walls of ice the Austrians lay waiting the approach of the exhausted French. The grenadiers, clambering up the slippery path, formed in column and advanced with firm step on the strong entrenchments. A sheet of fire ran along their sides, strewing the rocks with the dead. Pressing on, however, they carried the external palisades, but the fire here becoming so destructive they were compelled to retreat, and brought word to Macdonald that the entrenchments could not be forced. Eight days after, however, he ordered a fresh column under Vandamme to attempt to carry them by assault. Under a terrible discharge the intrepid column moved up to the icy wall, and though a devouring fire mowed down the men, so fierce was the onset that the two external forts were carried. But the fire from the inner entrenchment and from a blockhouse that commanded the position of the French was too terrific to withstand; and after bravely struggling against such desperate odds they were compelled to retreat. On the snowy summit of the Tonal, among the glaciers, and scattered around on the huge blocks of ice, lay the brave dead, while the wintry sun flashed mournfully down on the bayonets of the retreating and wounded column. Nothing daunted, Macdonald by a circuitous route over two other mountain ridges at length reached the Adige, and fulfilled the extraordinary commands of Napoleon.

The passage of Napoleon over the St. Bernard was a magnificent feat, but the passage of the Splugen by Macdonald was a *desperate* one. One was attended with *difficulties* alone, the other with danger; one was executed in safety, the other with the loss of whole companies. This latter fact alone is sufficient to prove which was the more difficult and dangerous. Suwarrow was driven up his pass by the cannon of the French, and led his bleeding thousands over the snow, while the enemy's muskets were continually thinning his defenceless ranks. Macdonald led *his* column through an awful gorge, and up a naked Alpine peak, when the tempest was raging and the snow flying and the avalanches falling in all the terror of a wintry hurricane. Bonaparte led *his* army over the San Bernard in the delightful month of summer, when the genial sun subdues the asperity of the Alps, and without an enemy to molest him. Which achievement of these three stands lowest in the scale it is not difficult to determine.

Battle of Wagram

But it is at Wagram that we are to look for Macdonald's greatest deed. One never thinks of that terrific battle without feelings of the profoundest wonder at his desperate charge, that then and there saved Napoleon and the empire. The battle of Aspern had proved disastrous to the French. The utmost efforts of Napoleon could not wring victory from the hands of the Austrians. Massena had stood under a tree while the boughs were crashing with cannon balls overhead, and fought as never even *he* fought before. The brave Lannes had been mangled by a cannon shot, and died while the victorious guns of the enemy were still playing on his heroic but flying column; and the fragments of the magnificent army, that had in the morning moved from the banks of the Danube in all the confidence of victory, at nightfall were crowded and packed in the little island of Lobau. Rejecting the counsel of his officers, Bonaparte resolved to make a stand here, and wait for reinforcements to come up. Nowhere does his exhaustless genius show itself more than in this critical period of his life. He revived the drooping spirits of his soldiers by presents from his own hands, and visited in person the sick in the hospitals, while the most gigantic plans at the same time strung his vast energies to their utmost tension.

From the latter part of May to the first of July he had remained cooped up in this little island, but not inactive. He had done everything that could be done on the spot, while orders had been sent to the different armies to hasten to his relief; and never was there such an exhibition of the skill and promptitude with which orders had been issued and carried out. At two o'clock in the afternoon the different armies from all quarters first began to come in, and before the next night they had all arrived. First with music and streaming banners appeared the columns of Bernadotte, hastening from the banks of the Elbe, carrying joy to the desponding hearts of Napoleon's army. They had hardly reached the field before the stirring notes of the bugle, and the roll of drums in another quarter, announced the approach of Vandamme from the provinces on the Rhine. Wrede came next from the banks of the Lech, with his strong Bavarians, while the morning sun shone on Macdonald's victorious troops rushing down from Illyria and the Alpine summits to save Bonaparte and the Empire. As the bold Scotchman reined his steed up beside Napoleon, and pointed back to his advancing columns, he little thought that two days after the fate of Europe was to turn on his single will. Scarcely were his troops arranged in their appointed place before the brave Marmont appeared with glittering bayonets and waving plumes from the borders of Dalmatia. Like an exhaustless stream the magnificent armies kept pouring into that little isle, while, to crown the whole, Eugene came up with his veterans from the plains of Hungary. In two days they had all assembled and on the evening of the 4th of July Napoleon glanced with exultant eye over a hundred and eighty thousand warriors, crowded and packed into the small space of two miles and a half in breadth and a mile and a half in length. Congratulations were exchanged by soldiers who last saw each other on the same glorious battle-field, and universal joy and hope spread through the dense ranks that almost touched each other.

Bridges had been constructed to fling across the channel, and during that evening were brought out from their places of concealment and dragged to the bank. In *ten minutes* one was across and fastened at both ends. In a little longer time two others were thrown over and made firm to the opposite shore. Bonaparte was there, walking backward and forward in the mud, cheering on the men, and accelerating the work, which was driven with such wonderful rapidity that by three o'clock in the morning six bridges were finished and filled with the marching columns. He had constructed two bridges lower down the river, as if he intended to cross there, in order to distract the enemy from the *real* point of danger. On these the Austrians kept up an incessant fire of artillery, which was answered by the French from the island with a hundred cannon, lighting up the darkness of the night with their incessant blaze. The village of Erzerderf was set on fire, and burned with terrific fierceness, for a tempest arose, as if in harmony with the scene, and blew the flames into tenfold fury. Dark clouds swept the midnight heavens, as if gathering for a contest among themselves; the artillery of heaven was heard above the roar of cannon, and the bright lightning that ever and anon rent the gloom blent in with the incessant flashes below, while blazing bombs, traversing the sky in every direction, wove their fiery network over the heavens, making the night wild and awful as the last day of time. In the midst of this scene of terror Napoleon remained unmoved, heedless alike of the storm of the element and the storm of the artillery; and though the wind shrieked around him, and the dark Danube rolled its turbulent flood at his feet, his eye watched only the movements of his rapid columns over the bridges, while his sharp, quick voice gave redoubled energy to every effort. The time the scene the immense results at stake all harmonized with his stern and tempestuous nature. His perceptions became quicker, his will firmer, and his confidence of success stronger. By six o'clock in the morning a hundred and fifty thousand infantry and thirty thousand cavalry stood in battle array on the shores of the Danube, from whence a month before the Austrians had driven the army in affright. The clouds had vanished with the night, and when the glorious sun arose over the hilltops his beams glanced over a countless array of helmets, and nearly three hundred thousand bayonets glittered in his light. It was a glorious spectacle, those two mighty armies standing in the early sunlight amid the green fields while the air fairly sparkled with the flashing steel that rose like a forest over their heads. Nothing could exceed the surprise of the Austrians when they saw the French legions across the river and ready for battle. That bright scene was to see the fate of Europe settled for the next four years, and that glorious summer's sun, as it rolled over the heavens, was to look down on one of the most terrific battles the world ever saw.

The battle, the first day, was fierce and sanguinary, and clearly indicated that sternness with which the field would be contested. Bonaparte, at the outset, had his columns converged to a point resting at one end of the Danube, and radiating off into the field, like the spokes of a wheel. The Austrians, on the contrary, stood in a vast semicircle, as if about to enclose and swallow up their enemy. Macdonald's division was about the first brought into the engagement, and bravely hold its ground during the day. When night closed the scene of strife the Austrians had gained on the French. They nevertheless sounded a retreat while the exhausted army of Napoleon lay down on the field of blood to sleep.

Early in the morning the Austrians, taking advantage of their success the day before, commenced the attack, and the thunder of their guns at daylight brought Napoleon into his saddle. The field was again alive with charging squadrons and covered with the smoke of battle. From daylight to nearly noon had the conflict raged without a moments cessation. Everywhere, except against the Austrians' left, the French were defeated. From the steeples of Vienna the multitude gazed on the progress of the doubtful fight, till they heard the cheers of their countrymen above the roar of cannon, driving the flying enemy before them, when they shouted in joy and believed the victory gained. But Napoleon galloped up and, restoring order in the disorderly lines, ordered Davoust to make a circuit, and, ascending the plateau of Wagram, carry Neusiedel. While waiting the result of this movement, on the success of which depended all his future operations, the French lines under Napoleon's immediate charge were exposed to a most scourging fire from the enemy's artillery, which tore them into fragments. Unable to advance, and too distant to return the fire, they were compelled to stand as idle spectators and see the cannon-shot plough through them. Whole battalions, driven frantic by this inaction in the midst of such fearful carnage, broke and fled. But everything depended on the infantry holding firmly their position till the effect of Davoust's assault was seen. Yet nothing but Napoleon's heroic bravery kept them steady. Mounted on his milk- white charger, Euphrates, given him by the king of Persia, he slowly rode backward and forward before the lines, while the cannon-balls whistled and rattled like hail-stones about him, casting ever and anon an anxious look toward the spot where Davoust was expected to appear with his fifty thousand brave followers. For a *whole hour* he thus rode in front of his men, and though they expected every moment to see him shattered by a cannon-ball he moved unscathed amid the storm. At length Davoust was seen charging like fire over the plateau of Wagram, and finally appeared with his cannon on the farther side of Neusiedel. In a moment the plateau was covered with smoke as he opened his artillery on the exposed ranks of the enemy. A smile lighted up Napoleon's countenance, and the brow that had been knit like iron during the deadly strife of the two hours before, as word was constantly brought him of his successive losses and the steady progress of the Austrians, cleared up, and he ordered Macdonald, with eight battalions, to march straight on the enemy's centre, and pierce it.

Charge of Macdonald

This formed the crisis of the battle, and no sooner did the Archduke see the movement of this terrible column of eight battalions, composed of sixteen thousand men, upon his centre, than he knew that the hour of Europe's destiny and of his own army had arrived. He immediately doubled the lines at the threatened point, and brought up the reserve cavalry, while two hundred cannon were wheeled around the spot on which such destinies hung, and opened a steady fire on the approaching column. Macdonald immediately ordered a hundred cannon to precede him and answer the Austrian batteries, that swept every inch of ground like a storm of sleet. The cannoneers mounted their horses, and, starting on a rapid trot with their hundred pieces, approached to within a half cannon-shot, and then opened on the enemy's ranks. The column marched up to this battery, and with it at its head belching forth fire like some huge monster, steadily advanced. The Austrians fell back and closed in on each other, knowing that the final struggle had come. At this crisis of the battle nothing could exceed the sublimity and terror of the scene. The whole interest of the armies was concentrated here, where the incessant and rapid roll of cannon told how desperate was the conflict. Still Macdonald slowly advanced, though his numbers were diminishing and the fierce battery at his head was gradually becoming silent. Enveloped in the fire of its antagonist, the guns had one by one been dismounted, and at the distance of a mile and a half from the spot where he started on his awful mission Macdonald found himself without a protecting battery, and the centre still unbroken. Marching over the wreck of his guns, and pushing the naked head of his column into the open field, and into the devouring cross-fire of the Austrian artillery, he continued to advance. The carnage then became terrible. At every discharge the head of that column disappeared, as if it sank into the earth, while the outer ranks on either side melted away like snow-wreaths on the river's brink. No pen can describe the intense anxiety with which Napoleon watched its progress. On just such a charge rested his empire at Waterloo, and in its failure his doom was sealed. But all the lion in Macdonald's nature was roused, and he had fully resolved to execute the dread task given him or fall on the field. Still he towered unhurt amid his falling guard, and with his eye fixed steadily on the enemy's centre moved sternly on. At the close and fierce discharges of these cross-batteries on its mangled head that column would sometimes stop and stagger back, like a strong ship when smitten by a wave. The next moment the drums would beat their hurried charge, and the calm, steady voice of Macdonald ring back through his exhausted ranks, nerving them to the desperate valour that filled his own spirit. Never before was such a charge made, and it seemed at every moment that the torn and mangled mass must break and fly.

The Austrian cannon are gradually wheeled around till they stretch away in parallel lines like two walls of fire on each side of this band of heroes, and hurl an incessant tempest of lead against their bosoms. But the stern warriors close in and fill up the frightful gaps made at every charge, and still press forward. Macdonald has communicated his own settled purpose to conquer or die to his devoted followers. There is no excitement no enthusiasm such as Murat was wont to infuse into his men when pouring on the foe his terrible cavalry. No cries of "*Vive l'Empereur*" are heard along the lines; but in their place is an unalterable resolution that nothing but annihilation can shake. The eyes of the army and the world are on them, and they carry Napoleon's fate as they go. But human strength has its limits, and human effort the spot where it ceases forever. No living man could have carried that column to where it stands but the iron-hearted leader at its head. But now he halts and casts his eye over his little surviving band that stands all alone in the midst of the enemy. He looks back on his path, and as far as the eye can reach he sees the course of his heroes by the black swath of dead men that stretches like a huge serpent over the plain. Out of the *sixteen thousand men with which he started but fifteen hundred are left beside him. Ten out of every eleven have fallen*, and here at length the tired hero pauses and surveys with a stern and anxious eye his few remaining followers. The heart of Napoleon stops beating at the sight, and well it may, for his throne is where Macdonald stands. He bears the empire on his single brave heart *he is the* EMPIRE. Shall he turn at last and sound the retreat? The fate of nations wavers to and fro, for, like a speck in the distance, Macdonald is seen still to pause, while the cannon are piling the dead in heaps around him. "*Will he turn and fly?*" is the secret and agonizing question Napoleon puts to himself. No! he is worthy of the mighty trust committed to him. The empire stands or falls with him, but shall stand while *he* stands. Looking away to where his Emperor sits, he sees the dark masses of the Old Guard in motion, and the shining helmets of the brave cuirassiers sweeping to his relief. "Forward!" breaks from his iron lips. The roll of drums and the pealing of trumpets answer the volley that smites that exhausted column, and the next moment it is seen piercing the Austrian centre. The day is won the Empire saved and the whole Austrian army is in full retreat.

Such was the battle of Wagram, and such the charge of Macdonald. I know of nothing equal to it, except Ney's charge at Waterloo, and that was not equal, because it failed.

On riding over the victorious field Bonaparte came where Macdonald stood amid his troops. As his eye fell on the calm and collected hero, he stopped, and holding out his hand said, "*Shake hands, Macdonald no more hatred between us we must henceforth be friends, and as a pledge of my sincerity, I will send your marshal's staff, which, you have so gloriously earned.*" The frankness and kindness of Napoleon effected what all his neglect and coldness had failed to do *subdued him*. Grasping his hand, and with a voice choked with emotion, which the wildest uproar of battle could never agitate, he replied, "*Ah! sire, with us it is henceforth for life and death."* Noble man! Kindness could overcome him in a moment. It is no wonder that Bonaparte felt at last that he had not known Macdonald's true worth.

The last great conflict in which he was engaged was the disastrous battle of Leipzig. For two days he fought like a lion, and when all hope was abandoned he was appointed by Napoleon to form, with Lannistau and Poniatowski, the rearguard of the retreating army while it passed over the only remaining bridge of Lindenau across the Elster. Here he stood and kept the allies at bay, though they swarmed in countless multitudes into the city, making it fairly reel under their wild hurrahs, as they drove before them the scattered remnants of the rear of the French army. Carriages and baggage-wagons and chariots and artillery came thundering by, and Macdonald hurried them over the bridge, still maintaining his post against the headlong attacks of the victorious army. Slowly the confused and bleeding mass streamed over the crowded bridge, protected from the pursuing enemy by the steady resistance of Macdonald. The allies were struck with astonishment at this firm opposition in the midst of defeat. Half the disasters of that battle, so fatal to Napoleon, would have been saved but for the rashness of a single corporal. Bonaparte had ordered a mine to be constructed under this bridge, which was to be fired the moment the French army had passed. The corporal to whom this duty had been entrusted, hearing the shouts of the allies as they rolled like the sea into Leipzig, and seeing the tiralleurs amid the gardens on the side near the river, thought the army had all passed, and fired the train. The bridge was lifted into the air with a sound of thunder, and fell in fragments into the river. It is said the shriek of the French soldiers forming the rear guard, when they saw their only communication with the army cut off, was most appalling. They broke their ranks and rushed to the bank of the river, stretching out their arms toward the opposite shore, where were the retreating columns of their comrades. Thousands in desperation plunged into the stream, most Of whom perished, while the whole remaining fifteen thousand were made prisoners. But amid the melee that succeeded the blowing up of the bridge were seen two officers spurring their horses through the dense multitude that obstructed their way. At length, after most desperate efforts, they reached the banks. As they galloped up to the shore on their panting and blood-covered steeds one was seen to be Macdonald and the other the brave Poniatowski. Casting one look on the chaos of an army that struggled toward the chasm, they plunged in. Their strong chargers stemmed the torrent manfully, and struck the opposite shore. With one bold spring Macdonald cleared the bank and galloped away. But the brave and noble Pole reached it only to die. His exhausted steed struggled nobly to ascend the bank, but failing, fell back on his wounded rider, and both perished together in the flood.

Of Macdonald's after-career I have already spoken. He remained firm to Napoleon till his abdication, and then, like all his generals and marshals, gave in his allegiance to the Bourbon throne. His firmness of character, which rendered him in all emergencies so decided and invincible, prevented him also from indulging in those excesses and adopting those ultra principles which marred the character of some of the other marshals. His Scotch education may also have had some influence over him. He gave his adhesion to the Bourbons because it was in the compact with Napoleon, and because under the circumstances he considered it his duty to do so, and no after-excitement could shake his fidelity. He was a thorough Scotchman in his fixedness of will. He possessed none of the flexibility of the French character, and but little of its enthusiasm. Bold, unwavering, and determined, he naturally held great sway over the French soldiers. Versatile themselves, they have greater confidence in a character the reverse of their own, and will follow farther an iron-willed commander than one possessing nothing but enthusiasm. In a sudden charge you want the headlong excitement, but in the steady march into the very face of destruction, and the firm resistance in the midst of carnage, you need the cool, resolute man.

This trait in Macdonald's character was evinced in his conduct when sent to repel the invasion of Napoleon, who was drawing all hearts after him in his return from exile. He repaired to Lyons with his army, but, finding that his troops had caught the wildfire enthusiasm that was carrying everything before it, he addressed them on their duty. It was to no purpose, however, for, no sooner did they see the advanced guard of Napoleon's small company, and hear the shout of "*Vive l'Empereur*" with which they rent the air, than they rushed forward, shouting "*Vive l'Empereur*" in return, and clasped their old comrades to their bosoms. Ney, under similar circumstances, was also borne away by the enthusiasm of the moment, and, flinging his hat into the air, joined in the wild cry that shook Europe like an earthquake, and summoned a continent to arms again, and made kings tremble for their thrones. But Macdonald was not a being of such rapid impulses. His actions were the result of reflection rather than of feeling. True to his recent oath, he turned from his treacherous troops and fled, and narrowly escaped being taken prisoner by them.

He was a conscientious soldier kind in peace, sparing of his men in battle, unless sacrifice was imperiously demanded, and then spilling blood like water. Generous and open-hearted, he spoke his sentiments freely, and abhorred injustice and meanness. Dazzled, as all the world was, by the splendid talents and brilliant achievements of Bonaparte, he followed him with a constancy and devotion that evince a generous and noble heart.

To a watchfulness that never slept, and a spirit that never tired, he added exertion that overcame the most insurmountable difficulties and baffled the plans of all his enemies. He seemed to be unconscious of fatigue, and never for a moment indulged in that lassitude which is so epidemic in an army and so often ensures its destruction. One cannot put his finger on the spot in the man's life where he acted as if he felt discouraged or ready to abandon everything in despair. He seemed to lack enthusiasm, but had in its place a dogged resolution that was still more resistless. He quietly saw what was to be done, and then commenced doing it in the best possible manner, without the thought of failing in his designs. He was conscious of the mighty force of will, and knew by experience how difficulties vanish by pushing against them.

The Duke of Tarentum, as Macdonald was called in France, had no sons. He had three daughters, two of whom married nobles, and the third a rich banker.

Marshal Mortier

CHAPTER 9

Marshal Mortier

Edward Adolphe Casimer Joseph Mortier was born for a soldier; and though inferior as a commander to Soult, Ney, Massena, St. Cyr, and Suchet, he nevertheless played all important part in the great Napoleonic drama, and always exhibited the qualities of a good general.

He was born in Cambry in 1768, and his father, being a rich farmer, was able to give him a good education. Having adopted the republican side in the Revolution, he obtained for his son, when twenty-three years of age, a commission in a regiment of cavalry. Here by his knowledge and good behaviour he was soon promoted to the rank of adjutant-general. On the Rhine under Pichegru and Moreau, and in Switzerland under Massena, he fought bravely in his place, and was finally promoted to general of a division.

At the rupture of the peace of Amiens he was ordered to march into Hanover with 25,000 men. With scarcely any opposition he occupied the country and acted as humanely and uprightly as his orders allowed him, and on the assumption of the imperial crown by Napoleon was made Marshal of the Empire. He was in the campaigns of Austerlitz, Jena, Eylau, and Friedland, now operating with the main army, and now left by himself to act against detached portions of the enemy, and yet in all circumstances, whether victorious or defeated, exhibiting the same heroism and loftiness of character.

In 1808 he was placed over a part of the army in Spain, and reduced Badajos after a siege of fifty-five days; but his career in the Peninsula was marked by no brilliant actions. He was ever found humane, generous, and upright, while he bore a part in that unhappy war. In the expedition to Russia he commanded the Young Guard, but was not called to fight in any great battle till the retreat commenced. At Dresden, Lutzen, and around Paris, in that last death-struggle of Napoleon, he bore himself worthy of his renown and won laurels even in defeat.

After the abdication of Napoleon, Louis made him Peer of France and Knight of St. Louis, and bestowed on him the command of the sixteenth military division. On the return of the Emperor from Elba Mortier was appointed by Louis over the army of the north with the Duke of Orleans. But the prince, finding he could not secure the fidelity of the troops, which the mere mention of Napoleon's name was enough to shake, fled, leaving the command to Mortier, bidding him do what in his "excellent judgment and patriotism" he might think best. Mortier thought it best to join his former Emperor at Paris. He was immediately made peer, and appointed inspector of the frontiers on the East and North. Napoleon designed to have had him command the Young Guard at Waterloo, but he was taken sick and compelled to remain inactive till the second overthrow. Louis XVIII. on his restoration denied him a seat in the Chamber of Peers; but in 1816 he was elected member of the Chamber of Deputies and governor of the fifteenth military division, and three years after restored to the peerage.

After the Revolution of 1830 he gave in his adhesion to Louis Phillippe and retained his rank.

Mortier was a noble-hearted man, of great valour, tempered with prudence, and of incorruptible integrity. Napoleon loved some of his generals for their chivalric devotion to him, while he had no great admiration for their characters; others he tolerated because they were useful; while some few received both his respect and affection. Mortier was one of these. Napoleon loved the frank, unostentatious, and heroic chieftain, whom he had proved in so many trying circumstances.

Mortier was not an impulsive man, though capable of being strongly aroused. His excitement steadied him, and in the moment of extreme peril he was as calm as if in perfect safety. He would manoeuvre his men under the murderous fire of a hundred cannon as composedly as in a peaceful review. Having determined what he ought to do, he seemed to give himself no concern about the results to himself.

Tall and well formed, his splendid and commanding figure moved amid the chaos of a battle-field like some ancient hero, while his calm and powerful voice would restore confidence in the very moment of despair. He never murmured, like Bernadotte and St. Cyr, at the trying circumstances in which the Emperor placed him. If a sacrifice was to be made and he was selected as the victim, he made no complaint; and where his duty as a commander placed him, there he stood and fought, apparently caring little whether he fell or was saved in the struggle.

He was less ambitious and vain than many of the other marshals, and was governed by higher principles of action. His selfishness was not constantly interfering with his duty, and he always appears calm and self-sustained amid the tumultuous events in which his life was passed. Better educated than many of the other generals, his mind and feelings were better disciplined, so that the warrior never triumphed over the man. His very chivalry sprung not so much from the excitement of the moment as from his high sense of honour, which was a part of his nature.

Battle of Dirnstein

But in the campaign of Austerlitz, at the battle of Dirnstein, he appears in his most chivalric and determined character.

After the capitulation of Ulm, Napoleon continued his progress along the Danube, waiting the moment to strike a mortal blow at the enemy. The Austrians, hearing of the surrender of Mack, began to retreat toward Vienna, pressed by the victorious French. Napoleon was moving down the right bank of the Danube, while Mortier, at the head of twenty thousand men, was to keep nearly parallel on the left shore. Murat, with the advanced guard, was pressing with his accustomed audacity toward Vienna. In the mean time the Russian allies, finding they could not save the capital, crossed over the Danube to the left shore to escape the pursuit of Napoleon and effect a junction with reinforcements that were coming up. Mortier was aware of this, and pressed eagerly forward to intercept their march toward Moravia.

As you pass from Dirnstein to Stein, the only road winds by the Danube, and between it and a range of rocky hills, forming a deep and narrow defile. Mortier was at the former place hastening the march of his columns, and, eager to advance, pushed forward with only the single division of Gazan, leaving orders for the army to follow close in the rear. Passing through this defile, he approached

Stein at daybreak, and found the rearguard [*sic*] of the Russian army posted on heights in front of the town, sustained by powerful batteries which swept the road along which he was marching. Notwithstanding his inferiority of numbers, and the murderous fire he should be forced to encounter, he resolved immediately to attack the enemy's position.

As the broad daylight of a November morning spread over the Danube, he opened his fire on them, and rushed to the assault. In a short time the action became desperate, and the grenadiers on both sides could almost touch each other in the close encounter. The Russian troops came pouring back to sustain the rear-guard, while the French advanced with rapid step along the road to aid their companions. With headlong courage on the one side and steady firmness on the other, the struggle grew hotter every moment. Neither would yield, and Mortier stood hour after hour amid the wasting storm, till at length he began to grow anxious for the issue, and at eleven o'clock, to hurry up his troops, galloped back to Dirnstein. Spurring furiously along the defile, he came up to Dupont's division a little beyond the farther entrance, and urged him to redouble his speed. Then, putting spurs to his horse, he again hastened back to the scene of strife. But what was his astonishment, on emerging from the road, to behold a Russian army issuing from the hills and marching straight for its entrance. Doctoroff, with his whole division, had made a circuitous march during the combat, and, cutting off Mortier's retreat, was about to take possession of the defile. As the marshal left the main road to escape being taken prisoner himself, and wound along the hillsides and saw the dense masses pouring silently into that narrow pass, his heart for a moment stopped beating; for his own doom, and that of his brave troops, seemed to be sealed. Crushed between the two armies, there was no hope for him, unless Dupont came to his relief. The morning, that had dawned so brightly upon him, had suddenly become black as midnight. But his resolution was immediately taken. There was but one course left for him, unless he intended to surrender; and that was to march back and endeavour to cut his way through to his army.

Behold that single division pressed in front by the whole Russian army, and cut off in the rear, slowly retiring toward that silent gorge! Battling back the host that pressed after him and sent their destructive storms of grapeshot through his torn ranks, Mortier formed his men into a solid column, and, without a drum or trumpet note to cheer them on, moved with a firm step into the dark entrance, resolved to exit his way through or die in the effort. But a sight dread enough to appal the stoutest heart met his gaze as he looked along the narrow strip of road between the rocks and the Danube. As far as the eye could see, there was nothing but dense battalions of the enemy in order of battle. Without shrinking, however, the stead column moved with fixed bayonets into the living mass. A deadly fire received them, and the carnage at once became dreadful. With the cannon thundering on their rear, and burying their fiery loads in their ranks, swept in front by incessant discharges of musketry, trampled under foot by the cavalry, and crushed between two armies, the escape of that brave division seemed utterly hopeless. Indeed, the work of annihilation had begun with frightful rapidity. Mortier, after the most desperate fighting, had pierced but a little way into the pass, and hope grew fainter every moment as he surveyed his thinned and wasting ranks, when the thunder of cannon at the farther extremity shot a thrill of joy through his heart. No cannon-shot before ever carried such hope to his bosom, for he knew that Dupont was charging along that defile to his rescue. The Russians immediately faced this new foe also, and then commenced the complicated strife of four armies fighting in the form of one long protracted column Mortier hemmed in between two Russian armies, and Doctoroff between two French ones. But Mortier was naturally the first to go down in this unequal strife. Combating all the morning against overwhelming numbers, and struggling in the afternoon in a deep ravine crushed between two armies, his noble division had sunk away till nothing but the mutilated fragments remained; and now, as twilight deepened over the Danube, its last hour seemed striking. But perceiving that the fire of Dupont approached steadily nearer, he cheered on his men to another and still another effort. Under the light of the stars, that now and then twinkled through the volumes of smoke that curtained in the armies, and by the blaze of the artillery, the work of death went on, while an old castle, in which Richard Couer de Lion once lay imprisoned, stood on the hills above and looked sternly down on the strife. All along that gorge was one incessant thunder-peal of artillery, to which the blaze of musketry was as the lightning's flash. Amid the carnage that wasted around him, Mortier towered like a pillar of fire before men, as they closed sternly behind him. Nearly three-fourths of his whole division had fallen in this Thermopylae, and nothing but its skeleton was left standing, looking as if a hurricane had passed through it. Still he would not yield, but, rousing his men by his words and example, cleared a terrible path through the enemy with his sword. With his majestic form rising above the throng that tossed like a wreck on a strong current about him, he was visible to all his men. Sometimes he would be seen completely enveloped by the Russian grenadiers, while his dripping sabre swept in a rapid circle around his head, drinking the life of some poor wretch with every blow, as he moved steadily on in the lane he made for himself. Parrying sword-cut and bayonet-thrust, he trod amid this chaos and death as if above the power of fate. With friends and foes falling like autumn leaves around him, he still remained untouched; and it was owing to his strength alone, and the skill and power with which he wielded his sabre, that he escaped death. His strokes fell like lightning on every side, and under them the strongest grenadier bent like a smitten reed. Struck with admiration at his gallantry, and thinking all was lost, his officers besought him to step into a bark they saw moored to the shore and escape. "No," said he, in the spirit of true heroism, "keep that for the wounded. He who has the honour to command such brave soldiers should think himself happy to die with them. We have still two guns left, and a few boxes of grapeshot-we are almost through. *Close up the ranks for a last effort.*" And they did close up and move intrepidly into the fire. But the last of the ammunition was soon gone, and then nothing was left but the bayonet. But just then a cheer burst on their ears over the roar of battle the cheer of approaching deliverance and they answered it. That shout was like life to the dead, and that torn and mangled remnant of a column closed up for a final charge. The Russians flew up a side valley before the onset and with the shout, "France, France, you have saved us!" that weary but heroic band rushed into the arms of their deliverers. A loud hurrah rent the air, and the bloody conflict was done. Nearly six thousand men lay piled in ghastly heaps along the road, while broken muskets and twisted bayonets, scattered here and there, showed how close and fierce the struggle had been.

 The deep and solemn silence that succeeded this uproar was broken only by the groans of the wounded, or the sullen murmur of the Danube, that rolled its bright waters along as calmly as if no deadly strife had stained its banks with blood. The smoke of battle, which had rolled so fiercely over the scene, now hung above the river, or lay along the hillsides like thin vapour, calm and tranquil, while nature breathed long and peacefully.

Mortier had been out-generalled but not conquered; and his bearing on this occasion stamped him as a true hero. The decision to cut his way through the enemy or perish, the personal courage he exhibited, and the noble resolution to fall amid his brave followers when all hope seemed lost, exhibited not only the greatness of the warrior but the nobleness of the man.

His career, as has been remarked, in Spain was not a brilliant one; but he appears before us again in his true character in the expedition to Russia. The honourable post of commander of the Young Guard was given to him, and his place was near the Emperor's person. He took no active part in the great combats through which the Grand Army passed to Moscow, for Napoleon was sparing both of the Young and Old Guards, and would not allow them to be engaged. At Borodino Ney and Murat, in the midst of the conflict, sent frequently to Napoleon for its aid, and though it marched to the margin of the battle, ready to pour its massive columns on the enemy the moment the French should yield, it remained merely a spectator of the fight.

As the army approached Moscow, Murat and Mortier were ordered to advance on the city. They marched for two days with nothing to eat but bruised wheat and horseflesh, and at length came in sight of the enemy drawn up for battle in a strong position. Mortier remonstrated against an attack as hopeless and useless, but Murat, with his accustomed impetuosity, ordered a charge, and two thousand of that reserve of which Napoleon had been so sparing were left on the field. Mortier immediately wrote to the Emperor denouncing Murat, and declaring he would not serve under him.

At length Moscow, with its domes and towers and palaces, appeared in sight; and Napoleon, who had joined the advanced guard, gazed long and thoughtfully on that goal of his wishes. Murat went forward and entered the gates, with his splendid cavalry; but as he passed through the streets he was struck by the solitude that surrounded him. Nothing was heard but the heavy tramp of his squadrons as he passed along, for a deserted and abandoned city was the meagre prize for which such unparalleled efforts had been made. As night drew its curtain over the splendid capital, Napoleon entered the gates and immediately appointed Mortier governor. In his directions he commanded him to abstain from all pillage. "For this," said he, "you shall be answerable with your life. Defend Moscow against all, whether friend or foe."

The bright moon rose over the mighty city, tipping with silver the domes of more than two hundred churches, and pouring a flood of light over a thousand palaces and the dwellings of three hundred thousand inhabitants. The weary army sunk to rest; but there was no sleep for Mortier's eyes. Not the gorgeous and variegated palaces and their rich ornaments, nor the parks and gardens and oriental magnificence that everywhere surrounded him, kept him wakeful, but the ominous foreboding that some dire calamity was hanging over the silent capital. When he entered it, scarcely a living soul met his gaze as he looked down the long streets; and when he broke open the buildings he found parlours and bedrooms and chambers all furnished and in order, but no occupants. This sudden abandonment of their homes betokened some secret purpose yet to be fulfilled. The midnight moon was sailing over the city when the cry of "Fire!" reached the ears of Mortier; and the first light over Napoleon's falling empire was kindled, and that most wondrous scene of modern times commenced.

The Burning of Moscow

Mortier, as governor of the city, immediately issued his orders and was putting forth every exertion, when at daylight Napoleon hastened to him. Affecting to disbelieve the reports that the inhabitants were firing their own city, he put more rigid commands on Mortier to keep the soldiers from the work of destruction. The marshal simply pointed to some iron-covered houses that had not yet been opened, from every crevice of which smoke was issuing like steam from the sides of a pent-up volcano. Sad and thoughtful, Napoleon turned toward the Kremlin, the ancient palace of the Tzars, whose huge structure rose high above the surrounding edifices.

In the morning Mortier, by great exertions, was enabled to subdue the fire. But the next night, September 15, at midnight, the sentinels on watch upon the lofty Kremlin saw below them the flames bursting through the houses and palaces, and the cry of "Fire! Fire!" passed through the city. The dread scene had now fairly opened.

Fiery balloons were seen dropping from the air and lighting upon the houses, dull explosions were heard on every side from the shut-up dwellings, and the next moment a bright light burst forth and the flames were raging through the apartments. All was uproar and confusion. The serene air and moonlight of the night before had given way to driving clouds and a wild tempest that swept with the roar of the sea over the city. Flames arose on very side, blazing and crackling in the storm, while clouds of smoke and sparks in an incessant shower went driving toward the Kremlin. The clouds themselves seemed turned into fire, rolling in wrath over devoted Moscow. Mortier, crushed with the responsibility thus thrown upon his shoulders, moved with his Young Guard amid this desolation, blowing up the houses and facing the tempest and the flames struggling nobly to arrest the conflagration.

He hastened from place to place amid the blazing ruins, his face blackened with the smoke and his hair and eyebrows singed with the fierce heat. At length the day dawned a day of tempest and of flame and Mortier, who had strained every nerve for thirty-six hours, entered a palace and dropped down from fatigue. The manly form and stalwart arm, that had so often carried death into the ranks of the enemy, at length gave way, and the gloomy marshal lay and panted in utter exhaustion. But the night of tempests had been succeeded by a day of tempests; and when night again enveloped the city, it was one broad flame wavering to and fro in the blast. The wind had increased to a perfect hurricane, and shifted from quarter to quarter as if on purpose to swell the sea of fire and extinguish the last hope. The fire was approaching the Kremlin, and already the roar of the flames, and the crash of falling houses, and the crackling of burning timbers were borne to the ears of the startled Emperor. He arose and walked to and fro, stopping convulsively and gazing on the terrific scene. Murat, Eugene, and Berthier rushed into his presence, and on their knees besought him to flee; but he still clung to that haughty palace as if it were his Empire.

But at length the shout, "The Kremlin is on fire!" was heard above the roar of the conflagration, and Napoleon reluctantly consented to leave. He descended into the streets with his staff and looked about for a way of egress, but the flames blocked every passage. At length they discovered a Postern gate leading to the Moskwa, and entered it, but they had only entered still further into the danger. As Napoleon cast his eye around the open space, girdled and arched with fire, smoke, and cinders, he saw one single street yet open, but all on fire. Into this he rushed, and amid the crash of falling houses, and raging of the flames, over burning ruins, through clouds of rolling smoke, and between walls of fire, he pressed on, and at length, half suffocated, emerged in safety from the heated city, and took up his quarters in the imperial palace of Petrowsky, nearly three miles distant. Mortier, relieved from his anxiety for the Emperor, redoubled his efforts to arrest the conflagration. His men cheerfully rushed into every danger. Breathing nothing but smoke and ashes, canopied by fame and sparks and cinders, surrounded by walls of fire that rocked to and fro and fell with a crash amid the blazing ruins, carrying down with them red-hot roofs of iron, they struggled against an enemy that no boldness could awe or courage overcome. Those brave troops had heard the tramp of thousands of cavalry sweeping to battle without fear, but now they stood in still terror before the march of the conflagration, under whose burning footsteps was heard the incessant crash of falling houses and palaces and churches. The continuous roar of the raging hurricane, mingled with that of the flames, was more terrible than the thunder of artillery; and before this new foe, in the midst of this battle of the elements, the awestruck army stood powerless and affrighted.

When night again descended on the city, it presented a spectacle the like of which was never seen before, and which baffles all description. The streets were streets of fire, the heavens a canopy of fire, and the entire body of the city a mass of fire, fed by a hurricane that whirled the blazing fragments in a constant stream through the air. Incessant explosions from the blowing-up of stores of oil and tar and spirits shook the very foundations of the city and sent vast volumes of smoke rolling furiously toward the sky. Huge sheets of canvas on fire came floating like messengers of death through the flames, the towers and domes of the churches and palaces glowed with a red heat over the wild sea below, then, tottering a moment on their bases, were hurled by the tempest into the common ruin. Thousands of wretches, before unseen, were driven by the beat from the collars and hovels, and streamed in an incessant throng through the streets. Children were seen carrying their parents the strong, the weak; while thousands more were staggering under the loads of plunder they had snatched from the flames. This, too, would frequently take fire in the falling shower, and the miserable creatures would be compelled to drop it and flee for their lives. Oh, it was a scene of woo and fear inconceivable and indescribable. A mighty and close-packed city of houses and churches and palaces, wrapped from limit to limit in flames which are fed by a fierce hurricane, is a sight this world will seldom see.

But this was all within the city. To Napoleon without the spectacle was still more sublime and terrific. When the flames had overcome all obstacles, and had wrapped everything in their red mantle, that great city looked like a sea of rolling fire swept by a tempest that drove it into vast billows. Huge domes and towers, throwing off sparks like blazing firebrands, now towered above these waves and now disappeared in their maddening flow, as they rushed and broke high over their tops, scattering their spray of fire against the clouds. The heavens themselves seemed to have caught the conflagration, and the angry masses that swept them rolled over a bosom of fire. Columns of flame would rise and sink along the surf ace of this sea, and huge volumes of black smoke suddenly shoot into the air as if volcanoes were working below. The black form of the Kremlin alone towered above the chaos now wrapped in flame and smoke, and again emerging into view standing, amid this scene of desolation and terror, like virtue in the midst of a burning world, enveloped but unscathed by the devouring elements. Napoleon stood and gazed on this scene in silent awe. Though nearly three miles distant, the windows and walls of his apartment were so hot that he could scarcely bear his hand against them, Said he, years afterward: "*It was the spectacle of a sea and billows of fire, a sky of clouds and flame, mountains of red, rolling flame, like immense waves of the sea, alternately bursting forth and elevating themselves to skies of fire, and then sinking into the ocean of flame below. Oh! it was the most grand, the most sublime, and the most terrific sight the world ever beheld.*"

When the conflagration subsided Mortier found himself governor of a city of ashes. Nine-tenths of Moscow had sunk in the flames, and the gorgeous capital with its oriental magnificence its palaces and towers and gardens was a heap of smoking ruins, amid which wandered half-naked, starving wretches, like spectres around the place of the dead. Napoleon returned to the

Kremlin, but the spectacle the camps of the soldiers presented as he passed through them was one his eye had never rested on before.* The soldiers had here and there thrown together a few boards to shelter them from the weather, and sprinkled over the soft, wet ground with straw to keep off the dampness, and "there, reclining under silken canopies, or sitting in elegant chairs, with Cashmere shawls and the costliest furs, and all the apparel of the noble and wealthy strewed around them, they fed their camp-fires with mahogany furniture and ornamental work, which had a few days before decorated the palaces of the noble." The half-starved wretches were eating from silver plates, though their only food was a miserable black cake and half-boiled horseflesh. In the interval between them and the city were crowds of disbanded soldiers, staggering under the weight of plunder, and among them many Russians, men and women, seeking the camp-fires of their enemies. In the city it was still worse, and an insufferable stench arose from the smoking mass. All discipline was lost, and the disbanded army swarmed through the streets for plunder. This they gathered into the open places, and bartered away with their friends. Thus the poor creatures loaded themselves with gold and silver and costly apparel, little thinking how valueless the snow-drifts of Russia would soon make them. When Napoleon was again established in the Kremlin he put a stop to this disorder, and ordered the plundering to be carried on according to rule.

At length the reluctant Napoleon turned his back on the towers of Moscow, confessing to the world that after the loss of a hundred thousand men and incredible toil he had grasped only a phantom. It was necessary that some one should cover his retreat by remaining in the city, and Mortier was appointed to this unwelcome task. Had the Young Guard been left with him, it would not have been so hopeless an undertaking; but only eight thousand were put under his command, of which not more than a quarter could be relied upon. With this handful of men he was to cover Napoleon's retreat, and when he could hold out no longer, to blow up the Kremlin and join the rear-guard of the army. It was necessary for someone to do this for the safety of the army, and the lot fell more naturally on Mortier as governor of the city. That is, a sacrifice was demanded and it seemed proper that Mortier should be the victim. That he should escape the whole

---

* *Vide* Segur.

Russian army was not to be expected, and when his friends took their farewell it was as with one they should never see again. Mortier himself looked on his career as ended, but made no complaint. Without a murmur he set about fulfilling the task allotted to him.

As the army withdrew from the city, the Cossacks began to swarm around it, and finally drove Mortier and his feeble band into the Kremlin. These were followed by ten thousand Russians, who pressed around the French marshal. To perform the double task assigned him, of defending the city and blowing up the Kremlin, he was compelled, even while he occupied it, to gather immense quantities of powder within it, a single touch of which would send that massive structure broken and shattered toward the heavens. He placed a *hundred and eighty-three thousand pounds* in the vaults below, while he scattered barrels of it through the different apartments above. Over this volcano of his own creation he stood and fought for four days, when the slightest ignition from one of the enemy's guns would have buried him and his soldiers in one wild grave together.

At length, after he had kindled a slow firework whose combustion could be nicely calculated, he led his weary troops out of that ancient structure. But while he marched with rapid steps from the scene of danger, several Cossacks and Russians, finding the imperial palace deserted, rushed into it after plunder. The next moment the massive pile wavered to and fro like a column of sand, and, seeming to rise from the earth, fell with a crash that was heard thirty miles distant. The earth shook under Mortier as if an earthquake was on the march. Huge stones, fragments of wall, thirty thousand stand of arms, and mangled bodies and limbs were hurled in one fierce shower heavenward together, and then sunk over the ruined city. The second act in the great drama was now ended, and the last was about to commence.

On his arrival at the army he was again placed over the Young Guard. At the battle of Krasnoi, which Napoleon fought to save Davoust, and which was described in the chapter on that marshal, Mortier was the principal actor. When Bonaparte with his six thousand Imperial Guard marched into the centre of fifty thousand Russians, protected by powerful batteries, Mortier, with five thousand of the Young Guard all that was left of that splendid body was just in advance of him. He and General Roguet commenced the attack. The Russians, able by their overwhelming numbers to crush that handful of French at once, hesitated to advance, and began to cannonade them. Mortier stood with his noble Guard in the midst of this iron storm, willing victims to save Davoust. Having no artillery of his own to answer the murderous batteries of the Russians, and they being beyond the reach of musketry, he had nothing to do but remain inactive and let the cannon plough through his ranks. For three mortal hours he stood and saw the horrible gaps which every discharge made. Yet not a battalion broke; and that "Young Guard there proved themselves worthy to fight beside the Old Guard of the Empire. In those three hours two thousand of his little band had fallen, and then he was directed to retreat. Steadily and in perfect order, though the enemy were rapidly hemming them in, did that heroic Guard retire before those fifty thousand Russians. Mortier gave orders for them to retreat slowly, and General Laborde, repeating his orders, exclaimed, "*Do you hear, soldiers? The marshal orders ordinary time. Ordinary time, soldiers!*" and amid that incessant tempest of grapeshot and balls it *was* "*ordinary time*" with them. The brave fellows never hastened their steps by a single movement, but marched as calmly out of that storm as if going to their bivouacs.

At Lutzen and Dresden he fought worthy of his former glory, and at the disastrous battle of Leipzig commanded the Old Guard. He battled for France till the last moment, and when the allied forces invaded his country and were marching towards Paris, he and Marmont alone were left to arrest them. Napoleon, thinking to draw the enemy after him, had hung on their rear till they were out of his reach and on the march for the French capital.

But previous to his separation from Napoleon, Mortier combated bravely by his side in those stupendous efforts he put forth to save his empire. At the battle of Montmirail he fought beside Ney with the greatest heroism. At the commencement of the action he was not on the field, but amid the roar of artillery and the shocks of the bayonet he came up, bringing with him the Old Guard, the cuirassiers, and the Guards of Honour. Napoleon immediately ordered a grand attack on the centre, and while victory stood balancing in the conflict, he brought up the cuirassiers and Guards of Honour. As they rode in their splendid array past him, he said, "Brave young men! there is the enemy! will you let them march on Paris?" "We will not," was the ready response, and shaking their glittering sabres over their heads, they burst with a loud hurrah on the enemy, scattering them like a whirlwind from their path.

At the bloody battle of Craon he fought on foot at the head of his columns, and, amid one of the most wasting fires artillery troops were perhaps ever exposed to, steadied his men by his example, and was seen, again and again, with his tall, commanding form rising above his soldiers, to move straight into the blaze of the enemy's batteries, When the smoke cleared away there he still stood amid his rent and shattered ranks, sending his calm voice over the tumult, and animating, for the third time, his troops by his courageous words and still more courageous actions.

But when Marmont and Mortier, who had held the positions at Rheims and Soissons, as Napoleon had directed, found themselves exit off from all communication with the Emperor by the interposition of the Russian army, their case became desperate. With only twenty thousand men in all, they slowly retired toward Paris before the formidable masses of the allied forces. The weary army was toiling on, striving to gain the village of Fere-Champanoise, fighting as it went, when twenty thousand horse came thundering upon it, and a hundred and thirty guns opened their fire on its shaking squares. Bravely combating, Mortier struggled with his wonted firmness to steady his troops. His five thousand cavalry met the shock of these twenty thousand bravely, but in vain; the hundred and eighty guns sent havoc amid the squares, making hue [*sic*] rents into which the Russian cuirassiers galloped with fierce valour, treading down everything in their passage. A heavy rolling fire of musketry met each charge, but at length order was lost, and the army, which had patiently dragged its bleeding form over the plain; rushed in one confused mass into Fere-Champanoise. A gallant charge of horse from the village, right through the broken ranks, arrested the pursuit till Mortier and Marmont could rally their troops behind the houses.

The next day a division under General Pacthod, coming up to join the French army, was surrounded by the Imperial Guards of Alexander, commanded by the Emperor in person, and, refusing to surrender, was utterly annihilated. It could not he helped, though the valour the soldiers exhibited deserved a better reward. Completely surrounded, they formed themselves into squares, and kept up a rolling fire as they retreated toward Fere-Champanoise. Thirteen thousand cavalry galloped around this worn band of six thousand, filling the air with dust, and fell in successive shocks on them in vain, till a battery, brought to bear with fatal effect, made a lane through one square, into which they dashed and sabred it to pieces. The Emperor Alexander, admiring their valour, wished to save them, and ordered them to surrender. General Pacthod refused, and, cheering his men by his actions and words, roused them to the highest pitch of enthusiasm; and though the cannonballs crushed through them with frightful havoc, they moved unshaken amid the storm, rent and torn into fragments, then, weeping in indignation that they had fired their last cartridge of ammunition, charged bayonet. At length, when half of the whole division had fallen, and the enemy's cavalry was riding through their broken ranks with irresistible fury, General Pacthod delivered up his sword.

A most touching incident occurred during this engagement. In the midst of the fight, Lord Londonderry saw a young and beautiful lady, the wife of a French officer, dragged from a *calèche* by three wretches who were making off with their prey. Galloping up to her rescue, he snatched her from their hands and delivered her to his orderly, to be taken to his own quarters, who, lifting her to the horse behind him, started off, but was scarcely out of sight when a band of Cossacks rushed upon him, and, piercing him through with a lance, bore off the lady. She was never heard of more. Every exertion was made to discover her fate, but it was never known. Whether, a prey to lawless violence, she was released from her sufferings by death, or whether she dragged out her existence a helpless captive, no one can tell.

After this defeat, Mortier and Marmont could no longer keep the field, and fell back on Paris. There they made the last stand for their country, and fought till valour and resistance were no longer of avail, and then delivered up their swords to the enemy. But though together in their retreat, and equally brave in their last defence, they were not alike in their surrender of the city. Mortier's honour is free from the stain that dims the lustre of Marmont's fame.

Sickness, as before stated, prevented Mortier from striking a last blow for Napoleon at Waterloo. If he had commanded the Young Guard on that day, and Murat the cavalry, the fate of the battle and the world might have been changed.

He was retained in the confidence of Louis Phillippe, until at length he, who had passed through so many battles unscathed, fell a victim to an assassin. On the 28th of July, 1835, as Louis Phillippe was going to a review of the National Guard, Mortier, on horseback close behind, was killed by the explosion of Fieschi's infernal machine. A little delay had allowed the King to pass the spot of danger, but when the smoke lifted, Mortier was seen falling from his horse, dead. He was the most distinguished victim in that attempt to assassinate the King.

Marshal Soult

CHAPTER 10

Marshal Soult

No American has visited the Chamber of Peers within the last few years without being struck with the appearance of Marshal Soult. The old warrior, with his grave and severe look, comes limping into the hall, almost the sole representative of that band of heroes to whom Napoleon committed his empire, and whose names are indissolubly linked with his through all coming time. He is now about seventy-seven years of age, though erect as a soldier. His head is bald on the top, and the thin hair that remains is whitened by the frosts of age. He is, perhaps, a little over the middle height, rather square built, and evidently once possessed great muscular power. His eye is dark, and now and then exhibits something of its ancient fire, while his brown visage looks as if he had just returned from a long campaign, rather than lived at his ease in Paris. He is extremely bow-legged, which is evidently increased by the wound that makes him limp, and though he wears ample pantaloons to conceal the defect, nothing but petticoats can ever prevent the lower extremities of the marshal from presenting the appearance of a parenthesis. He received his wound in storming Monte Creto, at the time when Massena was besieged in Genoa. His voice is rather guttural, and its tone severe, as if belonging to a man who had passed his life in the camp.

No one acquainted with his history can behold the old veteran limping to his seat without emotion. One of the chief props and pillars of Napoleon's throne, and one of the principal actors in that great drama which he enacted on the plains of Europe, his presence calls to mind many a fierce-fought battle, and many a victory too. During some of those frequently stupid séances of the Chamber, I have often wondered, as I looked down on Soult in his seat whether he too was not thinking of his struggles along the Rhine, or his bivouacs in the Alps, or of some of those fearful scenes he witnessed in Spain.

Nicholas-Jean-de-Dieu Soult was born in the small town of Amans, Department of Tarn, the 29th of March, 1769, or about four months before Bonaparte. His father was a country notary of no distinction, and, apparently unable to control the restless spirit of his boy, let him choose his own course of life. Young Soult could not brook the confinement of study, and read little, and that not of the most instructive kind; and, becoming perfectly disgusted with the old parchments of his father, at the age of sixteen entered as a volunteer in a regiment of the Royal Infantry. The revolution opened an ample field for his genius, and during the first struggles of the Republic he distinguished himself by his skill and bravery, and rapidly went up from sergeant to under-lieutenant, adjutant, major, captain, chief of battalion, and colonel learning the art of war under Luckner, Hoche, Lefebvre, and Jourdan.

At the battle of Fleurus, in 1794, he was chief of the staff under Lefebvre, and there exhibited that admirable coolness and penetration in the hour of danger which afterward made him so conspicuous as a military leader. General Marceau commanded the right of the army, and his division at Ardennes was hurled back by a charge of the enemy and thrown into disorder. Marceau, in despair, hurried to Soult and asked for four battalions to help him restore the combat. But the latter saw he could not grant his request without endangering Lefebvre's division, and refused. Marceau, in the agony and confusion of the moment, threatened to shoot himself if he was not aided. Soult told him to be calm and steady. "Rally your men to the charge," said he, "and the four battalions shall come as soon as possible." The words were scarcely out of his mouth before Prince Coburg was on him like a rolling torrent, and Soult was in a moment in the thickest of the fight. After the battle was over Marceau sought him out, and generously begged his pardon for his rudeness and praised him for his valour.

Promoted to general of brigade this year, he fought bravely at the battles of Altenkirchen, Lahn, and Friedberg. Being detached one day with three battalions and a hundred and fifty cavalry to cover the left of the army stationed at Herban, he suddenly found himself in the course of his march surrounded by four thousand cavalry. His destruction seemed inevitable; but, immediately forming his men into squares, he coolly met the shock, while a devouring fire, rolling round the steady ranks, emptied the enemy's saddles with frightful rapidity. But the Austrian commander, thinking this little band must go down before his fierce squadrons, rallied his men at a distance and again ordered the charge. The trumpets sounded, and these four thousand riders moved to the onset. Advancing first on a plunging trot, they at length broke into a fierce gallop, and with an impetuosity and strength that made the ground thunder and smoke in their passage, burst with a loud shout upon the ranks. The smoke covered both for a moment, and when it lifted the shattered squadrons were recoiling over the field. Again and again did that splendid body of cavalry reform and rush to the charge, and as often retire before the steady valour that opposed it. Thus for five hours did Soult stand amid his little band, animating them by his voice and example, till five successive shocks had been repulsed, and then continued his march without having left a single man in the hands of the enemy.

After the peace of Campo Formio, Soult rested for a while; but in 1798, while Bonaparte was in Egypt, he is found again in the field of battle. At the village of Ostrach, with only 6000 men, composing the advanced guard of the army, he was attacked by 25,000 Austrians under the Archduke Charles. Under the murderous fire of such superior numbers his comparatively feeble band began to shake. One battalion bent backward and was on the point of flying, when Soult seized a standard, and, rushing to its head, called on the soldiers to follow him, and, boldly charged into the very midst of the enemy, and thus saved his army from a rout.

The next month he was made general of division, and passed through the campaign of Switzerland under Massena. While the latter was winning the battle of Zurich, Soult, stationed between Lake Zurich and Wallenstadt to prevent the junction of the Austrians and Russians, was equally successful. The enemy was encamped on the farther side of the Linth in a secure position; but Soult organized a company of a hundred and fifty swimmers, who, with their sabres in their teeth, and holding their muskets in one hand over their heads, boldly dashed into the river at midnight and swam to the opposite shore.

They here made a stand till some grenadiers could he got over, and then attacked the camp of the enemy, putting it to rout, slay-ing and taking four thousand men. While these brilliant victories by Massena and Soult were sending a few rays of light across the gloom that hung over the French armies, Bonaparte returned from Egypt. Massena was immediately appointed to Genoa; and in assuming the command he requested that Soult might be attached to him. He had seen his skill and bravery in Switzerland, and he needed him in the desperate undertaking which was now before him. Elevated to the rank of lieutenant-general, he passed the Alps; and after fighting bravely was driven with Massena into Genoa. Here, by his fierce onsets, which perfectly stunned the enemy, and by his brilliant victories, fighting heroically and victoriously against the most overwhelming numbers, he showed that Massena was not deceived in the spirit he had sought to aid him in this campaign. The last effort that was made before the French were completely shut up in the city was the assault on Mount Creto conducted by Soult. It was a desperate undertaking at the best, and in the midst of the bloody combat a thunder-storm swept over the mountain, and enveloped the two hosts. In the midst of the roar of the artillery and louder roll of thunder, and flashes of lightning that outshone the girdle of fire that wrapped the enemy, Soult headed a last charge in one more effort to save the day. Pressing boldly on into the midst of the fire, he was struck by a ball and fell. Supposing he was killed, his men turned and fled. With a broken leg he was taken prisoner, and soon after sent to Alexandria. Here news was finally brought him that Genoa had capitulated, and immediately after that Bonaparte was in the plains of Italy, having fallen like an avalanche from the Alps.

Lying on his back, he heard one morning the departure of the Austrian army, as it issued forth over the Bormida to battle. The heavy tread of the marching columns, the rumbling of the artillery, and the thrilling strains of martial music, had scarcely died away on his ear, before the thunder of cannon shook the house in which he lay a helpless captive. All day long the windows in his room rattled to the jar which the tremendous cannonading on the field of Marengo sent for miles around. Hour after hour he lay and listened to the fast and fierce explosions which told how deadly the strife was, until at length the retiring tumult declared too well to his practiced ear that France was retreating. Next he heard shouts of victory through the streets, and his eye flashed fire in the eagerness to help stem the tide of battle. All was lost, and he turned uneasily on his couch; when suddenly, toward evening, the battle seemed to open with treble violence. Again he listened; and as the sound drew near, his heart beat quick and anxiously; and as night came on, and through the darkness the fierce uproar approached the city, till the cannon seemed to be playing almost on its very walls a smile of joy passed over his countenance. The next moment a crowd of fugitives burst through the gates, and the cry of "All is lost," told the wounded chieftain that Italy was won.

Being soon after exchanged for some Austrian officer, he was presented to Napoleon, who had heretofore known little of him except by report. He asked Massena if he was deserving of the high reputation he had gained. The hero of Genoa replied, "For judgment and courage he has few equals." He had fought beside him in three desperate *sorties* from the city, and had seen him charge with a coolness and intrepidity against overwhelming odds that won his admiration and esteem.

In consequence of this high encomium, Soult was appointed chief commander in Piedmont, to quell the brigands, called *Barbets*, and soon after was made colonel general of the Consular Guard, and given the command of the camp of St. Omer.

When Napoleon meditated his grand descent on England, Soult was placed over the army between Boulogne and Calais. Knowing well what kind of an enemy England was, and the character of her troops, he commenced a course of discipline to which French soldiers had never before been subject. With a frame of iron and a will that matched it, he concentrated all his energies to the task before him. From daylight till dark he was seen moving about, now on horseback inspecting his troops, and drilling them to the limit of human endurance, and now passing through the entrenchments and directing their progress. The constant exercise he demanded of the soldiers caused them to complain to Bonaparte, and the latter finally expostulated with him, saying that he feared the men would sink under it. Soult replied, "Those who cannot endure what I myself do will remain at home; while those who bear it will be fit to undertake the conquest of the world." He could not have returned a reply more grateful to Napoleon; and when the latter became Emperor of France he made him Marshal of the Empire.

He commanded the right wing at Austerlitz; and at Jena assailed the centre of the enemy with desperate energy. At Eylau he, with

Augereau, was first engaged; and although enveloped in the middle of the field by a snowstorm that blotted out everything from view, while two hundred cannon incessantly played on his staggering column, he was enabled to fall back in good order. At Heilsberg he fought with unrivalled courage; and after the battle of Friedland marched into Konigsberg, after having forced the enemy from the city.

Soon after he was sent into Spain to repair the disasters of King Joseph, whom no experience or instructions could make a great military leader. Ordered to invade Portugal, he carried Oporto by assault with great slaughter, but was compelled finally to retreat before the superior force of Wellesley. To put an end to the rivalry among the various generals in Spain, Napoleon at length appointed him major-general of the French army there, thus showing the high opinion he had of his military abilities. The victory of Ocana soon after justified the confidence placed in him.

For several years he carried on this unhappy war in Spain now pursuing, and now retreating until after the disastrous issue of the Russian campaign, when he was called by Napoleon in 1813 to support his falling empire in the north. After the battles of Lutzen and Bautzen, news reached Napoleon of his losses in the peninsula, and the defeat of his armies at the battle of Vittoria. He immediately looked around among his generals to see who could best repair the follies of his royal brother, and Soult was again selected. But the wife of the obedient marshal did not wish to return to a country where there was such obstinate fighting with so few laurels, and used all her persuasion, not only with her husband, but with the Emperor, to have him remain. Napoleon repulsed her rudely; and Soult hastened, as fast as horses could carry him, to Paris. Stopping there only a few hours, he pressed onto Spain. Scarcely had he arrived at headquarters before the army was in motion; and though he did all that human energy could do, he was finally beaten at every point. He, however, fought the last battle fired the last cannon for Napoleon; and at length, on the news of the abdication, transferred his command to the Duke of Angoulême, and returned to Paris. Confirmed in his ranks and titles by Louis XVIII., he was appointed to the thirteenth military division. He was soon after named Minister of War; and in urging the sequestration of the property of the Bonaparte family, and in bringing General Excelmans before a council of war, he showed a great deal of gratuitous zeal for his new master.

When Napoleon returned from Elba, Soult published his famous order of the day, in which the Emperor was stigmatized as an adventurer and usurper. Louis, however, suspected him, and took from him his appointment as Minister of War. Soon after Napoleon's arrival in Paris Soult sought an interview with him, and though it is not known what passed between them, the latter, in a few days, was appointed major-general, and published another order of the day, which showed a wonderful change he had undergone respecting the "adventurer and usurper." He fought at Fleurus and Waterloo, but not with the energy of his younger days. On the second restoration of the Bourbons he was put on the proscribed list, and, fearing he should be brought to trial, published a justification of himself, in which he referred to Napoleon in disparaging terms-an act that must forever be a stain on his character.

Exiled with other French generals, he retired to Düsseldorf, where he remained three years, employed chiefly in preparing his memoirs, which, on his death, will probably be given to the world. In 1819 he was permitted to return to Paris, and the next year received again his marshal's baton. In 1829 Charles X. made him Peer of France, and conferred on him the collar of Saint Esprit. Under Louis Phillippe he became Minister of War, and finally President of the Council. He took an active part in the agitations and struggles of April, 1834. His course, however, not being approved, he retired into private life till 1839, when he again became President of the Council.

Representing the court of France at the coronation of Queen Victoria, he was everywhere received with the greatest enthusiasm, and the multitude pressed eagerly around him to see one who had been such a prominent actor in the great drama of the French Revolution. Marshal Soult had less genius but more intellect than most of the distinguished French marshals. He had none of the high chivalric feeling which so frequently bore them triumphantly over the battle-field; but he had in its place a clear, sound judgment, and a fearless heart. It required no thunder of cannon to clear his ideas his thoughts were always clear, and his hand ever ready to strike. He depended on the conclusions of reason rather than on the inspiration of genius for victory. He calculated the chances beforehand, and when his purpose was taken it was no ordinary obstacle or danger that could shake it. Such men as Murat and Lannes and Augereau relied very much on the enthusiasm of their soldiers, and the power which intense excitement always imparts; Soult, on the contrary, on the discipline of his troops, and the firmness and steadiness it gives either in assault or retreat; and hence, when left alone, could be depended on as an able and efficient general. Though impetuous as a storm in the early part of his life, it was the impetuosity of youth rather than of character; and one familiar with his career ever thinks of him as the stern and steady Soult. He was more of an Englishman than Frenchman in his natural character, and succeeded better than most of the other French generals when opposed to English troops. But though methodical and practical in all his plans, he knew the value of a headlong charge, and could make it. Still he does not seem to rise with the danger that surrounds him, but rather meets it with the firmness of one who has settled beforehand that it shall not overcome him. In the tumult and terror of a mighty battle he moves before us not so, much as the genius of the storm itself, as like one who has made up his mind to take its peltings with composure. He stands when the tide of battle flows like a rock over which the surge beats in vain; and his calm, stern voice arrests the panic that has begun, and turns the shaking ranks into walls of iron before the foe.

He did not possess that versatility of genius which enabled Bonaparte so frequently to turn his very defeats into victory; he depended rather on the strength and terror of the blow he had planned, and if that failed, it became him to pause before he gave another. Like the lion, he measured his leap before he took it, and if he fell short measured it over again. But with all this coolness and forethought his blow was sometimes sudden and deadly as a falling thunderbolt. A more prompt and decisive man in action was not to be found in the army. As cool amid the falling ranks and fire of three hundred cannon as on a parade, his onset was nevertheless a most terrible thing to meet. He carried such an iron will with him into the battle, and disputed every inch of ground with such tenacity of purpose, that the courage of the boldest gave way before him. Though he performed perhaps fewer personal heroic deeds than many others, he also committed fewer faults. After seeing him a few times in battle, one unconsciously gets such an opinion of his invincibility that he never sees his columns moving to the assault without expecting sudden victory, or one of the most terrific struggles to which brave men are ever exposed. We do not expect the pomp and splendour of one of Murat's charges of cavalry, nor the majesty of Ney's mighty columns, as he hurls them on the foe; but the firm step and stern purpose and restless onset of one who lets his naked deeds report his power. Soult's eye measured a battle-field with the correctness of Napoleon's, and his judgment was as good upon a drawn battle as upon a victory. Not having those fluctuations of feeling to which more excitable temperaments are subject, a defeat produced no discouragement, and hence a victory gave the enemy no moral power over him. It was singular to see in what a matter-of-fact way he took a beating, and how little his confidence in himself was destroyed by the greatest disasters. A man that is not humbled or rendered fearful by defeat can never be conquered till he is slain.

Soult possessed a strong mind and great character, and in his military life the warrior sinks before the man of intellect, and even British pride condescends to render him homage as an able and great commander.

He has been charged with rapacity while in Spain, and his plunders commented freely on by his enemies, but the charge has never been clearly made out. Still there is no doubt he did not let the wealth the chances of war flung into his hands slip through his fingers; and he managed, amid all his tergiversations, and from all the changes he passed through, to acquire large estates, which now enable him to support his rank with splendour.

Soult was not cruel in his disposition, and exhibits none of the ferocity of the warrior in his career. A bold, skilful, and inflexible man in the field, he ranks among the first of Napoleon's marshals.

Napoleon, who, after the battle of Marengo, had asked Massena if Soult really deserved his high reputation, and on being answered in the affirmative had attached him to his person, gave him command of the army at Boulogne, and afterward made him Marshal of the Empire, soon after testing his great qualities at the....

BATTLE OF AUSTERLITZ

It was in the latter part of November, 1805, that Napoleon, on riding over the country around Austerlitz, determined to make it the battle-field on which he would overthrow the combined armies of Austria and Russia. Rapidly concentrating his forces here, he on the last night of November found himself at the head of nearly eighty thousand men. His army was drawn up in a plain, with the right resting on Lake Moenitz, and the left six miles distant on a hill, which was covered with artillery. Two little streams flowed past the army into the lake, bordered with marshes to protect it, while on a high slope was pitched the Emperor's tent, overlooking the whole scene. Opposite the French army was a waving line of heights, the highest of which, Mount Pratzen, a few miles distant, formed the centre of the allied forces, numbering ninety thousand men, commanded by the emperors of Russia and Austria in person. Under Soult was placed the finest corps in the army, for the weight of the battle was designed to rest on him, and the heights of Pratzen, forming the enemy's centre, was to be his field of combat.

Napoleon had been on horseback all day long, and after dark was riding along the lines previous to his departure to his tent, when the news of his approach spread like lightning through the whole army. Suddenly the soldiers seized the bundles of straw that had been supplied them for their beds, and, lighting them at one end lifted them on poles over their heads, making an illumination as splendid as it was unexpected. All along through the valley those blazing torches lighted the path of the astonished Napoleon *the first anniversary of his coronation*. Suddenly the enthusiastic shout of "*Vive l'Empereur!*" burst around him. The cry was caught by the next and the next battalion as he advanced, and prolonged by those he had left, till the shout of that immense host filled all the valley, and rose like the roar of the sea over the heights, miles away, falling, with an ominous sound, on the camp of the enemy. It was a scene that baffles description. Those myriad torches, blazing and swinging to and fro in the darkness a broad mass of flame losing itself in the distance and the shout of that army, rolling in such deafening accents after Napoleon, formed together a far more imposing ceremony than his coronation in the capital.

Next morning at four o'clock Napoleon was on horseback beside his tent. The moon had just gone down, the stars shone pale and tremulous in the sky, and all was silent and tranquil around [Pratzen]. Not a sound broke from the immense host that slumbered below, over which the motionless fog lay like a white covering or it might be a shroud in anticipation of the thousands that ere night would there lie stark and stiff in their last sleep. But amid the deep hush his quick ear caught a low, continuous sound beyond the heights of Pratzen, like the heavy tread of marching columns and rumbling of artillery carriages over the ground. The deep murmur passed steadily from right to left, showing that the allies were gathering their force against his right wing. At length the sun rose slowly above the horizon, tingeing with gold the heights of Pratzen, on which were seen moving dense masses of infantry, and poured its glorious light over the sea of mist that slept in the valleys below. It was the "*Sun of Austerlitz.*" The hour, the scene, the immense results at stake, and the sudden bursting of that blazing fire-ball on his vision, made a profound impression on Napoleon, which he never forgot.

The allies, intent on outflanking the French, were weakening their centre by drawing off the troops to the left. The marshals who stood around the Emperor saw the fault of the enemy, and eagerly asked permission to take advantage of it. But he, turning to Soult, whose troops were massed in the bottom of the valley near the heights, covered by the fog, asked him how long it would take to reach the summit of Pratzen. "Less than twenty minutes," replied the marshal. "Wait a little, then," said Napoleon; "when the enemy is making a false movement, it is necessary to be careful not to interrupt him." It was now eight o'clock in the morning, and soon after he gave the impatiently expected signal, and Murat, Lannes, Bernadotte, and Soult, who had stood around him, parted like lightning from his side, and swept in a headlong gallop to their respective corps. Napoleon rode toward the centre, and as he passed through the troops, said: "Soldiers! the enemy has imprudently exposed himself to your strokes. *Finish the campaign by a clap of thunder!*" "*Vive l'Empereur,*" answered him in one long, protracted shout.

In the mean time Soult emerged, with his strong battalions, from the covering mist, and, clothed in the rich sunlight, ascended, with an intrepid step, the slopes of Pratzen. It was a magnificent sight, and Napoleon watched with intense anxiety the advance of that splendid army. With banners fluttering in the morning sunlight, and drums and trumpets rending the air, the massive columns streamed upward and onward. In a moment the top of Pratzen was covered with smoke, from whose bosom issued thunder and lightning, as if a volcano was there hurling its fiery fragments in the air. Covered from sight, those two hosts mixed in mortal combat struggled for the mastery, while the curtain of smoke that folded them in waved to and fro, and rent before the heavy artillery, and closed again, and rolled in rapid circles round the hill, telling to the armies below what wild work the stern Soult was making with the foe. At length the fire and smoke which Pratzen had belched forth for two hours grew less, the sulphurous cloud lifted in the midday sun, and lo! there waved the French standards, while a victorious shout went pealing over the armies struggling in the valley.

Soult, having pierced the enemy's centre, next descended like an avalanche on their left wing. Bessières was charging like fire below with the Imperial Guard, and the whole field shook with the shock of cavalry and thunder of cannon, while the, entire valley was filled with rolling smoke, in which were moving dark masses of infantry. There was Murat, with his headlong valour, and Lannes, Davoust, and Augereau, strewing the field with the dead. At length, help being sent to Soult, the left of the enemy was borne away, and the allied army routed. Fleeing before the victorious marshal, Buxhowden bravely attempted to cover the retreat, and, forming his men into close column, strove gallantly to direct the reversed tide of battle. But, pierced through and trodden under foot, seven thousand fell before the victorious French, while the remainder attempted to escape by crossing a frozen lake near by with the artillery and cavalry. In a moment the white frozen surface was covered with dark masses of infantry, amid which were seen the carefully advancing squadrons of cavalry. Pressed by the enormous weight, the ice could scarcely sustain the multitude, when Soult suddenly ordered his cannon to play upon it. The iron storm crushed through the yielding mass, the whole gave way, and with one terrific yell that rose over the tumult of battle more than two thousand men sank to rise no more. Amid the swimming multitude the frighted cavalry-horses plunged to and fro, while on the struggling mass the artillery continued to play with deadly precision.

On the left Bernadotte, Murat, and Lannes were equally successful, and the bloody battle of Austerlitz was won. Nearly thirty thousand bodies strewed the field, and when night again closed over the scene Napoleon, weakened only by twelve thousand men, saw his menaced throne firmly established. Soult was the hero of the day, and after the battle was over Napoleon rode up to him and said, in presence of all his staff, "Marshal Soult, I consider you the ablest tactician in my empire."

Bonaparte never forgot the brilliant conduct of his marshal on this occasion, and years afterward, when he was told that the latter was aiming at the throne of Portugal, he made known to him that he had heard the reports, but added, "*I remember nothing but Austerlitz.*"

But Soult exhibited his great qualities as a commander in his campaigns in Spain. He showed himself there superior as a tactician to all the other marshals, except Suchet, and was more than a match at any time for the Duke of Wellington. His very first movements convinced Napoleon of his superior ability. Arriving together at Bayonne, the Emperor immediately planned the campaign, and issued his orders. Soult was to supersede Bessières in the command of the second corps, in the path of which Napoleon, with his Imperial Guard, was to follow. In a few hours after he received his orders Soult's army was in motion. In fifty hours he travelled from Bayonne to Burgos, took the latter town, gained the battle of Gamonal; and, still on the post-horse he had mounted at Briviesca, where he took command of the army, pushed on his columns in every direction; and in a few days laid prostrate the whole north of Spain. Following up his successes, he marched against Sir John Moore, and, forcing him back step by step for a fortnight, across rivers and through mountains covered with snow, finally drove him into Corunna. There the English commander fortified himself, to await the transports that had been ordered round to receive his army. Soult opened his cannon on the place, and with his weary troops pressed his assaults vigorously, in the hope of forcing the English army to surrender before the arrival of the expected vessels. But Sir John Moore resolved to combat to the last, and prepared for a final battle. In the mean time, to prevent an immense magazine of powder of four thousand barrels from falling into the hands of the French, he ordered it to be blown up. A smaller quantity in a storehouse near it was first fired. The explosion of this first was like the discharge of a thousand cannon at once; but when the great magazine took fire, and those four thousand barrels exploded at once, the town rocked to and fro as if an earthquake was lifting its foundations. Rocks were uprooted by the shock, the ships in the harbour rose and fell on the sudden billows that swept under them; while a sound like the crash of nature itself startled the two armies as it rolled away before the blast.

At length the transports arrived, and the embarkation commenced, while Soult advanced to the attack. The battle soon became general, and Sir John Moore, while watching the progress of the fight, was struck by a cannon-ball on the breast and hurled from his horse. Rallying his energies, he sat up on the ground, and without a movement or expression of pain again fixed his eye on the conflict.

Seeing that his men were gaining ground, he allowed himself to be carried to the rear. At the first glance it was plain that the ghastly wound was mortal. "The shoulder was shattered to pieces, the arm was hanging by a piece of the skin, the ribs over the heart were broken and bared of the flesh, and the muscles of the breast torn into long strips, which were interlaced by their recoil from the draggling of the shot. As the soldiers placed him in a blanket, his sword got entangled, and the hilt entered the wound; Captain Hardinge, a staff officer, who was near, attempted to take it off, but the dying man stopped him, saying, '*It is well as it is. I had rather it should go out of the field with me.*'" Thus was the hero borne from the field of battle. He died before night, and was buried in the citadel of Corunna, the thunder of Soult's guns being the mournful salute fired above his grave. Actuated by a noble feeling, the brave marshal erected a monument to him on the spot where he fell.

The great ability which Soult exhibited in this pursuit caused Napoleon to rely on him chiefly in those operations removed from his personal observation, and he was ordered to invade Portugal. In the midst of the rainy season he set out from Corunna, and against the most overwhelming obstacles steadily and firmly pursued his way, until at length he arrived at Oporto, and sat down before the city.

Storming of Oporto

A summons to surrender being disregarded, he waited for the morning to carry the place by assault. But at midnight a terrific thunder-storm arose; the clouds in dark and angry masses swept the heavens; the wind blew with frightful fury, and the alarmed inhabitants, mistaking the roar of the blast for the tread of the advancing armies, set all their bells ringing, while two hundred cannon suddenly opened into the storm, and one fierce fire of musketry swept the whole circuit of the entrenchments. The loud and rapid ringing of so many bells in the midst of the midnight storm; the thunder of cannon replying to the thunders of heaven, as clap after clap broke over the city the fierce lightning outshining the flash of musketry; the roar of the wind and the confused cries of the inhabitants, as they rushed by thousands through the streets, combined to render it a scene of indescribable sublimity and terror. The French stood to their arms wondering what this strange uproar meant.

But at length the morning broke serene and clear, and the waving of standards in the air, the beat of drums, and the loud strains of the trumpets, told the inhabitants that Soult was finally leading his strong battalions to the assault. After an obstinate struggle the entrenchments were carried at all points, and the victorious army burst with loud shouts into the city. The routed army divided; a part fled towards the fort of St. Jao, the remainder toward the mouth of the Douro, in the hopeless attempt to cross by boats or by swimming. Their general, while expostulating with them on the madness of the effort, was shot by them in presence of the enemy, and the terror-stricken host rushed headlong into the river, and were almost to a man drowned.

But the battle still raged within the city, and the barricades of the streets being forced open, more than four thousand men, women, and children went pouring in one disordered mass to the single bridge of boats that crossed the river. But as if the frenzy, and tumult, and carnage were not yet sufficiently great, just then a defeated troop of Portuguese cavalry came in a wild gallop down the street, and with remorseless fury burst through the shrieking multitude, trampling all ages and sexes under their feet. Clearing a bloody pathway for themselves, they rushed on to the bridge, followed by the frantic crowd. The boats sunk, and where they went down floated a dense mass of human bodies, filling all the space between. The French soldiers as they came up, struck with amazement at the sight, forgot the work of death, and throwing down their muskets, nobly strained every nerve to save the sinking throng. Meanwhile the city rang with firearms and shrieks of the dying. Frantic as soldiers ever are in sacking a city, they were made doubly so by a spectacle that met them in one of the public squares. There, were several of their comrades who had been taken prisoners their eyes burst asunder, their tongues torn out, and their whole bodies mutilated; while the breath of life still remained. Fierce cries of revenge now blent with the shouts of victory. The officers lost all control, though they mingled with the soldiers, and by their voice and efforts strove to stay the carnage of violence. Their efforts were in vain, and even the authority of Soult was, for a while, no more than threads of gossamer before the maddened passions of the soldiers. Ten thousand Portuguese fell in this single assault, and the streets of Oporto ran blood. Only five hundred Frenchmen were slain.

This sanguinary affair being over, Soult immediately established order, and by his vigorous measures, great kindness, and humanity, so won the esteem of the Portuguese that addresses came pouring in upon him from all quarters, and offers were made him of the throne of Portugal.

But this brilliant opening of his campaign was destined soon to meet with sad reverses. A large English force, unknown to him, had assembled in his vicinity, and were rapidly marching against him. In the mean time treason in his own camp began to show itself. Many of the French officers had resolved to deliver the army into the hands of the English. This conspiracy, extending more or less through the different armies in the peninsula, was set on foot to overthrow Napoleon. It was a long time before Soult could fathom these secret machinations. His own forces their position and destination were all known to the English, while he was left in utter uncertainty of *their* strength and plans. But at length his eyes were opened, and he saw at once the appalling dangers which surrounded him. It was then he exhibited the immense energy and strength of character he possessed. An abyss had opened under his feet, but he stood and looked into its impenetrable depths without a shudder. Not knowing whom to trust almost enveloped by a superior enemy he nevertheless took his decision with the calmness of a great mind. Compelled to fall back, he escaped as by a miracle the grasp of the enemy, and once more entered Oporto. Compelled to abandon the city, he continued to fall back, resting his hope on Loison, whom he had ordered to hold Amarante. But that general had departed, leaving his commander-in-chief to destruction. Soult heard of this new calamity at midnight, just after he had crossed the Souza River. The news spread through the dismayed army, and insubordination broke forth, and voices were heard calling for a capitulation. But Soult rose calmly above the storm, and learning from a Spanish peddler that there was a by-path across the mountains, instantly resolved to lead his troops over it. The treacherous and discontented were alike paralyzed by his firmness, and saw without a movement of resistance all the artillery and baggage destroyed; and with their muskets on their shoulders started over the mountains, and finally effected a junction with the retreating Loison. Nothing can be more sublime than the bearing of Soult in this retreat. Superior to treason, to complaints, and danger, he moved at the head of his distracted army with a firmness and constancy that awed rebellion and crushed all opposition.

Instead of retreating on the high road, which must have ensured his destruction, he commanded that all the artillery of Loison's corps also should be destroyed in presence of the army. Knowing when to sacrifice, and doing it with inflexibility of purpose that quelled resistance, he bent his great energies on the salvation of his army. Taking again to the mountains he gained a day's march on his pursuers. Reorganizing his ill-conditioned army, he took command of the rear-guard himself, and thus kept his stern eye on the enemy, while the mutinous and traitorous were held before him and in reach of his certain stroke. Thus retreating the despoiled, starving army at length approached the river Cavado, when word was brought the marshal that the peasantry were destroying the only bridge across it. Should they succeed the last hour of his army had struck; for there it must halt, and by morning the English guns would be thundering on his rear while he had not a single cannon to answer them. The abyss opened wider beneath him, but over his marble features passed no shadow of fear. Calling Major Dulong to him the bravest man in his ranks he told him the enemy were destroying the bridge across the river ahead, and he had chosen him out of the whole army to save it. He ordered him to pick out a hundred grenadiers and twenty-five horsemen and surprise the guard and secure the passage. "If you succeed," said he, "send me word; but *if you fail, send none* your silence will be sufficient." One would be glad to know what the last desperate resolution of that iron-willed commander was, should silence follow the bold undertaking of the brave Dulong.

He departed, while Soult waited with the intensest anxiety the result. The rain fell in torrents, the wind went howling fiercely by, and midnight blackness wrapped the drenched and staggering army as they stood barefoot and unsheltered in the storm. After a long and painful suspense a messenger arrived. "The bridge is won," fell on Soult's ear like hope on the dying. A flash of joy passed over his inflexible features, for he still might escape the pain of a surrender. The bold Dulong, with his strong grenadiers, covered by the darkness, had reached the bridge unseen and slain the sentinel before he could utter a cry of alarm. But what a sight met their eyes! The swollen river went roaring and foaming by, over which only a narrow strip of mason-work was seen the wreck of the destroyed bridge. Nothing daunted, Dulong advanced on to the slender fragment, and with twelve grenadiers at his back began to crawl along his perilous path.

One grenadier slipped and fell with a sudden plunge into the torrent below. But the wind and the waves together drowned his shriek, and the remaining eleven passed in safety and fell with a shout on the affrighted peasantry, who immediately turned and fled. The bridge was repaired, and by daylight the heads of the column were marching over. Soult had not a moment to spare, for the English cannon had already opened on his rear-guard.

But no sooner was this bridge passed than another flying with a single arch over a deep gulf, and called the Saltador or Leaper rose before him, defended by several hundred Portuguese. Only three men could move abreast over this lofty arch, and two attempts to carry it were repulsed, when the brave Dulong advanced and swept it with his strong grenadiers, though he himself fell in the assault, dreadfully wounded.

The army was saved, and by the courageous energy, skill, and heroism of its commander; and at length entered Orense barefooted, without ammunition, baggage, or a single cannon.

Soult has been blamed for his management at the outset of this retreat, especially for being surprised as he was at Oporto; but let one surrounded by conspirators, and uncertain whom to trust among his officers, do better or show that any leader has acted more worthily in similar circumstances, before exceptions are taken. It would be uninteresting to follow Soult through all his after-operations in Spain. Napoleon had gone, and between the quarrelling of the rival chiefs and the imbecility of Joseph, affairs were not managed with the greatest wisdom.

Soult was crippled in all his movements his sound policy neglected and his best combinations thwarted by Joseph. The disastrous battle of Talavera was fought in direct opposition to his advice; nevertheless he soon after had the pleasure of chasing Sir Arthur Wellesley out of Spain. His operations in Andalusia and Estramadura, and the firmness with which he resisted the avarice of Joseph, all exhibited his well-balanced character. In Andalusia he firmly held his ground, although hedged in with hostile armies and surrounded by an insurgent population, while a wide territory had to be covered with his troops. His vast and skilful combinations during this period show the intellect he brought to the task before him. King Joseph could not comprehend the operations of such a mind as Soult's, and constantly impeded his success. When, without ruin to the army, the stubborn marshal might yield to his commands, he did; but where the king's projects would plunge him into irredeemable errors, he openly and firmly withstood him. The anger and threats of Joseph were alike in vain; the inflexible old soldier professed his willingness to obey, but declared he would not, with his eyes open, commit a great military blunder. King Joseph would dispatch loud and vehement complaints to Napoleon, but the Emperor knew too well the ability of Soult to heed them. Had the latter been on the Spanish throne instead of Joseph, the country would have been long before subdued and French power established.

But it would be impossible, without going into the entire complicated history of the peninsular war, to give any correct idea of the prodigious efforts he put forth of his skilful combinations, or of the military genius he exhibited, in his successful career. Yet, arduous as was the duty assigned him, he drove Wellington out of the country; and, though fettered by the foolish orders of a foolish King, maintained French power in Spain till he was recalled to steady Napoleon's rocking throne in Germany. Cautious in attack, yet terrible in his onset, and endless in his resources when beaten, no general could have accomplished more than he, and he adopted the only method that could at all be successful in the kind of war he was compelled to wage.

The bloodiest battle during the peninsular war was fought by Soult, and lost in the very moment of victory. In May, 1811, he rapidly concentrated his forces, and moving from Seville, advanced on Beresford, occupying the heights before Albuera.

Battle of Albuera

Soult had twenty-one thousand men under him, while the Spanish and French armies together numbered over thirty thousand. The French marshal, however, relying on the steadiness and bravery of his troops, and not relying the Spaniards at more than half their numerical strength, resolved to give battle. The allies were stationed along a ridge, three miles in extent. The action commenced by an attack of French cavalry, but soon Soult's massive columns began to move over the field and ascend with a firm step the opposing heights. The artillery opened on the heads of those columns with terrible precision, but their batteries replied with such rapidity that they seemed moving volcanoes traversing the field of death. Amid the charges of infantry, the shocks of cavalry, and the carnage of the batteries, they continued to press on, while their advancing fire spread like an ascending conflagration up the hill. Everything went down in their passage. Over infantry, artillery, and cavalry they passed on to the summit of the heights. Beresford, in this crisis of the battle, ordered up the British divisions from the centre. These, too, were overborne and trampled under foot, the heights won, the battle to all appearance gained, and Beresford was preparing to retreat.

Suddenly an English officer, Colonel Hardinge, took the responsibility of ordering up a division not yet engaged, and Abercromby with his reserve brigade. Advancing with a firm and intrepid step, in face of the victorious enemy, they arrested the disorder, and began to pour a destructive fire on the dense masses of Soult. His columns had penetrated so far into the very heart of the army that not only their front, but their entire flanks, were exposed to a most severe fire. Thus did Macdonald press into the Austrian lines, and taking the cross fire of the enemy's batteries, see his mighty columns dissolve beside him. Soult endeavoured to deploy his men, so as to return a more effectual fire. But the discharges of the enemy were so rapid and close, that every effort was in vain. The steady ranks melted away before the storm, but still refused to yield. Soult saw the crisis this sudden check had brought upon him, and strained every nerve to save the day. His stern voice was heard above the roar of battle cheering on his men, while he was seen passing to and fro through the ranks, encouraging them by his gestures and example to maintain the fight. Vain valour. That charge was like one of Napoleon's Imperial Guards', and the tide of battle was reversed before it. Those brave British soldiers closed sternly on their foes as in a death-struggle. Says Napier: "In vain did Soult, by voice and gesture, animate his Frenchmen; in vain did the hardiest veterans, extricating themselves from the crowded columns, sacrifice their lives to gain time for the mass to open out on such a fair field; in vain did the mass itself bear up, and, fiercely striving, fire indiscriminately upon friends and foes, while the horsemen, hovering on the flank, threatened to charge the advancing lines. Nothing could stop that astonishing infantry. No sudden burst of undisciplined valour, no nervous enthusiasm, weakened the stability of their order; their flashing eyes were bent on the dark columns in their front, their measured tread shook the ground, their dreadful volleys swept away the head of every formation, their deafening shouts overpowered the dissonant cries that broke from all parts of the tumultuous crowd, as, slowly and with a horrid carnage, it was pushed by the incessant vigour of the attack to the farthest edge of the height. There the French reserves mixing with the struggling multitude, endeavoured to sustain the fight, but the effort only increased the irremediable confusion; the mighty mass gave way, and like a loosened cliff, went headlong down the steep. The rain flowed after in streams, discoloured with blood, and *fifteen hundred unwounded men, the remnant of six thousand unconquerable British soldiers, stood triumphant on the hill.*"

The fight was done, and fifteen thousand men lay piled in mangled heaps along that hill and in the valley. The rain came down in torrents, and night set in, dark and gloomy, over the scene of conflict. But from the dreadful field groans and cries arose through the long night, as the wounded writhed in their pain. The pitiless storm, and the moaning wind, and the murky night, and heart-breaking cries of the suffering and the dying, combined to render it a scene of unmingled terror. Soult took five hundred prisoners and several stand of colours, while the British had only the bloody field for their trophy. The next day, however, Soult still hung like a thunder-cloud on the army of the English. But they having received reinforcements on the third day, he deemed it prudent to retire. Marmont, however, joining him soon after, he again took the offensive, and drove the English before him, and over the Spanish borders.

It is impossible to follow the marshal through his chequered career. For five years he struggled manfully against the most harassing obstacles, and finally, when Spain was delivered from the enemy, he hastened, as before remarked, to Napoleon, to help him stem the torrent that was threatening to bear him away. With his departure victory also departed, and soon the disastrous battle of Vittoria threw Spain again into the hands of the English.

The appointment by Napoleon of Soult to retrieve these losses showed what his opinion was of the marshal as a military leader. Not the complaints and false representations of his own brother, nor the reports of rival generals, could blind his penetrating eye to the great ability of the Duke of Dalmatia. No higher eulogy could be passed on him than this single appointment.

The frontiers of France were threatened through the passes of the Pyrenees, and these Soult was ordered to defend to the last extremity. He found at Bayonne but the fragments of the armies that had battled in Spain, but with his accustomed energy he set about their organization, and with such untiring perseverance did he work that in a fortnight he was ready to take the field. Bearing down on Wellington, he poured his strong columns like a resistless torrent through the pass of the Roncesvalles. The gorges and precipices of the Pyrenees rang to the peal of musketry, the roll of the drum, and the roar of cannon, and Soult's conquering troops broke with the shout of victors into Spain.

It was his design to succour St. Sebastian, which with a small garrison had withstood a long siege, and been most heroically defended. But the energy which he had imparted to his army was only momentary. The soldiers were exhausted and worn down, and could not be held to the contest like fresh troops, and Soult was compelled to retire before superior force. The sudden abyss that had opened under Wellington closed again, and having repulsed his able antagonist, he sat down anew before St. Sebastian. Soult had given his word to his brave garrison that if they would hold out a short time longer he would march to their relief, and he now set about fulfilling his promise, hopeless as the task was, and moved to within eight miles of the place with his army. But the besiegers, in the mean time, had not been idle. The siege was pressed vigorously, and a hundred and eighteen guns were dragged before the doomed town. Before Soult broke so rash and sudden through the Pyrenees, Wellington had made an ineffectual assault on the place, and though the fortifications had been weakened and many of the houses burned, withdrawing his forces to meet the French marshal, the garrison had a breathing spell, and made good use of their time to repair their defences.

Terrible Assault of St. Sebastian

Wellington at length placed in battery sixty cannon, some of them sixty-three pounders, and began to play on the walls. The thunder of these heavy guns shook the hills around, and was echoed in sullen shocks on the ear of the distant Soult. For four days did this fierce volcano belch forth its stream of fire against St. Sebastian, carrying terror and dismay to the hearts of the inhabitants. Nothing could withstand such batteries, and the iron storm smote against the walls till a frightful gap appeared, furnishing foothold for the assaulting companies.

St. Sebastian stands by the sea, with the river Uremea flowing close under its walls, which in low tide can be forded. On the farther side of this river were the British troops, and on the 31st of August, at half-past ten, the forlorn hope took its station in the trenches, waiting for the ebbing tide to allow them to cross. As this devoted band stood in silence watching the slow settling of the waters, they could see the wall they were to mount lined with shells and fire-barrels, ready to explode at a touch, while bayonet points gleamed beyond, showing into what destruction they were to move. Soldiers hate to think, and the suspense which they were now forced to endure was dreadful. These brave men could rush on death at the sound of the bugle, but to stand and gaze into the very jaws of destruction till the slowly retiring waters would let them enter was too much for the firmest heart. Minutes seemed lengthened into hours, and in the still terror of that delay the sternest became almost delirious with excitement. Some laughed outright, not knowing what they did; others shouted and sung; while others prayed aloud. It was a scene at which the heart stands still. The air was hot and sulphurous dark and lurid thunderclouds were lifting heavily above the horizon, and the deep hush of that assaulting column was rendered more awful by the hush of nature which betokens the coming tempest.

Noon at length came; the tide was down, and the order to advance was given, and that devoted band moved to the centre of the stream. A tempest of grapeshot and bullets scattered them like autumn leaves over its bosom, but the survivors pressed boldly on, and, reaching the opposite shore, mounted the breach and gained the summit. But as they stood amid the wasting fire, they hesitated to descend on the farther side, for they saw they must leap down twelve feet to reach the ground; while the base of the wall bristled with sword-blades, and pikes, and pointed weapons of every description, fastened upright in the earth. While they still delayed to precipitate themselves on these steel points, the fire from the inner rampart swept them all away. Still column after column poured across the river and filled up the dreadful gaps made in the ranks of their comrades, and crowded the breach, and still the fierce volleys crushed them down, while the few who passed met the bayonet-point, and fell at the feet of the heroic defenders. After two hours of this murderous strife, the breach was left empty of all but the dead, and the shout of the French was heard in the pause of the storm. In the crisis the English soldiers were ordered to lie down at the foot of the ramparts, while forty-seven cannon were brought to bear on the high curtain within, from whence the fire swept the breach. The batteries opened, and the balls, flying only two feet over the soldiers' heads, crushed with resistless power through the enemy's works. At this moment an accident completed what the besiegers had begun, and overwhelmed the defenders. A shell bursting amid the hand-grenades, shells, trains of fire-barrels, and all kinds of explosive materials which the garrison had laid along the ramparts for a last defence, the whole took fire. A sheet of flame ran along the walls, and then the mouth of a volcano seemed to open, followed by an explosion that shook the city to its foundations, sending fierce columns of smoke and broken fragments into the air, and strewing the bodies of three hundred French soldiers amid the ruins. As the smoke lifted, the assailants rushed with a deafening shout forward, and though firmly met by the bayonet, their increasing numbers overwhelmed every obstacle, and they poured into the town. Soult, eight miles distant, had just been defeated in attempting to march to the relief of the garrison, and from the heights of Bidassoa heard that terrific explosion that followed the cannonading, and saw the fiercely ascending columns of smoke that told that St. Sebastian was won.

At this moment, when the shouts of the conquerors, maddened by every passion that makes man a monster and a fiend, were paralyzing the hearts of the inhabitants with fear, the long-gathering thunderstorm burst on the town. Sudden darkness wrapped everything, through which the lightning incessantly streamed, followed by crash after crash of thunder, till the very heavens seemed ready to fall. Amid this stern language of skies and war of the elements, and roar of the conflagration that, fanned by the tempest, wrapped the dwellings, scenes were transpiring over which history must draw a veil. Rapine, revenge, drunkenness, lust, and murder burst forth without restraint, making a wilder hell than man ever dreamed of before. The inhabitants fled from their burning houses and crowded into a quarter where the flames had not yet come. As men, women, and children stood thus packed together, the brutal soldiery reeled and staggered around them, firing into the shrieking mass, and plunging their bayonets into the old and young alike. Lust, too, was abroad, and the cries of violated women mingled with the oaths and blasphemies and shouts of the soldiers. Wives were ravished in presence of their husbands, mothers in presence of their daughters, and one girl of seventeen was violated on the corpse of her mother. For three days did the rapine, and murder and cruelty continue, and scenes were enacted which may not be described, and before which even friends would blush. Such is war, and such its horrors.

The governor retreated to the citadel, and bravely defended himself with a handful of men for several days, still hoping the arrival of Soult. But that marshal had his hands full to keep Wellington at bay. At length, compelled to retreat, he yielded the ground step by step, fighting his way as he went. He delivered the bloody battles of Bidassoa and Neville, disputed the passage of the Nive, and fought at St. Pierre worthy of a better result. He showed a depth of combination, an energy of character, and a tenacity of purpose seldom equalled by any general. Had his shock in battle been equal to Ney's, he would have been irresistible. As it was, with half the force brought against him, he baffled every effort of the enemy to overwhelm him, and being driven into France disputed every inch of his native soil with a heroism and patriotism that have rendered him immortal. Now enforcing discipline, now encouraging his troops in the onset, and now on foot at the head of the columns, periling his life like the meanest soldier, he strained every nerve to resist the advance of his overpowering adversary. He had arrived at Bayonne and taken command of the disorganized and humble army in July. He had reorganized it, broken like a thunderbolt into Spain, fought seven pitched battles, lost thirty thousand men, and in December is again seen at Bayonne showing a firm front to the enemy. For five months he had struggled against the most overwhelming obstacles; fought with troops that would have ruined the cause of a less stern general; struck blows that, even against the odds they were directed, well-nigh gave him the victory; and amid the complaints of the soldiers and the desertion of his German troops, never once gave way to discouragement. Self-sustained and resolute, his iron will would bend before no reverses, and in that last struggle for Napoleon in Spain and France, and his masterly retreat, he has placed himself among the first military chieftains of the world. It is true he preferred a less laborious field, and one where constant defeat was not to be expected, and wrote to Napoleon requesting to be near him. But no one could supply his place, and he was compelled to struggle on. He then submitted a plan for the defence of France to the Emperor, which the latter, it seems, had not time to attend to; and instead of rendering aid to his distressed general, he drew away a large force to assist in the defence of Paris. But Soult had served under Massena in Genoa and knew how to endure. With his army thinned by the demands of Napoleon and constant desertion, in the midst of a murmuring population, he bore up with a constancy that fills the mind with wonder and admiration. To his requests for help Napoleon at last replied: "*I have given you my confidence, I can do nothing more.*" Never was confidence more worthily bestowed; and though left in such peril, Soult continued to dispute bravely the country over which he retreated from Bayonne, and at Orthez burst on the enemy with such impetuosity that he had well-nigh gained the victory. Retiring, fighting as he went, he at length entrenched himself at Toulouse, and here, after Napoleon's abdication, though before the news had reached him, fought the famous battle of Toulouse.

Each side claimed the victory; but, according to English historians themselves, Wellington's loss was far greater than Soult's; and the latter was ready next morning to begin the fight, while the former was not. As the two armies thus stood menacing each other, the news of Napoleon's abdication arrived. Soult, however, not having received authentic and full information of the terms of the abdication, refused to make any change in his operations, except to grant an armistice till farther reports could be received. Even if Napoleon had abdicated, he did not know that the Bourbons would be reinstated, or that the army should not retain its present hostile attitude. In the uncertain state of affairs the two leaders again prepared for battle, but the useless waste of blood was spared by orders from the Minister of War; and Soult delivered up is command to the Duke of Augouléme. As before remarked, he struck the last blow and fired the last cannon-shot for Napoleon and the Empire.

His conduct at Waterloo has caused many remarks and subjected him to some heavy accusations. But the most that can be made of it is that he did not act with his accustomed vigour. At Waterloo he was not the hero of Austerlitz.

Soult has committed many errors; and it could not well be otherwise. A life passed in such an agitated political sea as his has been must now and then exhibit some contradictions and inconsistencies. But these minor faults are buried beneath his noble deeds; and his blood so freely shed on so many battle-fields for France, the great talents he has placed at the service of his country, and the glory with which he has covered her armies, will render him dear to her long after his eventful life has closed.

The Duke of Dalmatia is now seventy-seven years of age; and though he has resigned his office of Minister of War, he is still President of the Council, and takes an active part in the political affairs of France.

Nothing shows more plainly the ridiculous self-conceit of English historians in drawing a parallel between Wellington and Bonaparte merely because the former won the battle of Waterloo, or rather was Commander-in-Chief when it *was* won, than this long struggle between him and Soult in Spain. The French marshal showed himself a match for him at any time; nay, beat him oftener and longer than he was beaten. The advantage, if any, was on the side of the French marshal; for while he possessed equal coolness and prudence, he carried greater force in his onsets. Yet who would think of drawing a parallel between Soult and Napoleon with the least intention of making them equal; Wellington was no ordinary general; and he receives all the merit he deserves when put beside Soult as an equal. Pitted against each other for years, they were so nearly balanced that there seems little to choose between them; but to place either beside Napoleon as his equal excites a smile in any but an Englishman.

Marshal Murat

Chapter 11

Marshal Murat

Achille, the eldest son of Murat, formerly king of the two Sicilies, is now a planter in Florida. Fleeing from France, he came to our country, and found an asylum on our shores, the place of refuge to so many of those stern and restless spirits that once unsettled Europe from her repose. Kings, and princes, and marshals, and nobles, have in turn been forced to take shelter under our eagle, to escape imprisonment and death at home.

There are three classes of men which a state of war brings to the surface to astonish the world by their deeds. The first is composed of those stern and powerful men whose whole inherent force must out in action or slumber on forever. In peaceful times they acquire no eminence, for there is nothing on which they can expend the prodigious active energy they possess; agitated times, when a throne can be won by a arm and a daring spirit, they arouse themselves, and move amid the tumult completely at home. At the head of this class stands Marshal Ney-the proud, stern, invincible soldier, who acquired the title of "the bravest of the brave."

A second class of reckless, daring spirits, who love the excitement of danger, and the still greater excitement of gaining or losing every thing on a single throw, always flourish in great commotions. In times of peace they would be distinguished only as roving adventurers or reckless, dissipated youth of some country village. In war they often perform desperate deeds, and by their headlong valour secure for themselves a place among those who go down to immortality. At the head of this class stands Marshal Junot, who acquired the sobriquet of *la tempête*, "the tempest."

A third class is composed of the few men left of a chivalric age.

They have an innate love of glory from their youth, and live more by imagination in the days of knighthood, than amid the practical scenes that surround them. Longing for the field where great *deeds* are to be done, they cannot be forced into the severe and steady mental labour necessary to success in ordinary times. To them life is worthless, destitute of brilliant achievements, and there is nothing brilliant that is not *outwardly* so. In peace such men simply do nothing, and dream away half their life, while the other half is made up of blunders, and good and bad impulses. But in turbulent scenes, they are your decided characters. The doubts and opposing reasons that distract others have no influence over them. Following their impulses, they move to a higher feeling than the mere calculator of good and evil. At the head of this class stands, as a patriot, the lazy Patrick Henry, and as a warrior, the chivalric Murat. The latter, however, was an active, rather than a passive dreamer-pursuing, rather than contemplating, a fancied good, and he acquired the name of the "*prieux chevalier.*"

Joachim Murat was born March 25th, 1767, in Bastide, a little village, twelve miles from Cahors. His father was the landlord of a little tavern in the place. He was honest and industrious, with a large family of children, none of which exhibited any striking qualities with the exception of Joachim, who was regarded the most reckless, daring boy in the village. He rode a horse like a young Bedouin, and it was around his father's stable he first acquired that firm and easy seat in the saddle, that afterwards made him the most remarkable horseman of his time. The high and fiery spirit of the boy marked him out, at an early age, as a child of promise, and he became the Benjamin of his parents. The father had once been a steward in the Talleyrand family, and through its influence young Murat was received, when nine years old, into the college of Cahors, and entered on a course of studies, preparatory to the church.

Young Murat was destined by his parents to the priestly office, for which he was about as much fitted by nature as Talleyrand himself. But nothing could make a scholar of him. Neglecting his studies and engaged in every frolic, he was disliked by his instructors and beloved by his companions. The "Abbe Murat," as he was jocularly termed, did nothing that corresponded to his title, but on the contrary every thing opposed to it. His teachers prophesied evil of him, and declared him, at length, fit for nothing but a soldier, and they, for once, were right. Leaving Cahors, he entered the college at Toulouse no wiser than when he commenced his ecclesiastical education. Many adventures are told of him while at the latter place, which, whether apocryphal or not, were all worthy of the reckless young libertine. At length, falling in love with a pretty girl of the city, he fought for her, and carrying off his prize, lived with her concealed till the last *sous* was gone, and then appeared among his companions again. This put an end to his clerical hopes, and throwing off his professional garb, he enlisted, in a fit of desperation, into a regiment of chasseurs that happened at that time to be passing through the city. Becoming tired of the restraint of the camp, he wrote to his brother to obtain his dismissal, which was promised, on condition he would resume his theological studies. The promise was given, and be returned to his books, but the ennui of such a life was greater than that of a camp, and he soon left school and went to his father's house, and again employed himself in the stables. Disgusted with the business of an ostler, be again entered the army. The second time be became sick of his employment, and asked for his dismissal. It was about this time he cheated an old miser out of a hundred francs, by passing off a gilded snuff-box for a gold one. But money was not the motive that prompted him to this trick. A young friend had enlisted in the army, and had no way of escape except by raising a certain sum of money, which was out of his power to do. It was to obtain this for his friend, Murat cheated the old man.

But the revolution beginning now to agitate Paris, Murat's spirit took fire, and having obtained a situation in the constitutional guard of Louis Sixteenth, he hastened with young Bessières, born in the same department, to the capital, and there laid the foundation of his after career, which made him the most distinguished of Napoleon's marshals. An ultra-republican, his sentiments, of which he made no secret, often brought him into difficulty, so that it is said he fought six duels in a single month. At this time he was twenty-two years of age, tall, handsome, and almost perfectly formed, and with a gait and bearing that made him the admiration of every beholder.

During the reign of terror he was a violent republican, and advanced through the grades of lieutenant and captain to that of major. In 1795, having aided Napoleon in quelling the sections, the latter, when he was appointed to command the army in Italy, made him a member of his personal staff. Here, beside the rising Corsican, commenced his brilliant career. With the words, "Honour and the Ladies," engraved on the blade of his sword-words characteristic of the chivalric spirit of the man-he passed through the Italian campaign second only to Bonaparte in the valorous deeds that were wrought. At Montenotte, Milesimo, Dego, Alondovi, Rivoli, &c., he proved the clear-sightedness of Napoleon in selecting him for a companion in the perilous path he had marked out for himself. He was made the bearer of the colours taken in this campaign, to the Directory, and was promoted to the rank of general of brigade.

He soon after accompanied Bonaparte to Egypt, where he grew weary and discontented in the new warfare he had to encounter. In the first place, cavalry was less efficient than infantry against the wild Mamelukes. When twenty thousand of those fierce warriors, mounted on the fleet steeds of the desert, came flying down on their mad gallop, nothing but the close and serried ranks of infantry and the fixed bayonet could arrest their progress. Besides, what was a charge of cavalry against those fleet horsemen, whose onset and retreat were too rapid for the heavy-armed French cuirassiers to return or pursue? Besides, the taking of pyramids and deserts was not the kind of victory that suited his nature.

But at Aboukir, where he was appointed by Napoleon to force the centre of the Turkish lines, he showed what wild work he could make with his cavalry. He rode straight through the Turkish ranks, and drove column after column into the sea; and in one of his fierce charges dashed into the camp of Mustapha Pacha, and rode straight up to the Turkish chieftain as, surrounded by two hundred Janizaries, he stood bravely defending himself. As the Pacha saw him approach he advanced rapidly to meet him, and drawing a pistol, aimed it at his head. The bullet grazed his cheek, just starting the blood, and the next moment Murat's glittering sword gleamed before the eyes of the Pacha as it descended on his hand, crushing two of his fingers with the blow. The Pacha was seized, and carried a prisoner into the French camp. His brilliant achievements in this battle fixed him forever in the affections of Napoleon, who soon after made him one of the few who were to return with him to France. During that long and anxious voyage Murat was by his side, and when the vessel in which they sailed was forced by adverse winds into the port of Ajaccio, he visited with the bold Corsican the scenes of his childhood.

In the revolution of the 18th Brumaire, which placed Bonaparte in power, Joachim took a conspicuous part, and did perhaps more than any other single general for him in that trying hour. In that crisis of Napoleon's life, when he stalked into the Council of the Five Hundred, already thrown into tumultuous excitement by the news of his usurpation; and the startling cry, "Down with the tyrant" met his ear, Murat was by to save him. "Charge bayonets," said he to the battalion of soldiers under him, and with firm step and levelled pieces they marched into the hall and dissolved the Assembly.

Soon after, being at the time thirty-three years of age, he married Caroline Bonaparte, the youngest sister of the Emperor, then in all the bloom and freshness of eighteen. The handsome person and dashing manners of Murat pleased her more than the higher-born Moreau. In a fortnight after his marriage he was on his way with his brother-in-law to cross the San Bernard into Italy. At Marengo he commanded the cavalry, and for his great exploits in this important battle, received from the consular government a magnificent sword.

Bonaparte, as Emperor, never ceased lavishing honours on his favourite brother-in-law. He went up from General of Brigade to General of Division, then to Commander of the National Guard, Marshal, Grand Admiral, Prince of the Empire, Grand Eagle of the Legion of Honour, Grand Duke of Berg and Cleves, and was finally made King of Naples.

"The Abbé Murat" had gone through some changes since he was studying theology at Toulouse.

It is not my design to enter in detail into the history of Murat, but having given the steps by which he ascended to greatness, speak only of those acts which illustrate the great points of his character. In the campaign of 1805 at Wertingen, Vienna and Austerlitz, and other fields of fame in 1806-7 at Jena, Lubeck, Eylau and Friedland in 1808 overthrowing the Spanish Bourbons, and placing the crown in Napoleon's hands, he is the same victorious leader and intrepid man.

His three distinguishing characteristics were, high chivalric courage, great skill as a general, and almost unparalleled coolness in the hour of peril. Added to all this, Nature had lavished her gifts on the mere physical man. His form was tall and finely proportioned his tread like that of a king his face striking and noble, while his piercing glance few men could bear. This was Murat on foot, but place him on horseback, and he was still more imposing. He never mounted a steed that was not worthy of the boldest knight of ancient days, and his incomparable seat made both horse and rider an object of universal admiration. The English invariably condemn the theatrical costume he always wore, as an evidence of folly, but it was in perfect keeping with his character. He was not a man of deep thought and compact mind, but resembled an oriental in his tastes, and loved every thing gorgeous and imposing. He usually wore a rich Polish dress, with the collar ornamented with gold brocade, ample pantaloons, scarlet or purple, and embroidered with gold; boots of yellow leather, while a straight diamond-hilted sword, like that worn by the ancient Romans, hanging from a girdle of gold brocade, completed his dashing exterior. He had heavy black whiskers, and long black locks, which, streaming over his shoulders, contrasted singularly with his fiery blue eye. On his head he wore a three-cornered chapeau, from which rose a magnificent white plume that bent under its profusion of ostrich feathers, while beside it, and in the same gold band, towered away a splendid heron plume. Over all this brilliant costume, he wore in cold weather a pelisse of green velvet, lined and fringed with the costliest sables.

Neither did he forget his horse in this gorgeous apparelling, but had him adorned with the rich Turkish stirrup and bridle, and almost covered with azure-coloured trappings. Had all this finery been piled on a diminutive man, or an indifferent rider like Bonaparte, it would have appeared ridiculous; but on the splendid charger and still more majestic figure of Murat, with his lofty bearing, it seemed all in place and keeping. This dazzling exterior always made him a mark for the enemy's bullets in battle, and it is a wonder that so conspicuous an object was never shot down. Perhaps there never was a greater contrast between two men, than between Murat and Napoleon, when they rode together along the lines previous to battle. The square figure, plain three-cornered hat, leather breeches, brown *surtout*, and careless seat of Napoleon, were the direct counterpart of the magnificent display and imposing attitude of his chivalric brother-in-law. To see Murat decked out in this extravagant costume at a review, might create a smile, but whoever once saw that gaily-caparisoned steed with its commanding rider in the front of battle, plunging like a thunderbolt through the broken ranks, or watched the progress of that towering white plume, as floating high over the tens of thousands that struggled behind it a constant mark to the balls that whistled like hailstones around it never felt like smiling again at him. Especially would he forget those gilded trappings when he saw him return from a charge, with his diamond-hilted sword dripping with blood, his gay uniform riddled with balls and singed and blackened with powder, while his strong war-horse was streaked with foam and blood, and reeking with sweat. That white plume was the banner to the host be led, and while it continued fluttering over the field of the slain, hope was never relinquished. Many a time has Napoleon seen it glancing like a beam of light to the charge, and watched its progress like the star of his destiny, as it struggled for awhile in the hottest of the fight, and then smiled in joy as he beheld it burst through the thick ranks of infantry, scattering them from his path like chaff before the wind.

Napoleon once said, that in battle he was probably the bravest man in the world. There was something more than mere success to him in it. He invested it with a sort of glory in itself threw an air of romance about it all, and doubtless fought frequently, almost in an imaginary world. The device on his sword, so like the knights of old his very costume copied from those warriors who lived in more chivalric days, and his heroic manner and bearing, as he led his troops into battle, prove him to be wholly unlike all other generals of that time. In his person at least, he restored the days of knighthood. He himself unconsciously lets out this peculiarity, in speaking of the battle of Mount Tabor. At the foot of this hill, Kleber, with 5,000 men, found himself hemmed in by 30,000 Turks. Fifteen thousand cavalry first came thundering down on this band of 5,000, arranged in the form of a square. For six hours they maintained the unequal combat, when Napoleon arrived with succour on Mount Tabor. As he looked down on the plain, he could see nothing but a countless multitude covering the tumultuous field, and swaying and tossing amid the smoke that curtained them in. It was only by the steady vollies and simultaneous flashes of musketry, that he could distinguish where his own brave soldiers maintained their ground. The shot of a solitary twelve-pounder, which he fired, first announced to his exhausted countrymen that relief was at hand. The ranks then, for the first time, ceased acting on the defensive, and extending themselves, charged bayonet. Murat was on the banks of the Jordan and took the enemy as they rolled towards the bridge, and with his little band performed prodigies of valour and outdid himself. Once he was nearly alone in the centre of a large body of Turkish cavalry. All around, nothing was visible but a mass of turbaned heads and flashing scimitars, except in the centre, where was seen a single white plume, tossing like a rent banner over the throng. For awhile the battle thickened where it stooped and rose, as Murat's strong war-horse reared and plunged amid the sabre strokes that fell like lightning on every side, and then the multitude surged back, as a single rider burst through covered with his own blood and those of his foes, and his arm red to the elbow that grasped his dripping sword. His steed staggered under him and seemed ready to fall, while the blood poured in streams from his sides. But Murat's eye seemed to burn with four-fold lustre, and with a shout, those who surrounded him never forgot to their latest day, he wheeled his exhausted steed on the foe, and at the head of a body of his own cavalry trampled everything down that opposed his progress. Speaking of this terrible fight, Murat said that in the hottest of it he thought of Christ, and his transfiguration on that same spot nearly two thousand years before, and it gave him ten-fold courage and strength. He was promoted in rank on the spot. This single fact throws a flood of light on Murat's character, and shows what visions of glory often rose before him in battle, giving to his whole movement and aspect, a greatness and dignity that could not be assumed.

None could appreciate this chivalrous bearing of Murat more than the wild Cossacks. In the memorable Russian campaign, he was called from his throne at Naples to take command of the cavalry, and performed prodigies of valour in that disastrous war. When the steeples and towers of Moscow at length rose on the sight, Murat, looking at his soiled and battle-worn garments, declared them unbecoming so great an occasion as the triumphal entrance into the Russian capital, and retired and dressed himself in his most magnificent costume, and thus apparelled, rode at the head of his squadrons into the deserted city. The Cossacks bad never seen a man that would compare with Murat in the splendour of his garb, the beauty of his horsemanship, and, more than all, in his incredible daring in battle. Those wild children of the desert would often stop, amazed, and gaze in silent admiration, as they saw him dash, single-handed, into the thickest of their ranks, and scatter a score of their most renowned warriors from his path, as if be were a bolt from heaven. His effect upon these children of nature, and the prodigies he wrought among them, seem to belong to the age of romance rather than to our practical times. They never saw him on his magnificent steed, sweeping to the charge, his tall white plume streaming behind him, without sending up a shout of admiration before they closed in conflict.

In approaching Moscow, Murat, with a few troops, had left Gjatz somewhat in advance of the grand army, and finding himself constantly annoyed by the hordes of Cossacks that hovered around him, now wheeling away in the distance, and now dashing up to his columns, compelling them to deploy; lost all patience, and obeying one of those chivalric, impulses that so often hurled him into the most desperate straits, put spurs to his horse, and galloping all alone up to the astonished squadrons, halted right in front of them, and cried out in a tone of command, "Clear the way, reptiles!" Awed by his manner and voice, they immediately dispersed. During the armistice, while the Russians were evacuating Moscow, these sons of the wilderness flocked by thousands around him. As they saw him reining his high-spirited steed towards them, they sent up a shout of applause, and rushed forward to gaze, on one they had seen carrying such terror through their ranks. One called him his "hetman," the highest honour that could be conferred on him. They would now point to his steed and now to his costume, while they fairly recoiled before his piercing glance. Murat was so much pleased by the homage of these simple-hearted warriors, that be distributed among them all the money he had, and all he could borrow from the officers about him, and finally his watch, and then the watches of his friends. He had made many presents to them before; for often, in battle, he would select out the most distinguished Cossack warrior, and plunging directly into the midst of the enemy, engage him single-handed, and take him prisoner, and afterwards dismiss him with a gold chain about his neck or some other rich ornament attached to his person.

He was also a good general, though I know this is often disputed. Nothing is more common than the belief that an impulsive, headlong man cannot be clear-headed, while history proves that few others ever accomplish anything. From Alexander down to Bonaparte, your impetuous beings have always had the grandest plans, and executed them. Yet, men will retain their prejudices, and you cannot convince them that the silent, grave owl is not wiser than the talkative parrot, though the reverse is indisputably true. There could hardly be a more impetuous man than Bonaparte, and he had a clearer head and a sounder judgment than all his generals put together. Murat's impulses were often stronger than his reason, and in that way detracted from his generalship. Besides, he was *too* brave, and never counted his enemy. He seemed to think he was not made to be killed in battle, or to be defeated. Bonaparte had great confidence in his judgment when be was cool, and consulted him perhaps more than any other of his generals upon the plan of an anticipated battle. On these occasions Murat never flattered, but expressed his opinions in the plainest, most direct language, and often differed materially from his brother-in-law. Perhaps no one ever had greater skill than Napoleon in judging of the position of the enemy; and in the midst of battle, and in the confusion of conflicting columns, his perceptions were like lightning. Yet, in these great qualities, Murat was nearly his equal. His plans were never reckless, but the manner he carried them out was desperation itself. Said Bonaparte of him, "He was my right arm he was a paladin in the field the best cavalry officer in the world."

Murat loved Bonaparte with supreme devotion, and bore with his impatience and irascibility, and even dissipated them by his good-humour. Once, however, Bonaparte irritated him beyond endurance. Murat foresaw the result of a march to Moscow, and expostulated with his brother-in-law on the perilous undertaking. The dispute ran high, and Murat pointed to the lateness of the season, and the inevitable ruin in which the winter, so close at hand, would involve the army. Bonaparte, more passionate than usual, because Murat had the right of it, as he had, a few days before, when he besought him not to attack Smolensk because the Russians would evacuate it of their own accord; made some reply which was heard only by the latter, but which stung him so to the quick that he simply replied, "A march to Moscow will be the destruction of the army," and spurred his horse straight into the fire of a Russian battery. Bonaparte had touched him in some sore spot, and he determined to wipe out the disgrace by his death. He ordered all his guard to leave him, and dismounting from his magnificent steed, with his piercing eye turned full on the battery, stood calmly waiting the ball that should shatter him. A more striking subject for a picture was scarce ever furnished than he exhibited in that attitude. There stood his high-mettled and richly-caparisoned charger, with arching neck and dilated eye, giving ever and anon a slight shiver at each explosion of the artillery that ploughed up the turf at his feet, while Murat, in his splendid attire, stood beside him with his ample breast turned full on the fire, and his proud lip curled in defiance, and his tall white-plume waving to and fro in the air as the bullets whistled by it the impersonation of calm courage and heroic daring. At length, casting his eye round, he saw General Belliard still by his side. He asked him why he did not withdraw. "Every man," he replied, is master of his own life, and as your Majesty seems determined to dispose of your own, I must be allowed to fall beside you." This fidelity and love struck the generous heart of Murat, and he turned his horse and galloped out of the fire. The affection of a single man could conquer him, at any time, whom the enemy seemed unable to overcome. His own life was nothing, but the life of a friend was surpassingly dear to him.

As proof that he was an able general as well as a brave man, it is necessary only to refer to the campaign of 1805. He commenced this campaign by the victory of Wertingen took three thousand prisoners at Languertau, advanced upon Neresheim, charged the enemy and made three thousand prisoners, marched to Norlingen and compelled the whole division of Weernesk to surrender, beat Prince Ferdinand, and hurrying after the enemy, overtook the rear-guard of the Austrians, charged them and took 500 prisoners took Ems, and again beat the enemy on the heights of Amstetten, and made 1800 prisoners pushed on to Saint Polten, entered Vienna, and without stopping, pressed on after the Russians, and overtaking their rear-guard, made 2000 prisoners, and crowned his rapid, brilliant career with prodigies of valour that filled all Europe with admiration, on the field of Austerlitz.

Bonaparte usually put from ten to twenty thousand cavalry under Murat, and placed them in reserve behind the lines, and when he ordered the charge be was almost certain of victory. After a long and wasting fight, in which the infantry struggled with almost equal success, and separate bodies of horse had effected but little, Bonaparte would order him down with his enormous weight of cavalry. It is said that his eye always brightened as he saw that magnificent body begin to move, and he watched the progress of that single white plume, which was ever visible above the throng with the intensest interest. *Where* it went he knew were broken ranks and trampled men, and *while* it went he knew that defeat was impossible. Like Ney, he carried immense moral force with him. Not only were his followers inspired by his personal appearance and incredible daring, but he had acquired the reputation of being invincible, and when he ordered the charge, every man, both friend and foe, knew it was to be the most desperate one human power could make. And then the appearance of twenty thousand horsemen coming down on the dead gallop, led by such a man, was enough to send terror through any infantry.

The battle of Valentina exhibited an instance of this moral force of Murat. He had ordered Junot to cross a marshy flat and charge the flank of the Russians while he poured his strong *cuirassiers* on the centre. Charging like a storm with his own men, he was surprised to find that Junot had not obeyed his command. Without waiting for his guard, he wheeled his horse, and galloping alone through the wasting fire, rode up to him and demanded why be had not obeyed his order. Junot replied that he could not induce the Westphalian cavalry to stir, so dreadful was the fire where they were ordered to advance. Murat made no reply, but reining his steed up in front of the squadrons, waved his sword over his head and dashed straight into the sharp shooters, followed by that hitherto wavering cavalry as if they had forgotten there was such a thing as danger. The Russians were scattered like pebbles from his path; then turning to Junot, he said, "There, thy marshal's staff is half earned for thee; do the rest thyself."

Soon after, at the battle of Borodino, as the redoubts were carried and Bagration was driven back, and while, he was endeavouring to rally his men disordered with victory, the second Russian line advanced, and the latter became entirely surrounded before he was aware of it. To escape being made prisoner, he threw himself into one of the redoubts, where he found only a few soldiers, panic stricken, and running in affright around the fort seeking a way of retreat. Instantly calling them to halt, he stood and waved his plume, as a banner, over his head, and finally rallied them to resistance, and held the redoubt till Ney advanced to his deliverance. As these two heroes stood and breasted the terrible tempest that then burst upon them, Murat saw the soldiers of Friand's division beginning to break, and heard one of the officers order a retreat. Running up to him, he seized him by the collar, and exclaimed, "What are you about?" The colonel pointed to the ground, on which lay half his troops, and said,

"You see it is impossible to stand here." "Very well," replied Murat, "*I* will remain." The officer stopped, looked at him a moment in surprise, and then turning round, coolly said, "You are right! soldiers, face the enemy; let us go and be killed!"

Throughout this fatal campaign he bore himself like one who could not be killed, and when the mournful retreat commenced, he fought with the same unshaken courage. Though his cavalry had melted away, and his gorgeous apparel had given place to the soiled and tattered garments of a fugitive, and the gay and brilliant knight had disappeared before the rigors of winter, the claims of hunger, toil, and defeat; he still charged with the same impetuosity as ever. His apparel, dazzling as it was, had nothing to do with his courage. He once said to Miot, at the siege of Jaffa, who asked him what be would do if the enemy should surprise him in the night, "Well, I would mount on horseback in my shirt, and I should be the better distinguished in the dark." His showy exterior simply corresponded with his chivalric sentiments.

But it is impossible to speak of all the engagements in which he took a part. He was in constant service, and he never fought a battle without performing some heroic deed. On the plains of Italy, over the sands of Egypt, by the waters of Jordan, by the Danube and Rhine, through the snow-drifts of Russia, everywhere, over hundreds of battle-fields, be moves the same intrepid leader and chivalric warrior. Resistless in the onset, deadly in the pursuit, he flies from one scene of strife to another, as if war were his element.

CHARGE AT EYLAU

But it is at Eylau that he always appears in his most terrible aspect. This battle, fought in mid winter, in 1807, was the most important and bloody one that had yet occurred. France and Russia had never before opposed such strength to each other, and a *complete* victory on either side would have settled the fate of Europe. Bonaparte remained in possession of the field, and that was all no victory was ever so like a defeat.

The field of Eylau was covered with snow, and the little ponds that lay scattered over it were frozen sufficiently hard to bear the artillery. Seventy-five thousand men on one side, and eighty-five thousand on the other, arose from the frozen field on which they had slept the night of the 7th of February, without tent or covering, to battle for a continent. Augereau, on the left, as described in the preceding volume, was utterly routed early in the morning. Advancing through a snow-storm so thick he could not see the enemy, the Russian cannon mowed down his ranks with their destructive fire, while the Cossack cavalry, which were ordered to charge, came thundering on, almost hitting the French infantry with their long lances before they were visible through the storm. Hemmed in and overthrown, the whole division, composed of 16,000 men, with the exception of 1,500, were captured or slain. Just then the snow-storm clearing up, revealed to Napoleon the peril to which he was brought, and he immediately ordered a grand charge by the Imperial Guard and the whole cavalry. Nothing was farther from Bonaparte's wishes or expectations than the bringing of his reserve into the engagement at this early stage of the battle but there was no other resource left him. Murat sustained his high reputation on this occasion, and proved himself for the hundredth time worthy of the great confidence Napoleon placed in him. Nothing could be more imposing than the battle-field at this moment. Bonaparte and the Empire trembled in the balance, while Murat prepared to lead down his cavalry to save them. *Seventy squadrons*, making in all 14,000 well-mounted men, began to move over the slope, with the Old Guard moving sternly behind. Bonaparte, it is said, was more agitated at this crisis than when, a moment before, he was so near being captured by the Russians. But as he saw those seventy squadrons come down on a plunging trot, pressing hard after the white plume of Murat, that streamed through the snow-storm far in front, a smile passed over his countenance. The earth groaned and trembled as they passed, and the thousands of glittering helmets and flashing sabres above the dark and angry mass below, looked like the foam of a sea wave as it crests on the deep. The rattling of their armour and the muffled thunder of their tread drowned all the roar of battle, as with firm set array and swift, steady motion, they bore down with their terrible front on the foe. The shock of that immense host was like a falling mountain, and the front line of the Russian army went down like frost-work before it. Then commenced a protracted fight of hand-to-hand and sword-to-sword, as in the cavalry action at Eckmuhl. The clashing of steel was like the ringing of countless hammers, and horses and riders were blended in wild confusion together. The Russian reserve were ordered up, and on these Murat fell with his fierce horsemen, crushing and trampling them down by thousands. But the obstinate Russians disdained to fly, and rallied again and again, so that it was no longer cavalry charging on infantry, but squadrons of horse galloping through a broken host that, gathering into knots, still disputed with unparalleled bravery the red and rent field.

It was during this strange fight that Murat was seen to perform one of those desperate deeds for which he was so renowned. Excited to the highest pitch of passion by the obstacles that opposed him, he seemed endowed with ten-fold strength, and looked more like a superhuman being treading down helpless mortals, than an ordinary man. Amid the roar of artillery and rattle of musketry, and falling of sabre-strokes like lightning about him, that lofty white plume never once went down, while ever and anon it was seen glancing through the smoke of battle the star of hope to Napoleon, and that his "right arm" was still uplifted and striking for victory. He raged like an unloosed lion amid the foe; and his eye, always terrible in battle, burned with increased lustre, while his clear and steady voice, heard above the tumult of the strife, was worth more than a thousand trumpets to cheer on his followers. At length, seeing a knot of Russian soldiers that, for a long time, had kept up a devouring fire on his men, he wheeled his horse and drove in full gallop upon their levelled muskets. A few of his guard, that never allowed that white plume to leave their sight, charged after. Without waiting to count his foes, he seized the bridle in his teeth, and with a pistol in one hand and his drawn sword in the other, burst in headlong fury upon them, and scattered them as if a hurricane had swept by.

Though the cavalry were at length compelled to retire, the Russians had received a check that alone saved the day. Previously, without bringing up their reserve, they were steadily advancing over the field, but now they were glad to cease the combat and wait for further reinforcements under Lestocq, before they renewed the battle. I have spoken of the progress of the fight during the day in another place. Prodigies of valour were performed on all sides, and men slain by tens of thousands, till night at length closed the awful scene, and the Russians began to retire from the field.

Such was the battle of Eylau, fought in the midst of a piercing snow-storm. Murat was a thunderbolt on that day, and the deeds that were wrought by him will ever furnish themes for the poet and painter. But let the enthusiast go over the scene on the morning after the battle, if he would find a cure for his love of glory. *Fifty-two thousand men* lay piled across each other in the short space of six miles, while the snow, giving back the stain of blood, made the field look like one great slaughter-house. The frosts of a wintry morning were all unheeded in the burning fever of ghastly wounds, and the air was loaded with cries for help, and groans, and blasphemies, and cursings. Six thousand horses lay amid the slain, some stiff and cold in death, others rendering the scene still more fearful by their shrill cries of pain. The cold heavens looked down on this fallen multitude, while the pale faces of the thousands that were already stiff in death, appeared still more appalling in their vast winding-sheet of snow. Foemen had fallen across each other as they fought, and lay like brothers clasped in the last embrace; while dismembered limbs and disembowelled corpses were scattered thick as autumn leaves over the field. Every form of wound, and every modification of wound were here visible. No modern war had hitherto exhibited such carnage, and where Murat's cavalry had charged, there the slain lay thickest. *Two days* after the battle *five thousand* wounded Russians lay on the frozen field, where they had dragged out the weary nights and days in pain. The dead were still unburied, and lay amid wrecks of cannons, and munitions wagons, and bullets, and howitzers; whole lines had sunk where they stood, while epaulettes, and neglected sabres, and muskets without owners, were strewed on every side, and thrown into still more terrible relief by the white ground of snow, over which they lay. Said Napoleon, in his bulletin home, after describing the dreadful appearance the field presented, "The spectacle is sufficient to inspire princes with the love of peace and horror of war."

I have said little of his conquest of Madrid, because it was done without effort. The sudden rising of the population of the city, in which were slaughtered seven hundred Frenchmen, was followed by the public execution of forty of the mob. Much effort has been made to fix a stain on Murat by this execution, and the destruction of some hundred previously, in the attempt to quell the insurrection; by calling it a premeditated massacre. But it was evidently not so. Murat was imprudent, there is no doubt, and acted with duplicity, nay, treachery, in all his dealings with the royal family of Spain, but also acted under instructions. He doubtless hoped to receive the crown of Spain, but Bonaparte forced it on his brother Joseph, then king of Naples, and put Murat in his place.

Of his civil administration, one cannot say much in praise. He was too ignorant for a king, and was worthless in the cabinet. The diplomacy of a battle-field he understood, and the management of 20,000 cavalry was an easier thing than the superintendence of a province. Strength of resolution, courage, and military skill he was not wanting in, while in the qualities necessary to the administration of a government, he was utterly deficient. He was conscious of his inferiority here, and knew that his imperial brother-in-law, who gazed on him in admiration, almost in awe, in the midst of battle, made sport of him as a king. These things, together with some unsuccessful efforts of his own, exasperated him to such a degree that he became sick and irresolute. Four years of his life passed away in comparative idleness, and it was only the extensive preparations of Napoleon in 1812 to invade Russia, that roused him to be his former self. Bonaparte's treatment of him while occupying his throne at Naples, together with some things that transpired in the Russian campaign, conspired to embitter Murat's feelings towards his imperious brother-in-law; for his affection, which till that time was unwavering, began then to vacillate.

It is probable that it had been more than hinted to him by the emperor that he intended to deprive him of his crown. At least, not long after Bonaparte left the wreck of the grand army in its retreat from Russia in his hands, he abandoned his post, and travelled night and day till he reached Naples. It is also said by an acquaintance of Murat, that Bonaparte, at the birth of the young Duke of Parma, announced to the King of Naples, who had come to Paris to congratulate him, that he must lay down his crown. Murat asked to be allowed to give his reply the next morning, but no sooner was he out of the Emperor's presence than he mounted his horse and started for his kingdom. He rode night and day till he reached Naples, where he immediately set on foot preparations for the defence of his throne. Being summoned anew by a marshal of France, sent to him for that purpose, to give up his sceptre, he replied, "Go, tell your master to come and take it, and, he shall find how well sixty thousand men can defend it." Rather than come to open conflict with one of his bravest generals, he abandoned the project, and let Murat occupy his throne. If this be true it accounts for the estrangement and final desertion of Napoleon by his brother-in-law. Still, in Napoleon's last struggle for his throne on the plains of Germany, Murat fought nobly for him, and helped to gain the battle of Dresden, and chased Blucher over the Elbe. But after the disastrous battle of Leipzig, he returned to Naples and immediately entered into negotiations with the allied powers, and in this act sullied forever his fame.

In 1814 he concluded a treaty with Austria, by which he was to retain his crown on the condition he would furnish 30,000 troops for the common cause. Bonaparte could not a first credit this defection of the husband of his sister, and wrote to him twice on the subject. These letters show that Murat was playing a double game, and endeavouring, in the uncertainty of things, to secure his throne. In his first letter Napoleon says, "You are a good soldier on the field of battle, but, excepting there, you have no vigour and no character. Take advantage of an act of treachery, therefore, which I attribute only to fear, in order to serve me *by useful information*. I rely upon your intentions, upon your promises. I suppose you are one of those who imagine the lion is dead; if such are your calculations, they are false. . . . The title of king has turned your head. If you wish to preserve the power, behave right and keep your word." The second commences, "Sir my brother, I have already communicated to you my opinion of your conduct. Your situation had turned your head. My reverses have finished you. You have surrounded yourself with men who hate France, and who wish to ruin you. What you wrote to me is at variance with your actions. I shall, however, see by your behaviour at Ancona if your heart be still French, and if you yield to necessity alone. Recollect that your kingdom, which has cost so much blood and trouble to France, is yours only for the benefit of those who gave it you. . . . Remember that I have made you king solely for the interest of my system."

The truth is, Bonaparte tampered with the affection of Murat. The latter had so often yielded to him on points where they differed, and had followed him through his wondrous career with such constant devotion, that Napoleon believed he could twist him round his finger as he liked, and became reckless of his feelings. But he found the intrepid soldier could be trifled with too far, and came to his senses barely in time to prevent an utter estrangement.

Shortly after, Napoleon abdicated, and was sent to Elba. But before the different allied powers had decided whether they should allow Murat to retain his throne, Europe was thrown into consternation by the announcement that Bonaparte was again on the shores of France. Joachim immediately declared in favour of his brother-in-law, and attempted to rouse Italy. But his army deserted him, and hastening back to Naples, he threw himself into the arms of his wife, exclaiming, "All is lost, Caroline, but my life, and that I have not been able to cast away." Finding himself betrayed on every side, he fled in disguise to Ischia. Sailing thence to France, he landed at Cannes, and dispatched a courier to Fouché, requesting him to inform Napoleon of his arrival. Bonaparte, irritated at his former defection, and still more vexed that he had precipitated things so in Italy, contrary to his express directions, sent back the simple reply, "to remain where he was until the Emperor's pleasure with regard to him was-known." This cold answer threw Murat in a tempest of passion. He railed against his brother-in-law, loading him with accusations, for whom, he said, he had lost his throne and his kingdom. Wishing, however, to be nearer Paris, he started for Lyons, but while changing horses at Aubagne, near Marseilles, he was told of the disastrous battle of Waterloo.

Hastening back to Toulon, he lay concealed in a house near the city, to await the result of this last overthrow of Napoleon. When he was informed of his abdication, he scarcely knew what to do. At first he wished to get to Paris, to treat personally with the allied sovereigns for his safety. Being unable to accomplish his purpose, he thought of flying to England, but hesitated to do this also, without a promise of protection from that government, he finally, through Fouché, obtained permission of the Emperor of Austria to settle in his dominions. But while be was preparing to set out, he was told that a band of men were on the way to seize him, in order to get the 40,000 francs which the Bourbons had offered for his head; and fled with a single servant to a desolate place on the sea-shore near Toulon. Thither his friends from the city secretly visited him, and informed him what were the designs respecting him. Resolving at last to proceed to Paris by sea, he engaged the captain of a vessel bound to Havre, to send a boat at night to take him off. But by some strange fatality, the seamen could not find Murat, nor he the seamen, though searching for each other half the night; and the sea beginning to rise, the boat was compelled to return to the ship without him. As the morning broke over the coast, the dejected wanderer saw the vessel, with all her sails set, standing boldly out to sea. He gazed for awhile on the lessening masts, and then fled to the woods, where he wandered about for two days, without rest or food. At length, drenched with rain, exhausted and weary, he stumbled on a miserable cabin, where he found an old woman, who kindly gave him food and shelter. He gave himself out as belonging to the garrison at Toulon, and he looked worn and haggard enough to be the commonest soldier. The white plume was gone, that had floated over so many battle-fields, and the dazzling costume, that had glanced like a meteor through the cloud of war, was exchanged for the soiled garments of an outcast. Not even his good steed was left, that had borne him through so many dangers, and as that tall and majestic, form stooped to enter the low door of the cabin, he felt how changeful was human fortune. The fields of his fame were far away his throne was gone, and the wife of his bosom ignorant of the fate of her lord.

While he sat at his humble fare, the owner of the cabin, a soldier belonging to the garrison of Toulon, entered, and bade him welcome. But there was something about the wanderer's face that struck him, and at length remembering to have seen those features on some French coin, he fell on his knees before him, and called him king Murat. His wife followed his example. Murat was astonished at the discovery; and then overwhelmed at the evidence of affection these poor, unknown people offered him, be raised them to his bosom, and gave them his blessing. Forty thousand francs were no temptation to this honest soldier and his wife.

Here he lay concealed, till one night the old woman saw lights approaching the cabin, and immediately suspecting the cause, aroused Murat, and hastening him into the garden, thrust him into a hole, and piled him over with vine branches. She then returned to the house, and, arranged the couch from which he had escaped and began herself to undress for bed, as if nothing had occurred to disturb her ordinary household arrangements. In a few moments sixty *gens d'armes* entered, and ransacked the house and garden, passing again and again by the spot where Murat was concealed. Foiled in their search, they at length went away.

But such a spirit as Murat's could not long endure this mode of existence, and he determined to put to sea. Having, through his friends at Toulon, obtained a skiff, he on the night of the 22d of August, with only three attendants, boldly pushed his frail boat from the beach, and launched out into the broad Mediterranean, and when about thirty miles from the shore, they saw and hailed a vessel, but she passed them. The wind now began to rise, and amid the deepening gloom was heard the moaning of the sea, as it gathered itself for the tempest. The foam-crested waves leaped by, deluging the frail skiff, that struggled almost hopelessly with the perils that environed it. The haughty chieftain saw dangers gathering round him that no charge of cavalry could scatter, but he sat and looked out on the rising deep, with the with the same composure he so often had sat on his gallant steed, when the artillery was mowing down every thing at his side. At length the post-office-packet-vessel for Corsica was seen advancing towards them. Scarcely had Murat and his three faithful followers stepped aboard of it, before the frail skiff sunk to the bottom. It would have been better for him had it sunk sooner. He landed at Corsica in the disguise of a common soldier. The mayor of the Commune of Bastia, the port where the vessel anchored, seeing a man at his door, with a black silk bonnet over his brows, his beard neglected, and coarsely clad, was about to question him, when he looked up, and "judge of my astonishment," says the mayor, "when I discovered that this was Joachim, the splendid king of Naples! I uttered a cry; and fell on my knees." Yes, this was Murat the plume exchanged for the old silk bonnet, and the gold brocade for the coarse gaiters of a common soldier.

The Corsicans received him with enthusiasm, and as he entered Ajaccio, the troops on the ramparts, and the populace received him with deafening cheers. But this last shadow of his old glory consummated his ruin. It brought back to his memory the shouts that were wont to rend Naples when he returned from the army to his kingdom, loaded with horrors and heralded by great deeds. In the enthusiasm of the moment, he resolved to return to Naples, and make another stand for his throne. At this critical period the passports of the emperor of Austria arrived. Murat was promised a safe passage into Austria, and an unmolested residence in any city of Bohemia, with the title of Count, if he, in return, would renounce the throne of Naples, and live in obedience to the laws. Disdaining the condition he would a few weeks before have gladly accepted, he madly resolved to re-enter his kingdom.

With two hundred and fifty recruits and a few small vessels, he sailed for his dominions. The little fleet, beat back by adverse winds, that seemed rebuking the rash attempt, did not arrive in sight of Calabria till the sixth of October, or eight days after his embarkation. On that very night a storm scattered the vessels, and when the morning broke, Murat's bark was the only one seen standing in for land. Two others at length joined him, but that night one of the captains deserted him, and returned with fifty of his best soldiers to Corsica. His remaining followers, seeing that this desertion rendered their cause hopeless, besought him to abandon his project, sail for Trieste, and accept the terms of Austria. He consented and throwing the proclamations he had designed for the Neapolitans into the sea, ordered the captain to steer for the Adriatic. He refused, on the ground that he was not sufficiently provisioned for so long a voyage. He promised, however, to obtain stores at Pizzo, but refused to go on shore without the Austrian passports, which Murat still had in his possession, to use in case of need. This irritated Murat to such a degree, that he resolved to go ashore himself, and ordering his officers to dress in full uniform, they approached Pizzo. His officers wished to land first, to feel the pulse of the people, but Murat,, with his accustomed chivalric feeling, stopped them, and with the exclamation, "I must be the first on shore!" sprang to land, followed by twenty-eight soldiers and three domestics. Some few mariners cried out, "Long live King Joachim!" and Murat advanced to the principal square of the town, where the soldiers were exercising, while his, followers unfurled his standard, and shouted, "Joachim for ever!" but the soldiers made no response. Had Murat been less infatuated, this would have sufficed to convince him of the hopelessness of his cause. He pressed on, to Monte Leone, the capital of the province, but had not gone far before he found himself pursued by a large company of *gens d'armes*. Hoping to subdue them by his presence, be turned towards them and addressed them. The only answer he received was a volley of musketry. Forbidding his followers to return the fire, with the declaration that his landing should not cost the blood of one of his people, he turned to flee to the shore. Leaping from rock to rock and crag to crag, while the bullets whistled about him, he at length reached the beach, when, lo! the vessel that landed him had disappeared. The infamous captain had purposely left him to perish. A fishing-boat lay on the sand, and Murat sprang against it to shove it off, but it was fast. His few followers now came up, but before the boat could be launched they were surrounded by the blood-thirsty populace. Seeing it was all over, Murat advanced towards them, and holding out his sword, said, "People of Pizzo! take this sword, which has been so often drawn at the head of armies, but spare the lives of the brave men with me." But they heeded him not, and kept up a rapid discharge of musketry; and though every bullet was aimed at Murat, not one touched him, while almost every man by his side was shot down. Being at length seized, be was hurried away to prison. Soon after, an order came from Naples to have him tried on the spot. One adjutant-general, one colonel, two lieutenant-colonels, and the same number of captains and lieutenants, constituted the commission to try a King. Murat refused to appear before such a tribunal, and disdained to make any defence.

During the trial he conversed in prison with his friends in a manner worthy of his great reputation. He exhibited a loftiness of thought and character that surprised even his friends that had known him longest. Once after a pause in conversation, be said: "Both in the court and camp, the national welfare has been my sole object. I have used the public revenues for the public service alone. I did nothing for myself, and now at my death I have no wealth but my actions. They are all my glory and my consolation." After talking in this strain for some time, the door opened and one of the commissioners entered and read the sentence. Murat showed no agitation, but immediately sat down and wrote to his wife the following letter.

My Dear Caroline
My last hour has arrived; in a few moments more I shall have ceased to live in a few moments more you will have no husband. Never forget me; my life has been stained by no injustice. Farewell my Achille, farewell my Letitia, farewell my Lucien, farewell my Louise. I leave you without kingdom or fortune, in the midst of the multitude of my enemies. Be always united: prove yourselves superior to misfortune; remember what you are and what you have been, and God

will bless you. Do not reproach my memory. Believe that my greatest suffering in my last moments is dying far from my children. Receive your father's blessing; receive my embraces and my tears.

Keep always present to you the memory of your unfortunate father.

Joachim Napoleon
Pizzo, 13th October, 1815

Having then enclosed some locks of his hair to his wife, and given his watch to his faithful valet, Amand, he walked out to the place of execution. His tall form was drawn up to its loftiest height, and that piercing blue eye that had flashed so brightly over more than a hundred battle-fields, was now calmly turned on the soldiers who were to fire on him. Not a breath of agitation disturbed the perfect composure of his face, and when all was ready he kissed a cornelian be held in his hand, on which was cut the head of his wife, and then fixing his eyes steadily upon it, said, "Save my face, aim at my heart!" A volley of musketry answered, and Murat was no more.

He had fought two hundred battles, and exposed himself to death more frequently than any other officer in Napoleon's army. By his white plume and gorgeous costume a constant mark for the enemy's bullets, he notwithstanding always plunged into the thickest dangers, and it seems almost a miracle that he escaped death. His self-composure was wonderful, especially when we remember what a creature of impulse be was. In the most appalling dangers, under the fire of the most terrific battery, all alone amid his dead followers, while the bullets were piercing his uniform and whistling in an incessant shower around his head, he would sit on his steed and watch every discharge with the coolness of an iron statue. A lofty feeling in the hour of peril bore him above all fear, and through clouds of smoke and the roar of five hundred cannon, he would detect at a glance the weak point of the enemy, and charge like fire upon it.

As a general he failed frequently, as has been remarked, from yielding his judgment to his impulses. As a man and king he did the same thing, and hence was generous to a fault, and liberal and indulgent to his people. But his want of education in early life rendered him unfit for a statesman. Yet his impulses, had they been less strong, would not have made him the officer he was. His cavalry was the terror of Europe. Besides, in obeying his generous feelings, he performed many of those deeds of heroism exposing his life for others, and sacrificing everything he had, to render those happy around him, which make us love his character. He was romantic even till his death, and lived in an atmosphere of his own creation. But unlike Ney, he was ashamed of his low origin, and took every method to conceal it. He loved his wife and children and country with the most devoted affections. His life was the strangest romance ever written, and his ignominious death, an everlasting blot on Ferdinand's Character.

That the moral character of Murat could not be very correct according to our standard, is evident from the fact that his life was spent in the camp. The only way to judge such a man, is to balance his actions, and see whether the good or evil preponderate.

But whatever his faults were, it will be a long time before the word will see another such man.

Marshal Lefebvre

CHAPTER 12

Marshal Lefebvre

It was not my intention to speak of those four Marshals whose appointments were designed as honorary by Napoleon, but Lefebvre continued in active life to the close of the war, and hence belongs to the history of the Empire. Old age did not drive him into repose, and he battled bravely for freedom and for France till Paris capitulated. Though nearly fifty years of age when created Marshal, having fought for the republic on the Rhine and in Germany, he did not retire on his honours, but followed Napoleon through his wonderful career, and though verging on sixty, survived even the terrible Russian campaign.

François Joseph Lefebvre was born at Ruffach, in the department of the Upper Rhine, Oct. 25th, 1755. His parents were poor, ignorant, and belonged to the humblest rank of citizens. They were unable to give their son even a common education, but they instilled in his mind principles of honesty and incorruptible integrity, from which he never departed. A youth of eighteen, he enlisted as a private in the Guards, but did not reach even the rank of a sergeant till thirty-three years of age. At thirty-seven he found himself captain of the Light Infantry, and in the midst of the French Revolution. He was in Paris during those terrible scenes, amid which the Bourbon throne went down, and though a good republican, was twice was twice wounded in endeavouring to shield the king from popular violence.

In 1793, war being declared, Lefebvre's promotion became rapid, for in a few months he went up to adjutant-general, general of brigade, and general of division. Under the first republican generals, Hoche, Jourdan, Moreau, and Pichegru, he fought with a bravery that showed him worthy of his command. At the terrible battle of Fleurus he covered his division with glory, and at Stockach, where one of the fiercest actions that had occurred during the war took place, he proved himself worthy to fight beside St. Cyr and Soult, who that day performed prodigies of valour. Amid the most wasting fire, he, with eight thousand men, withstood, hour after hour, the shock of thirty thousand Austrians, holding his men by his example and personal exposure to the shock as if the had been walls of iron, until at length he was borne severely wounded from the field. Fighting for liberty and his country, he continued his career of glory till Napoleon's return from Egypt; and on the 18th Brumaire helped to place him in the Consular seat. He commanded the guards of the Ancients and Council of Five Hundred, and was supposed to be in favour of the Directory, and he undoubtedly was. But it was of the utmost importance to Napoleon that the commander of the guards of the Legislative bodies should operate with him in his bold attempt to overthrow the government, and so the night before, at midnight, he sent an aide-de-camp to Lefebvre, requesting the latter to call on him at six o'clock in the morning. In the morning early all was in commotion. The cavalry went pouring along the streets, and distinguished generals were seen hastening, in full uniform to the Rue Chautereine. Lefebvre, as he was passing along, in compliance with Bonaparte's invitation, was surprised to find his troops in motion without his orders, and asked Colonel Sebastiani what it meant. Without answering him, the latter told him to go to Bonaparte. The old veteran marched into the presence of the general-in-chief with a cloud on his brow, but the latter turning to him, said, "Well, Lefebvre; you, one of the pillars of the republic, will you suffer it to perish in the hands of these *lawyers*? Join me and assist me to save it." As he was about to depart, Napoleon stopped him, and offering him a beautiful sword, said, "Here is a sabre which I wore at the Pyramids; I give it to you as a token of my esteem and confidence." "Yes," replied Lefebvre, now fairly brought over by the confidence and generosity of Napoleon, "let us throw the lawyers into the river." During all that stormy day and the next he was faithful to his new master.

In 1804 he was made Marshal of the Empire, and went through the campaigns of 1805 and '6 with honour, and fought on foot at the head of the Guards at Jena. In 1807 he invested Dantzick and took it, and in 1808 was placed over the fourth corps of the army in Spain. He fought and won the battle of Durango, but though he gained the victory, his conduct displeased Napoleon, as it opened the campaign before his Plans were all matured. In 1809 be is found bravely fighting at Landshut, and Eckmuhl, and Wagram, and soon after struggling heroically amid the mountain passes of the Tyrol. He commanded the Old Guard in the Russian campaign, and though approaching his threescore years, bravely met the wintry storm, and cold, and with the remnant of his devoted followers closed sternly around the Emperor, stemming the tide to the last. In the campaigns that followed, the old veteran, still unsubdued, marched at the head of his columns, and in the last struggle of Napoleon for his Empire defended the soil of his native land inch by inch, and led his children (as he was wont to call his soldiers) into the battle at Montmirail, Arcis-sur-Aube, and Champ Aubert. Wherever the soldiers saw those grey locks streaming they would follow, if into certain death. In almost the last battle he ever fought he had a horse shot under him.

After Napoleon's abdication, Louis made him Peer of France and a Knight of St. Louis. When the Emperor returned from Elba, Lefebvre gave in his adhesion, and accepted a seat in the Chamber of Peers. He remained inactive, however, during the short struggle that followed. At the second restoration be was deprived of his honours and rank for a while, but the next year he received again his Marshal's truncheon, and three years afterward his seat in the Chamber of Peers. This was in 1819, and, on the occasion of his taking his seat, Marshal Suchet pronounced a eulogium on the brave old soldier, now sixty-four years of age.

Lefebvre was one of those few characters that circumstances never change. Simple in his manners, rank and honours brought no extravagance in dress or appearance. Honest and frugal in his youth, he never practiced extortion when in power, or retained the wealth that fortune flung into his hands. Of incorruptible integrity, no temptations could shake his truth, or provoke an ignoble action. Generous to a fault, he was weak only when his gratitude or affection were assailed. Born in poverty, and of humble parentage, he passed through the horrors of the Revolution, the corruptions of the camp, and a long military life, and finally became Duke of Dantzic and Marshal of the Empire, without losing any of his simplicity of character or love of virtue. A child of nature, he was never ashamed of his parentage. He owed nothing to education, but all to himself. He had not the genius of many of the other marshals, but he possessed in its place a well-balanced mind and strong common sense. He affected neither sumptuousness of living nor brilliancy of style. There was the same simplicity and naïveté in his language when Marshal of the Empire, as when a private in the Guards. He seemed utterly unconscious of the petty ambitions and rivalries that disturbed the happiness of others, and moved straight forward in the path of duty, without any concern for himself. His disinterestedness was proverbial, and the needy never left his door empty-handed. The tear of a poor soldier moved him more than the baubles of rank or fame; and it is the greatest eulogium that can be passed upon him when it is said that, amid all the changes, and turbulent scenes, and temptations he passed through, he never *lost his heart.* His soldiers worshipped him, and no wonder. Not one of them ever asked his help in vain, and his fatherly treatment of all bound him to them with cords of iron. In the latter part of his career, they were more anxious for his life in battle than for their own, and whenever a desperate charge was to be made, they besought him to retire.

In early life he married a servant girl, similar in character to himself. Honest, affectionate, disinterested, truthful, and simple, she never changed with her change of rank, and was as plain-spoken and good-hearted when duchess as when a servant girl. Like her husband, she appreciated excellence of character alone, and seemed utterly unconscious that rank gave any claim to respect. Lefebvre loved her to the last, and cared no more than she for the jokes her ignorance of etiquette and good language gave rise to in the gay circles of Paris.

Lefebvre was bravery itself. The most impulsive man in the army would not face death with more composure than he. Through the blaze of artillery, the close fire of musketry, and on the point of the bayonet, he would move with unflinching firmness. He could not carry his soldiers so far as a more impetuous man would have done, but he would hold them in their place as long. Still, when thoroughly aroused, he was a terrible man in battle, and moved amid its chaos and carnage with fearful energy and strength. He was also an excellent tactician on the field, and would bring his men into position with admirable order. His coolness was not so much the steadiness of a determined man as the composure of one perfectly unconscious of surrounding danger. This gave to his manner a quietness in executing a dangerous movement, or making a desperate assault, that robbed it, in the view of the soldier, of half of its power to injure. This peculiarity increased with years. He was more impetuous in youth, but age and long familiarity with danger made a battle like a common occurrence to him, and he viewed it apparently with as much *sang froid* as he would an ordinary review.

He loved his country with devotion, and those who see nothing but fierce fighters in Napoleon's marshals, would do well to take a lesson of patriotism and disinterestedness from Lefebvre. Though giving his youth, manhood, and old age, all to the service of France, be was so poor that be could not send his son to college.

After the peace of 1799, he was without the means of subsistence, and wrote thus to the Directory: "The definitive conclusion of peace enables the country to dispense with my services. I beg you to grant me a pension, that I may live in comfort. I want neither carriage nor horses, I wish only for bread. You know my services as well as I do. I shall not reckon up my victories, and I have no defeats to count." Noble man! after pouring out his blood like water for his country, the only return he asked was simply bread.

But, during Bonaparte's career, he exhibited nowhere, perhaps, his great qualities as a commander, and the steadiness with which he prosecuted his plans, amid the most discouraging circumstances, than in the....

Siege of Dantzic

Before the battle of Eylau, Lefebvre had made some progress towards reducing this town, but that great conflict had suspended for awhile his operations. But after the battle he was again sent to invest it with twenty-seven thousand soldiers, of whom but twenty thousand were effective troops.

Dantzic, which, in the last unholy partition of Poland, had been given to Prussia, was an important place, not only as a fortress into which the enemy could at any time throw a large army, but situated as it was at the mouth of the Vistula, was the great commercial depot of all Poland. At the time Lefebvre invested it, it was surrounded by a firm rampart and a deep ditch filled with water, strong palisades, and all the outworks necessary for its defence. Added to all this, the ground around was marshy and soft, impeding all the operations of a besieging army, while the inhabitants, by opening the sluices of the Vistula, could at any time deluge two-thirds of the entire flat that surrounded the city with water, till the walls of the town became a mere island in a lake several miles broad. Seventeen thousand Russian and Prussian soldiers garrisoned the place, who, with the armed inhabitants, could present double the force Lefebvre could bring to the assault. To complete this formidable defence, nine hundred cannon stood ready to open their thunder on the daring enemy that should presume to approach the ramparts.

From this statement it will be seen that it was no ordinary task Lefebvre had given him; and it was no ordinary energy and skill he brought to its fulfilment. He sat down before the city the middle of February, and marched his victorious army into it the latter part of May. For more than three months he struggled against the most overwhelming obstacles, and exhibited bravery and greatness him of resource, which stamp him the great general.

After a fierce combat, he declared the narrow strip of land called the Peninsula of Nehrung, and completed the investment of the town on one side. The siege was fairly commenced by an attack on the fort of Hagelsberg, which stood on a little eminence outside the walls. Its elevation prevented it from being inundated, so that approaches to it could be made. After several weeks' incessant toil, and amid desperate sorties from the garrison, the second parallel was finished, and nearly sixty cannon and mortars together opened their fire within twenty-two rods of the wall. This tremendous battery, as if on purpose to add terror to the scene, commenced its thunder at night. Night and day the earth groaned under its heavy and constant explosions, while the cannon of the besieged answered it till it was one succession of deafening thunder-claps over the city, and it shook and trembled on its strong foundations. Amid storms of sleet and hail-in the full blaze of the noonday sun at solemn twilight and at deep midnight without cessation or relief, for an entire week, that volcano thundered on, driving sleep from the alarmed inhabitants, while the bombs hissed and blazed above their dwellings and fell in their midst, and the heavy shot came crashing into their apartments, and the cry of "fire" rung through every street. Nothing can be more terrible than this incessant play of heavy cannon on a town. During this week, Lefebvre worked his guns with a rapidity and skill that threatened to leave not one stone upon another. The only intermission to the fire was when the garrison made some desperate sortie on the batteries, when the musketry and the bayonet took the place of cannon.

But this tremendous cannonade produced but little effect on the ramparts, for they were covered with earth, which broke the force of the balls, and Lefebvre, finding that he could not make a breach for the assaulting companies, commenced sapping the place. He, ran mines under the walls, but the besieged countermined, and thus week after week wore away before any serious demonstration could be made.

But the mines at length being completed, so as to render the defence of the place much longer hopeless, and the garrison not being strong enough to cut its way through Lefebvre's army, the Emperor Alexander determined to relieve it by a combined attack both by sea and land. His arrangements were kept secret from the enemy, and in order to prevent reinforcements being sent to Lefebvre, a feigned attack was to be made on the other portions of the army more remote at the same time. Oudinot and Lannes, with their strong corps, to prevent the Russians from interrupting the operations of the besiegers, while they also formed the rearguard of the army. The Russian emperor had arranged every thing skilfully, and the storm that was ready to burst on Lefebvre threatened to destroy him utterly. But some little delay in the arrival of a Swedish man-of-war enabled Napoleon to get wind of the intended attack, and immediately perceiving the imminent danger to which his marshal was exposed, he ordered Lannes and Oudinot to advance to his help. They came not a moment too soon; for, on the 15th of May, the enemy were seen to issue in formidable numbers from the trenches and march swiftly on Lefebvre's fortifications, which they swept away with irresistible fury. But, while the shouts of victory were still ringing, Lannes, at the head of the brave grenadiers of Oudinot, moved sternly to the assault. The entrenchments were carried, and the Russians driven back. Rallying again, however, they returned to the attack with such impetuosity that the French were again driven out, and Oudinot's horse being shot under him, he fell upon Marshal Lannes, and the two chieftains after that fought on foot, side by side, leading the repeated charges till the Russians were compelled to retire into the city.

This settled the fate of Dantzic, but for more than a week the resistance was kept up. Several sorties were made by the garrison, one of which was successful, and a redoubt was carried of great importance to the French. No sooner did Lefebvre see his troops flying before the enemy, than he put himself at the head of his brave grenadiers, saying, "*Now for our turn, my children,*" and moved intrepidly to the assault. But the redoubt was fiercely contested, and so deadly was the fire to which he was exposed, that the bullets rattled like hailstones around him. Fearing for their beloved chief, and forgetful of all danger to themselves, those grenadiers his "children," as he termed them closed darkly around to form a rampart with their bodies. But the old veteran pushed them affectionately one side, saying, "No, no, let me fight as you do," and marching straight through the storm, swept over the redoubt, carrying every thing before him. Those "children" would have died every one in his footsteps before he would have left the side of Lefebvre.

Resistance at length became useless, and on the 24th the place capitulated. Lefebvre, with a generosity and nobleness of heart that always characterized him, delayed entering the town in order to send to Oudinot and Lannes, who had so bravely succoured him on the 15th, requesting them to be present at the capitulation, and share the honour of entering the city. But with equal nobleness those brave generals refused to pluck one laurel from the head of the old veteran, and re-passed the Vistula on purpose to compel him to enter the city alone and receive all the glory.

Four days after the capitulation, Napoleon conferred on him the title of Duke of Dantzic, and never was an honour more worthily bestowed.

But two years after this, he was destined to count at least one defeat among his victories. After the battle of Wagram, and during the armistice that followed, Napoleon sent him, as before remarked, into the Tyrol, to quell the inhabitants that had taken up arms with Austria.

Campaign in the Tyrol

With thirty thousand men he marched on Innsbruck, the Tyrolese capital, while ten thousand more advanced from the northern side. The armies met at Innsbruck, and to all appearance the war was terminated. The Archduke John issued proclamations, informing the people that peace was established, and recommending submission. But these brave mountaineers determined t carry on the war in their own strength, and letting the Austrian army depart without a murmur, began to assemble on all their hills to defend their country; and on the 4th of August fell on the advanced guard of Lefebvre, who was leading his army down the Brenner mountains, along the banks of the Eisach torrent. He was pushing for a bridge below, the entrance to which was through a deep and dark defile made by the overhanging cliffs. The forest around was silent, and not a living man was seen, to excite any fear of an attack, and the army marched boldly into the mountain gorge. The green fir-trees stood silent in the summer air; and the huge cliffs, that, with their ragged fronts, rent here and there the leafy curtain that fell down the face of the mountain, stood motionless as ever. But no sooner had the head of the army moved partly through the defile, than the whole breast of the mountain was covered with smoke, as the rapid vollies of the sharp-shooters sent death amid the ranks. Not an enemy was visible, and yet the ranks melted like wax before the deadly aim of those mountaineers. The affrighted column stopped, uncertain whether to advance or recede, when the Tyrolese rushed from their ambuscade, and with their thrilling war shouts, rolled, like one of their own mountain torrents, on the foe, and pouring themselves through the confused ranks, fought hand to hand with the soldiers. Lefebvre, however, hurried up other troops, who moved with the stern front of disciplined bravery through the confusion, rolling the disordered mountaineers from the sides of their close column, as a strong ship cleaves the waves. The Tyrolese were routed, and the column, now relieved, pushed on through the defile. All was still again as the hush of death, and the mountain seemed to have swallowed up the enemy, when suddenly some loose stones came rolling down the steep, frightening the horsemen in front. The officers had scarcely turned their eyes up the cliffs to see what this new movement betokened, when the rapid blows of axes were heard, and several immense fir-trees began to wave to and fro above them as if swept by a sudden wind. This was succeeded by a crackling sound, and the next moment the huge trunks pitched heavily forward, and fell headlong down the mountain, followed by avalanches of rocks, earth, and logs, which crushed with the sound of thunder on the column, burying whole squadrons in one wild grave. This immense mass of rubbish had been piled against the trees, which were then cut nearly asunder, so that a few blows of the axe, with the pressure behind, would overthrow them and send the whole mass down the steep. So awful was the shock, and so sudden the death, that the column, broken through and shattered into fragments, again halted, and amid the deep silence that followed, was heard distinctly the roar of the Eisach through the forest as it poured its turbulent flood down the mountain. The silence, however, was but momentary the Tyrolese immediately opened a destructive fire, but the intrepid column moved steadily forward those behind mounting over the heaps of ruins that lay piled above their buried comrades and reached the bridge. But alas! it was on fire, and the crackling, blazing timbers were rapidly falling, one after another, into the waters below. A bold Bavarian spurred forward and rushed in a gallop on the flaming arch the smoke covered him from sight, and the next moment both horse and rider were seen falling together through the broken and blackened timbers into the torrent that swept fiercely beneath. The bridge was destroyed, and the two armies separated by an impassable gulf.

Lefebvre attempted to lead his army over the Brenner, into the Italian Tyrol. It was twenty miles to the top of the pass, and up this steep ascent the marshal was compelled to lead his twenty thousand men. After the most wasting toil, he had succeeded in carrying his army part way up the heights, when from every cliff, and hollow, and tree, a sudden rapid fire opened on his men. Unable to manoeuvre on the steep ascent, and his cannot being almost useless, he saw at once the peril of his position. Without any field on which to deploy his men without room for his cavalry, or even footing for a single division to manoeuvre, he was compelled to trust so solely to the almost useless fire of his infantry. The enemy being half concealed, the bullets only rattled against the cliffs, or buried themselves harmlessly in the trunks of trees, while their own ranks, crowded together in a narrow path, presented an unerring mark to the Tyrolese sharpshooters. Lefebvre struggled bravely to carry his men through this wasting fire, and his troops sustained, for some time, the unequal contest; but no soldiers will long contend in such a useless struggle, and the head of the column began to give way, and settle heavily back upon the army below. For a moment, the mighty mass balanced along the steep, and then, like a loosened cliff, broke headlong down the mountain, rolling horses and cannon, cavalry and infantry, in irretrievable confusion to the bottom. Lefebvre, borne back in the refluent tide, narrowly escaped being made prisoner; and the next night, disguised as a common trooper, entered again Innsbruck. The next day, a general battle took place before the town. It opened at six in the morning, and ended at midnight. All day long did Lefebvre manfully maintain his ground, and roll back the hardy mountaineers from the shock; and when darkness curtained in the mountain valley, it was one broad blaze of light over the struggling hosts, and the Alpine heights shook to the incessant thunder of cannon. But at midnight the French were compelled to give way, and fall back into the town.

Lefebvre lost six thousand men in this bloody struggle, and immediately evacuated Innsbruck, and marching out of the Tyrolese territory, finally collected the fragments of his army at Salzburg.

Bonaparte, however, sending reinforcements, Tyrol was again invaded, and after some hard fighting conquered.

For six years after this he continued in active service, and, as before mentioned, finished his honourable and glorious career, by fighting bravely beside Napoleon, in his last struggle for France and his empire.

He died in Paris, September 14th, 1820, at the age of sixty-five. He left no children, and but little property. His wife, who was devotedly attached to him, wishing to raise a monument over his grave, and having no money with which to defray the expenses, with a nobleness of heart, that always characterized her, sold all her jewels for that purpose, and reared the present splendid sarcophagus, of white marble, which stands in *Père la chaise*. On it is inscribed *Soldat, Marechal, Duc de Dantzick, pair de France: Fleurus, Avante-Garde, Passage du Rhin, Altenkirchen, Dantzick, Montmirail* names which recall the fields of his fame, and many a hard-fought battle, where the sleeping hero once poured out his blood for France.

Though Duchess of Dantzic, his wife was utterly unfitted by her education, for the refined circles of Paris. Plain, direct, blunt, and honest, like her husband, she, by her frank, fearless manner of expressing herself, committed many blunders, which, for a time, made her the joke of the drawing-rooms of the French capital. In Paris, moral worth is at such a discount, that the good heart, generosity, and kindness of the ignorant duchess went for nothing.

She might have broken the rules of morality every day without exciting a remark, by to violate the laws of etiquette, and exhibit ignorance of the conventional forms of the society in which she moved, was an unpardonable offence. She could have possessed a doubtful reputation as a wife without injury, but ignorance made her the jest of the elegant.

Calling one day with Madame Lannes on the Empress Josephine, word was returned that her Majesty would see no one. "What! what." said she, "not see any one? Tell her that it is Lefebvre's wife and *la celle à Lannes*" meaning to say, Lefebvre's wife and the wife of Lannes. But the Parisians, following the pronunciation instead of the spelling, seemed never to weary of saying, Lefebvre's wife and "*la selle à l'âne.*"

But notwithstanding her ignorance of etiquette, she was not destitute of true delicacy of feeling. Generous to a fault, she seemed to love all soldiers for her husband's sake, and a poor officer especially called forth her sympathy. Hearing once that an old emigrant officer had returned to Paris poor, she went to the Marchioness of Valady, in whose house she served as a domestic when Lefebvre was private in the Guards, and said with her usual bluntness, but no less truth, "How little generosity there is among you folks of quality! We who have risen from the ranks know our duty better. We have just heard that M, one of our old officers, has returned from emigration, and is starving from want. Now we were fearful of offending him by offering him assistance, but it is quite different with you. A kind act on your part will be grateful to him, so pray give him this as coming from yourself," handing her as she spoke a hundred *louis*. This delicate act of generosity shows a heart that is pure gold, and outweighs all the external accomplishments with which she could be invested. Such a heart could appreciate the upright and truthful character of Lefebvre, and was worthy the confidence and affection of the brave old soldier.

Marshal Massena

CHAPTER 13

Marshal Massena

No one can visit Genoa without being reminded of the history of Massena. The heights around the city in which he struggled the crippled and deformed beings that meet one at every turn, pointed to as the results of the fearful famine he brought on the inhabitants, when besieged by sea and land he obstinately refused to surrender are constant mementoes of that iron-hearted man.

Andrea Massena's birth-place was only a hundred miles from Genoa. He was born at Nice on the 6th of May, 1758, and, while still an infant, was left an orphan in the world. Growing up without parental care, his education was neglected, and he was left to the mercy of almost any impulse that might move him. An uncle, captain of an ordinary merchant vessel, took him to sea with him while yet a mere boy. But after having made two voyages, the young Andrea, then only seventeen years of age, enlisted as a private soldier in the royal Italian regiment, in which another uncle ranked as captain. This service seemed more fitted to his tastes, and he performed its duties with such regularity and care that he was soon made corporal. Long after, when scarred with his many battles, and standing on the highest pinnacle of military fame Marshal of France and Duke of Rivoli he frequently spoke of this first promotion as affording him more happiness than all the after honours that were heaped upon him. From this he went up (gradually enough, it is true) to sergeant and, finally, adjutant, where he stopped. Unable by the most strenuous exertions and unimpeachable fidelity to reach the rank of under-lieutenant, he at, length, after fourteen years' service, left the army in indignation, and, marrying the daughter of a shop-keeper, settled down in Nice. Here he doubtless would have remained and died a common man, but for the outbreak of the Revolution. Massena, like those other stern-hearted men who afterwards shook Europe so, heard the call for brave and daring spirits, and immediately re-entered the army. At the age of thirty-five he found himself general of division, and had acquired in the army of Italy, where he served, the reputation of a man of great courage and skill. He was present at Montenotte, Millesimo, Arcole, Lodi, and through all that brilliant campaign of Napoleon in 1796, in Italy. He did not long escape the eye of the young Corsican who was astonishing Europe by his victories, and he soon began to look upon him as he did upon Ney, Lannes, and Murat. He once said to him during this campaign, "Your corps is stronger than that of any other general you, yourself, are equivalent to six thousand men." When peace was concluded with Austria, he was chosen to convey the ratification of it to the Directory, which received him in the most flattering manner.

While Bonaparte was in Egypt, Massena commanded the army on the eastern frontiers of France, and after the return of the former, was entrusted with the defence of Genoa, invested by the Austrians and blockaded by the English. The next two or three years were passed at Paris or Ruel in comparative idleness. He bought the magnificent chateau of Richelieu at the latter place, and scarce ever appeared at court. He was a strong republican, and disliked the pomp and show the First Consul began to gather around him. Bonaparte was aware of this, but still he felt he could not do without him, and so, when made emperor in 1804, he created him Marshal of France. The next year the defence of Italy was entrusted to him, and at Verona, and afterwards at Caldiero, he beat and completely routed the Archduke Charles and drove him out of the country. The year following this, he commanded the army that accompanied Joseph Bonaparte to Naples, and by the successful siege of Gaeta, fixed the new king firmly on his throne. These were years of glory to him; and the next year, 1807, he commanded the right wing of the Grand Army in Poland. At the close of this campaign he was created Duke of Rivoli, and presented by Bonaparte with a large sum of money with which to support his new title.

In 1810, Napoleon placed him over the army in Portugal. Reducing Ciudad Rodrigo, after three months' siege, and taking Almeida, he advanced on Wellington, who retreated to the Torres Vedras. Here the English commander entrenched himself, and bid defiance to Massena, who, finding himself unable to dislodge him, and famine and sickness in the mean time wasting his army, was compelled to commence a disastrous and barbarous retreat into Spain. He was shortly after recalled, and from his infirm health and shattered constitution, was left behind in the fatal Russian Expedition, though against his earnest request.

This ended his military career. He was at Toulon when told that Bonaparte landed from Elba. He could not at first believe the report, but was soon convinced of its truth by a letter from Napoleon himself. "Prince," said he, "hoist the banner of Essling on the walls of Toulon and follow me." But the old Marshal refused to break his new allegiance till the surrounding cities had gone over, and the Bourbon cause was evidently lost. He took no part in the military preparations during the Hundred Days, and after the overthrow of the Emperor at Waterloo was appointed by Louis commander of the National Guard, and was one of the council appointed to try Ney. But the old Marshal declared the court incompetent to perform such a task, and would have nothing to do with the dishonour and murder of his old comrade in arms.

Massena possessed scarcely a trait either of the Italian or French character, though, from his birth-place, he might be supposed to exhibit something of both. He was not an impulsive man like Junot or Murat, nor an impetuous creature like Lannes. He was not easily excited, but when once aroused he was one of the most terrible men in Bonaparte's army. He was like an enormous wheel that requires a great deal of force to set it in motion, but when it does move it crushes every thing in its passage. Perhaps the prominent trait in his character was fixedness of purpose. He was more like Ney in this respect than any other of Napoleon's marshals. His tenacity was like death itself. A battle with him never seemed over, unless he gained it. This obstinacy of resolution never forsook him. I do not know an instance in his whole career, where he appeared the least affected by the panic of others. The cry of *sauve qui peut*, never hastened his footsteps, or disturbed the regular movement of his thoughts. His own iron will was sufficient for any emergency. He wished no aid or sympathy from others to steady him, but fell back on himself in the most desperate straits with a confidence that was sublime. Amid the wildest hurricane of cavalry face to face, with a hotly-worked battery, while his dead and dying guard lay in heaps around him, or retreating before an overwhelming force he was the same self-collected and self-poised man. Amid the disordered ranks he stood like a rock amid the waves, and hurled back from his firm breast the chaos that threatened to sweep every thing away. His stubbornness of will, however, was not mere mulish obstinacy, which is simply aversive to change of purpose, but was based on decisions which evinced the soundest judgment and a most active and vigorous mind. It is true that his hatred of defeat, combined with his stubborn resolution, sometimes caused him to err in exposing his men to useless slaughter.

He was brave as courage itself, and constitutionally so. It required no excitement to bring him up. He did not seem to be aware of danger, and acted, not so much like a man who has made up his mind to meet the perils that environ him heroically, as like one who is perfectly unconscious of their existence. His frame corresponded with his character, and seemed made of iron; his endurance was wonderful. He had one peculiar trait he grew clearheaded amid the disorder of battle. It is said that on ordinary occasions he appeared dull and heavy, and his remarks were of the most ordinary kind; but the thunder of cannon cleared up his ideas and set his mind in motion. The effect of the first report of cannon, as it rolled heavily away over the field, shaking the plain with its sullen jar, was almost instantaneous, and his mind not only became active, but cheerful. It was the kind of music he liked, and his strong, ambitious nature beat time to it. Neither was this a momentary excitement, but a steady effect continuing throughout the contest. Amid the wildest uproar of conflicting thousands buried in the smoke and tumult of a headlong charge his thoughts were not only clear and forcible, but indicated the man of genius. Great emergencies often call out great mental and physical efforts; but there are few men whose minds the confusion and disorder of a fierce-fought battlefield brighten up into its clearest moods. Such a man must have within him the most terrible elements of our nature. This singular characteristic gave wonderful collectedness to his manner in the midst of the fight. In front of the deadliest fire, struggling against the most desperate odds, he gave his orders and performed his evolutions without the least agitation or alarm. He never seemed disheartened by any reverses, and fought after a defeat with the same energy he did after a victory.

This self-control this wonderful power of will rendering a man equal in himself to any emergency is one of the rarest qualities in man. Those who judge of Massena's ability as a general seem to overlook this characteristic entirely, or place it on a par with mere animal courage. But blind, dogged resistance is one thing the same tenacity of will, combined with the powerful action of a clear and vigorous mind, is quite another. The former the most common man may possess, but the latter is found only in great men. It is mind alone that imparts that prodigious power.

Mere obstinacy secures about as many disasters as successes, but Massena acquired the title in the French army of "The Favoured Child of Victory." No man could have won that title, without genius. Nothing is more common than the absurd echo of the statement, that Napoleon's generals could do nothing of themselves, and were mere engines terrible, it is true which he brought to act on the enemy's ranks. Men talk as if those conquerors of Europe the Marshals of Napoleon were mere senseless avalanches which he hurled where he wished. But said Napoleon, when on St. Helena, "Massena was a superior man; he was eminently noble and brilliant when surrounded by the fire and the disorder of battle. The sound of guns cleared his ideas, and gave him understanding, penetration, and cheerfulness. He was endowed with extraordinary courage and firmness, which seemed to increase in excess of danger. When defeated, he was always ready to fight the battle again, as though he had been the conqueror."

This is as true as any criticism Bonaparte ever passed on any of his marshals. The remark respecting his courage increasing "in excess of danger," is especially so. There seemed an exhaustless reserve force in him, which came forth as the storm gathered darker and the dangers thickened around him. That force his will could not summon up perilous crises alone could do it, and then his very look and voice were terrible. Towering in front of his shattered column, he moved like the God of War, amid the tempest that beat upon him. Sometimes, when moving into the very teeth of destruction, he would encourage his shrinking troops by putting his hat on his sword and lifting it over his head, and thus, like a pillar of fire to his men, march straight on death. There cannot be a more touching eulogy than that passed on Massena and others by Napoleon when, sad and disheartened, he wrote from before

Mantua to the Directory, informing it of his perilous position. Said he, "I despair of preventing the rising of the blockade of Mantua; should that disaster arise, we shall soon be behind the Adda, and perhaps over the Alps. The wounded are few, but they are the *élite* of the army. Our best officers are struck down; the army of Italy, reduced to a handful of heroes, is exhausted. The heroes of Lodi, of Millesimo, of Castiglione, of Bassano, are dead or in hospitals. Joubert, Lanusse, Victor, Murat, and Charlot are wounded; we are abandoned in the extremity of Italy. Perhaps the hour of the brave Augereau, of the intrepid Massena, of Berthier, is about to strike; what then will become of these brave soldiers?" In his moments of despondency he confesses how he leans on such men as Massena. Well he might, for a short time after, in the terrible fight on the dikes of Ronco, and at the passage of Arcole, another of his props went down in Lannes, and Massena escaped almost by a miracle. In the wasting fire to which he was exposed, Massena could not bring his men to charge, except by placing himself at the head of the column, and lifting his chapeau on the point of his sword above his head, and thus moving to the onset. It is said that his bearing on this occasion was magnificent. As his column moved along the dike, he was seen in front bareheaded, with his glittering sword stretched high over his head, on the point of which swung his hat as a banner to the ranks that pressed after; while his hair streamed in the storm of battle, and his piercing eye flashed fire, as it surveyed the dangers that encompassed him. Thus, again and again did he charge on a run through the tempest of shot that swept everything down around him, and by this course alone was enabled to maintain his ground during the day.

But with all Massena's bravery, and firmness, and genius, he had some traits of character that stained his reputation and dimmed his glory. He was rapacious, it cannot be denied though not to the extent his enemies assert and at times cruel. He seemed almost entirely wanting in human sympathy, and cared no more for the lives of others than for his own, which was apparently not at all.

In the battle of Rivoli, which took place the winter after that of Arcole, Massena exhibited that insensibility to fatigue which always characterized him, and which he, by constant, unwearied discipline, imparted to his soldiers. In this engagement, Bonaparte opposed thirty thousand men to forty thousand. He arrived on the elevated plain of Rivoli at 2 o'clock on the Morning Of the 14th of January. The heights around were illuminated by the innumerable fires of the bivouacs of the enemy, revealing the immense force he was about to struggle against. Nothing daunted, however, he formed his army under the light of the silver moon that was sailing through the midnight heavens, shedding its quiet light on the snow-covered Alps, and casting in deeper shadow the dark fir-trees that clasped their precipitous sides; and by nine in the morning was ready for action. The Austrian columns, moving down from the heights of the Montebaldo, which lay in a semicircle around the French army, fell on the left with such power that it was forced back and overthrown. While the Austrians were following up this success, and the position of the French was every moment becoming more critical, the village of Rivoli, near by, suddenly rang with the clatter of horses' hoofs. Bonaparte, with his guard, was plunging through on a fierce gallop, to the head-quarters of Massena. This indomitable chief had marched the whole night, and was now resting his troops before leading them into action. In a moment Massena was on horseback, and, forming his weary troops into column, charged the Austrians in front with such desperation that they were forced to fall back, and the combat was restored. Bonaparte never called on the intrepid Massena in vain, and all that day he fought with resistless bravery.

The doubtful and bloody contest was at length at nightfall decided in favour of the French. But there was another Austrian army farther down, on the Lower Adige, where Augereau's position was every hour becoming more critical. With Massena and a part of his division, which had marched all the previous night, and fought with unconquerable resolution the whole day, he started for Mantua. These indomitable troops, with their chief at their head, moved off as if fresh from their bivouacs, rather than wearied with a whole night's rapid march, and a succeeding day of hard fighting, and marched all that night and the following day, and arrived after dark in the neighbourhood of Mantua. At day-break the battle was again raging, and, before night, Bonaparte was a second time victorious.

The next year found Berthier governor of Rome, and practicing the most extensive system of pillage on the poor pope and his Ecclesiastical States. The soldiers at length became exasperated with the excesses of their commander, and to check the insubordination, Massena was appointed to supersede him. All the officers, from the captains down, had assembled and drawn up a protest against the conduct of Berthier. Massena, as soon as he assumed the command, ordered the insubordinate troops, except three thousand, to leave the capital. But they refused to march, and assembling again, drew up another remonstrance complained of Massena accused him of pillaging the Venetian States, and practicing extortion and immoralities of every kind. Even his iron hand was not strong enough to reduce the soldiers to allegiance, and, throwing up the command, he retired to Arona.

While Bonaparte was in Egypt, Massena was first appointed commander-in-chief over the army of Switzerland, and afterward superseded Jourdan over those of the Switzerland and the Rhine together. After suffering various losses, and being finally driven from Zurich, he at length retrieved his fame by a masterly movement and great victory, and evinced not only his unconquerable tenacity by fighting his lost battles over again, but also his consummate skill as a general in arranging his plan of attack.

The battle of Zurich, to which reference is made also in the articles on Oudinot and Soult, was perhaps one of the most glorious ones he ever fought. After a series of disasters and repulses, he found himself between two armies, for Suwarrow was marching over the St. Gallord on his rear, while Korsakow occupied Zurich in front. In this critical position he determined to fall on Korsakow before Suwarrow could come up. By a series of able movements, he succeeded completely in his plans, and hemming in Zurich, crashed with a single blow the Russian army. He then directed his concentrated strength on the victorious Sawarrow, as he came pouring his columns over the Alps. He turned this Russian bear at Lucerne, and forced him over a succession of mountains, along paths where only one man could tread at a time. He met him in the Muthenthal, and sending havoc through his ranks, compelled him again to take to the mountains. He followed on his flying traces, and while the disordered army was dragging its weary length over the precipices and Alpine passes, and through the snow, leaving its weary soldiers as bloody testimonials of its passage on every cliff and foot of ground, he thundered on it with his fierce battalions, and strewed the Alpine summits with the dead. In a fortnight he had beaten two armies, and slain and wounded nearly thirty thousand Austrians and Russians. He broke up the coalition between Austria and Russia, and saved France, when midnight darkness was enveloping her prospects. Says

Thiers, in speaking of these victories, "Everlasting glory to Massena, who thus executed one of the most admirable operations recorded in the history of the war, and who saved us at a more perilous moment than that of Valmi and Fleurus! .... Zurich is the brightest jewel in Massena's coronet, and there is not a military coronet that bears one more brilliant."

But perhaps there is no greater illustration of Massena's firmness, courage, and force combined, than the manner in which he sustained....

THE SIEGE OF GENOA

After Bonaparte's return from Egypt, he appointed Massena over the army of Italy. Moreau, at the head of a hundred and thirty thousand men, was to advance on Swabia, while Napoleon himself, at the head of forty thousand, was to march over the Alps.

The 60,000 soldiers given to Massena had dwindled down through fever and famine to about 36,000 fighting men, which were required to defend both Genoa and Nice, though a hundred and twenty miles apart. Melas, with 120,000 soldiers in good condition, was the enemy he had to oppose. Leaving, 50,000 in Piedmont to watch the passes of the Alps, Melas bore down with 70,000 on the gorges of the Apennines, for the purpose of cutting the French army in two, and shutting one half up in Nice, and the other half in Genoa. This he succeeded in doing; and though Suchet and Soult fought with unexampled bravery, the French line was divided, and the former separated from each other. The latter was now compelled to fall back on Genoa, with only 18,000 men. On the evening of the 6th of April, the Austrian flag was flying on the heights that overlooked the city; while at the same time a British squadron was seen slowly moving up the gulf to shut it in seaward. Without the speedy appearance of a French army over the Alps, that of Massena was evidently a doomed one. He knew that he could hold the place against all the force that could be brought against it; but the convoys of provisions, which had been kept back by adverse winds, were now effectually shut out by the English blockading squadron; while the Austrians, sweeping in an entire line round the walls of the city, were rapidly cutting off all supplies from the country, so that famine would soon waste his army. But it was in the midst of difficulties like these, that Massena's spirit rose in its strength. He seemed to multiply with exigencies, and there commenced with the siege of Genoa one of the most heroic struggles witnessed during the War.

Genoa is defended, both by nature and art, as I have never seen any other seaport. The Ligurian Gulf strikes it head deep into the Apennines, so that the ground slopes from the very verge of the water up to the mountain. Two moles running from the opposite shores, almost cross each other, cutting off the extreme point of the bay for the port of the city. Perpendicular walls rise from the water, forming the base of the houses that line the shore. Around these cannon are planted, while forts are on every commanding point above the city. Added to this, a double wall surrounds the town, one six miles in circumference, the other thirteen. The outer walls, corresponding to the shape of the hill, ascend it somewhat in the form of a triangle.

Two forts, the Spur and the Diamond, stood at the top of this triangle, protecting the fortified walls down on either side by their commanding fire. There were three other forts on the east side of the city, protecting commanding eminences that rose from the river Bisagno. On the west, or towards Nice, there were no forts, and the Polcevera came pouring its waters into the gulf without furnishing any strong positions.

Thus defended, Massena saw the immense Austrian army slowly contracting its lines around the city, like a huge anaconda tightening its folds about its victim. He immediately resolved to attempt two desperate projects first, to sally out on the east with his handful of men, and drive the enemy over the Apennines and afterwards to sally forth on the west side and endeavour to cut the Austrian army in two, and restore his junction with Suchet. Following out his daring plans, he on the 7th of April took Gen. Miollis's division, strengthened by some of the reserve, and dividing it into two columns, marched forth at their head to storm the heights of Monte Ratti. The Austrians were driven from every position by the desperate charges of the French columns, and forced over the Apennines; and Massena returned at evening, marching before him fifteen hundred prisoners, and among others the Baron D'Aspres, who had incited the peasants to a revolt. The inhabitants were crazy with excitement, rending the air with acclamations and shouts of joy bringing litters for the wounded, and soup for the brave soldiers, and urging them into their houses proud of the honour of sheltering one of the defenders of their city.

Allowing only one day to intervene, Massena on the 9th of April sallied forth on the west side of the town, in order to carry out his plan of effecting his junction with Suchet. Word had been sent to the latter general of the premeditated attack, with orders to rush on the Austrian forces on the opposite side, and cut his way through. Massena took ten thousand men with him, leaving the remainder to protect the city. Gazan's division he put under Soult, with orders to keep along the ridge of the Apennines, while he, at the head of Gardanne's division, kept along the sea-coast below, the junction to take place at Sassello. Ten thousand French were on the march to meet forty thousand Austrians, under Melas. Soult, reaching Aqua Santa, made a brilliant charge on a superior body of Austrians, which threatened to cut off the retreat to Genoa. But this fierce battle prevented him from being at Sassello, when Massena expected him, which broke up the plans of the latter so entirely, that had he been a less resolute and invincible man, it would have secured his ruin.

Marching unmolested along the beautiful riviera or sea coast the first day, he came the second day upon the enemy. His force was divided into two columns, one of which he led in person. Supposing Soult to be at Sassello, and wishing to establish a communication with him, he had pushed on with only twelve hundred men, relying on big right column, now far in the rear, and Soult, to sustain him.

In this position nearly ten thousand Austrians moved down upon him, and endeavoured to enclose and crush him. Then commenced one of those desperate struggles for which Massena was so remarkable. With his 1200 men he kept the whole 10,000 at bay, while he slowly retreated in search of his lost column. Charge after charge of the overwhelming force of the Austrians was made on his little band; but he held it by his presence to the shock, with a firmness that perfectly surprised the enemy. Now it would be perfectly enveloped and lost in the cloud of the enemy that curtained it in, and the next moment it would emerge from the thick masses of infantry, and appear unbroken with its indomitable chief still at its head. Unable to find the column which had lagged far behind, on account of the tardy distribution of provisions, he scaled precipices, plunged into ravines, and cast himself among bands of hostile peasantry, fighting all the while like a lion. Having, at length found it, he rallied his troops, and determined to cross the Apennines, and reach Soult, also. But his men were worn out with the desperate fighting of the day, and could not be rallied soon enough to make the attempt successful. So, sending off all that were ready to march, as a reinforcement to Soult, who was struggling in the mountains against the most desperate odds, he fell back along the sea-coast to protect the entrance to the city. His company now being dwindled to a mere handful, it seemed as if every charge of the mighty force that rushed on it must sweep it away. But still Massena, a host in himself, towered unhurt at its head. At length, however, his overthrow seemed inevitable. A sudden charge of Austrian hussars had surprised one of his battalions, and it was just laying down its arms, when, seeing the danger, he rallied with incredible rapidity thirty horsemen about him, and fell like a thunderbolt on the entire company. Stunned and driven back, they lost their advantage, and the battalion was saved. At length Soult, after proving himself fifty times a hero, joined him: and together, cutting their way through the enemy, they re-entered Genoa with *four thousand prisoners* more than half the number of the whole army that led them captive. When the Genoese saw him return with his handful of men, preceded by such a column of prisoners, their admiration and wonder knew no bounds, and Massena's power at once became supreme.

But now he was fairly shut in. His army of eighteen thousand had become reduced to about twelve thousand fighting men. These, and over five thousand prisoners and the population, were to be fed from the scanty provisions which the city contained. But in the midst of the darkness that now hung over his prospects, Massena walked with a calm and resolute demeanour,

looking the sufferings that awaited him and his army full in the face, without one thought of surrendering.

At length, one morning about a fortnight after this last sally, a general cannonading was heard all around the city, even from the gunboats on the sea, telling of some movement of the enemy. A general assault was making on Fort Diamond, which, if taken, would shut up the army in the inner wall of the city. The plateau in front of the fort was carried by them, and the fort itself summoned to surrender. The Austrians were gaining ground every moment, and threatened to carry the position of the Madonna del Monte, from which the city could be cannonaded. Fort Quezzi had been taken, and Fort Richelieu was now threatened. The French were driven back on all sides, when Massena at noon hastened to the spot. He ordered Soult, with two demi-brigades, to retake the plateau in front of Fort Diamond, while he himself advanced on Fort Quezzi. Around the latter place the struggle became desperate. Col. Mouton, after performing almost incredible deeds of daring, fell, pierced by a musket ball. The combatants had advanced so close to each other that they could not fire, and fought with stones and clubbed muskets. But superior numbers were fast telling on the French, and they were on the point of breaking, when Massena hurled his reserve, composed of only half a battalion, on the enemy. He himself was at its head, cheering it by his presence and voice; and, dividing the enemy before him as the rock flings aside the stream, he swept the dense masses of the enemy over their own dead and wounded from the field.

Soult was equally successful, and Massena returned at evening with 1600 prisoners, having slain and wounded 2400 more. For three weeks be had fought an army of 40,000 men with one of 12,000 in the open country, and had slain and taken prisoners in all nearly 15,000 men, or almost the entire number of the whole army he had led into Genoa. Nearly every man had killed or taken his man, and yet there were 12,000 left to struggle on.

On the 10th of May Massena made another successful sally with his diminished army. General Ott, of the Austrians, had sent a boast to him that he had gained a victory over Suchet, which was a falsehood. The only reply the marshal made to it was to fall on him with his brave columns. The Austrians were hurled back by his irresistible onset, and he returned at evening with 1500 more prisoners. Nothing shows the indomitable resolution and power of the man more than these successive assaults.

Nothing could much longer withstand such superiority of numbers; still, three days after his last victory, another assault was made on Monte Creto. Massena was opposed to this movement, for he saw that his exhausted army was not equal to storming a position so strongly defended as this. But he yielded to the urgent solicitation of his under officers; and the iron-souled Soult was allowed, at his own urgent request, to make the attempt. He ascended the slope with a firm step, and fought, as he ever had done, with a valour that threatened to overleap every obstacle, when suddenly amid the uproar of battle a thunder-cloud was seen to sweep over the mountain. The lightning mingled in with the flash of musketry, while the rapid thunder-peals rolled over the struggling hosts, presenting to the spectators a scene of indescribable sublimity. In the midst of this war of the elements and war of men, Soult fell on the field. This decided the contest, and the French were driven for the first time before the enemy. Soult, with a broken leg, was taken prisoner.

This ended the severe fighting with the enemy, and now the whole struggle was to be with famine. Bonaparte knew the distress of his general, and he wrote to Moreau to accelerate his movements on the Rhine, so that Massena could be assisted. "That general," said he in his letter to Moreau, "wants provisions. For fifteen days he has been enduring with his debilitated soldiers the struggle of despair." And, indeed, it was the struggle of despair. Napoleon was doing, but too late, what could be done. His magnificent army was hanging along the Alpine cliffs of San Bernard, while Lannes was pouring his victorious columns into the plains of Italy. But famine was advancing as fast as they. The women ran furiously through the city ringing bells and calling out for food. Loaded cannon were arranged in the streets to restrain the maddened populace, The corn was all gone even the beans and oats had failed them. The meat was consumed, and the starving soldiers fell on their horses. These, too, were at length consumed, and then the most loathsome animals were brought out and slain for food. Massena, still unyielding and unsubdued, collected all the starch, linseed and cacao in the city, and had them made into bread, which even many of the hardy soldiers could not digest. But they submitted to their sufferings without a murmur. On its being suggested to them that their general would now surrender "*He* surrender!" they exclaimed; "he would sooner make us eat our very boots." They knew the character of the chieftain who had so often led them into battle, and he held over them the sway of a great and lofty mind.

But the distress increased every day. Wan and wretched beings strolled about the streets, and, wasted with famine, fell dead beside the walls of the palaces. Emaciated women, no longer able to nourish their infants, roamed about with piteous cries, reaching out their starving offspring for help. The brave soldiers who had struggled for the past month so heroically against the foe, now went staggering through the streets faint for want of food. The sentinels could no longer stand at their posts, and were allowed to mount guard seated. The most desolate cries and lamentations loaded the midnight air; while at intervals came the thunder of cannon and the light of the blazing bomb as it hung like a messenger of death over the city. Added to all, rumours were abroad that the inhabitants were about to revolt and fall on the exhaust army. Still Massena remained unshaken. Amid the dead he moved with the same calm resolute mien that he was wont to do amid the storm of battle. He, who could stand unmoved amid the shock of armies, could also meet without fear the slow terrors of famine. His *moral* power was now more controlling than the command he held. He disdained to reserve any food for himself, but fared like the most common soldier. Though burdened with the cares and responsibilities that pressed him down, he ate the miserable soup and more disgusting bread of the starving soldier, sharing cheerfully with him his dangers and his sufferings. He, too, felt the power of famine on his own nature. Day by day he felt the blood course more sluggishly through his veins, and night by night he lay down gnawed by the pangs of hunger. His iron frame grew thin, and his bronze cheek emaciated, yet his brave heart beat calm and resolute as ever. The eye that never blenched even at the cannon's mouth now surveyed the distress and woe about him with the composure of one who is above the power of fate.

But now a new cause of alarm arose. The seven or eight thousand prisoners, grown desperate with famine, threatened every day to break out in open revolt. Massena had furnished them the same supplies he did his own soldiers, and sent first to the Austrian commander and then to Lord Kieth to supply them with provisions, giving his word of honour that none of them should go to the garrison. They refusing to obey his request, he was compelled, in self-defence, to shut up the miserable creatures in some old bulks of vessels which he anchored out in the port, and then directed some of his heaviest guns to be trained on them to sink them the moment the sufferers should break loose. The cries and howls of these wretched thousands struck terror to the boldest heart; and the muffled sound rising night and day over the city, drew tears of pity even from those who themselves were slowly perishing with famine.

Still Massena would not yield. A courier sent from Bonaparte had passed by night through the English fleet in an open boat, and though discovered in the morning, and pursued, had boldly leaped into the sea with his sword in his mouth, and, amid the bullets that hailed around him, swam safely to the shore. Massena thus knew that Bonaparte was on the Alps, and determined to hold out till the last. But several days had now passed, and no farther tidings were heard of him. Many of the soldiers in despair broke their arms, and others plotted a revolt. In this desperate strait Massena issued a proclamation to them, appealing to their bravery and honour, and pointing to the example of their officers enduring the same privations with themselves. He told them Bonaparte was marching towards the city, and would soon deliver them. But the weary days seemed ages, and when nearly a fortnight had passed without tidings, the last gleam of hope seemed about to expire. But suddenly one morning a heavy rumbling sound was heard rolling over the Apennines, like the dull report of distant cannon. The joy of the soldiers and populace knew no bounds. "Bonaparte is come!" ran like wild-fire through the city. "We hear his cannon towards Bochetta!" they exclaimed in transport, and rushed into each other's arms, and ran in crowds towards the ramparts to catch more distinctly the joyful sound. Massena himself hurried to the heights of Tanailles. Hope quickened his steps as the faint but heavy echo broke over the city and a gleam of joy shot over his countenance as he should be saved the mortification of a surrender. But as he stood on the ramparts and gazed off in the direction of the sound that had awakened such extravagant joy in the hearts of the besieged, he saw only the edge of a thunder-cloud on the distant horizon; and what had been taken for the thunder of Bonaparte's cannon was only the hoarse "mutterings of the storm in the gorges of the Apennines." The reaction on the soldiers and people was dreadful. Blank melancholy and utter despair settled on every face, and Massena that he must at last yield; for even of the loathsome bread on which they had been kept alive there remained only two ounces to each man, and if they subsisted any longer it must be on each other. But the indomitable veteran did not despair until even these two ounces were gone, and even then he delayed. "*Give me*," said lie to the Genoese, in the anguish of his great heart, "*give me only two days' provisions, or one, and I will save you from the Austrian yoke, and my army the pain of a surrender.*" But it could not be done, and he who deserved to be crowned thrice conqueror, was compelled to treat with the enemy he had so often vanquished.

The Austrian general, knowing his desperate condition, demanded that he should surrender at discretion. Massena, in reply, told him that his army must be allowed to march out with colours flying, with all their arms and baggage, and not as prisoners of war, but liberty to fight when and where they pleased the moment they were outside the Austrian lines. "*If you do not grant me this,*" said the iron-willed chieftain, "*I will sally forth from Genoa sword in hand. With eight thousand famished men I will attack your camp, and I will fight till I cut my way through it*" and he would have done it, too. General Ott, fearing the action of such a leader the moment he should join Suchet, agreed to the terms if Massena would surrender *himself* prisoner of war. This the old soldier indignantly refused. It was then proposed that the troops should depart by sea, so as not to join Suchet's corps in time to render any assistance in the opening campaign of Bonaparte. To all these propositions Massena had but one reply: "Take my terms, or I will cut my way through your army." General Ott knew the character of the man he bad to deal with too well to allow things to come to such an issue, and so granted him his own terms. When leaving, Massena said to the Austrian general, "I give you notice that ere fifteen days are passed I shall be once more in Genoa" and he was.

Thus fell Genoa, defended by one of the bravest men that ever trod a battle-field. Nine days after, the battle of Marengo was fought, and Italy was once more in the hands of France.

I have thus gone over the particulars of this siege, because it exhibits all the great traits of Massena's character. His talents as a commander are seen in the skill with which he planned his repeatedly successful attacks, and the subordination in which he kept his soldiers and the populace amid all the horrors of famine his bravery, in the courage with which he resisted forces outnumbering his own ten to one, and the personal exposure he was compelled to make to save himself from defeat and his invincible firmness, in the tenacity with which he fought every battle, and the calmness with which he endured the privations and horrors of famine. His fixed resolution to cut his way through the Austrian host with his famished band, rather than yield himself prisoner of war, shows the unconquerable nature he possessed. With such leaders, no wonder Bonaparte swept Europe with his victorious armies. Neither is it surprising that, five years after, we find Napoleon intrusting him with the entire command of the army in Italy, although the Archduke Charles was his antagonist. He conducted himself worthy of his former glory in this short but brilliant campaign; and after forcing the Adige at Verona, he assailed the whole Austrian lines at Caldiero. After two days' hard fighting repeatedly charging at the head of his column, and exposing himself to the fire of the enemy like the meanest soldier he at length, with 50,000, gained the victory over 70,000, and drove the Archduke out of Italy.

After the campaign of Eylau, in 1807, Massena returned to Paris, and appeared at court. But his blunt, stern nature could not bend to its etiquette and idle ceremonies and he grew restless and irritable. It was no place for a man like him. But this peaceful spot proved more dangerous than the field of battle; for, hunting one day with a party of officers at St. Cloud, a shot from the grand huntsman's gun pierced his left eye and destroyed it forever. He had gone through fifty pitched battles, stormed batteries, and walked unhurt amid the most wasting fire, and received his first wound in a hunting excursion.

In 1809, in the campaigns of Aspern and Wagram, he added to his former renown, and was one of the firm props of Napoleon's empire on those fiercely fought battle-fields. Previously to the battle of Aspern, and after that of Eckmuhl, while Bonaparte was on the march for Vienna, chasing the Archduke Charles before him, Massena had command of the advance-guard. Following hard after the retreating army of the Archduke, as he had done before in Italy, he came at length to the river Traun, at Ebersberg, or Ebersdorf, a small village on its banks, just above where it falls into the Danube. Here, for a while, an effectual stop seemed put to his victorious career, for this stream, opposite Ebersberg, was crossed by a single long, narrow wooden bridge. From shore to shore, across the sandbanks, islands, &c., it was nearly half a mile, and a single narrow causeway traversed the entire distance to the bridge, which itself was about sixty rods long. Over this half mile of narrow path the whole army was to pass, and the columns to charge; for the deep, impetuous torrent could not be forded. But a gate closed the farther end of the bridge, while the houses filled with soldiers enfiladed the entire opening, and the artillery planted on the heights over it commanded every inch of the passage. The high-rolling ground along the river was black with the masses of infantry, sustained by heavy batteries, all trained on that devoted bridge, apparently enough in themselves to tear it into fragments. To crown the whole, an old castle frowned over the stream, on whose crumbling battlements cannon were planted so as also to command the bridge. As if this were not enough to deter any man from attempting the passage, another row of heights, over which the road passed, rose behind the first, covered with pine-trees, affording a strong position for the enemy to retire to if driven from their first.

Thus defended, thirty-five thousand men, supported by eighty cannon, waited to see if the French would attempt to pass. Even the genius and boldness of Massena might have been staggered at the spectacle before him. It seemed like marching his army into the mouth of the volcano to advance on the batteries that commanded that long, narrow passage. It was not to be a sudden charge over a short causeway, but a steady march along a close defile through a perfect tempest of balls. But this was the key to Vienna, and the Marshal resolved to make the attempt hoping that Lannes, who was to cross some distance farther up, would aid him by a movement on the enemy's flank.

The Austrians had foolishly left four battalions on the side from which the French approached. These attacked, were driven from their position, and forced along the causeway at the point of the bayonet, and on the bridge, followed by the pursuing French. But the moment the French column touched the bridge, those hitherto silent batteries opened their dreadful fire on its head. It sank like a sand-bank that caves under the torrent. To advance seemed impossible; but the heroic Cohorn, flinging himself in front, cheered them on, and they returned to the charge, driving like an impetuous torrent over the crashing timbers. Amid the confusion and chaos of the fight between these flying battalions and their pursuers, the Austrians on the shore saw the French colours flying, and fearing the irruption of the enemy with their friends, closed the gate and poured their tempest of bullets on friend and foe alike. The carnage then became awful. Smitten in front by the deadly fire of their friends, and pressed with the bayonets behind by their foes, those battalions threw selves into the torrent below, or were trampled under foot by the steadily advancing column. Amid the explosion of ammunition wagons in the midst, blowing men into the air, and the crashing fire of the enemy's cannon, the French beat down the gate and palisades and rushed with headlong speed into the streets of the village. But here, met by fresh battalions in front and riddled through by a destructive cross-fire from the houses, while the old castle burled its storm of lead on their heads, these brave soldiers were compelled to retire, leaving two thirds of their number stretched on the pavement. But Massena ordered up fresh battalions, which, marching through the tempest that swept the bridge, joined their companions, and regaining the village, stormed the castle itself. Along the narrow lanes that led to it, the dead lay in swathes, and no sooner did the mangled head of the column reach the castle walls, than it disappeared before the plunging fire from the battlements, as if it sunk into the earth. Strengthened by a new reinforcement, the dauntless French returned to the assault, and, battering down the doors, compelled the garrison to surrender. The Austrian army, however, made good their position on the pine-covered ridge behind the village, and disputed every inch with the most stubborn resolution. The French cavalry, now across, came on a furious gallop through the streets of the village, trampling on the dead and dying, and amid the flames of the burning houses, and through the smoke that rolled over their pathway, hurried forward with exulting shouts and rattling armour to the charge. Still the Austrians held out, till, threatened with a flank attack, they were compelled to retreat.

There was not a more desperate passage in the whole war than this. Massena was compelled to throw his brave soldiers, whether dead or wounded, into the stream, to clear a passage for the columns. Whole companies falling at a time, they choked up the way and increased the obstacles to be overcome. These must be sacrificed; or the whole shattered column that was maintaining their desperate position on the farther side be annihilated. It was an appalling spectacle to see the advancing soldiers, amid the most destructive fire themselves, pitch their wounded comrades, while calling out most piteously to be spared, by scores and hundreds into the torrent. Le Grand fought nobly that day. Amid the choked-up defile and the close fire of the batteries, he fiercely pressed on, and in answer to the advice of his superior officer, deigned only the stern "*Room for the head of my columns none of your advice!*" and rushed up to the very walls of the castle.

The nature of the contest, and the narrow bridge and streets in which it ranged, gave to the field of battle a most horrid aspect. The dead lay in heaps and ridges piled one across the other, mangled and torn in the most dreadful manner by the hoofs of the cavalry and the wheels of the artillery which were compelled to pass over them. *Twelve thousand* men thus lay heaped, packed and trampled together, while across them were stretched burning rafters and timbers which wrung still more heart-rending cries and shrieks from the dying mass. Even Bonaparte, when he arrived, shuddered at the appalling sight, and turned with horror from the scene. The streets were one mass of mangled, bleeding, trampled men, overlaid with burning ruins. Napoleon blamed Massena for this act, saying he should have waited for the flank movement of Lannes; but I suspect this was done simply as a salvo to his own conscience as he looked at the spectacle before him.- If Massena had not made the attempt, he would, undoubtedly, have been blamed still more.

This opened Vienna to the French army, and eighteen days after, the battle of Aspern was fought. I have already, when speaking of Marshal Lannes, described that engagement. It will be seen by referring to that description that Massena and Lannes were the two heroes of that disastrous battle. They occupied the two villages of Aspern and Essling, which formed the two extremities of the French lines. At the commencement of the fight, Massena's position was in the cemetery of Aspern. Here he stood under the trees that overshadowed the church, and directed the defence. Calm and collected as he ever was in the heat of the conflict, he surveyed without alarm the dangers that environed him. The onset of the Austrian battalions was tremendous, as they came on with shouts that rang over the roar of cannon. But Massena calmly stood, and watching every assailed point, supported it in the moment of need, while the huge branches above his head were constantly rending with the storm of cannon balls that swept through them, and the steeple and roof of the church rattled with the hail-storm of bullets that the close batteries hurled upon them. The conflict, became murderous, but never did he exhibit greater courage or more heroic firmness. He was everywhere present, steadying his men by his calm, stern voice, and reckless exposure of his person, and again and again wringing victory out of the very grasp of the enemy. Thus, hour after hour, he fought, until night closed over the scene and then, by the light of blazing bombs and burning houses, and flash of Austrian batteries, he continued the contest with the determination of one who would not be beat. When an advancing column recoiled before the close and fatal fire to which it was exposed, he would rush to its head, and crying "Forward!" to his men, carry them into the very jaws of death. In the midst of one of these desperate charges, every one of his guard fell by his side dead or wounded, and he stood all amid the storm that wasted so fearfully around him; yet, strange to say, he was not even wounded.

But at length, after the most superhuman efforts, he was forced from the village amid the victorious shouts of the Austrians. But he would not be driven off, and returned to the attack with unbroken courage, and succeeded in wringing some of the houses from the victors, which he retained through the night. The next morning, being always ready to fight a lost battle over again he made a desperate assault on Aspern, and carried it. Again he stood in the churchyard where he so calmly commenced the battle; but it was now literally loaded with the dead, which outnumbered those above whose tombs they lay. But after the most heroic defence he was again driven out, and the repulse of Lannes' column on the centre, soon after, completed the disaster.

In the disastrous retreat of the French army across the Danube in the midst of the battle, Massena exhibited his unconquerable tenacity of will, and disputed every inch of ground as if his life were there. When the victorious Austrians pressed upon the ranks, crowded on the banks of the river, he and Lannes, as before remarked, alone prevented an utter rout. They fought side by side with a heroism that astonished even Napoleon. Lannes fell, but this only increased Massena's almost superhuman exertions to save the army. Now on horseback, while the artillery swept down everything around him, and now on foot to steady the shaking ranks or head a desperate charge, he multiplied with the dangers that encompassed him. He acted as if he bore a charmed life, and rode and charged through the tempest of balls with a daring that filled the soldiers with astonishment, and animated them with tenfold courage. His eye burned like fire, and his countenance, lit up by the terrible excitement that mastered him, gave him the most heroic appearance as he stormed through the battle. No wonder that Bonaparte, as he leaned on his shoulder afterwards, exclaimed, "Behold my right arm!" For the assistance he rendered in this engagement he received the title of "Prince of Essling."

Massena was with Bonaparte while he lay cooped up in the island of Lobau waiting for reinforcements, so that he could retrieve his heavy losses. Here again he was the victim of an accident that well nigh deprived him of life. Though he had moved unharmed amid so many conflicts, and bore a charmed life when death was abroad on the battle-field mowing down men by thousands, and exposed his person with a recklessness that seemed downright madness, with perfect impunity; yet here, while superintending some works on the Danube, his horse stumbling, he fell to the ground, and was so injured that he was unable for a long time to sit on horseback. There seems a fatality about some men. Massena had more than once fallen from his dying steed in the headlong fight, and moved in front of his column into a perfect storm of musketry without receiving a scratch; and yet in a peaceful hunt, where there was no apparent danger, he lost an eye, and, riding leisurely along the shores of the Danube, was well nigh killed by a fall from his horse. But this last accident did not keep him out of battle. He was too important a leader to be missed from the field. Lannes was gone, and to lose two such men was like losing thirty thousand soldiers.

At the battle of Wagram, which took place soon after, he went into the field at the head of his corps in a calash. Being still an invalid, one of the surgeons belonging to the medical staff accompanied him, as he did in several other battles. It is said that Massena was exceedingly amused by the agitation the timorous doctor exhibited the moment the carriage came within range of the enemy's batteries. He would start at every explosion of the artillery, and then address some remark to the old marshal, as much as to say, "You see I am not frightened at all;" and again, as a cannon ball went whizzing by, or ploughed up the ground near the wheels, would grow pale, and turn and twist in the greatest alarm, asking of the probability and chances of being hit. The old veteran enjoyed his distress exceedingly, and would laugh and joke at his fears in great delight. But when the storm grew thick, and the battle hot, his face would take its stern aspect, and, forgetful of the poor doctor by his side, he would drive hither and thither amid the falling ranks, giving his orders in a tone that startled this son of Esculapius almost as much as the explosion of cannon.

On the second day of the fight at Wagram, Massena's troops, after having carried the village of Aderklaa, were repulsed by a terrible discharge of grape shot and musketry, and a charge of Austrian cavalry. This being followed up by an onset from the Archduke Charles himself with his grenadiers, they fell back in confusion on the German soldiers, who, also breaking and fleeing, overturned Massena in his carriage. He was so enraged at the panic of his soldiers, that he ordered the dragoons about his person to charge them as enemies. But it seemed impossible to arrest the disorder. Spreading every moment, this part of the field appeared about to be lost. Massena, unable to mount his horse or head his columns, chafed like a lion in the toils. Disdaining to fly, he strove with his wonted bravery to rally his fugitive army. It was all in vain, and the disabled veteran was left almost alone in his chariot in the midst of the plain. Bonaparte, in the distance, saw the distress of his marshal, and came on a swift gallop over the field, pressed hard after by his brave cuirassiers and the horse artillery of the guard, which made the plain smoke and tremble in their passage. Reining up his steed beside Massena's carriage, he dismounted, and springing into the seat beside him, began to discourse, in his rapid way, of his plans. With his finger pointing now towards the steeples of Wagram, and now towards the tower of Neusiedel, he explained in a few seconds the grand movement he was about to make. Remounting his milk-white charger he restored order by his presence and personal exposure, so that the designed movements were successfully made.

Massena commanded the advance guard after this battle, and pursued the Archduke to Znaym, where the Austrians made a stand. The position was an admirable one for defence, and there was evidently to be a hard struggle before it could be carried. But Massena advanced boldly to the assault. After various successes and defeats amid the most dreadful carnage, enraged at the obstinacy of the resistance and the frequent recoil of his own troops, he declared his resolution, disabled as he was, to mount on horseback and charge at the head of his troops in person. His staff strove in vain to prevent him. With a single glance at his recoiling columns, he leaped from his carriage and sprung to his saddle, but his feet had scarcely touched the earth, before a cannon ball crushed through the centre of the vehicle, tearing it into fragments. If he had remained a moment longer he would have been killed instantaneously. Fate seemed to have a peculiar watch over him in battle, leaving him quite at the mercy of the most ordinary chance when out of it.

His conduct of the invasion of Portugal was a master-piece of generalship. With a force of between seventy and eighty thousand men, he was directed to drive Wellington out of the kingdom. Probably, Massena in no part of his military career, exhibited the qualities of a great commander so strikingly as in this campaign. Resistless in a charge firm as a rock in the hour of disaster possessed with a power of endurance seldom equalled by any man he here demonstrated also his great abilities when left alone to plan and execute a protracted war.

It would be uninteresting to go over the details of this memorable pursuit and retreat. From the first of June to the middle of October, he chased Wellington through Portugal, and for four months and a half crowded the ablest general of England backwards until he came to the lines of the Torres Vedras. The English had been engaged on these lines for a year, and they now rose before Massena, an impregnable barrier from which the tide of success must at last recoil. This monument of human skill and enterprise consisted of three lines of entrenchments one within another extending for nearly thirty miles. On these lines were a hundred and fifty redoubts and six hundred mounted cannon. This impregnable defence received Wellington and his exhausted army into its bosom, and Massena saw his foe retire from his grasp, and take up his position where his utmost exertions to dislodge him must prove abortive. To add to the security of Wellington, he here received reinforcements that swelled his army to a hundred and thirty thousand men, or more than double that of the French Marshal. To march his weary and diminished troops on these stupendous fortifications, defended by such a host, Massena saw would be utter madness. His experienced eye could sometimes see the way to success through the most overwhelming obstacles, but here there was none.

Besides the defences which here protected Wellington, there were twenty British ships of the line, and a hundred transports ready to receive the army if forced to retire. Unwilling to retreat, Massena sat down before the Torres Vedras, hoping first to draw Wellington forth with his superior force to a pitched battle in the open field. But the British commander was too wary to do this, and chose rather to provoke an assault on his entrenchments, or starve his enemy into a retreat. Massena sent off to the emperor for instructions, and then began to look about for means to provision his army. For a month the scenes of Genoa were acted over again. The army was reduced to starvation, but still he, with his wonted tenacity, refused to retreat. Wellington, in speaking of the position of the French at this time, declared that Massena provisioned his 60,000 men and 20,000 horses for two months where he could not have maintained a single division of English soldiers.

But at length, driven to the last extremity, and seeing that he must either commence a retreat at once, or his famine-stricken army would be too weak to march, he broke up his position, and began slowly to retrace his victorious steps. Arranging his troops into a compact mass, he covered it with a rear-guard under the command of Ney, and without confusion or disorder, deliberately retired from the Torres Vedras. Wellington immediately commenced the pursuit, and hovered like a destroying angel on his flight. But it was here that the extraordinary abilities of Massena shone forth in their greatest splendour, and this retreat will ever stand as a model in military history. He showed no haste or perturbation in his movements, but retired in such order and with such skill, that Wellington found it impossible to assail him with success. Taking advantage of every position offered by the country, the French Marshal would make a stand till the main body of the army and the military wagons passed on, then slowly, and in perfect order, fall back, still presenting the same adamantine wall to the foe.

Thus for more than four months in the dead of winter from the middle of November to the first of May did Massena slowly retreat towards the frontier of Portugal. At Almeida he made a stand, and the two armies prepared for battle. Wellington was posted along the heights opposite the town. The French commenced the assault, and fell with such vehemence on the British that they were driven from their position in the village of Fuentes d'Onoro. A counter-charge by the e English retrieved a part of the village, and night closed the conflict. Early next morning Massena again commenced the attack, and in a short time the battle became general. So severely was Wellington handled, he was compelled to abandon his position and take up another on a row of heights in rear of the first. In his retreat he had to cross a plateau four miles in breadth which was perfectly curtained in with French cavalry. Making his left wing a pivot, he swung his entire right in admirable order across the plain to the heights he wished to occupy. None but English infantry could have performed this perilous movement. Formed into squares, they moved steadily forward while the artillery of Ney wag thundering in their rear, and his strong columns rolling in an unbroken torrent against them. Those brave squares would at times be lost to view in the cloud of the enemy that enveloped them, and then emerge from the disorder and smoke of battle, without a formation broken, steadily executing the required movement on which the contest hung. Had they given way, Wellington would have been lost.

It was during this day that three regiments of English soldiers met the Imperial Guard in full shock, and both disdaining to yield, for the first time during the war, bayonets crossed, and the forest of steel of those two formidable masses of infantry lay levelled against each others' bosoms. The onset was made by the British, and so terrible was the shock that many of the steadfast Guard were lifted from the ground, and sent, as if hurled from a catapult, into the air. The clatter of the crossing steel and the intermingling in such wild conflict of two such bodies of men, is described as having been terrible in the extreme.

At night the English were forced back from all their positions; but the new stand Wellington had made was too formidable to be assailed, and after remaining three days before it, Massena again commenced his retreat. This ended the pursuit, and the latter fell back to Salamanca, having lost since his invasion of Portugal more than a third of his army.

The cruelties practiced during this retreat have given rise to severe accusations on the part of the British. But it remains to be shown, before they can be made good, that these were not necessary both to save himself and to harass the enemy. All war is cruel; and the desolation and barrenness that followed in the track of the French army, wasting the inhabitants with famine, were a powerful check on Wellington in his pursuit. The sympathy of the inhabitants with the English doubtless made Massena less careful of their wants and sufferings; but his barbarity has been greatly exaggerated by Walter Scott and other English historians. The track of a retreating and starving army must always be covered with woe; and one might as well complain of the cruelty of a besieging force, because the innocent women and children of the invested town die by thousands with hunger.

In 1816 the old marshal was accused in the Chamber of Deputies of plotting a conspiracy to bring back Napoleon. He indignantly and successfully repelled the charge, but the blow it gave his feelings hastened, it is thought, his death; and he died the next year at age of fifty-nine.

Massena had two sons and one daughter. The daughter married his favourite aid-de-camp, Count Reille. The eldest son having died, the second succeeded to the father's estates and titles.

Marshal Marmont

CHAPTER 14

Marshal Marmont

In contemplating the beginning and close of Marmont's life one seems to look on two different individuals. They present a contradiction, or, at least, an inconsistency very unfavourable to his fame. The truth is, he lived too long. If his career had closed nobly with that of Napoleon, his character would have presented greater harmony and completeness than now. To be moulded under the genius of Napoleon, and then have the life of activity passed under his direction transferred to the control of a Bourbon, must produce anomalies and changes that his admirers cannot but regret. If it be hard to serve two masters, it must be peculiarly so to serve two so unlike as Napoleon and Charles X. Still, by betraying Napoleon, instead of ending with him, he showed it needed no Charles X. to ruin his character.

Augustus-Frederic-Louis Viesse de Marmont was an exception to most of the other Marshals, in that he belonged to a noble family, and, like a gentleman's son, was destined at an early age to the profession of arms. Born on July 20, 1774, at Chatillon-sur-Seine, he was, at the age of fifteen, placed in the infantry as sub-lieutenant. Leaving this department for the artillery, he was present at the siege of Toulon. The young Bonaparte, commanding the artillery on that occasion, was so pleased with the bravery and skill of Marmont, that after he quelled the revolt of the sections, he made him his aid-de-camp, and the next year took him to Italy, to lay there the foundation of his future fame. At Lodi he charged the enemy's artillery at the head of a body of cavalry, and though his horse was shot under him, he succeeded in bringing off a cannon. For his gallantry on this occasion he received a sabre of honour. In this first campaign of Bonaparte, young Marmont exhibited all the impetuosity, daring, and devotion, that could be wished. For, leading a battalion of grenadiers into the thickest of the fight, in the battle of St. George, and aiding essentially in securing the victory, he was selected to present the colours taken in that action to the Directory. Ardent, joyous, and elated, the young soldier proceeded to Paris, and, amid all the pomp and solemnity befitting the occasion, presented the standards in an enthusiastic address, in which he showered eulogies on the army of Italy, and on the young chief at its head.

Returning to Italy, he went through the campaign of 1797 with honour, and, after the fall of Venice, returned to Paris. Being now twenty-three years of age, full of hope, and with a bright future before him, he, through the influence of Napoleon, obtained the hand of the daughter of M. Perregaud, one of the wealthiest bankers of Paris. Only a few weeks of leisure, however, were allowed to him, and he was summoned away from his young bride to accompany Bonaparte to Egypt.

On landing at Malta, he was one of the first ashore, and, in repelling a sortie of the besieged, took the standard of the Knights, and for his bravery was made, on the spot, general of brigade. He fought gallantly before Alexandria, and while Napoleon was in Syria, remained governor of the city.

Returning with him to France, he stood by him in the revolution that overthrew the Directory, and, as a reward for his services, was made Counsellor of State, and invested with the chief command of the artillery and army of reserve. Young Marmont had gone up rapidly, and now stood in all the freshness of youth beside Bonaparte, who was just entering on his wondrous career. His youthful imagination was fired by the boundless field that opened before him, and it was with joyous feelings he found himself chosen by the First Consul to accompany him over the San Bernard. One of the most energetic and efficient officers during that Alpine March, he won the admiration of all by his activity, force, and bravery. Descending with that shouting army into the plains of Lombardy, he commanded the artillery at the battle of Marengo. Borne away by his boiling courage, and panting after distinction, he showed on this terrible day the traits of a true warrior. He moved his hotly-worked guns up to within ten rods of the enemy's lines, and there poured his destructive fire into their ranks.

The rank of general of division was given him as a reward for his services during this campaign, and he was selected to negotiate the treaty of Campo Fornio.

On his return to Paris he was made inspector-general of the artillery. After the rupture of the treaty of Amiens by England, and the commencement of war, he was sent into Holland, and thence into Styria, and afterwards into Dalmatia, where, with a small army, he occupied Ragusa, and defended himself, successfully, against the most overwhelming numbers. He fulfilled Napoleon's most sanguine expectations, and, day after day, marched or fought fourteen out of every twenty-four hours. For his able conduct he was made Duke of Ragusa. He employed his men, during the peace, in making over two hundred miles of road across marshes and over mountains. He was recalled from this province with other corps in different parts of the continent to relieve Napoleon, waiting for reinforcements, in the island of Lobau, whither he had been driven after the battle of Aspern. To fulfil the urgent commands of the Emperor, he was forced to fight his way through mountain gorges, and across hostile territory, to the shores of the Danube. Pushing the enemy before him, he steadily advanced, and finally brought his victorious columns in safety to that fearful rendezvous the night before the battle of Wagram. His corps formed a part of the reserve in this great conflict, and he was one of those ordered up to sustain the heroic Macdonald in his unparalleled charge on the Austrian centre. Pressing on after the retreating army, he fought desperately at Znaym, and was made Marshal of the Empire. Soon after, he was appointed governor of the Illyrian provinces, and during an administration of eighteen months, exhibited the attributes of mercy and justice, and won the respect and love of the inhabitants.

In 1811 he was sent into Spain to take Massena's place over the army of Portugal. Napoleon's orders to him were precise and peremptory, but Marmont, discouraged, and averse to the position in which he was placed, showed a dilatoriness and want of energy, that materially injured the plan of operations marked out for him. He, however, restored order among the dispirited and ill-conditioned troops over which he was placed, and effected a junction with Soult. The two marched together to relieve Badajos, and Wellington was forced to retreat. Marmont followed after, and occupying Salamanca, erected forts at Almarez. At length Wellington invested Cuidad Rodrigo, and took it before Marmont, though on the march, could arrive to its rescue. The French Marshal then re-collected his troops at Salamanca. Wellington, in the mean time, marched back to Badajos, and after a short siege, carried it by assault. Marmont then made a demonstration on Cuidad Rodrigo, and after several combats, in which he was victorious, fell back to Salamanca. Eight months had now passed away, and nothing had been accomplished towards driving the English commander out of Spain. The Duke of Ragusa had certainly shown want of energy, but the truth is, the French generals were divided in, their opinion somewhat jealous of each other, and possessing no confidence in King Joseph. There was a head wanting to give force and activity to affairs. Marmont felt this, and earnestly desired to be recalled and join the army about to invade Russia. Besides, some of the best troops in Spain bad been drawn off to swell the army that was to perish in the wars of the north, and every thing languished.

At length, however, he showed he was an enemy to be feared. He was fairly pitted against Wellington, but a great portion of his forces being scattered over the country, his immediate army furnished no adequate opposition to that of his adversary. He had retreated, therefore, to Salamanca. But the forts there being stormed and taken, he continued to retreat to the Duero. Separated from reinforcements which he needed, he dare not hazard a battle, and things began to look threatening around the French Marshal.

But soon after, he first redeemed his errors, then, crowned them by one greater than all, at the. . . .

Battle of Salamanca

Having succeeded in concentrating his scattered forces, he finally, after two months more skirmishing and retreating, resumed the offensive, and determined to open his communication with King Joseph, which had been cut off by Wellington. The former was marching up to his relief, and if the two armies could effect a junction, the English general was lost, and he strained every effort to prevent it. Then commenced a series of marches, manoeuvres, and military evolutions, seldom, if ever, surpassed by any army. If Marmont's genius, or even good judgment, had been equal to his military science, statues to the Duke of Wellington would not have filled, as now, the public squares and edifices of England.

The French Marshal had taken the bold resolution to pass the Duero, and advance to the Guarena, and thus not only open his communication with Joseph, but outflank Wellington. To effect this he made several deceptive movements to bewilder the allies, and on the 16th and 17th of July began his march. Ascending the river, he crossed it in safety, and on the 17th, concentrated his army at Navadel, having marched some of his divisions forty and forty-five miles without halting to rest. At day break he was on the Trabancos, over which he had driven the English cavalry posts; and immediately made preparations to cross. The British troops under Colton, stationed here, endeavoured to dispute the passage, and a most singular scene presented itself. A heavy fog lay along the river, which concealed the French army from view, and Colton, seeing nothing but horsemen there, advanced to the shore with his cavalry. The artillery, however, opening, followed by, the rattle of musketry, he ordered up a regiment to support the horse. The conflict now became warm, and before the heavy explosions of the cannon in the bosom of the fog, the upper lighter portions sprung skyward in spiral columns, which, as they reached the rising sun, turned gold and red in its beams, while through the dark, dense stratum below, were seen the black masses of cavalry, plunging about in the gloom, now appearing, and now lost to the eye mere phantoms careering through the mist. A hill across the river showed dimly through the fog, covered with French infantry, that seemed as they marched down to battle to crumble off and slide noiselessly away. The English infantry stood and watched this strange spectacle, when suddenly, a single cavalry officer was seen to emerge on foot from the edge of the mist, and stalk towards them. He seemed to press a bloody handkerchief to his breast, as he strode firmly on. But that red spot was a ghastly wound a cannon ball had torn away his breast, and his beating heart lay exposed to view.

From daylight till seven o'clock the combat raged, when Wellington came hastily up, and began to examine the movements of Marmont. Just then a body of French horsemen came galloping across the valley, and rode straight up the hill on which Colton's left wing was posted, and with unparalleled audacity drove back a whole line of English cavalry. The English reserve were brought up, and these brave fellows were rode under and hewn down without mercy. Still forty horsemen swept boldly up and onward, and dipped over the further edge of the hill right in the midst of the enemy's lines. At the bottom of the hill were a body of infantry, and part way up, a whole squadron of cavalry in order of battle. The bold officer at the head of these forty horsemen suddenly reined up his steed at this sudden apparition, and his followers gathered hastily around him. His destruction seemed inevitable, for the British were already rushing to the charge. But the next moment those reckless riders wheeled, and with a shout, rushed in a tearing gallop on the advancing squadron, and driving it back over its own guns, rolled it down the slope carrying away the Duke of Wellington and all to the bottom. Here the mad irruption was stayed by another squadron of heavy dragoons, and the little band that made it, cut to pieces. The officer that led them on, however, escaped almost by a miracle. Surrounded by three troopers, he stretched one on the earth, then putting spurs to his noble steed fled back towards the French lines. For a quarter of a mile the two pursuing horsemen galloped side by side with him, hewing and hacking away at him with their swords, yet by his extraordinary strength and skill he escaped in safety.

At length Wellington began to retreat towards the Guarena, whither Marmont was already marching. The great struggle now was to see which should reach the Guarena first, and there prepare for battle. Then occurred a spectacle seldom witnessed in war. The two armies, in beautiful order, began to stretch forward. It was a hot July noon the air was close and oppressive, rendered still more so by the clouds of dust kicked up by the cavalry and artillery as they thundered along. But in close array, and in splendid order, the panting soldiers pressed after their leaders; and the two armies, only a few rods apart, strained every nerve to out-match each other. The long black columns streamed forward, and the two hostile hosts, side by side within hailing distance of each other, did not fire a single shot, and to a careless spectator seemed but one army executing some grand manoeuvre on a day of parade. A few cannon balls crushing through the ranks, from some of the heights, alone told they were foes. Under a broiling sun, covered with clouds of dust, they thus marched for *ten miles* side by side; while the officers, wrought up to the highest excitement, were seen pointing with their swords forward, hurrying on the columns, already moving in double quick time to the rapid beat of the drum pausing now and then only to touch their chapeaus to each other in courtesy across the narrow space that intervened. The heavy German cavalry went thundering along this narrow lane as if on purpose to keep peace between the hostile ranks; and thus together they swept over the rolling country, and at night reached the Guarena. After some fighting, darkness closed over the armies, and the tired warriors slept.

Marmont had marched his army for two days and nights without cessation, and hence next morning was in no condition to fight, while Wellington was equally averse to a battle. The day wore away with a few skirmishes, and Marmont, who had fairly outmanoeuvred the English general, instead of giving battle, rested till the following morning, then began to march up the Guarena to outflank more perfectly his enemy and open his communication with, his reinforcements, now rapidly coming up. Wellington, perceiving his design, immediately put his army in motion also to prevent it; and here the strange scene of two days before, was enacted over again on a grander scale. Only a narrow stream divided the two armies as on two parallel ridges they marched rapidly up the river. He who reached Contalpino first would win this battle of manoeuvres. Forty-five thousand men on either side, massed together, moved all day in order of battle, within musket-shot of each other the opposing officers waving their swords in recognition across the narrow interval as they strained every nerve to push the mighty columns onward, whose heavy, measured tread shook the banks of the stream. The long lines of bayonets flashed in the sun-light, while now and then, as the ground favoured, the cannon opened on either side, and the English cavalry marched threateningly between, waiting for some disorder or unskilful movement in the French ranks to dash in and impede their march. But Marmont did not make a single mistake, and his forty-five thousand men moved in one solid wall beside the enemy, presenting the same beautiful array and the same resistless barrier of steel. You could almost hear the panting of the tired hosts as they strained forward like racers on the course; but towards evening, it was plain that Marmont had outmanoeuvred and outmarched the English general; and at night Wellington halted his troops with the painful conviction that he was fairly outflanked, and unless some unexpected good fortune turned up, must commence his retreat. Marmont, in these few days, had restored all that he had lost, and had exhibited a skill and ability in manoeuvring an army unsurpassed by any general of his time. He had regained the offensive, and unless he committed some unpardonable blunder, could drive Wellington before him in confusion. His hitherto dilatory and unskilful management of the war seemed about to be forgotten obliterated in a glorious victory. The communication with King Joseph was open the reinforcements were already coming up, and all was bright and cheering.

But at this crisis he overturned all his hopes, and by one of those rash and inconsiderate movements ruined his army and deeply tarnished his fame. The two armies occupied opposite heights, with a deep basin between. This basin was a mile broad and two miles long, and Marmont, who was in a splendid position, having steadily outmanoeuvred Wellington, had nothing to do but wait for the reinforcements to arrive, and then fall on him like a thunderbolt. But, knowing if he delayed the attack till the junction of the forces under Joseph and Jourdan be should be superseded in his command, and the glory of the victory be taken from him, and having become over-confident, from his great success for the last few days, and a little too contemptuous of his adversary's skill, he executed a manoeuvre that was as rash and unmilitary as it well could be. Seeing that the English were about to fall back, and wishing to strike the blow before the arrival of the king, he determined to cut off their retreat, and force Wellington into a battle. As I remarked, the two armies occupied opposite heights Marmont on the east, and Wellington on the west, with a valley two miles long between. The French Marshal, about three o'clock on the 22d, sent forward his left wing, to threaten the road to Ciudad Rodrigo, along which he expected the allies to retreat. This wing pressing on too rapidly, gradually became entirely separated from the centre. When the report of this movement was brought to Wellington, he could hardly believe it. It did not seem possible that a general, who had exhibited such striking ability for the last few days, could commit a blunder that would be unpardonable in the most ordinary general. Hastening up to the higher ground, however, he beheld with inexpressible delight that it was true, for there, in the basin below, was the left wing of the enemy marching forward in beautiful order to cut off his retreat, while a huge chasm appeared between it and the centre of the army. As he took the glass from his eye he exclaimed, "At last I have them Marmont is lost!" His resolution was immediately taken, and orders flew like lightning to different portions of the army. The dark and hitherto motionless masses that covered the heights began to move, as if suddenly penetrated by some invisible agency, and the next moment they came rolling rapidly down the slope into the basin, and, moving through a hurricane of bullets, crossed the line of the enemy's march. Marmont, from the summit of the heights on which he rested, saw at once the whole valley filled with the English columns, and the battle thrown upon him in the midst of a difficult evolution, and while his army was separated by a wide interval. He, however, strove gallantly to recover his advantage. He despatched officer after officer in haste, ordering the left wing to fall back on the centre, and the centre to close up to the menaced wing, but before his commands could be executed, the scarlet uniforms of the English troops were seen moving like one broad wave on the dark masses of the French infantry. Amid the rolling fire of musketry, and heavy crash of artillery, the British bayonets steadily advanced, and Marmont saw that his hour had come. Hastening forward to the point of greatest danger, a shell stretched him on the ground with a broken arm and two deep wounds in his side.

This completed the disaster, for the French army, in its most critical state, was deprived of its head. But for his fall, the issue of the battle, desperate as it appeared, might have been different, for the bravery of the French troops seemed to overbalance all advantages. As it was, Clauzel, on whom the command devolved, did restore the fight. He succeeded in bringing the left wing and the centre together, and put forth almost superhuman exertions to stem the tide that was setting so heavily against him, and bore up in the storm with a heroism and constancy that filled his foes with surprise and admiration. Notwithstanding the odds he was compelled to struggle against, he still hoped to redeem the day, but nature herself helped to baffle his efforts, for the sun, now stooping to the western horizon, sent his flashing beams full in the eyes of a part of his troops, distracting their aim, while a brisk west wind, just then arising, carried the dust, which the cavalry and infantry trampling over the loose soil, stirred up, full in the soldiers' faces. Still, he kept pouring his brave columns in such stern, and fierce valour on the foe, that for awhile he steadily gained ground. Sixty thousand men were packed into that basin, on whose dark masses the artillery from the heights played with pitiless fury, while clouds of dust, mingling with the smoke of battle, rolled over them as they struggled in the embrace of death. The wounded Marmont heard the uproar, but his brave heart sunk in despair as he remembered how the battle stood when he fell.

Still, Clauzel did well nigh save him from defeat. As the sun sunk behind the western heights, be was driven back through the basin, but making a gallant effort at the base of the hill he arrested the onward movement of the enemy, and, following up his success, rolled the victorious columns back through the valley, and victory once more quivered in the balance. As twilight deepened over the bloody field, he had driven Wellington so hard that a crisis arrived when every thing rested on the reserves. The general who could bring the greatest number to the conflict would win the day. Fortune again favoured the English commander, and the heroic Clauzel, with his thinned and wasted ranks, retreated into the forest beyond the heights, and the battle was done. That basin was piled with the slain, and trampled into dust which lay sifted over the wounded and dead thousands that had fallen there. Groans and shrieks loaded the night air, and Marmont, faint and wounded, was borne through the darkness, suffering more from the wound in his heart than from the one his mangled body exhibited.

The army was routed, and the report of this sad defeat reached Napoleon just before the battle of Borodino. Fabvier, one of Marmont's aid-de-camps, brought the news; and a few days after, as if to retrieve the disgrace that had befallen the army in Spain, fought on foot at the head of the sharp-shooters, and fell wounded in a most obstinate fight of the regiment he was in, as it sustained for a while the shock of the whole Russian army.

Marmont had conducted the whole forepart of the campaign badly. Discontented and listless, he evinced no energy, and brought himself and his army to the verge of ruin. Rousing himself, however, at last, he had executed one of the most brilliant manoeuvres the history of the war could exhibit, and having outflanked the enemy, had got him in his power. But in the very midst of his good fortune he showed himself unworthy of it, and lost his advantage by a rash and foolish movement. Bonaparte was filled with indignation at the management of his Marshal, In his letter to the minister of war, directing an examination to be made of this affair he declared that Marmont's dispatch to him, explaining his defeat, had more trash and complication in it than a clock. He ordered him to demand of the Duke of Ragusa why he had delivered battle without orders from the king why he had not followed out the general plan of She campaign why he had taken the offensive, when sixteen or seventeen thousand men were in two days' march to reinforce him. In conclusion, he declared that he was forced to think that he had sacrificed to vanity, the glory of his country and the good of the common cause. Still, remembering his old friendship, he, in the height of his just wrath, ordered all these questions to be delayed, till Marmont had entirely recovered from his wounds.

Hearing afterwards that it was possible he was not aware of the near approach of reinforcements, he poured his complaints and recriminations on his inefficient brother, for not coming up to the Marshal's help sooner. The truth is, the whole war was managed miserably, and it could not well be otherwise with Joseph at the head of affairs.

Marmont said afterwards, that he would willingly have received a mortal blow at the close of the combat, could he only have retained the faculty of command at that trying moment when the shock of the armies took place. His wound was so severe, that it was necessary to amputate his arm, and he did not recover sufficiently to resume his command, till after the expedition to Russia, when he again fought bravely at Lutzen, Bautzen; Dresden, and Leipzig. Napoleon retained no ill will against his marshal, and restored him to favour and confidence the moment his wound was healed an act of generosity and kindness, that must, at this day, be like a sting in the memory of the latter.

But he well nigh recovered his fame, in the last struggle of Napoleon for his throne. At Bautzen he attacked the centre of the allied army with resistless fury at Dresden, he was also stationed in the centre, beside the Emperor, and at Leipzig, fought beside Ney, worthy of his former renown. Five times did the overwhelming enemy break into the village of Schoenbrun, in which he was stationed, and five times did he fiercely hurl them back; and it was not till reinforcements were brought up that he at length gave way. An aid-de-camp was shot by his side, and he himself was wounded in his remaining hand. He fought beside Napoleon, in his mighty efforts to roll back the armies of Europe from his capital, and at Brienne, Champ Aubert, Vauxchamps, Montmirail, &c., exhibited energy and heroism that received his highest commendation.

But at Laon he was utterly routed. Bonaparte had his army drawn up in order of battle before that of Blucher, but delayed his attack till the arrival of Marmont from Rheims. The eighth of March saw a sublime spectacle around Laon, as the two armies moved in the plain, and the long lines of fire from the advancing or retiring infantry, and the deep black columns moving to the charge to the music of cannon, met the eye on every side, and were lost in the distance.

The next day word reached Napoleon that Marmont was rapidly approaching, and he immediately recommenced the attack. He fought, however, merely to gain time, for his force was too inferior to hazard a general battle, until reinforcements came up. But that night, as this Marshal, with his troops, worn down with fatigue, were reposing in their cold bivouacs, dreaming of no danger, Prince William, who had been despatched by Blucher for that purpose, fell suddenly upon him with his Prussians. So unexpected was the onset, that at the first fire the soldiers fled in every direction, and the whole corps was dispersed through the darkness, and became a cloud of fugitives, whom no effort could rally.

Afterwards, when left alone with Mortier, to arrest the tide that was setting on Paris, he disputed the soil of his country with heroic courage. And at last, when driven into the capital, he continued to struggle on, as if he were determined to wipe out every error of his life by his noble self-devotion to France. Foremost in the lines, he exposed himself like the meanest soldier, and cheered on his men against the most overwhelming numbers. The world looked with admiration on his conduct, and Napoleon stood ready to cover him with honour, and France to load him with blessings. But he shamefully capitulated, and let the infamous coalition, which had struggled so long to crush his country, triumph by marching its armies into the capital.

English historians, and the enemies of Napoleon, never condemn Marmont for his conduct, in surrendering Paris, but rather praise him, declaring he fought as long as he could, and that farther resistance would have been madness. No doubt he was advised to this course by the influential men of the city. Lafitte, the great financier, among others, used his utmost endeavours to prevent an assault on the place, and well he might. The loss of property would have been immense, to say nothing of the dreadful carnage that would ensue; and Marmont was persuaded to capitulate. But he should have learned his duty from Massena in Genoa, St. Cyr in Dresden, and Davoust in Hamburg, and fought as long as one gleam of hope remained. Had Bonaparte not been near, or had he been ignorant of the state of affairs, then he might have been excusable, and his prudence proper; but he knew the only man who had a right to deed away the throne was marching rapidly up. He had received orders from the Emperor, who had promised to be in the city by the second of April with seventy thousand men, to hold out to the last. Aware of his proximity, and conscious that he alone could save France, he transgressed his commands, and exercised a power, which, under the circumstances, he did not rightly possess.

Napoleon was within a few hours' ride of the city when it was surrendered, and could not at first believe the reports that were brought him of its fall. His great heart broke under the blow.

Marmont was inexcusable, for he had seen enough of that mighty wizard's working to know that his presence in the capital would entirely change the state of affairs Paris would have thronged around him the very canaille would have gathered in a countless array about his standard. Hope would have taken the place of despair, and to every blow been given tenfold power. Besides, the very fact that he was with the army would have made the allies circumspect and careful. He knew the ground around Paris better than he did the rooms of his palace, and the amazing resources of his mind would have found means to check the enemy till his advancing troops should arrive, as they did at Dresden, and then he would have rolled the allied thousands back on the Rhine. But no, Marmont took on himself the responsibility of settling the whole matter not only the safety of the capital, and the extent of the dominions of France but to barter away the throne of Napoleon, when he himself would be there in a few hours, to do it for himself, if necessary. He doubtless thought he was doing a very generous deed, when he stipulated for the life and liberty of the Emperor. No wonder the indignant heart of the latter spurned him as a traitor, and when Marmont remembers the kindness of Napoleon to him, after his folly had ruined the French cause in Spain, his heart must be filled with remorse at his base surrender.

Napoleon never forgave him, and he always spoke of him afterwards with the greatest bitterness. To have a general on whom he had lavished honours take upon himself to dispose of France, his crown, and throne, was a wrong almost as great as deliberate treason.

Said he afterwards at St. Helena, "Marmont will be an object of horror to posterity. As long as France exists, the name of Marmont will not be mentioned without shuddering. He feels it, and is at this moment probably the most miserable man in existence. He cannot forgive himself, and will yet terminate his life. like Judas."

No wonder on the accession of Louis XVIII. he was made Peer of France and captain of the body guard. He could be trusted to defend a monarch for whose welfare he had betrayed his benefactor and his country.

When Bonaparte returned from Elba, he proclaimed Marmont a traitor. The marshal, truer to his last than to his first benefactor, commanded the army that conducted the King from Paris to Ghent. Finding, however, there was treachery among some one of his staff, and not knowing who was the guilty one, he determined to write all his secret orders himself. But his right arm was gone and his left hand writing was so illegible, that nobody but himself could read it. The Duke of Montmartre, who commanded the rear guard, could not make out the despatches that directed his march, though he spent the whole night over them, and was consequently left to his own conjectures, and the two portions of the army no longer acting in unison, he and his rear guard were taken prisoners.

During the short reign of Napoleon, Marmont remained at Aix-la-Chapelle, to whose waters he had repaired, ostensibly for his health. At the second restoration, he resumed his former rank and titles. Ten years after, he was sent to quell an insurrection in Lyons, after which he devoted himself principally to agricultural pursuits in his native province, till 1826, when he was sent as ambassador to the coronation of Nicholas at Moscow. In 1830 he was appointed by Charles X. over the troops of Paris. On the memorable 25th of July, when the imbecile King, utterly unable to learn wisdom from past events, issued his two tyrannical decrees one abolishing the liberty of the press, and the other annulling the election of the deputies, he relied on Marmont to quell the violence he expected would follow.

He took the command on the 27th, and succeeded in quelling the disorders; but, early next morning, the populace was again abroad, and armed. In attempting to disperse them a fierce battle ensued, and Marmont fired on his countrymen. The revolution was now fairly commenced, and the poor marshal was in a painful dilemma. To sustain the king he must fight it out, and strew the streets of Paris with its dead citizens, and thus become forever obnoxious to his countrymen. Besides, the people had become so thoroughly aroused that it was doubtful whether they would not conquer then, woe to his fame!

The Hotel de Ville was first attacked and taken, but the troops stormed and retook it. Again, however, did the brave citizens rush to the assault with loud shouts, and though its walls and passage-ways were drenched in blood, again wrench it from the soldiers and hold it against every assault. The Tuilieries and Louvre were the next objects of attack. The Louvre, though deemed impregnable, was carried through the panic of the Swiss Guards, and Marmont, in attempting to rally his men, came near being killed, and fought worthy of a better cause, under the clock pavilion of the Louvre; but the people were every where triumphant. The students of the Polytechnic school rushed on the guns and the bayonets of the infantry, with the coolness of veterans, and women became heroes. During these three terrible days he acted like a fool or one demented. Now, beseeching the king to retreat with the insurgents, and now opening his cannon on them he neither saved his monarch nor his reputation, and finally was compelled to depart with the dethroned king to England, consoled with the reflection that he had scattered the bodies of more than five thousand of his countrymen over the pavements of Paris, to carry out an unjust and tyrannical act. It is nonsense to talk of his duty as a soldier. It was not a lawless *mob* he was called to quell, but the people of France, who had risen against a lawless *monarch*, and he knew it. It was a struggle *for* law, not *against* it, and Marmont, who had passed through one revolution, and been a warm advocate of republican principles, should have seen his remaining arm chopped from his body before he would have any thing to do with such a piece of villainy.

On his way to England he seems to have awakened from his delusion, and deprecated, though too late, his unenviable position. In a letter to a friend, dated the 6th of August, he says, "Have you ever seen any thing like it? to fight against our fellow citizens in spite of us. Is there any thing wanting to make me completely miserable? And the future! what unjust opinions will be had of me! My only refuge is my conscience. I accompany the king to Cherbourg; when he is in safety my mission will end. I shall leave France, and wait to see what the future has in store for me." His conscience must be a singular thing to furnish refuge in such a case as this. To uphold a villainous king in violating the sacred rights guaranteed to the people, he shoots down several thousands of citizens, and then takes refuge in his conscience.

But Marmont was not a cold-blooded, selfish man. He seemed to have a mental weakness that came on him like a spasm, and just at the time when there was no occasion for it. Thus, in Spain, be exhibited great military skill, and a clear, sound head in his manoeuvres with Wellington before the battle of Salamanca, and till he had acquired all the advantage, and then he showed the imbecility of a weak mind. So at Paris, circumstances had placed him where he could cover himself with glory, and he fought like one who appreciated his position and felt his responsibility, but after he had gone through a part of the trial honourably, he tipped over the whole structure he was rearing, and lost instead of gained by the power he held.

He lost his head in the same way during the revolution of 1830, and he has ever been his own worst enemy. He was a brilliant man, but not a safe one. Unequal in his feelings, he was also unequal in his actions. He seemed capable of reaching a certain limit in an emergency, but not of staying there and struggling a single moment; and went back as fast as he went forward. A brave and a good general he was, not a great one. He lacked strength of mind, and that breadth of character and fixedness of will which belong to a strong man. In action, he was heroic and fearless, but he had not that reserve power to fall back upon in moments of despair, when fate seemed resolved to push her victim to the last extremity.

Ever since the unfortunate part he took in the last revolution, he has been a voluntary exile from France, and it is doubtful whether he will ever venture to show himself in the streets of Paris. He has passed part of his time in Transylvania, and a part in Constantinople, and now, though seventy-two years of age, wanders over the world like a spirit that cannot rest, afraid to set foot on his native soil. His noble deeds are all obscured, his early glory dimmed, and the name that might have gone down to posterity with a halo of light about it, has a spot upon it which no time nor change can wipe away.

Napoleon's prophecy has proved true, and Marmont's name is abhorred in France.

Marshal Victor

Chapter 15
Marshal Victor

Victor Perrin was born at Marche, in the department of Vosges in 1766. His parents were humble, and his early advantages nothing. Ignorant of books and the world in which he was to play such a conspicuous part, he entered, when but fifteen years of age, the artillery as a private.

His first appearance on the surface of things is at the siege of Toulon, where Napoleon also took his first step toward power. These two young soldiers, both in the artillery, had then an opportunity to see how each other fought. In the fierce attack on Fort Eguillette, Victor exhibited his two great characteristics, coolness in the midst of danger, and impetuosity in attack. He was then twenty-seven years old, and three years after, Napoleon, not forgetting the fearless artilleryman of Toulon, called him to his side in his first campaigns in Italy. During those three years, however, he was not idle, but conducted himself gallantly in the eastern Pyrenees, where he fought as a general of brigade.

There could be no better school for Victor than the campaigns he passed through by the side of Bonaparte. Amid the excitement of those constant battles and astounding victories, he seemed to have a new life imparted to him; and catching the inspiration which the whole army seemed to have derived from Bonaparte, he stormed over the battlefields of Laono, Dego, La Favorita, Alexandria and Novi, like one who thought himself invulnerable. At Mantua, whither Bonaparte had marched with such rapidity day and night after the battle of Rivoli, to succour Augereau, he astonished oven Massena by the overwhelming fury of his attack.

Provera was coming up to succour Wurmser, who had been driven into Mantua, and it was to prevent the junction of these two generals that Bonaparte had made such an unparalleled march from Rivoli. Massena was placed on one an of Provera, and Victor on the other, on the morning of the combat. Both were successful in the execution of their orders, but Victor, at the head of the 57th regiment, surpassed even the renowned Massena. When the signal for the attack was given, he rushed on and over the enemy with such ferocity and astonishing power that they were perfectly stunned. Amid the impetuous onsets and unparalleled bravery that characterized the whole campaign, nothing like it had been seen. The charge at Lodi and Arcola seemed the measured tread of self-collected soldiers compared to it. It was not the onset of determined or enthusiastic men not the headlong charge of Augereau, sweeping furiously through the ranks. It was something more than excitement the whole regiment, with Victor at its head, seemed suddenly to have been carried away, one and all, by a fierce frenzy, which imparts unnatural physical strength. Resistance was useless. The steady ranks went down before them, like grass before the mower. Rolled back on themselves, they parted, and fell along the sides of that resistless regiment, as if it were made of adamant. With his eye flashing fire, and the smoke of battle wreathing in clouds around him, Victor strode on in front, like some war-god of old. Artillery, infantry, cavalry, went down, one after another, in their passage the close fire of batteries and the firm charge of the bayonet, all disappeared where they moved. Heedless alike of danger or destruction, they took the storms of grape-shot that tore through the ranks without a shudder. Their rapid tread shook the ground over which they passed, and their firm array was like a wall of iron against every assault. Bonaparte had charged at Lodi and Arcola, as he had seen no man do before, and, fresh from the fierce-fought battle of Rivoli, was not likely to be astonished at any deed of daring; but Victor's charge for a moment took his mind from everything else. The whole army, which had been accustomed to heroic deeds, beheld it with amazement, and when the battle was over, and the victory won, it gave that regiment, by general acclamation, the name of "*The Terrible*," which it ever after bore. What a fearful baptism that must have been which could compel the "Army of Italy" to affix such a name to the regiment that received it! For Augereau, Massena, and Bonaparte to apply such a title, signifies more than words can convey.

At Austerlitz, Napoleon reminded this regiment of its name, and saw it with pleasure sustain its dread title. At the battle of Tann, twelve years after its christening, it also maintained its old reputation, breaking six regiments to pieces in succession, in a charge. In his bulletin home, Napoleon made honourable mention of it.

At Marengo, he also exhibited those great qualities, which made him so conspicuous in the after wars of the Empire. He opened that great battle, and was second to none but Lannes on that eventful day. Stationed along the little stream of Fontanone, he received the first shock of the Austrian army, as it defiled over the Bormida. Bonaparte was ignorant of the design of the Austrians to give battle on the plains of Marengo, but with the first thunder of cannon, an aid-de-camp from Victor came galloping into his presence, informing him that the enemy, with all his force, was deploying from the bridge. I have already spoken, in my description of the battle of Marengo, of the firmness with which he met the shock of the whole Austrian army, and stood muzzle to muzzle with their ranks for two hours, till Lannes came up. Perhaps there never was an instance in which such an inferior force was held so long in an open field exposed to so close, constant and murderous a fire. The discharges on both sides were rapid as lightning, and it was one incessant flash and peal of musketry and cannon along the Fontanone, till the line formed by Victor's and Lannes's divisions as it stretched across the field, now sallying backward, and now springing to its place again, looked like a vast serpent of fire waving to and fro in the plain.

For his heroism on this day he received a sabre of honour, which he most richly deserved.

At the peace of Amiens, he was appointed ambassador to the court of Denmark, where he remained till the rupture of the treaty by England, and the commencement of the war. At Jena, while leading his division forward, he received a contusion from a spent ball, which confined him to his bed for several days.

A few days before the battle of Eylau, while going to Stettin at the command of the Emperor, he was taken prisoner. Apprehending no danger, he was riding along in his carriage, with only one aid-de-camp and a servant, when twenty-five Russian hussars came galloping up, and seized him as a prisoner of war.

Being exchanged, he was sent to besiege the strongly fortified town of Graudetz, and soon after led the first corps into battle at

Friedland. When Ney's mighty column was checked in its advance and rolled back over the field, it fell on Victor moving rapidly to the attack. The latter, steadying his troops by a powerful effort, checked both friend and foe, and allowed Ney to rally his men again to the charge. These two chieftains then moved together upon Friedland stormed through its streets, though defended desperately at every step, and finally drove the routed enemy over the Alle. Side by side with Ney, Victor did not suffer this day by the comparison. His charge was as terrible, and the movement of his column as steady, as that of the "bravest of the brave"; and for the great services he rendered, was made, after the battle, Marshal of the Empire.

The peace of Tilsit soon followed, and Victor was appointed Governor of Berlin, and during the fifteen months of his administration exhibited the high qualities of a good and wise ruler, and left with the esteem and love of all the inhabitants.

In 1808 he was sent to Spain. He won the battle of Espinosa for Soult, and the next year, while operating in La Mancha, routed the Spaniards at Ucles, and took 15,000 prisoners. Being then ordered to support Soult in his invasion of Portugal, he proceeded on his mission, though with a tardiness that has not left him free from blame. He, however, defeated the enemy at Cuidad Real, and pushed on to the Gaudiana. Here be won the battle of Medellin, routing an army of 35,000 men, with one of little over 16,000 took several thousand prisoners, and left the field covered with the dead. So utter was the rout, that Cuesta, the Spanish general, was not able for several days to rally a single battalion.

Battle of Talavera

The next July the useless battle of Talavera was delivered, ostensibly by King Joseph, but in fact by Victor. Disregarding the sound advice of Soult, and following that of Victor, Joseph met with a defeat, which though of no advantage to the enemy, might have been prevented. Jourdan was opposed to the marshal's combinations, but the latter was so well convinced of their excellence that he declared, if they failed, military science was useless. It was a scorching day on which the battle was fought, and from morning till noon all was quiet, while the soldiers of the two armies descended to a stream in the valley between, to quench their thirst, and accosted each other in terms of familiarity across the narrow space that separated them. But about one o'clock the rolling of drums along the French lines announced to the allies that the enemy was preparing for the attack. Victor gave the signal, and eighty cannon opened their destructive fire, and the light troops went sweeping onward with the rapidity of a thundercloud over the heavens while the deep, dark columns marched sternly after, and charged with terrible strength the English lines. But the close and well directed fire of the artillery, and the rapid volleys of the infantry as they closed around the heads of these columns, enveloping them in one sheet of flame, that swept like billows along, their sides, was too much for human courage, and after bravely struggling, they fell back in disorder.

After various successes and reverses, the French seemed about to gain the day. The English centre was broken, and Victor's column's marching triumphantly through it. But one brave English regiment, advancing amid the routed and disordered multitude, and opening to let the fugitives through, and forming in beautiful order when they had passed, marched straight upon the pursuing columns from the right side, and poured its rapid fire into the dense ranks. Closing on the foe in such steadiness and firmness, these few soldiers arrested the progress of the entire mass, and the artillery being brought to bear, and the cavalry charging in flank, the tide of success was turned; and victory, which seemed a moment before in the hands of the French, was wrested from their grasp, and amid the loud shouts of the British, they retreated in firm and good order to their former position, and the battle was over. The French had failed in their attack, and nothing more and this was the great victory of Talavera, about which so much has been said. Two thousand men had been killed on both sides, and about eight thousand wounded and the ground was strewed with human bodies. Then followed a scene at which the heart turns faint. The battle was hardly over when the long dry grass took fire, and one broad flame swept furiously over the field, wrapping the dead and the wounded in its fiery mantle. The shrieks of the scorched and writhing victims, that struggled up through the thick folds of smoke that rolled darkly over them, were far more appalling than the uproar of battle, and filled both armies with consternation.

A short time after, the army effected a junction with Soult, and Sir Arthur Wellesley was compelled to retreat. Victor erred, but if he had been successful, as he might have been had the commander-in-chief been a different man, he would have received praise rather than blame from the battle of Talavera.

The retreat of the English, and his re-occupation of Talavera, gave an opportunity for Victor to show the kindness and generosity of his character. When he entered the town, he found the public square covered with the sick and maimed of both armies scattered around on the pavement, without any one to care for them. He immediately sent his soldiers into the houses, commanding the inhabitants to receive the wounded sufferers. He spoke kindly to the English, and ordered that one English and one French soldier should be lodged together the English always to be served first thus not only softening the asperities of war, but furnishing an example to his foes, that they might, but never did, follow.

Marching on to Cadiz, he set down before the town in a regular siege, and would soon have reduced it, but for the reinforcements the English were able from time to time to throw into it. While his forces yet encircled the place, and the works were still progressing, he was called by Bonaparte to command a corps of the grand army in the invasion of Russia.

He conducted himself nobly, and won new laurels in this campaign, and in the retreat from Moscow saved the army at the....

Terrible Passage of the Beresina

As the broken remnants of that once magnificent army now a cloud of despairing fugitives approached this river, in their retreat to Wilna, Napoleon sent Oudinot forward to defend the only bridge by which the army could pass. Supposing his orders had been fulfilled, he continued to advance, when the astounding news was brought him that this marshal had been driven back across the river, and the bridge destroyed. Napoleon's fate now seemed brought to a crisis. A river twenty rods wide and six feet deep was before him, while a victorious enemy stood on the farther bank with a powerful artillery to contest the passage. Another immense host was also thundering in the rear, and the knell of the grand army seemed slowly tolling amid the gloom of a Russian winter. At night, as Napoleon lay on his troubled couch, he was heard speaking of the dreadful alternatives before him, and began already to contemplate the disaster of a surrender; but when morning broke, his stern soul again summoned its energies to the danger that threatened him. First he ordered the reports of his ministers to be burnt, then the eagles of the separate corps, then the useless carriages and wagons, while all the remaining mounted officers, to the number of five hundred, were formed into a *sacred squadron*, and closed firmly around their chief. This being done, before daylight next morning he, with his tattered, dying army, plunged into the gloomy forest of Minsk, whose sullen echoes were already alive with the thunder of Russian cannon. In the midst of a northern winter, through this desolate and untrodden wilderness, he pressed on till at length he reached Victor's army.

This marshal had been stationed at Smolensk, while Napoleon marched to Moscow, and afterward sent forward to secure the retreat, so that he had seen neither the Emperor nor the army since they moved away from him, in all the pride and pomp of war, toward the Russian capital. And now, as the Emperor appeared, the way was cleared for him to pass by, and Victor's corps received him with the old shout of "*Vive l'Empereur*," which had long since been forgotten in the Russian solitudes. This brave marshal expected to see once more that magnificent host in all its ancient strength and proud array; but what was his consternation and dismay, when he beheld before him a motley and miserable crowd of wretches, without uniform, wrapped in female garments, old blankets and pieces of carpet, burnt and torn into tatters; while officers, with no troops to command, were marching on foot in their midst. Instead of shoes, this savage-looking horde had their feet wrapped in rags to protect them from the cold, and lean, unshaven, unwashed, haggard, famine-struck, and spiritless, with their eyes bent on the earth, they staggered by, the wreck of the Grand Army. Victor could not believe his eyes, and his soldiers were filled with astonishment and gloomy forebodings, and lost all heart. Oudinot was joined to Victor, and the eyes of the two chiefs were filled with tears as they asked where was the *corps d'armée*. The fugitives pointed to those five hundred horsemen, all that was left of the brave cuirassiers of the Emperor. The pine-trees rocked and roared above them in the fierce blast, and an unutterable sadness took the place of hope, as the two commanders turned away to fulfil their respective orders.

On the 25th of November this ghost of an army approached the Beresina; but, lo! what a sight met the anxious eye of the Emperor. An army of 33,000 men darkened the opposite banks, with thirty pieces of artillery pointing on the broken parapets of the destroyed bridge; while the sullen, angry river, loaded with floating ice, went rushing by, and 40,000 victorious Russians were pressing fiercely in rear. But amid these disasters, Napoleon moved with the same calm and marble-like brow and the same unconquerable spirit as ever. Murat advised him to fly and save himself, but he scorned the proposal, resolved to stand or fall with his army. He immediately ordered two bridges to be built, while he made a demonstration lower down the river, as if he designed to effect a passage there. The task seemed hopeless, for the enemy's cannon could destroy faster than the engineers could build. The sappers, nevertheless, plunged boldly into the stream, and, up to their arms in the cold water, began to lay the foundations of the first bridge. All night long the blows of the hammer echoed along the banks of the stream, and the workmen toiled by the light of the bivouac fires of the enemy that lined the opposite shore; and as daylight dawned, the troops stood to their arms to wait the fire of the Russians; when lo! to their astonishment, they were in full retreat. A gleam of joy shot over Napoleon's countenance at this unexpected good fortune. One well-directed cannon-shot would have crushed the labours of the whole night; but fate had decreed it otherwise. Napoleon immediately pointed to the opposite bank as the prize of the bravest. A French aide-de-camp and a Lithuanian count spurred into the stream, and plunging amid the cakes of ice that cut the chests and flanks of their horses, at length, dripping and chilled, mounted the farther shore. Forty or fifty horsemen, each carrying a soldier behind him, followed after, while two small rafts, each carrying ten soldiers, were pushed across, and at one o'clock four hundred men stood on the opposite bank. One bridge was soon completed. Oudinot's division began their march, and, with the joyful shout of *Vive l'Empereur*, streamed triumphantly across. When the excited and anxious Emperor saw these brave troops at length in battle array on the farther shore, he exclaimed in transport, "Behold my star again appear!" The other bridge for the artillery was also finished by four o'clock, and the cannon crowded rapidly across. Oudinot, with his corps, now protected the passage from the enemy on the farther side, but 40,000 Russians, under Wettgenstein, were pressing in the rear to force the disordered mass into the Beresina. Victor, with his 6,000 men, was ordered to hold this imposing array in check, while the wreck of the Grand Army passed over.

Then commenced a scene unparalleled in the history of war. The days and nights of the 26th, 27th, and 28th of November were days and nights of excitement, of woe, and terror, and carnage, from which the heart turns away overwhelmed and bleeding. Bonaparte, after trampling down the living to clear a passage, had reached the opposite bank with the relics of the Old and Young Guard, forming a reserve to Oudinot and Ney, who were to keep in check the Russian army of 27,000 men, that were now bearing down on the bridges; while, on the other side, the brave Victor was to cover with his 6,000 veterans, the disordered army of 40,000 that was hurrying across the river. Imagine the spectacle that now presented itself. Here was a broad and swollen current filled with floating ice, spanned by two frail and narrow bridges, around the entrance to which 40,000 worn, haggard, and despairing wretches were crowding in one dense and confused mass. Before them, whither they were hastening, the thunder of cannon was shaking the banks of the stream as the foe pressed up to their last remaining hope. Behind them was an army of 40,000 men closing steadily upon their retreat, kept back only by a curtain of 6,000 enfeebled soldiers, which the stern Victor was holding in the very jaws of death. It was a wintry day, and the bridges creaked and groaned under the descending ice, as the mighty throng commenced their march. All that day (the 26th), and all night, the hurrying thousands streamed across, except when now and then when the timbers gave way, and the multitude surged back till the gap was closed up.

But the next morning, as daylight dawned over the wintry scene, the stragglers that had been wandering hither and thither through the forest came hurrying by thousands towards the bridges, the entrances to which were now completely choked by the throng. Confusion and terror bore down all discipline, and the low, buzzing sound of excited and struggling men, mingled now and then with piercing shrieks, as some poor wretch fell under the remorseless feet of his companions, filled all the air. The strong crowded off the weak, and women and children and soldiers were seen dropping by scores into the stream.

But that night the tumult on the bridges ceased, and, seized by one of those strange impulses that nothing can resist, the whole multitude deserted the passage and began to pull the little village of Studzianki to pieces, in which they had been encamped, and with the fragments make bivouacs to shelter them from the piercing cold. But in the morning, as they heard the thunder of the Russian cannon on Victor's army, alarm took the place of indifference, and the entire mass again pushed in one confused torrent over the bridges. This last day was the most fearful of all; and, as if the woe, and terror, and despair, and suffering were not already great enough, a furious snow-storm set in, and the cold, driving north wind shrieked and howled through the pine-trees as if the infernal regions had been emptied to complete the horrors of the scene. While the terrified crowd in advance blocked the passage in their alarm and haste, those from behind kept pushing forward, rolling the helpless mass into the stream, and trampling over the fallen with reckless indifference.

In the meantime Victor hung like a protecting angel around them, furnishing a striking and touching contrast to the dreadful struggle on the shore. Putting his little army between them and the foe, he took the cannon balls destined for them into his own steady ranks, and bearing bravely up with his veterans against those 40,000 unwearied troops, stood, the only hope of the army. Forgetful of himself of the narrow plank that lay between him and safety thinking only of the helpless sufferers crowding the banks of the river, he fought with the energy of despair now steadily hurling back the overwhelming columns of the foe, and now pouring his exhausted troops on the advancing batteries. Forced slowly back towards the river, he disputed every inch of ground as if it were his last hope, and though he knew his retreating comrades were placing the Beresina between them and the enemy, be resolved to perish where he stood or save the army. His was a glorious, though perilous task, and right nobly did he fulfil it.

But it was not in the power of man to wholly check the advance of such superior force, and he fell gradually back, and the Russian batteries, in one huge semi-circle, advanced till they commanded the bridges. As the first shots fell among the multitude, terror and despair reached their extremest limit. All order and all restraint were lost, and every passion of our nature burst forth in its fury and strength. Rage, terror, cruelty, love, pity, and generosity were mingled, like heaven and hell, together. The strong and furious, with sword in hand, mowed a path for themselves through the living mass; the selfish drove their carriages over the feeble and helpless, heedless alike of the prayers of the pleading or the groans and curses of the dying, as their bones crushed under their wheels. Horses reared and plunged amid the chaos, trampling down men, women, and children under their iron hoofs as their riders spurred furiously on; while, to crown all, at this terrible moment the artillery bridge gave way, and the crowd upon it fell with a shriek into the stream. Those behind, ignorant of the disaster, kept pushing onward those before, and for a long time the dropping of a head of the column over the edge of the chasm formed a living cataract of men. When at length it was abandoned, and the artillery and baggage-wagons came rolling over the frozen ground toward the remaining bridge below, the scene became, if possible, more terrific. Under their ponderous wheels the close-packed ranks were crushed like grass, and they went trundling steadily on over the pavement of bodies they made for themselves, while the living multitude, trampling on the dying multitude, smothered the stifling groans ere they were half uttered. Those who fell seized the heels and feet of those who trampled on them, with their teeth, in despair. Mothers and wives were seen tossing their arms frantically about, calling in vain on their children and husbands, and the next moment fell under the carriage-wheels, or were pushed into the river. Some, as they disappeared in the icy stream, were seen holding their infants in their up stretched and stiffened arms, after they themselves had been swept under by the strong current. Oh, it was a sight to freeze the heart! On a narrow bridge struggled a frighted multitude, trampling down and pushing each other off, in the effort for life; and under them swept a cold river, and on either side, thundered the cannon of the enemy, the balls and shells crashing and exploding in their midst; while, as if to drown the shrieks, and cries, and groans and supplications that loaded the air, a furious tempest raved by, sifting the snow in one vast winding sheet over them. The heavens were blotted out the clouds themselves were invisible, and the snow, whirled aloft, and borne in fierce eddies onward, gave ten-fold power to the freezing cold that already benumbed and palsied their limbs.

But amid these exhibitions of cruelty and selfishness, there were also examples of heroism and generosity that ennoble our nature. While hundreds were destroying life to save their own, others were risking theirs to protect the helpless and wretched. Soldiers, and even officers, were seen harnessing themselves to sledges, to drag over their wounded comrades, one artilleryman, seeing a mother and her two children carried by the current under the ice, leaped from the bridge on which he was struggling for life, and snatching the youngest, a mere infant, bore it in safety to the shore, and was heard stilling its cries with words of tenderness. Soldiers took infants from the breasts of their dying mothers, and amidst that fierce hurricane, and storm of cannon-balls, and struggle, and terror, adopted them as their own, with solemn oaths, and carried them in their stiffened arms through the danger. Along the bank, others were seen standing around their wounded officers, who had been borne back from Victor's army, and amid the driving snow and frost watched their receding life; and, though urged again and again to save themselves, nobly preferred to perish beside their dying commanders.

While this scene was passing on the bridge, Victor was sternly battling back the Russian army, and saw his ranks dissolve around him without one thought of retreating. All that dreadful day he held his troops to the fire that wasted them: but at length the night, dark and tempestuous, came on. The disordered masses were still crowding rapidly over, and though the falling snow darkened all the atmosphere, yet the black line of the dense column contrasted with the icy current below sufficiently to render it a mark for the Russian guns, which kept playing through the storm with frightful effect. Bivouac-fires were kindled on the opposite shore, but they shone dim and obscure through the thick tempest, while those cannon kept thundering on in the gloom. That single bridge groaned under the burden it bore; and the muffled tread of the multitude the heavy rumbling of artillery and carriages over the planks the confused words of command, and all the tumult of a terrified and maddened throng rushing from danger and death, were born back to Victor's ear, as he stood amid the storm and darkness, and listened. He knew that the fate of his army rested on a single plank, and he knew also that the heavy mass might crush that any moment in twain, as they had done the upper bridge; still he would not stir.

But at length, when nearly all were over, and he must save his army if ever, and there was time for those behind to cross after if they would, he gave the orders to retreat. Over the snow-covered ground, the distracted multitude heard the measured tread of his advance columns, and crowded still more frantically forward. Refusing to open a passage for him, he trampled them underfoot. The tenderness of sympathy had given place to the sternness of duty, and Victor cleared a terrible path for himself through the mass, and, treading those down he had been so nobly protecting, poured his tired columns over the bridge. He used every exertion to make the remaining stragglers follow in the rear of his army, but, held by some strange infatuation, some thousands still clung to the fatal shore. He even set fire to their baggage to compel them to leave. It was all in vain, and not until he, towards daylight, ordered the bridge to be fired, did they faintly arouse. But it was then too late, the fierce flame wrapped everything, and though some in their despair rushed over the burning timbers, they only precipitated their death. Others threw themselves on cakes of ice and endeavoured to float across, while the remainder, stiffened with cold, and covered with snow, wandered up and down the shore in despairing groups, or sat down on the cold ground, and with their elbows on their knees gazed vacantly on the opposite shore.

The bridges were consumed and sunk in the river, and at ten o'clock the Russian army lined the shores where Victor had so bravely covered the retreat. When the ice and snow melted away in the spring, *twelve thousand dead bodies* were strewed along the banks of the Beresina, where this fearful passage had been made.

Victor continued to struggle manfully the remainder of this disastrous retreat, and was one of Napoleon's chief reliances in the succeeding efforts he made to save his empire. At Leipzig, Wochau, and Dresden, he maintained his high reputation, and finally, on the soil of France, side by side with his Emperor, strained every nerve to save Paris.

At length, being sent forward to Montereau to take possession of the bridges of the town, his soldiers were compelled to fight their way, so that when they arrived at the place they were too weary to make an attack, and a large portion of the enemy escaped. This so exasperated Napoleon, that he disgraced him on the spot. Putting forth superhuman exertions himself, and feeling that ordinary efforts would ruin his hopes, he deprived Victor of his command, for refusing to do, what, in ordinary circumstances, would be considered impracticable. The latter, who had fought bravely, and in endeavouring to carry out his Emperor's commands, had seen his son-in-law fall before his eyes, felt the injustice of the act, and hastened to remonstrate with him. The Emperor would not listen to his complaints until the disgraced marshal turning away said, "Well, I will shoulder a musket then. Victor has not forgotten his old occupation. I will take my place in the Guard." This noble devotion disarmed Napoleon, who was unjust, because be was balancing on the edge of irretrievable ruin, and could not look with complaisance on any one, who by failing to fulfil his orders, had added to his danger. "Well, Victor," said he, reaching out his hand, "remain with us. I cannot restore you to your corps, which I have given to Gerard, but I give you two brigades of my Guard. Go, take the command, and let us be friends."

The marshal continued to fight bravely, and at the terrible battle of Craon he led his column again and again into the very mouth of a most murderous battery; and after performing prodigies of valour, and seeing his men cut down like corn before the reaper, was at length struck by a cannon-shot in the thigh, and, dreadfully lacerated, borne from the field.

When the Bourbons re-ascended the throne, he was appointed over the second military division. On Napoleon's return from Elba he did all he could to retain the fidelity of his troops, but finding his efforts of no avail followed the King. At the second restoration he was made peer of France, and major-general of the royal household. n 1821 he was made minister of war, and on resigning his office two years after, was appointed ambassador to the Court of Vienna, though be never proceeded on his mission. In 1830 he gave in his adhesion to Louis Philippe. He died in 1841.

Marshal Brune

CHAPTER 16

Marshal Brune

Marshal Brune is here introduced not so much for the services be rendered Napoleon, or for his achievements in battle, as to make the list of marshals created by Bonaparte complete. The only ones omitted in this work are Kellerman, Serrurier, and Perignon, and they are left out because their titles were purely honorary, and they took little or no part in the events that make up the history of France under Napoleon. Covered with honourable scars, and respected by both friends and foes, they occupied seats in the senate after their appointment, and passed the remainder of their lives in peaceful avocations. Hence they belong to the history of the Republic rather than to that of the Empire.

Guillaume-Marie-Anne-Brune was born the 13th of May, 1763, at Brives-la-Gaillarde. His father was a lawyer of the place, and young Brune, was designed for the same profession. After remaining a while in his father's office he went to Paris to complete his studies. In a short time, however, he turned literary man, and wrote for a living. He published a book entitled, *A Picturesque and Sentimental Voyage in several of the Western Provinces of France*. It was written both in prose and verse, and published anonymously. He soon after became proprietor of a paper devoted to the aristocracy, which he edited till the Revolution broke forth in all its fury. Being a fierce republican he plunged headlong into the agitation and excitement of those times. Enrolled in the National Guard, his fine figure, martial bearing, and ardent patriotism soon made him conspicuous. A full-blooded Jacobin, he attended all the meetings of the club took a part in their intrigues, and was foremost in all their acts of violence. At the revolt of Champ de Mars his press was seized, and he himself thrown into prison. But as the indiscriminate sword of popular vengeance was about to descend on his head Danton interposed and effected his deliverance. Out of gratitude to his benefactor, he immediately swore fidelity to his interests, and became a willing instrument in his hand to carry out all the bloody measures of the Jacobins.

Promoted to the rank of adjutant in a battalion of volunteers, he continued in the army until the fatal 10th of August, and overthrow of royalty, when he returned to Paris, and was made adjutant-general of the interior. This was in 1792, just before the horrid massacre of the fifth of September, when the prisons and streets of Paris ran blood. It is said that Brune was one of the agents of the Jacobins in this bloody deed, but there is no reason to believe the charge is true, though he was immediately promoted to the rank of colonel, and in that capacity joined the army under Doumouriez, in Belgium. He showed great courage as an under-officer, and throughout this miserable campaign proved himself better fitted to command than many of those who held rank above him. After the defeat at Nerwinde, and the partial disbanding of the army, he put forth great efforts to rally the troops, and succeeded so well that the government made honourable mention of him, and he was looked upon as one of the most promising young officers of the army.

Having returned to Paris, he was sent against the federalists of Cavados, whom be soon quelled. Again returning to Paris he claimed, as a reward for his services, the office of Minister of War, but Danton soon drove that arrogant expectation from his head. To console him for his disappointment, however, he caused him to be made general of brigade. Joining the Army of the North, he fought bravely in several engagements, and soon after was sent by the Committee of Public Safety to quell the insurrection in the Gironde. He executed his mission like a Jacobin, and showed himself a fit instrument for the Terrorists. At the death of Danton, he was left for a while without employment. Barras, however, at the time he placed Bonaparte over the troops at Paris to quell the sections, gave Brune an appointment at Feydeau for the same purpose.

After having shown great energy on the 10th of September, 1796, against the Babouvists, he joined the Army of Italy, and as a commander of a brigade under Massena, went through the remainder of the campaign with great honour to himself. Arriving at Rivoli with him, after marching the whole night, he led his brigade to the assault with great intrepidity, and was one of the most active, energetic, and brave officers in the division. He was always seen in the front lines in battle, and by his commanding form and great daring attracted the admiration of all. In the successive engagements he here in a short time passed through, seven bullets pierced his uniform without inflicting a wound. No toil seemed to exhaust, no danger daunt, and no obstacles discourage him. Young, ardent, fearless, and ambitious, he pursued his career with an energy and success that promised rapid promotion.

At the peace of Leoben, Massena was sent to Paris with the terms of the treaty, and Brune was given the command of his division. He was soon after made general of division on the field of battle, and took the place of Augereau, when the latter also departed for Paris. After the treaty of Campio Formio, he was sent into Switzerland as commander-in-chief of the French forces there, and while Bonaparte was in Egypt, he was busy reducing the distracted and divided Helvetian States. By negotiation, promises, a good deal of deception, and some hard fighting, he at length subjugated the country. The immense treasures of Berne fell into his hands, which he pretended to send to the Directory, without any very lucid account, however, of the amount he originally received. At all events, it so happened that he received some $150,000 as his portion of the spoils.

After the reduction of the country, he assumed the office of legislator, and proposed divisions of states, and laws, and constitutions, in a manner that highly displeased the Directory, and he was transferred to the Army of Italy. He intrigued in Piedmont, till, in fact, he intrigued the King from his throne.

Being recalled again he was sent to Holland to repel the invasion of England and Russia. These two powers had entered into an alliance by which the former was to furnish 13,000 and the latter 17,000 men, and make a descent on Holland for the purpose of striking a blow at France by threatening her northern provinces, and causing a diversion in favour of the armies in the Alps and on the Rhine.

The English, under Sir Ralph Abercromby, effected a landing at Helder, but were compelled to wait the arrival of the Russians, before they could assume the offensive. General Brune, seeing the condition of the English commander, rapidly concentrated his troops and advanced to the attack, but was repulsed. The field of battle, like that of Arcola, was a collection of dikes and causeways, where everything depended on the firmness of the heads of the columns.

At length, the reinforcements having all arrived, the whole army, amounting to 35,000 men, was placed under the command of the Duke of York, and boldly advanced in four massive columns against the republicans, posted at Alkmaer. The Russians rushed impetuously to the attack, and were at first successful, but at length, being arrested, they were driven back at the point of the bayonet in utter confusion. The English also, after a dreadful slaughter, were forced to retreat, and Brune remained master of the field, on which were strewn 7000 killed and wounded. A fortnight after, the allies, having received reinforcements, again assumed the offensive, and after an obstinate combat, in which nearly five thousand more fell, forced the French from their position. Four days subsequent to this (October 6), following up their advantage, they again made a violent assault on the French. The battle raged all day with almost equal success, and when night ended the carnage, nearly four thousand men were left on the hard-fought field.

But reinforcements having now come up to Brune, he took the offensive, and driving the allies before him, swept them from the land, and ended victoriously this bloody campaign of two months.

In the mean time, Bonaparte returned from Egypt, and assumed the reins of government. Brune, however, kept aloof till he saw him firmly fixed in power, and then professed acquiescence in the change. But Bonaparte distrusted his professions, and, to get rid of him, sent him into Venice to command the army there. Being in a short time superseded by Bernadotte, he was dispatched into the Grisons, and after the battle of Marengo was placed over the army in the north of Italy. Macdonald, after his passage of the Splugen, had the mortification to find himself under the orders of Brune, of whose army he was to form the left wing.

The latter, in the mean time, was concentrating his forces in large masses on the Mincio, where the Austrians, occupying the left bank, stood ready to dispute the passage. He was hesitating what course to adopt, when the news of the victory of Hohenlinden reached the army, rousing the enthusiasm of the soldiers to the highest pitch; and they demanded eagerly to be led against the enemy.

No longer able to restrain their ardour, he, on the 20th of December, approached the Mincio in four columns. The right, under Dupont, first got over and was hotly engaged when a dispatch from the commander-in-chief arrived, desiring him not to cross, but cover the bridge he had secured by a heavy fire of artillery. It was too late, and Dupont determined to maintain himself where he was. The enemy, however, coming down on him with an overwhelming force, he would have been driven into the river but for the timely arrival of Suchet, who commanded the centre column. This brave general, hearing of the desperate condition in which he was placed, advanced, without waiting for orders, to his relief, and pouring his eager divisions over the bridge, rushed to the conflict. A moment later and Dupont would have been lost. As it was, it required all the firmness these two brave leaders possessed to hold their position against the greatly superior numbers of the enemy. The heavy cavalry came thundering on them in repeated and apparently resistless onsets, but were as often steadily hurled back. The Austrians, however, bringing up fresh troops, at length bore down before them, and were sweeping victoriously over the field when Suchet threw himself with his division in their path. The contest then became fearful. The overwhelming numbers would bear back Suchet; and then the steady valour of the latter, leading his men with levelled bayonets against the dense masses as they swept onward, would again triumph. Thus backward and forward the two armies swung in the smoke of battle, till darkness separated them. Suchet was a host in himself in this unequal conflict, and fought with a desperation that scorned superior numbers and scoffed at death.

But even the wintry night did not long divide the enraged combatants. About midnight, Suchet and Dupont saw by the fitful light of the cold moon, as it now and then broke through the tempestuous clouds, two dark and massive columns moving in dead silence on their entrenchments. Suddenly the very ground seemed to open with fire, and artillery and musketry, flashing through the gloom, lit up the banks of the Mincio, like noonday. The shattered columns of the enemy, arrested before the destructive storm that received them, at length, after vainly endeavouring to bear up, turned and fled.

During all this bloody conflict, Brune remained inactive. Not having designed originally to effect a passage where Dupont and Suchet had crossed, he could not consent to abandon his first project, and did not. He acted without judgment in this, and was severely censured by Napoleon. He was, however, able to carry the army over, as the Austrians had already been beaten the day before.

Following up his victory, he pressed on after the enemy, who now, defeated at every point, requested an armistice. Brune consented, and a convention was called, but in arranging the terms he agreed to give up Mantua, the very fortress of all others which Bonaparte wished to hold. This so enraged the latter, that he for a long time would not entrust him with any important command. This, in reality, ended his military career, although he afterwards commanded the army of the invasion of Sweden.

In 1802, he was sent ambassador to Turkey, where he behaved foolishly for two years, and was then recalled and made Marshal of the Empire. He had seen much service, and acquired a great reputation in the army, yet it is hard to understand why he was elevated to the rank of marshal, when there were so many, more deserving than he, passed by.

The next year he was placed at Boulogne, to superintend some of the preparations for the invasion of England. Being, however, soon superseded by St. Cyr, be was sent to Hamburg as governor of the Hanseatic villages, and afterwards placed over a corps of the Grand Army, when there was no more fighting to be done.

In 1807 Napoleon put him over an army of 30,000 men with directions to invade Sweden. He showed great activity and energy in this expedition, and soon brought the King to terms. But not having effected as much as was expected, or, more probably, from having compromised the dignity of Napoleon in his negotiations with the King, allowing the latter to treat his title of Emperor with neglect, and conducting himself foolishly throughout, he was permanently disgraced. His rapacity may also have had something to do with it; at all events this Marshal of France, in the very heat and crisis of the continental struggle, was sent to preside over the electoral college in the department of Ercaut. Bonaparte could not have shown his contempt for the man more effectually than by this appointment.

Brune, now laid aside forever, began to fear he should lose his estates too, and commenced playing the sycophant both to the Emperor and to Berthier. He continued, however, unmolested, while years of great events rolled by; and when at length Napoleon abdicated, he gave in his adhesion to Louis XVIII., and was honoured by him with the Cross of St. Louis. The Bourbon seemed to take Bonaparte's measurement of men in graduating his honours, and this miserable bauble was all the degraded marshal could obtain.

Mortified and indignant, he hailed with delight the return of the Emperor from Elba, and was placed by him over the corps of observation at Var. Acting the tyrant and Jacobin here, he ravaged the provinces, and enraged the royalists, and gathered a storm which was soon to burst on his own head.

On the second abdication, Brune threw up his command and hastened to Paris. At Aix the people assembled to mob him, but the Austrian soldiers prevented them from executing their design. From thence he went to Avignon, though warned of the consequences, as the town was the scene of frightful disorder and violence. He, however, would not be dissuaded from his purpose, nor even change his military dress, and with two of his aid-de-camps drove boldly into the place, and alighting at the hotel, ordered his dinner. After remaining an hour, he again entered his carriage, and was about to drive away, when a hundred or more of the populace gathered around him and blocked his passage. Stones were hurled into his carriage; and, amid curses, shouts, and cries of vengeance, he was forced back to the hotel. The enraged mob, increasing every moment, swarmed in a confused mass around the house, and demanded the head of him who they declared was the assassin of Madame Lamballe. The *gens d'armes* endeavoured to quell the tumult, but not being seconded by the national guard, they finally retired from the scene. The prefect of the place then interposed, but in vain; and the mayor at length placed himself at the head of a detachment of the national guard, and defended the gate of the hotel. But the infuriated mob would not be deprived of their prey, and mounting the walls in the rear of the hotel, and passing along the tops of the neighbouring houses, finally penetrated into the chamber of the unfortunate marshal. One of the leaders, a young man, then accused him of the murder of the princess. He denied the charge with scorn, declaring that be had never slain any one but on the field of battle. He saw, however, that his hour had come, and that he was to expect no mercy from the hands of the assassins. He had seen too many mobs in Paris to be deceived with false hopes, and he asked for paper that he might write his will, and for his arms, that he might put an end to his own life. Both requests were refused. His will was doubtless already made, and as for his arms, if he had but once got them in his possession he would have made wild work with the rabble.

He was a determined man, and his chamber would have flowed in blood, and more than one soul gone to the next world before he would have been taken.

But finding it was all over with him, he drew himself up haughtily, and received a pistol ball without falling. He dropped at the second fire, when a rope was immediately placed around his neck, and he was dragged down the stairs and over the pavement, mangled and torn, to the brink of the river. The mob then drew up in front of the lifeless body and fired five volleys, ten shots in the volley, into it. While this revolting scene was enacted on the banks of the Rhone, a troop of women, in the hotel, were dancing in horrid mirth around the blood-spots in the apartment where the murdered marshal fell.

The mangled body was left on the shore of the river, and that tall and martial form, that had so often moved in the front rank of battle, in the strength and pride of a victor, was covered with dirt and gore the clotted hair wrapped around the pallid features, and the brilliant uniform torn and soiled by the hands of assassins. But, still, vengeance was not satisfied. As the corpse was borne, by order of the town authorities, to the place of sepulture, the mob rushed upon the procession, and wresting it away, returned, and cast it into the river. The current threw it back upon the shore, and there it lay for two days unburied, while crowds came and looked upon it; yet none dared to give it a burial.

In 1819 his wife endeavoured to bring the assassins to justice but royalists were not eager either to avenge a dead republican general, or involve themselves in a difficulty with the people of Avignon for the sake of his wife.

Brune is an evidence that the French Marshals were something more than brave men mere instruments in the hands of Napoleon. With undoubted courage, he still possessed so little ability, that he could not hold the place to which he was entitled by his rank. He was tried and abandoned like a worthless vessel, and that too, when Napoleon needed all the military talent he could command. All men commit errors, and must now and then suffer defeats, and the French marshals did not escape the common lot of mortals. They, however, still retained their places, while Brune was disgraced. Augereau, another weak-headed man, was trusted but slightly in great emergencies. Those on whom Napoleon leaned, were many of them one-sided men, yet they possessed great mental power, as well as physical energy.

Marshal Oudinot

CHAPTER 17

Marshal Oudinot

Oudinot will probably be the last marshal that will ever act as Governor of the Invalides, and be the last representative of those veteran soldiers of the Emperor, for whom they fought. One of the few remaining props of Napoleon's throne, he, too, is slowly crumbling beside the tomb of the proud monarch, and will soon sleep with the heroes by whose side he struggled.

He was born at Bar, April 2, 1767, and was christened Charles Nicolas. His father was a brewer, and young Nicolas followed the same occupation, and bid fair to see, some day, "Charles Nicolas Oudinot" stamped in large characters on beer barrels. In ordinary times he would have lived and died around his own vats, contented with the moderate circumstances in which fortune had placed him; but the Revolution called him to sterner employment, and to fields of toil and fame. An ardent republican, be adopted with all the fervour of youth those principles of equality and universal liberty, which the French armies had brought back from our shores. But, though a republican, he was not a Jacobin; and his native town being plundered, and about to be burned, he rallied his companions, and forming them into a military company, attacked and frightened away the revolutionary robbers. He soon after obtained a commission in the army, and his career fairly commenced. He fought gallantly for his country under the first republican generals, Hoche, Pichegru, Moreau, etc., and rose rapidly in rank. He defended the castle of Ritche successfully against an attack of the Prussians, and evinced that rash bravery which afterward distinguished him. In 1799 he was made general of division, and while Lannes and Murat and Davoust were struggling around the Pyramids, he was winning laurels in the

Alps under Massena. He advanced upon Feldkirch, in which the Austrians were strongly entrenched, but was met in his passage by an army sent out to arrest his progress. This he attacked with his usual impetuosity, charging repeatedly at the head of his grenadiers into the very centre of the enemy's fire, but was as often compelled to recoil before the shock. Thus, for a whole day, he fought; but at length succeeded in driving the enemy before him into Feldkirch.

The capture of this fortified place was extremely important to the French; and Jourdan, then on the Danube, sent orders to Massena to strain every nerve to take it. But seated on a rocky eminence, with a river at its base, and flanked by strong entrenchments, it bade defiance to every assault. Still, Oudinot, at the head of his grenadiers, crossed the stream, and steadily moved up the rocky ascent, to the very walls of the fortifications under Massena. He advanced upon Feldkirch, in which the Austrians were strongly entrenched, but was met in his passage by an army sent out to arrest his progress. This he attacked with his usual impetuosity, charging repeatedly at the head of his grenadiers into the very centre of the enemy's fire, but was as often compelled to recoil before the shock. Thus, for a whole day, he fought; but at length succeeded in driving the enemy before him into Feldkirch.

The capture of this fortified place was extremely important to the French; and Jourdan, then on the Danube, sent orders to Massena to strain every nerve to take it. But seated on a rocky eminence, with a river at its base, and flanked by strong entrenchments, it bade defiance to every assault. Still, Oudinot, at the head of his grenadiers, crossed the stream, and steadily moved up the rocky ascent, to the very walls of the fortifications but in vain. Before the heavy and well-directed fire that received them, they were compelled to fall back, though they bore up a long time against the storm. Oudinot, enraged at the repeated failure of his attempts, again put himself at their head, and, amid the most sweeping volleys, led them into the very muzzles of the guns, and there, with his sword waving over his head, cheered them on. But it was impossible to beat down the walls which protected the enemy, and Oudinot, after making a succession of most desperate onsets, exposing his person like a common soldier, and urging his men by his enthusiastic words and example, was compelled to acknowledge that he could not carry the place. Massena, however, feeling how important it was to take it, as it commanded the chief passage into the Tyrol, came up with another division, and joining it to the grenadiers, put himself at their head, and once more sounded the charge. This intrepid chief, with Oudinot by his side, rushed furiously on the entrenchments, and struggled long and obstinately to carry them, but in vain. Mangled, shattered, and thinned, those brave troops were compelled to withdraw, after leaving three thousand of their companions at the foot of the walls. The flower of the army lay there, and where Oudinot had led his grenadiers the slain were thickest.

Soon after a general attack was made On Massena's lines and be was driven from the Grisons. Oudinot, however, attacked an Austrian division, and after a severe combat defeated it, taking 1500 prisoners.

In the mean time, the victorious Suwarrow, after beating Macdonald at the Trebbia and Joubert and Moreau at Novi, began to pour his conquering legions over the Alps, to drive Massena from Switzerland. The latter occupied the pass at St. Gothard, and was threatening seriously Zurich, which Korsakow still held, when intelligence was brought him that Suwarrow was hastening up. He had been reinforced till his army amounted to 80,000 men, and with these he bore down on Zurich.

This partial recapitulation is made in order to explain the movements purposely emitted in the article on Massena. Oudinot, at the head of 15,000 men, was the right arm of Massena on this occasion.

As the last night previous to the assault approached, the little town presented a scene of indescribable confusion. The Russian army forced back from all points, filled the streets, artillery and ammunition wagons, and excited cavalry, forcing their way through the crowd, added to the chaos; while cries, and shouts, and sounds of alarm mingled together in ceaseless discord. As darkness fell over this beautiful Swiss village, the heights back of it glowed with the innumerable watch fires of the French, while blazing bombs began to descend in huge semicircles, throwing wrathful streaks over the tranquil lake that stretched away on the other side, and sending terror and dismay among the inhabitants. All night long was heard the heavy tramp of infantry, mingled with words of command, as Korsakow prepared to cut his way through the enemy. At daybreak his army sallied forth along the only road by which it could retreat, and fell with the energy of despair on the French columns. Over heaps of the slain, and amid the most horrid carnage, it steadily made its way, until it broke the array of the republicans. But thrown into confusion by repeated charges, it rushed in utter disorder along the road, leaving its cannon, military chest, and ammunition wagons with the victors.

While this fierce conflict was going on along the road, Oudinot came pouring down into the town like an Alpine torrent, sweeping everything before him. A fierce struggle ensued in the streets with the garrison, but his victorious battalions bore down all opposition, and the remaining troops surrendered. Eight thousand Russians lay piled in the streets and along the road, and Zurich ran blood.

Massena did not forget the service that Oudinot rendered him during this campaign, and the next year, when sent by Bonaparte to defend Genoa, he selected him chief of his staff. During all the fierce struggle around the city, he brought efficient aid to the leader who had chosen him, and, amid the horrors of the siege that followed, proved himself a hero in endurance as well as in daring. When Massena resolved to force his way through the Austrian lines, and restore his communication with Suchet, he sent him with orders to the latter to co-operate with him in the attack he designed to make on the enemy. To fulfil his mission, Oudinot was compelled to pass by night, in an open boat, through the entire English fleet: after incredible toil, he reached the headquarters of Suchet in safety.

When Napoleon became Emperor, he made him Count of the Empire, and gave him command of a corps of grenadiers. He was just the man to be at the head of those stern warriors, and he made wild work with them in the campaign of Austerlitz.

After the capitulation of Ulm, Napoleon marched on Vienna. As he approached the city, he was anxious to get possession of a bridge across the Danube, which led from it to the northern provinces of the Empire, in order to cut off the communication of the enemy, and sent forward a part of his troops for that purpose. Just as day began to dawn on the 13th of November, a brigade of cavalry entered the capital, followed by General Belliard, Murat, Lannes, and Oudinot, with the grenadiers of the latter. Traversing the city, they marched straight for the wooden bridge (Tabor) on the farther side. But the Austrians were prepared for them, and an advanced guard held the farther bank while the combustibles were laid the matches and all ready, to wrap the whole structure in flames. Added to this, a powerful battery was stationed so as to sweep the entire passage. A word, a touch, and that bridge would be a mass of flame, and every foot of its surface scourged by grapeshot and cannon-balls. To undertake to carry it by storm would ensure its destruction, and so resort was had to stratagem. These generals, on foot, advanced carelessly toward the entrance, at the head of their troops, their hands behind their backs, and surrounded by a multitude of stragglers, as if they were strolling about merely to gratify their curiosity. Sauntering along, they began to cross the bridge, and called out to the officers on the farther side not to fire, as "an armistice was concluded." Deceived by their friendly manner and the peaceful appearance of the soldiers, who, though in column, had their muskets slung on their shoulders as if war was over, the Austrians advanced to meet them, and began to converse about the armistice. In the mean time, the grenadiers gradually worked themselves over the bridge: but at length the Austrian officer in command, observing their movements, and seeing them already beginning to quicken their pace, became alarmed. The troops still advancing, contrary to his request, he shouted for his men to fire. The gunners instantly stood to their pieces, the lighted matches were uplifted, and the next moment, apparently, must witness the bold column, officers and all, swept to one wild death together. In this terrible crisis, Lannes and Oudinot rushed forward, the former, exclaiming in a loud voice, "What are you about? do you not see? The gunners hesitated a moment in doubt; but one, more self-possessed than the others, was just bringing his match to his gun, which would have been the signal of a general discharge, when Oudinot sprang upon him and, snatched the descending match from his hand. In an instant the grenadiers rushed forward and seized the guns, followed by the intrepid column, which threw the combustibles into the river. Then, pouring back, they took the batteries they had passed so quietly a few moments previous, before the artillerymen could recover their surprise.

Soon after, while pursuing the Russians, Oudinot and Murat, and Lannes together, maintained a terrible combat with them at Grund. The grenadiers of the former moved again and again in solid column into the most destructive fire, and finally, breaking over every obstacle, rushed in resistless strength and with loud cries through the street. Austerlitz followed, and the campaigns of 1807, through all of which he still maintained his character as a brave and skilful general.

After the battle of Eylau, Napoleon, in one of his bulletins, speaking of an attack made on the enemy by him, calls him "the intrepid General Oudinot." Soon after he was taken sick, and remained for a time inactive; but he was able, with his brave grenadiers, to succour Lefebvre, as he was hard pressed by the enemy, at the siege of Dantzic.

He fought bravely at Heilsberg, and in the battle of Friedland, that followed soon after, commanded under Lannes, and had an aid-de-camp killed by his side. But in 1809, at Wagram, he excelled all his former exploits. In the previous battle of Aspern he arrested the attention of the Emperor by the manner in which he carried his division into action, and by the terrible impetuosity with which be tore through the hostile ranks; and he placed him beside Lannes in that last decisive attack on the Austrian centre. He marched beside that unfortunate chief into the enemy's batteries, and put forth almost superhuman exertions to deploy his men, so as to return the fire that devoured his column. In the retreat he struggled heroically with Massena and Lannes to steady the wavering current that was setting so wildly on the Danube; and on the death of the latter received the command of the second corps.

At the battle of Wagram he was placed in the centre, and was directed to carry the village of Wagram. Bernadotte was to support the attack, but his Saxon troops turned and fled, and the whole weight of the conflict fell upon him alone, and right nobly did he sustain it; and on that day of great deeds was outdone by none, unless it were Macdonald. Six times in one hour he carried Wagram by assault, and as often was compelled to retire before superior force; but at length, at noon, swept it for the last time with his battalions, and held it. Unshrinking and undaunted, he maintained his position amid the wreck of that battlefield with a tenacity that brought the highest encomiums from Napoleon. Conscious of the great trust committed to him, and mindful of the dead chieftain in whose footsteps he stood, his excitement was tempered by prudence, his impetuosity by forethought, and he exhibited the highest qualities of a brave and skilful commander.

Bernadotte, in the proclamation he issued after the battle complimenting his Saxon troops on their behaviour, refers to the manner with which Wagram was contested, as a proof that their ranks were like "walls of iron." Napoleon in his bulletin declares, in so many words, that the whole glory was due to Oudinot alone, and takes pains to follow his statement with the very significant sentence: "*Bernadotte has gone to the springs for his health.*"

For his valour on this occasion, Oudinot received the long expected marshal's baton. He deserved it, for, to use Napoleon's own expression, he had been "tried in a hundred battles, and showed equal intrepidity and wisdom." Not satisfied with creating him marshal, he also made him Duke of Reggio.

Three years after, he commanded the second corps of the Grand Army in the invasion of Russia. This was his first campaign as marshal, and he seemed eager to distinguish himself. He delivered several battles, while other portions of the army were comparatively idle; and at length, at Polotsk, was so severely wounded in the shoulder that he was compelled to return to Wilna, and was superseded by St. Cyr. But when Napoleon began his retreat from Moscow, having recovered from his wound, he again took command of his corps, which had been joined by that of Victor at Smolensko. These two leaders, as mentioned in the sketch of Victor, were sent on to take possession of Minsk and the bridge across the Beresina, so as to protect the retreat of the enemy.

But they had not performed their task the bridge was broken down and destruction seemed inevitable; for a Russian army, protected by powerful batteries, lined the farther shore. Oudinot was the first to approach the river, and drew up his dispirited troops and planted his cannon on the bank. All night long his shivering battalions lined that icy stream, and daylight had hardly broke when Napoleon approached, and gazed long and anxiously on the opposite shore, dark with the masses of the enemy, and then retired to his tent to ponder on his position. It was at this juncture, that the Russian army, impelled by some unaccountable fear, began to retreat. Oudinot brought the glad tidings to the astonished Emperor. Rushing into his presence, he cried out, "Sire, the enemy has just raised his camp and quitted his position!" "It is not possible!" exclaimed Napoleon. Ney and Murat at that moment hastening in and confirming the statement, he sprang up and ran out to the bank. As he saw the long columns disappearing in the forest, a smile of exultation and delight passed over his countenance, and he exclaimed, "I have outwitted the admiral!"

When the bridges were finished, Oudinot, as before said, and his corps were the first across, and took up their station on the farther side, to protect the passage. While Victor was so nobly covering the retreat, and stretching his little army like a protecting arm around the disordered multitude, Oudinot, on the farther side, was sternly beating back the Russians, who had now returned to the attack. With 8000 men be boldly withstood and kept at bay 27,000 of the enemy. But, in endeavouring in a close engagement to rally a legion that was giving way, he was struck by a shot and borne wounded from the field of battle. Carried to a small village several miles in advance of the army to have his wounds cared for, he supposed himself out of reach of danger. But the next day nearly six hundred Russians and Cossacks together stormed into the place, and his capture seemed inevitable. Rallying, however, seventeen men, the wounded marshal shut himself up in a wooden house, and defended it so fiercely and boldly, that the Russian soldiers were struck with astonishment and fear, and fled from the village. But, having two cannon, they planted them on a small eminence, and brought them to bear upon that wooden building. Still, Oudinot would not surrender, and though no longer able to offer any resistance, as the enemy were out of musket shot, he lay and let the cannon-balls crash through the house. At length, as if on purpose to drive him to despair, a splinter of wood, shot away by a cannon-ball, flew and struck him, wounding him again severely. Still he would not let his few remaining followers surrender, and held out, till at length, toward night, the advance guard of Napoleon arrived, and effected his deliverance.

The cold and exposure of that terrible retreat, together with his wounds, were too much for even his iron constitution, and for some time after he reached Paris his health was feeble and languishing.

Recovering at length, be hastened to the seat of war, to help to arrest the tide of war that was setting toward France. He fought bravely at Lutzen, and was one of the few marshals who won for Napoleon the....

Battle of Bautzen

The allies, a hundred and fifty or sixty thousand strong, were drawn up in a semi-circle, on the heights of the Bohemian Mountains, their lines stretching six miles across the country. Before them, in the valley, was the river Spree, with several villages along its banks.

The plain on every side was thickly studded with conical hills, whose tops were black with cannon; while those villages were so many forts, from which, when necessary, the troops could retire to the semi-circular heights where the main army was posted.

At nine o'clock on the morning of the 20th of May, Napoleon stood on a commanding eminence which overlooked the entire battlefield, and issued his orders. Nothing could exceed the excitement and magnificence of the scene that met his gaze. As far as the eye could reach was one mass of moving men at first confused and commingled, but gradually assuming shape and regularity as the columns of infantry, the squadrons of cavalry, and the artillery fell into their appropriate places, and advanced steadily and firmly toward the Spree. The long, black lines of the columns, with the tens of thousands of bayonets glittering in the morning light above them, the splendid array and movements of the cavalry, and the constant flashes and thunder of the artillery, as it moved its way toward the river, combined to render it one of the most sublime spectacles that war ever presents. Napoleon gazed long and proudly at this scene at his feet, conscious that his touch had created it all, and by a word he would change it all.

On swept the mighty mass, while from every cone-like hill that dotted the plain issued fire and smoke, as if a volcano were working there. Each dark summit suddenly became illuminated, while the guns, thundering at the heads of the columns below, led them steadily on to the shock. The earth groaned under that living weight, and the deep roar that rose from its bosom rolled in ominous echoes over the heights on which Napoleon stood. Far-off shouts were heard in the pauses of the thunder, and fierce squadrons were seen with glittering helmets and flashing sabres galloping through the smoke.

Nothing could check the onward movement of that host, and by five o'clock it had passed the river at all points, and was moving darkly toward the heights beyond. The allies were steadily forced back, yet maintained, as they retired, a heavy and well-directed fire from their artillery on the heads of the pursuing columns. Only one advanced post was held, and that was a height on which the stern Blucher stood. All efforts to dislodge him were vain, and he kept the summit in a blaze with his heavy batteries.

It was now too late to make any serious demonstrations, and the battle could not be fought till next day. Oudinot, however, who formed the right wing of the army, advanced to the foot of the Bohemian Mountains, and fell furiously on the allied left. Carrying forward his columns with his usual impetuosity, he steadily pushed the enemy before him, while through the deepening twilight the incessant flashing of his advancing guns looked like a fierce flame ascending the hill. The forests seemed inherent with light, and the dark recesses shone with the glancing of musketry as the infantry moved amid the trees, "while the Bohemian mountains rolled back the roar of the artillery." All heedless of the approaching darkness, he continued to press on, threatening to sweep away the entire left wing of the army, when reinforcements were brought up, and he was arrested in his victorious career.

That night the French bivouacked in squares on the bloody field they had won, and both armies sank to rest. All was silent on mountain and plain, save when the low groans and prayers that rose from the thousands that were weltering in their blood swelled and died on the breeze. The smoke of battle hung in light clouds along the heights the stars looked tranquilly down on the slumbering hosts, and no one would have dreamed that the day had closed so wildly, but for the slain around, and the light of the burning villages, that blazed and crackled unheeded in the darkness. Innumerable watch-fires lined the hills and dotted the valley, till the flickering lights lost themselves in the distance.

Bonaparte had sent orders to Oudinot to recommence his attack at daylight; and when the first grey streaks of morning shot along the east, the weary marshal stood in order for battle. Neither was Bonaparte idle, and all through that valley was heard the rapid *reveillé* and the stirring blast of the bugle, starting thousands from their slumbers who, before another night, would take their last sleep; while the furious beat of drums and the clangour of trumpets, at the foot of the Bohemian Mountains, told that Oudinot was leading his strong columns to the attack. The battle-cloud rolled over the morning sun, and in a moment the field was in an uproar. The Emperor Alexander, alarmed at the fierce irruption of Oudinot on his left, had sent such reinforcements there during the night, that the marshal found himself overwhelmed by superior numbers. He, however, bore up bravely against this superior force, and struggled nobly to make head against it. But his efforts were in vain. First checked, then forced gradually back, he however contested every inch of ground with the energy of despair. His men rushed with shouts to the charge, and threw themselves in impetuous valour upon the enemy, but the immense masses that met them steadily advanced, and before their weight and fire he was compelled to fall back, step by step, down the slope. Napoleon, who had from his eminence seen the superior numbers against which his marshal was compelled to contend, and alarmed at the success of the allies in that quarter, ordered up Macdonald with his corps to support him. The bold Scotchman marched his columns rapidly up to Oudinot, and hurled them with such strength and impetuosity on the enemy that they were driven back up the height.

In the mean time the heavy batteries of Marmont and Bertrand were thundering on the centre, and the battle raged along the whole lines. At length the sound of Ney's guns on the extreme left the signal for a general attack reached the ear of Napoleon, and his orders were issued like lightning. The cavalry moved straight on the centre, while the Imperial Guard, in dark array, marched behind to support it. Eighty thousand men swept in one broad wave against the heights, and surging up its sides, rolled in resistless power over the summit. Ney, in the mean time, had turned the enemy's right, and settled the fate of the day.

The allied army was forced to retreat, followed by the victorious and enthusiastic French. The spectacle the field at this moment presented to Napoleon as he stood and looked off from a commanding height, was equally sublime and thrilling with that of the day before. He had ordered the whole army to advance; and, lo! a hundred and forty thousand men moved forward at his command. There were the long black columns of the enemy retiring over the field, and around their extremities clouds of cavalry hovering in protection; while on every side, over the immense plain, were spots of flame and wreaths of smoke, where the artillery blazed incessantly on the advancing battalions. There, too, were the victorious French moving in beautiful order and stern majesty after the retreating masses; while a hundred and twenty cannon in front, clearing a terrible path for the columns, shook the earth over which they trod, and eight thousand cuirassiers, cased in shining armour, and sending back the beams of the setting sun in dazzling splendour from their helmets, swept with fierce shouts to the onset. An interminable forest of bayonets glittered over this host; while between were long moving lines of light caused by the sunbeams, flashing on steel armour and sabres and helmets. Napoleon gazed long and triumphantly on the sublime spectacle, till the lessening columns and the receding thunder of cannon hastened him forward.

In the mean time the sun had gone down, and night, drawing her curtains over the earth, arrested the conflict, and the two tired armies again lay down to rest. But two dead armies were sleeping there also. More than thirty thousand had fallen in these two days of carnage, and men lay in heaps along the base of the heights, and were scattered thick as autumn leaves through the valley. But as the stars came out in the sky women were seen flocking over the field, and coarse-clad men treading amid the piles of human bodies, but not, as at Dresden, to plunder the dead, but to succour the dying. With hand-carts and wheelbarrows and litters, the kind-hearted peasantry had issued forth, moved by their own sympathies, and lifting up the wounded carried them to their houses, where they bound up their wounds and allayed their sufferings.

The next morning at daylight Napoleon renewed the pursuit, and pressed on the flying traces of the enemy with redoubled energy. All day long the fight continued, and the roads were blocked with the dead; but still the allies retained the firm order of battle. Enraged at their obstinacy, and still determined to turn that retreat into a route, he hurried to the front in person, and urged on the columns. He rode hither and thither, hastening up and concentrating his forces with amazing rapidity, and falling in terrible strength on the rear guard of the enemy. But all his efforts were vain; the disciplined bravery of the allied troops resisted every endeavour, and robbed him of half his victory.

Death of Duroc

But his greatest misfortune, that which wounded him deepest, was the death of his friend Duroc. As he made a last effort to break the enemy's ranks, and rode again to the advanced posts to direct the movements of his army, one of his escort was struck dead by his side. Turning to Duroc, he said, "Duroc, fate is determined to have one of us to-day." Soon after, as he was riding with his suite in a rapid trot along the road, a cannon-ball smote a tree beside him, and glancing, struck General Kirgener dead, and tore out the entrails of Duroc. Napoleon was ahead at the time, and his suite, four abreast, behind him. The cloud of dust their rapid movement raised around them prevented him from knowing at first who was struck. But when it was told him that Kirgener was killed and Duroc wounded, he dismounted, and gazed long and sternly on the battery from which the shot had been fired; then turned toward the cottage into which the wounded marshal had been carried.

Duroc was grand marshal of the palace, and a bosom friend of the Emperor. Of noble and generous character, of unshaken integrity and patriotism, and firm as steel in the hour of danger, he was beloved by all who knew him. There was a gentleness about him and a purity of feeling the life of a camp could never destroy. Napoleon loved him for through all the changes of his tumultuous life he had ever found his affection and truth the same and it was with anxious heart and sad countenance he entered the lowly cottage where he lay. His eyes were filled with tears, as he asked if there was hope. When told there was none, he advanced to the bedside without saying a word. The dying marshal seized him by the hand and said: "My whole life has been consecrated to your service, and now my only regret is, that I can no longer be useful to you." "Duroc!" replied Napoleon, with a voice choked with grief, "there is another life there you will await me, and we shall meet again." "Yes, sire," replied the fainting sufferer, "but thirty years shall first pass away, when you will have triumphed over your enemies, and realized all the hopes of our country. I have endeavoured to be an honest man; I have nothing with which to reproach myself." He then added, with faltering voice, "I have a daughter; your Majesty will be a father to her." Napoleon grasped his right hand, and sitting down by the bedside, and leaning his head on his left hand, remained with closed eyes, a quarter of an hour, in profound silence. Duroc first spoke. Seeing how deeply Bonaparte was moved, he exclaimed, "Ah! sire, leave me; this spectacle pains you!" The stricken Emperor rose, and, leaning on the arms of his equerry and Marshal Soult, left the apartment, saying, in heart breaking tones, as he went, "Farewell, then, my friend!"

The hot pursuit he had directed a moment before was forgotten victory, trophies, prisoners and all sunk into utter worthlessness, and, as at the battle of Aspern, when Lannes was brought to him mortally wounded, he forgot even his army, and the great interests at stake. He ordered his tent to be pitched near the cottage in which his friend was dying, and, entering it, passed the night all alone in inconsolable grief. The Imperial Guard formed their protecting squares, as usual, around him, and the fierce tumult of battle gave way to one of the most touching scenes in history. Twilight was deepening over the field, and the heavy tread of the ranks going to their bivouacs, the low rumbling of artillery wagons in the distance, and all the subdued yet confused sounds of a mighty host about sinking to repose, rose on the evening air, imparting still greater solemnity to the hour. Napoleon, with his grey great coat wrapped about him, his elbows on his knees, and his forehead resting on his hands, sat apart from all, buried in the profoundest melancholy. His most intimate friends dare not approach him, and his favourite officers stood in groups at a distance, gazing anxiously and sadly in that silent tent. But immense consequences were hanging on the movements of the next morning a powerful enemy was near, with their army yet unbroken and they at length ventured to approach and ask for orders. But the broken-hearted chieftain only shook his head, exclaiming, "Everything to-morrow!" and still kept his mournful attitude. Oh, how overwhelming was the grief that could so master that stern heart! The magnificent spectacle of the day that had passed, the glorious victory he had won, were remembered no more, and he saw only his dying friend before him. No sobs escaped him, but silent and motionless he sat, his pallid face buried in his hands, and his noble heart wrung with agony. Darkness drew her curtain over the scene, and the stars came out one after another upon the sky, and, at length, the moon rose above the hills, bathing in her soft beams the tented host, while the flames from burning villages in the distance shed a lurid light through the gloom-and all was sad, mournful, yet sublime. There was the dark cottage, with the sentinels at the door, in which Duroc lay dying, and there, too, was the solitary tent of Napoleon, and within, the bowed form of the Emperor. Around it, at a distance, stood the squares of the Old Guard, and nearer by, a silent group of chieftains, and over all lay the moonlight. Those brave soldiers, filled with grief to see their beloved chief borne down with such sorrow, stood for a long time silent and tearful. At length to break the mournful silence, and to express the sympathy they might not speak, the bands struck up a requiem for the dying marshal. The melancholy strains arose and fell in prolonged echoes over the field, and swept in softened cadences on the ear of the fainting warrior but still Napoleon moved not. They then changed the measure to a triumphant strain, and the thrilling trumpets breathed forth their most joyful notes, till the heavens rang with the melody. Such bursts of music had welcomed Napoleon as he returned flushed with victory, till his eye kindled in exultation; but now they fell on a dull and listless ear. It ceased, and again the mournful requiem filled the air. But nothing could arouse him from his agonizing reflections his friend lay dying, and the heart he loved more than his life was throbbing its last pulsations.

What a theme for a painter, and what a eulogy on Napoleon, was that scene! That noble heart which the enmity of the world could not shake, nor the terrors of a battlefield move from its calm repose, nor even the hatred and insults of his, at last, victorious enemies humble, here sank in the moment of victory before the tide of affection. What military chieftain ever mourned thus on the field of victory, and what soldiers ever loved a leader so?

The next morning, a little after sunrise, Duroc died.

When the mournful news was brought to Napoleon, he did not utter a word, but put into the bands of Berthier a paper directing a monument to be raised on the spot where he fell, with this inscription: "Here the general Duroc, Duke of Friuli, Grand Marshal of the palace of the Emperor Napoleon, gloriously fell and died in the arms of the Emperor his friend." He left two hundred napoleons in the hands of the owner of the house and the clergyman of the parish, to defray the expenses. But the monument was never erected, for after the defeats which soon followed, the allies, with a meatiness unparalleled in the history of civilized warfare, claimed this money as a part of the spoils of war. For the paltry sum of eight hundred dollars, they could prevent a monument from being raised to genius and true worth, and insult a noble heart by denying it this last tribute of affection to a dear friend. What a contrast does this present to the conduct of Marshal Soult at Corunna, who ordered a monument to be reared to Sir John Moore on the spot where he fell. Napoleon was as much above his enemies in magnanimity as he was in genius.

Three months subsequent to this, Oudinot was beaten in Bohemia, at Gross Beeren, by Bernadotte, after a severe struggle. The news of this defeat, coming as it did, in the midst of other losses, irritated

Napoleon, who was in that critical position where he must have a succession of victories or be lost, and he unjustly ordered Ney to supersede him. The disgraced marshal, however, did not refuse to fight under Ney, who was soon after worse beaten in a similar encounter.

In the October that followed, at Leipzig, be commanded two divisions of the Young Guard, and helped to stem the tide of that disastrous battle, till Napoleon ordered a retreat, and continued to struggle bravely for France and the empire to the last. At Brienne, Nangis, Montereau, Bar-sur-Aube, and other fields of fame, and side by side with Napoleon during all that fierce struggle to force the allies back from Paris, he exhibited his accustomed valour and patriotism.

On the abdication of the Emperor, be gave in his adherence to Louis XVIII, by whom he was made colonel-general of the grenadiers, and governor of Metz. He adhered to the royal cause during the hundred days of Napoleon's reign, after his return from Elba. On the second restoration he was made peer of France, Minister of State and given the command of the National Guard of Paris. In 1823, he served under the Duke of Angouléme in the invasion of Spain, and was appointed governor of Madrid. In 1830, he gave in his adhesion to Louis Philippe, and four years ago was appointed by him governor of the Invalides, which office he still holds.

Oudinot was brave even to rashness, sudden and terrible in a charge, and a good general in the field of battle. He needed, however, the oversight of Napoleon, and erred when left to himself. He was neither avaricious nor cruel, and through a long and tempestuous life sustained the honour of the arms of France, and struggled nobly for her freedom. He was careless of his person in battle, and now bears on his body the scars of twenty wounds received in the different engagements he passed through.

Marshal Bessieres

Chapter 18
Marshal Bessieres

It is difficult to make a fair estimate of one's military character who occupies the position Bessieres did during most of his career. As commander of the guards his place was near the Emperor, and hence he was seldom brought into action till toward its close, and then to make a single desperate charge, in order to arrest a disaster, or to complete a victory. Just as he had obtained the appointment best suited to his character, and where he would have occupied a more prominent position, he was slain.

Jean Baptiste Bessieres was born in Preissac, the capital of the department of Lot, the 6th of August, 1768. Murat was born in the same department about a year and a half before. Both of these future heroes were of humble origin, their parents being poor and ignorant. When Murat was twenty-four, and Bessieres twenty-three years of age, they started together for Paris to seek their fortunes. Both being romantic and chivalrous, they indulged in vague hopes of future renown as they passed on to the capital; but in the wildest flights of their imagination, one never dreamed of being king, nor the other of becoming a duke and marshal of the empire. The former had just come from the stables of a country landlord, and the latter from an equally democratic employment, and one would scarcely have marked them out as future heroes, as they jogged quietly on, buoyant with hope and youth.

The contrast between those two poor young men plodding their weary way to the capital, and Murat on the throne of Naples, and Bessieres a marshal of the empire beside Napoleon, is one of the best comments on republican institutions that could be furnished. To human appearance, nothing but an indifferent fortune awaited them;

and a subordinate situation in the army they sought to enter was all that could be reasonably expected. But a new era was to dawn on France, and its slumbering energies were to be called forth, and all men who had a soul in them were to be given a fair field and full scope. Murat and Bessieres were going into the heart of an earthquake, not to disappear in the abysses it opened beneath them, but to mount on its ruins to fame and honour.

These two young adventurers arrived in Paris, and both obtained situations as privates in the Constitutional Guard of Louis XVI. The next year, on the fatal 10th of August, Bessieres's services for the King closed. His first lesson in war was taken at the storming of the Tuileries, and the first battlefield his youthful eyes gazed upon was the Place du Carrousel and the palace garden, in which were strewed the mutilated bodies of the brave Swiss Guard. During the continuation of this horrid massacre, he strained every nerve to save the members of the Queen's household; and, at the risk of his own life, succeeded in snatching some of them from the hands of the mob. The Constitutional Guard being no more, he was transferred to a regiment of cavalry destined for the Pyrenees. His brave conduct in the north of Spain soon procured for him the rank of captain of chasseurs. A Short time after, Bonaparte received the command of the Army of Italy, to which Bessieres's regiment was luckily joined. His intrepidity and impetuous valour in the battles that followed the opening of the campaign soon attracted the attention of Napoleon. On one occasion, especially, did be win his admiration. He was charging at the head of his company an Austrian battery, when a shot tore his horse to pieces under him, and they fell entangled together on the plain. Releasing himself, however, by a strong effort, be leaped on a cannon, which was sending death through his ranks, and began immediately to lay about him with his sabre. Two of his followers seeing him thus defend himself against the gunners, who made furiously at him, put spurs to their steeds and galloped to his aid. Together they succeeded in capturing the piece, and brought it off in triumph. Bonaparte, at the time young and impetuous himself, was so pleased with this feat that, when he formed his Corps of Guides, Bessieres was made its commander. His fortune was now secure, and from this time on his history and that of the Consular and Imperial guards go together.

After the battle of Marengo, he was given the command of the

Consular Guard, with the rank of general; and when Bonaparte assumed the imperial crown, he created him Marshal of the Empire. Placed at the head of the Imperial Guard, he went through the campaigns of Austerlitz, Jena, Eylau, Friedland, Tilsit, and Wagram, now with his resistless riders stemming the reversed tide of battle, and now converting a defeat into a rout. The command of such a body as the Imperial Guard was an honour not lightly conferred, and was sufficient evidence in itself that he who held it was both a brave and an able officer. Still it did not give such scope to individual talent as the command of one of the corps of the army would have done. There was no manoeuvring, no separate responsibility; and, indeed, no protracted and vacillating conflict, bringing out the resources and exhibiting the higher qualities of a great leader. The Imperial Guard were ever about the person of the Emperor; their squares enfolded him by night and by day, wrapping his tent in the field where he bivouacked, and standing the tower of his strength amid the tumult of the fight, and hence were always under his immediate control. The position of Bessieres, therefore, however honourable, would never fit him for a separate command. Unaccustomed to plan for himself, being troubled with no combinations either of his own or others, he would naturally fail at the head of a corps that was to operate by itself, governed only by general directions. Resistless courage, unshrinking steadiness, and endurance that no toil could shake, were the great requisites of a commander of the Imperial Guard, as they were the great characteristics of the Guard itself. Perhaps Napoleon, who measured the capabilities of his generals with such accuracy, saw that he needed to be free from separate responsibility in order to be efficient. There is many a man who will be a hero when told what to do, yet shows great indecision and doubt when left to himself to decide on his own course. Such a position as Bessieres's would naturally produce such a character, even were it capable of a higher development. Acting constantly under the eye and direction of another, he would unconsciously acquire a feeling of dependence he never after could shake off. But Bessieres, who was a hero in action, seems naturally to have been exceedingly timorous in counsel. Cool, steady, and terrible at the head of his brave Guard, the moment he came into the cabinet his boldness and decision evaporated. His charge was as prompt and furious as Murat's, but his *advice* was that of one possessing an entirely opposite character.

Yet it was an honourable post to be at the head of the Old Guard. At once the prop and pride of Napoleon carrying his throne and empire over the battlefields of Europe the magnitude of the trust committed to it, and the awe its movements inspired, gave it a grandeur and, indeed, a power, no body of men, since the legions of Caesar, ever possessed. The appearance of those bear-skin caps, and of the helmets of the cuirassiers, always operated like an electric shock on the army. When they moved, the Emperor moved, and they came to stand as his representative. Their approach to a battlefield was like the shout of victory on the sinking courage of the soldiers. Taught to believe themselves invincible, and never employed till a crisis came, it was not their duty to struggle, but to conquer. So well known was it, when they were ordered up, that the final hour of one or the other army had come, that the contest along the different portions of the lines became apparently of no account, and everything waited the result of their shock. So perfect was their discipline, that their tread seemed unlike that of other soldiers, and one fancied he could see in their very movements a consciousness of power. Their shout of *Vive l' Empereur!* never rang over a battlefield without carrying dismay with it; and so resistless was their charge always found to be, that they became the terror of Europe.

Bessieres is linked in history with the Old Guard, and they go down to immortality together. Brave, generous, and noble, he was worthy of the trust that still honoured him, and commanded not only the admiration but the love of all who knew him. Disinterested and humane, he sought no emoluments from war, and never let the training of a camp numb his generous feelings, or weaken his love of justice. His enemies praised him, and those he conquered came to love his sway. The excitement of a fierce-fought battle could not make him cruel, nor even render him indifferent to the complaints of the suffering. In Spain even, where the French name became odious, he was beloved, and on his return to that country as governor of Old Castile and Leon, the people welcomed him with acclamations; and when, at last, the news of his death on a distant battlefield was received by them, several towns assembled to offer up masses for his soul. What a touching eulogium on his virtues! Even his enemies prayed for his departed spirit. There must have been in that nature something more humane and gentle than is usually found in the ranks of war, to have caused such a demonstration of feeling in those whose country he had invaded. In the very heat of one of his fierce charges at Marengo, and when one would think he had enough to do beside caring for individual suffering, he saved an Austrian horseman from death. The latter had been cast from his steed, and stood unsheltered right in front of the swiftly advancing squadron, with uplifted hands, imploring them not to trample him under foot. "Open your ranks, my friends," said Bessieres, "let us spare that unfortunate man," and the furious horsemen divided at his bidding around him. At Moscow, as he and his suite were sitting down to dinner, a crowd of famished, trembling wretches, fleeing from the flames, rushed into his palace for shelter. The sight of their misery was too much for his sympathetic heart; rising up, he said, "Gentlemen, let us seek a dinner elsewhere," and ordered the food prepared for himself to be given to them. Mitigating the horrors of war by his kindness to the wounded and vanquished, he moves before us as a brave and chivalric warrior, and at the same time a humane and generous man. The tenderness of feeling and warm sympathy he exhibited may seem inconsistent with his desperation in the hour of battle, and the carnage that followed where his strong squadrons swept. But he felt that he was fighting for his country and for freedom against invaders and despots, and hence was not accountable for the suffering he occasioned.

Charge of Cavalry at Austerlitz

At the battle of Austerlitz he exhibited that bravery and force which characterized him through all the after wars. While Soult, with his resistless battalions, was making such steady progress on the heights of Pratzen, Lannes and Bernadotte, commanding the left wing, were also gradually pushing the enemy before them. To check their advance the Grand Duke Constantine ordered up the Russian Imperial Guards. Descending from the heights, this imposing mass advanced boldly into the middle of the plain, where they were met by the division of Vandamme, and a furious conflict ensued. In the midst of the tumult, the Grand Duke put himself at the head of two thousand Russian cuirassiers of the Guard, and in the most beautiful order moved over the plain. The next moment they burst on the flank of Vandamme's column, and cutting it through and through, trampled it under foot; then wheeling amid the torn ranks, mowed down the soldiers like grass.

The quick eye of Napoleon seeing the overthrow, and knowing that in a few moments, without help, his left wing would be routed, he ordered up Bessieres with the cavalry of the Imperial Guard, and directed him to charge that mass of horsemen that were rioting so fearfully amid his infantry. Rapp headed the advance guard, crying out to his followers, "Soldiers! see how they are sabring your comrades below there! Let us fly to their rescue! "A fierce shout answered him; the bugles sounded the charge, and, moving forward in beautiful order, they broke into a trot, and then into a steady gallop, and fell like a rolling rock on the astonished foe. Driven back over the mutilated corpses of the square they were treading down with such fury, the Russian cavalry gave way, leaving their artillery in the hands of the French. The disorder, however, was but momentary. Rallying beautifully, the confused squadrons seemed to flow of their own accord into the array of battle, and returned gallantly to the charge. But now Bessieres, with his whole reserve, went sweeping to the onset, and both Imperial Guards met in full career. The shock of their wild meeting shook the plain, and for several minutes it was one cloud of tossing plumes and swaying helmets, and rising and falling standards; for neither mass gave way. The clashing of swords and ringing of armour, and steady blast of bugles, were heard over the volleys of musketry which the infantry still poured into each other's bosoms. Such a hand-to-hand cavalry fight had not been seen during the war before; for, equal in numbers and in courage, each resolved not to yield. The ground was soon covered with dead horses and men; while, to increase the chaos and confusion, the infantry on either side came pouring to the conflict. The sharp rattle of musketry and the thunder of cannon mingled with the fierce ringing of steel; while the fluttering of standards was seen amid the smoke, neither advanced nor forced back, showing that victory still wavered around them. At length, however, the Russians broke; a shout rang over the field; the trumpets sounded anew, and Bessieres poured his enthusiastic squadrons on the retiring foe.

The next year, after the campaigns of Friedland and Tilsit, in 1807, he was transferred to Spain, where a new field opened before him. Taken from the Imperial Guard, and from under the immediate eye of Napoleon, he was placed over the second corps, called the army of the "Western Pyrenees," and fixed his quarters at Burgos.

In the mean time, the insurrection broke out, and Bessieres divided his disposable force of 12,000 men into several movable columns, and pierced the country in every direction to put down the insurgents. But while by his activity and energy he was successful in his attempts, and was ranging unchecked the mountains of Austria and Biscay, the Spanish general Cuesta was gathering a large army to overwhelm him. Bessieres immediately collected the troops and advanced to give battle, before Blake, on his march to join the latter, could arrive. The junction, however, was effected, and Bessieres with less than fifteen thousand men found himself opposed to more than twenty-five thousand. It so happened that his position was of vital importance to the whole French army, and Bonaparte, knowing it, had ordered Savary to Marenna, so that, in case of need, he could be reinforced. Savary however, heaped blunder on blunder, and Bessieres was left alone to save himself as best he could. The Emperor was made aware of the danger that threatened him, and his anxiety in view of it may be gathered from his language afterwards to Savary, when he rebuked him for his bad management. Said he, "A check given to Dupont would have a slight effect, but a wound received by Bessieres would give a locked-jaw to the whole army. Not an inhabitant of Madrid, not a peasant of the valleys, that does not feel that the affairs of Spain are involved in the affairs of Bessieres." Notwithstanding the errors of his general, Napoleon relied, and not without reason, on the good sense and courage of Bessieres. With such responsibility on his shoulders, it maybe imagined, that it was with no slight anxiety the latter beheld, on the 14th of July, an army nearly three times as large as his own drawn up in order of battle before him. True, only 25,000 of these were regular troops, but this number was nearly double his own.

In two columns he drove in the advanced guard of the enemy, but when he came in front of their lines he made a halt, and for a moment hesitated whether he should hazard an attack on such superior forces.

Battle of Rio Seco

Perceiving at a glance, however, the vicious position Cuesta had assumed, he determined to advance. The Spanish general had posted his men in two lines, one directly behind the other, and nearly a mile and a half apart. Bessieres, who had learned the art of war under Napoleon, saw at once that a skilful manoeuvre would soon destroy the advantage of numbers. Although the approach in front was up an abrupt ascent, he ordered Lasalle to engage the attention of the enemy there with partial attacks of cavalry, until, by a flank movement, be could throw the weight of his troops in the space between the lines. Succeeding in his manoeuvre he fell on the rear of the first line, at the same time that Lasalle, hearing his guns, charged furiously in front; and, rending it asunder as if it had been mist, sent the fugitives in one tumultuous crowd over the field. But while the French, in the disorder of success, were pressing with shouts after the flying enemy, Cuesta boldly advanced his second line. The attack was bravely made, and the first battalions of the French went down before the charge, and the shout of victory was heard in the Spanish ranks. The confusion of the French increased, and for a while the result of the battle was doubtful. But Bessieres, who saw the disorder that was spreading through his army, perceived at once that the crisis had come, and putting himself at the head of twelve hundred horsemen, burst with appalling fury on the enemy's flank. Everything sank before him; and, just then, the division that had been pursuing the remnants of the first line returning, the attack was renewed with vigour, and after a short but fierce conflict the Spaniards were utterly routed. Nearly 6000 of their number were stretched on the field, while 1500 prisoners remained in the hands of the French.

When Napoleon heard of this victory he could not repress his joy. "Bessieres has placed Joseph on the throne of Spain!" he exclaimed; and it was true.

Soon after this the Emperor left for Paris, and when be again returned to restore the affairs of Spain, which had got into a most disastrous state, Bessieres was superseded in his command of the second corps by Soult, a man better fitted for that position than himself. The battle of Rio Seco was the only brilliant deed he performed, and he was in a short time recalled to the Imperial Guard. He showed, however, in his short career, that he possessed the elements of a good commander, although no training could have made him equal to Soult and Suchet.

He went through the campaigns of Aspern and Wagram, and at the former place performed one of those great actions which so often wrung victory from the enemy in the moment of defeat.

Cavalry Charge at Aspern

On the first day of this great battle, while Massena and Lannes were struggling with almost superhuman energy to hold the villages of Aspern and Essling, the space between them, occupied by the French army, was exposed to a tremendous fire from several hundred Austrian cannon, placed in battery. So destructive was the storm of grape-shot which they incessantly vomited forth, that the field was almost swept of the soldiers. Galled by this murderous fire, which nothing seemed able to withstand, Napoleon at length ordered up Bessieres to charge the guns with his cavalry. The marshal first sent forward the light horse of the Guard. They advanced at a furious gallop, and with noble enthusiasm to the onset; but those terrible batteries were too much for them. They reeled and bent backward before the volcano that opened in their faces, and though they bravely struggled to bear up against it, at length turned and fled, leaving the field strewed with mangled horses and their riders. Bessieres then put himself at the head of the heavy-armed cuirassiers, and ordered the trumpets to sound. They presented a noble sight as they moved away. In beautiful order the dark array swept into the field, and was soon seen passing like a rapid thunder-cloud over the plain. Around the base of the black and driving mass was a cloud of dust; midway it was one dense body of shining armour, while above shook the thousands of sabres, amid the fluttering standards, and *"Vive l'Empereur!"* came rolling back over the field, like the shout of victory. Their steady gallop made the earth tremble; and the rattling of their armour was more terrible than the thunder of cannon, as they rode fiercely on into the very months of the batteries. One discharge tore through them and then with a shout that rent the air, they rushed onward. The artillerymen hastily withdrew their guns to the rear, and the infantry threw themselves quickly into squares, to receive the shock. To human appearance nothing could resist it; but when the smoke of the sudden volley cleared away, those firm squares, instead of being scattered and trampled under foot stood unbroken and complete, gazing sternly and resolutely on the foe. A body of cavalry was brought up to sustain them; but these were scattered like leaves in the tempest before the cuirassiers; and then there was nothing but those naked formations standing in the open field to overpower, and on these Bessieres hurled his excited squadrons anew. But keeping up a rolling fire on every side that astonishing infantry stood firm against every shock. Made furious by their stern resistance, he rode at the head of his men, cheering them to the onset, and, foremost in the charge, precipitated them again and again on that girdle of bayonets.

Baffled in every effort, he rode round and round the blazing citadels, and fell against their steadfast sides in brave but vain valour. Nothing could break that array, and after leaving half his followers on the field, he was compelled to retire. This ended the fight for the day, and the two armies slept on the field of battle.

The next day, when the last effort was made to win the victory, and Lannes's intrepid column, in attempting to pierce the centre, was checked in its advance, and stood and melted away before the close and heavy fire of the enemy, Bessieres again made one of those charges with the Imperial Guard, which were usually so resistless. His brave cuirassiers bore down with appalling fury on the ranks, urging their horses against the bayonet points; and, cheered by his voice and example, made almost superhuman efforts to break the squares of the enemy. But it was all in vain: the day was lost, and the mighty mass was driven back toward the Danube. Bessieres performed prodigies of valour during these two days, and his noble bearing, boiling courage, and firm and steady action won the admiration of Napoleon.

He was shut up in the island of Lobau with the army, where it lay from May to July, waiting for reinforcements to make another struggle for victory. At the battle of Wagram, when Macdonald was carrying the Empire on his rapidly perishing column, and it at length stopped in its awful career, Bessieres were ordered to charge with the cavalry to sustain him. Riding through a tempest of cannon-balls, at the head of his men, he was spurring furiously on, when a heavy shot in full sweep struck his horse, and hurled it, torn and shattered, from under him. Pitched to a great distance, he fell, covered with blood and dust, apparently dead, while from the whole battalion in which be rode there arose a mournful cry at the sight. Walther succeeded to the command, and led on the column; but the charge was feeble. The men, no longer seeing Bessieres at their head, were dispirited, for no one, except Murat, could give such weight to a charge of cavalry as he. After the battle was over, Napoleon said to him, "The ball which struck you drew tears from all my Guard; return thanks for it; it ought to be dear to you." The cannon-ball which mangled his horse so dreadfully by some chance did not harm him, although it tore his pantaloons open from the thigh to the knee.

The year of 1811 he spent in Spain, as governor of Old Castile and Leon, but the next year was again beside Napoleon, and commanded the Imperial Guard through the Russian campaign. This Guard was always the Emperor's chief reliance, but especially during this disastrous invasion and retreat; and Bessieres, as commander, had his implicit confidence. He loved him, for he looked upon him as his child, a creation of his own. He had seen him fighting bravely by his side in his first Italian campaigns, and ever afterward kept him about his person, raising him from one post of honour to another, till he made him Duke of Istria, and Marshal of the Empire.

The night before the battle of Borodino, Napoleon, sick and suffering, and filled also with the deepest anxiety respecting the great battle that was to be fought on the morrow, sent for Bessieres and asked him if the Guard were in want of nothing. Calling him back, again and again, he repeated the question, and finally ordered him to distribute among them, from his own private stores, three days' provision of biscuit and rice. This favourite marshal could approach him, when he was in those moods that kept others at a distance. After the battle was over, Bonaparte, who had been worn down with business and a burning fever, finally lost his voice entirely from a severe cold. In this state, Bessieres read to him the long list of the slain and wounded generals. The dreadful mortality among his best officers, which it exhibited, filled him with such anguish that by one strong effort he recovered his voice, and exclaimed, "Eight days at Moscow, and there will be an end of it!"

The marshal, after the burning of Moscow, was one of the council he called to decide whether the army should retreat or advance. He gave his opinion against the impetuous Murat; and firmly and emphatically declared in favour of a retreat. Napoleon listened to him in silence, but broke up the council without giving his own opinion.

During all that retreat, he, with the faithful Guard, that no disaster could shake, and no losses dishearten, hovered, like a protecting spirit, around Napoleon. Though their thousands had dwindled down to hundreds, and toils that seemed endless wasted them at every step; and famine and cold, and a victorious enemy, thinned their ranks daily, and the most appalling sights that ever met the human eye, were constantly before them, and dismay and despair on every side they, with their worn yet firm-hearted leader, faithful to their trust, still maintained their order and their courage. Singing gaily past the batteries that tore their ranks asunder standing in squares around their emperor as he bivouacked in the cold snow, and furnishing him the last fragment of fuel that could be gathered, while they, one after another, dropped dead in their footsteps they fasten themselves on our affections, and stand, to remotest time, as a model of fidelity and firmness.

The next year he was again beside Napoleon in Germany, still with the Imperial Guard, but he did not share in the victories or disasters of that campaign, and was spared the pain of seeing his beloved commander, for whom he had so often periled his life, a fugitive and an exile.

As the army was approaching Lutzen, its foremost column came upon the advanced guard of the allies, posted on the heights of Poserna, and commanding a defile through which it was necessary to pass. Attempting to force this defile, Bessieres, rode forward, with his usual reckless exposure of his life, to reconnoitre the enemy's position more closely, when a cannon-ball struck one of his escort by his side and killed him instantly. "Inter that brave man," said he, with the utmost composure; but the words had hardly escaped his lips, when a musket ball struck him, and he reeled from his horse into the arms of his officers, dead. A white sheet was thrown over him to conceal his features and uniform from the soldiers as they passed by, lest the knowledge of his death spread discouragement among them. The next day the battle of Lutzen was fought, and the Imperial Guard wondered where their well-tried and beloved leader was, as they moved into the fight. Motionless and lifeless, his martial form lay near them, but unconscious of their wishes or their struggles. The genius of Napoleon was again shining out in its former splendour, and the star of his destiny was again mounting the heavens. The heavy tread of the tens of thousands that moved to battle was again heard the thunder of cannon rolled over the Bohemian Mountains and the cloud of war covered the plain, in which nearly two hundred thousand men were mingled in mortal combat. The empire was again battled for, and the Imperial Guard once more put their brave arms around the throne of Napoleon and bore it steadily through the fight, but their intrepid leader was heedless of it all. Through his form trembled under the explosion of cannon that shook the house in which he lay, and the confused tumult of the battle was borne loudly past, no change passed over those marble features. The voice that should have steadied his ranks was not beard in the conflict, and the good sword that had flashed foremost in the charge was no longer seen, like a guiding star to the thousands that crowded after. Silent and motionless as its master, it lay stretched by his side, its work also done, Bessieres bad fought his last battle; but while his spirit bad gone to that world where the shout of the warrior is never heard, his body still lay on the field where mighty armies were meeting.

At night it was known that Bessieres had fallen, and sadness filled the hearts of the Imperial Guard. Napoleon ordered the body to be embalmed, and sent to the Hôtel des Invalides, where he designed to give it great honours, but his overthrow prevented him. He wrote the following letter to the heart-broken widow:

> My Cousin: Your husband has died on the field of honour. The loss which you and your children have sustained is great, but mine is still greater. The Duke of Istria has died a noble death, and without suffering; he has left a reputation without spot, the best inheritance he could bequeath to his children. My protection is secured to them; they will inherit all the affection which I bore to their father.

The King of Saxony erected a monument to him on the spot where he fell; and for a year afterward the inconsolable widow kept lamps burning night and day around his tomb, and daily bedewed it with her tears.

He was a noble man, and, regardless of wealth in his struggle for his country, left his family poor and in debt. Napoleon, however, in his last will bequeathed his son about twenty thousand dollars, and Louis XVIII. afterwards made him peer of France. Had the former reigned, honours without end would have been heaped on the family, for his affection for Bessieres was something more than the stern love which one warrior bears another. Theirs was the friendship of two manly hearts that had moved together through scenes that try the firmest attachments, without once being divided.

Marshal Jourdan

CHAPTER 19

Marshal Jourdan

Jean Baptiste Jourdan, though in active service till the overthrow of Napoleon, performed his greatest military achievements in the early struggles of the Republic along the Rhine, and hence occupies less space than his real merit deserves, in these sketches of the marshals. The son of a surgeon, he was born April 29, 1762, at Limoges, and entered the army when but sixteen years old. Young, ardent, and of an age in which new impressions are most easily made, he came to this country, and fought side by side with the patriots of the Revolution, till the close of the war. Entering on his military career in a war of liberty against despotism, he naturally adopted the principles embodied in our Declaration of Independence, and became a stern republican, and continued so throughout all the violence and bloodshed he afterward witnessed in France even to his death. His character as a military man could not have been formed under better leaders than Washington and Lafayette.

Those who condemn the French Revolution, and the French generals who made Europe tremble, would do well to remember where many of them derived their first ideas of equality, that so alarmed the despots of the Continent. That fearful waking up which France had was caused in a great measure by our stirring appeal to the world, and our brave resistance to arbitrary power. The terrific and protracted struggle that covered Europe with armies, was but the successful strife on our shores transferred to a wider and more extended field. The French armies carried back with them our declaration of rights, and hurled it like a firebrand amid the despotisms of the Continent. When tyrants thought to quench it forever, they rushed to its defence, and whirled it aloft with shouts of vengeance, till Europe shook with the rising sound of arms. The French Revolution, with all its horrors, was the legitimate offspring of our Declaration of Independence, working amid the rotten monarchies, and ignorance and oppression and despair of the whole world; and those philanthropists, who never weary of singing the praises of Liberty in this land of peace and plenty, show themselves but bigots when they turn in disgust and horror from her more painful and revolting aspect there.

> Ariosto tells a pretty story of a fairy, who, by some mysterious law of her nature, was condemned to appear at certain seasons in the form of a foul and poisonous snake. Those who injured her during the period of her disguise were forever excluded from participation in the blessings she bestowed. But to those who, in spite of her loathsome aspect, pitied and protected her, she afterwards revealed herself in the beautiful and celestial form which was natural to her, accompanied their steps, granted all their wishes, filled their houses with wealth, made them happy in love, and victorious in war. Such a spirit is Liberty. At times she takes the form of a hateful reptile. She growls, she hisses, she stings; but woe to those, who in disgust, shall venture to crush her. And happy are those who, having dared to receive her in her degraded and frightful shape, shall at length be rewarded by her in the time of her beauty and her glory.[1]

I have made these remarks here, because they come more naturally under the sketch of Jourdan, who derived his first lessons of freedom from us, and was one of the first avid chief military leaders that helped to roll back the tide of aggression from the French borders, and opened the great tragedy that ended with the carnage at Waterloo. The marshals of Napoleon are regarded by many as so many ferocious animals let loose on the Continental armies: but let such except at least, Jourdan, the offspring of our own Revolution, and who won his renown in carrying out the very principles Washington and Lafayette implanted in his breast. True, where he was compelled to struggle, Liberty assumed the form of a hateful reptile, and dragged her slime over ruined altars and deserted firesides. But even there she will yet appear in her beauty, to cheer and to bless.

---

1. Macauley

Jourdan passed several years in the United States, so that his character and principles became settled under the influence of our institutions, and when he returned to France it was natural he should enter heart and soul into the Revolution. In 1791 he commanded a battalion under Doumouriez, and the next year fought bravely at the battle of Jemappe. In 1793 he was made general of division, and in October was appointed to take command of the army in Flanders in place of Houchard, who had been executed for want of energy in conducting the war. The Republican armies needed the most efficient man at their head in order to resist the coalitions against which they were forced to contend; and Houchard, having endangered the campaign by his tardiness, was tried and unjustly executed. Jourdan, who, a short time before at Handschoote, mounted the enemy's works with the greatest intrepidity, and showed himself a man of energy and daring, was put in his place, with the most peremptory orders to attack the enemy and drive them over the French borders. Young, untried in chief command, and fighting at the foot of the scaffold, he nevertheless did not shrink from the task; and at the head of a hundred thousand men boldly took the field. The Austrians were strongly posted at Wattignies, but Jourdan, obeying his orders, marched rapidly against them. After a severe action, in which he lost more than a thousand men, he was compelled to draw off his troops. The next day, however, be renewed the combat. Concentrating his forces on the most important point, he at daylight moved his army, in three massive columns on the enemy. The artillery opened with a heavy and rapid fire, but their steady roar could not drown the enthusiastic shouts and songs of freedom with which the French soldiers rushed to the attack. Like the shouts of Cromwell's army, they fell in ominous tones on the enemy's lines, telling to the world the spirit that impelled them on. Nothing could resist their headlong onset; and over the enemy's works, and over their ranks, the excited thousands went, treading down everything in their path, and strewing the field with six thousand bodies.

This victory relieved Flanders, and threw a ray of light across the darkened prospects of the Republic. Jourdan was hailed as the saviour of his country, and immediately summoned to Paris, to consult with the Committee of Public Safety, on future operations. Attending the Jacobin Society, he advanced to the tribune and vowed, that "the sword which be wore should only be unsheathed to oppose tyrants, and defend the rights of the people." Through the influence of Barère, however, he was deprived of his command, but soon after was appointed to the army of Moselle, and ordered up to the Sambre, to succour the French army there. He arrived just in time to prevent an utter defeat. Assuming the command of the combined forces, be crossed the Sambre, over which the Republicans, a few days before had been driven, advanced on Charleroi, and investing the place, after a short but vigorous siege, compelled the garrison to capitulate. The troops, however, had hardly left the gates, when the thunder of cannon in the distance announced the approach of the Austrians, hastening up to their relief.

The next day the battle of Fleurus took place. Jourdan had under him between eighty and ninety thousand men the Austrians numbered about eighty thousand. The Austrians commenced the attack at daylight, moving forward in five massive columns, and the battle raged with various success till nightfall, when the enemy retreated, and the French encamped on the field of victory. More than a hundred and fifty thousand men struggled in mortal combat from daylight till sunset, and ten thousand were left on the field of carnage. This was the second great victory of Jourdan, and it immediately placed him at the head of the Republican generals. Under him in this great and decisive battle fought many of the future marshals, and most distinguished generals of France. Bernadotte, Lefebvre, Kleber, Moreau, Soult, Championet, and others here exhibited those striking qualities to which they afterwards owed their elevation.

He continued to follow up his successes this and the following year, but in 1796 was badly defeated at Wurtsburg, and was forced to make a hurried and ruinous retreat. The loss of this battle, and the disasters that followed, wiped out the remembrance of his former victories, and he was recalled. Returning to Limoges, he kept aloof from public affairs till next year, when he was chosen member of the Council of Five Hundred. The Republican party considered him a great acquisition, and he took an active part in legislative matters during the session. He proposed the celebration of the 10th of August gave his influence in favour of the measures that brought about the revolution of 18th Fructidor opposed with violence the proposition of the Directory to interfere with the elections; and, finally, submitted a law to change the mode of recruiting for the army. When this law was passed, Jourdan declared that the act decided that the Republic was eternal.

In November, he was called from political strife to take command of the army of the Danube. After various manoeuvres, he was at length met at Stoekach by the Archduke Charles, with an army nearly a third larger than his own, and after a stubborn conflict, in which the republican troops exhibited a courage worthy of their cause, was severely beaten. He strove bravely to arrest the disorder in his ranks, riding among them, and calling the soldiers, by voice and gesture, to rally again to the attack. But the defeat was complete; and after leaving five thousand of his bravest troops on the field, he was compelled to retreat precipitately towards France.

The Directory immediately appointed Massena in his place, and accused him of inefficiency in this campaign; and, indeed, laid at his door the reverses that also befell Moreau, with whom he was to co-operate. To defend himself, he published a *Précis des Operations de l'Armée du Danube*, in which he showed that the disasters were all owing to the ignorance and stupidity of the Directory, who did nothing but heap blunder on blunder, and was fast bringing France to the verge of ruin.

Being soon after re-elected to the Council of Five Hundred, he proposed the following as the form of the civic oath: "I swear to oppose with all my power the restoration of royalty and every other form of despotism in France." He had already began [*sic*] to see whither things were tending, and threw in this impediment, while he could, to check the first attempt that should be made to overthrow the Republic.

During this summer, all the sessions of the legislative bodies were stormy. Divided into two great parties, they were engaged in perpetual wranglings, while defeat attended their armies abroad. Everything was tending toward an explosion of some sort, unless a strong hand should be found to steady the rocking structure of the Republic. The prospect grew darker continually, and in the autumn France seemed on the eve of another revolution. The moderates and the politicians were arrayed against the patriots, and a fierce conflict was kept up.

Jourdan belonged to the patriots, who were in the minority; and, in order to do something to check the disorders and arouse public spirit, proposed the resolution declaring the country in danger. This was strongly opposed, and the excitement running high the members of the clubs assembled in great numbers around the palace of the Five Hundred, and openly insulted the deputies. It was in the midst of this confusion the report spread that Bernadotte was about to put himself at the head of the patriots, and excite an insurrection. It was on this occasion, also, that the Directory, alarmed and agitated, dismissed him from office, under the form of an acceptance of his resignation. The news of this high-handed act reached the Council of Five Hundred, just as they were about to vote on Jourdan's resolution. Alarm instantly seized the patriots, and it was declared aloud that some extraordinary measures were in preparation. In the heat of the excitement caused by this announcement, Jourdan arose in his place, and in a stern voice exclaimed, "Let us swear to die in our curule chairs!" "My head shall fall," replied Augereau, "before any outrage shall be committed upon the national representation." The tumult increased, and before the house could be quieted the resolution to declare the country in danger was put and lost.

After this, things went on as they had done before, and every one was casting about for some one to arise and arrest the disasters abroad, and quell the tumult at home. Affairs were in this state when Bonaparte returned from Egypt, and, throwing himself into the chaos, soon showed that he was the spirit called for by the times. Jourdan, however, kept aloof, and with Augereau remained at St. Cloud, while this young general was wresting the power from the Directory, and placing it in his own hands.

But the next year, the new government being consolidated, he accepted the appointment of governor of Piedmont, and by his just and wise administration secured the respect and obedience of the inhabitants, and friendship of the King, who, sixteen years afterward, sent him his portrait set in diamonds as a token of his esteem. In 1812 he was called to the Council of State and chosen senator, and the next year appointed over the Army of Italy. When Napoleon became Emperor he was made marshal, and grand officer of the Legion of Honour. At the commencement of the war, in 1805, he was superseded by Massena, for Napoleon never had a high opinion of his military abilities.

When Joseph Bonaparte was put on the throne of Naples, he was appointed governor under him; and two years after, when the former was declared King of Spain, he joined him as his major-general. He was present at the battle of Talavera, and gave his opinion, as before remarked, against that of Victor, who insisted on an immediate attack. Although the result sustained that opinion, still, had he been sufficiently prompt and energetic, he could have recovered the battle as it was, and secured the victory. But "his glory belonged to another era"; he could not adapt himself to the new system of things, and looked on the wonderful career of Napoleon without that feverish ambition to join it which characterized the other marshals.

The reverses which the inefficient monarch experienced were charged over to him, and he was so constantly beaten that he at length acquired the sobriquet of "the anvil." But his position was the most discouraging one in which a man could well be placed. Acting in a subordinate capacity to one who was fit only to be a subordinate himself, all his actions were crippled and most of his counsels disregarded. He became discouraged and disgusted; for, while other generals were enjoying separate commands, he was kept as a mere companion to King Joseph, for whose follies and blunders be was held, in public opinion at least, responsible.

At the close of 1809 he asked to be recalled, and returning to the bosom of his family at Rouen, calmly waited the issue of the gigantic efforts of the being who was wielding the destinies of France and of Europe. All his favourite schemes of a Republic had disappeared like a dream; and, borne away by a current he could not stem, he had at last yielded to its force, though not partaking of the passion or energy that bore it on. Had Napoleon trusted him with his armies, and brought him under the influence of his genius in some of his great campaigns, it might have been different. But he entirely neglected him, or only put him in places calculated to break the spirit of any man.

Jourdan remained inactive for two years, but in 1812, when Napoleon set out on his expedition to Russia, he was ordered to return to Spain in his capacity of major-general. Here he sustained the appellation given him of "the anvil," and was called to very little active service, except to conduct inglorious retreats. No honour attended his marches; no success in his manoeuvres; and, overshadowed by King Joseph, he scarcely ever appears above the surface in that last effort to hold the Peninsula. He was present at the battle of Vittoria, in which the French army was utterly routed; and was so hotly pursued, after the retreat, or rather flight commenced, that he lost his marshal's truncheon. This most singular battle, in which the French army seemed to have been suddenly turned into cowardly Spaniards, gave a mortal blow to the prospects of Napoleon in Spain for, although Soult was afterwards sent to restore them, he achieved only transient success. As Napier remarks, there never was an army so badly used by its commanders as the French in this battle, for the soldiers were not half beaten when the flight began.

Jourdan, after this, remained idle, and took no part in the last struggle of Napoleon. On the abdication of the latter, he gave in his adhesion to Louis XVIII., and was made Knight of St. Louis. When the news of the Emperor's return from Elba reached Paris, he retired to the country, and for some time took sides with neither party; but at length he came over to his old allegiance, and was given a seat in the Chamber of Peers, and appointed to defend Besançon.

Soon after the second restoration, be was placed over the seventh military division, and restored to his seat in the Chamber of Peers.

In 1830, he gave in adhesion to Louis Philippe, who, years before, had fought under his command in the Republican armies; and was appointed by him governor of the Invalides, which office he continued to hold till his death in 1833.

Jourdan was a good general, but not a great one; at least not a great one under the system which Bonaparte introduced. All his habits of command, and modes of conducting a campaign or battle, were fixed before military science underwent such a change under the genius of the young Corsican. He was in advance of the military leaders with whom he was first brought in collision as commander-in-chief, and at Fleurus, in a great and decisive pitched battle, had proved himself a great and able general. But he could not adapt himself to the changes that were introduced. One or two important victories usually fix certain notions in the head of him who wins them, that nothing can afterwards root out. At least they give way so slowly, that he who possesses them is laid aside as a man belonging to another age. This was somewhat the case with Jourdan. He, as well as Moreau, could not consent to abandon the tactics in the practice of which they had won their renown, at the first bidding of a young man who had an idea he could storm through Europe. The consequence was, Moreau became at first jealous, then envious, and finally traitorous. Jourdan, having more sense and more patriotism, yielded to the popular feeling, and, instead of being exiled, was neglected. Napoleon could do nothing, except with those generals who came entirely into his system, and after he became Emperor he appointed no man commander-in-chief who had not won his right to the place, in his service. He, however, felt at last that he had not treated Jourdan right; and at St. Helena confessed it, saying, "He is a true patriot; and that is an answer to many things that have been said against him."

Marshal Bernadotte

CHAPTER 20

Marshal Bernadotte

Nothing could be more lucky for the reputation of Marshal Bernadotte than being elected Crown Prince of Sweden; and nothing could be more fortunate for the Crown Prince of Sweden than the failure of the Russian expedition. Too egotistical and self-inflated to perceive great qualities in other men, a querulous and unmitigated boaster, his career would have ended but sadly for himself, had he been left to pursue it as a Frenchman.

Jean Baptiste Jules Bernadotte was born at Pau, in the Lower Pyrenees, January 26, 1764. His father was a common attorney, and designed his son for the same profession. But at fifteen years of age young Bernadotte enlisted as a private in the royal marines and was sent to Corsica. The same year Bonaparte, then a boy of eleven years of age, left the island to enter the school of Brienne. It is not improbable that the vessels that bore these two youths, who were yet to cross each other's track so frequently in life, met in the passage. What actors in what scenes those two children were destined to be! Serving here two years he was sent to the East Indies, where, in a sortie, at Cuddalore, he was wounded and taken prisoner.

On his return to France, he designed to leave the service and prosecute the profession of law. But being promoted to the rank of sergeant it so inflamed his youthful ambition, that he determined to remain in the army; and from that time he steadily rose in his profession till he bore its highest honours.

Soon after, the Revolution broke out; and in an insurrection of the Marsellaise, the colonel that had promoted young Bernadotte was surrounded by the infuriated populace, and would have been destroyed, but for the latter, who threw himself into the crowd, and by his harangues calmed their fury and saved his benefactor.

Becoming a furious Republican, he was raised to the rank of colonel, and sent to the Rhine, where he fought bravely; and, at Fleurus, so distinguished himself that he was made general of brigade. Previous to this, however, he had, in the true affectation of Republicanism, so common at that time, refused this very appointment, and thus gained the credit for patriotic zeal which he knew to be the sure road to favour. Elevated to general of division, be fought gallantly during the campaign of 1795, and '96, on the Rhine, and though an unmitigated boaster, and utterly unworthy of confidence in his statements, especially of himself and his battles, was a brave, skilful, and efficient officer.

At the close of this campaign, he was sent with 20,000 men, detached from the army of Sambre-Meuse, into Italy, to aid the army under Bonaparte, who had just astonished Europe by his deeds. At the first interview between them a mutual dislike seemed to arise. Bernadotte said to his quarter-general, "I have seen a man of twenty-six or seven years of age, who assumes the air of one of fifty, and he presages anything but good to the Republic." The young Bonaparte dismissed *him* more summarily, saying simply, "He has a French head and a Roman heart." He, however, placed him over the advance guard in the campaign of 1797, terminating with the fall of Venice. At the battle of Tagliamento, with which it opened, he led his division into the river with the words, "Soldiers of the Rhine, the soldiers of Italy are watching your conduct." This stimulated them to the highest pitch of enthusiasm, and they plunged headlong into the stream, and moved side by side with "the army of Italy," into the fire of the enemy's batteries.

In honour of the bravery be exhibited in this battle, and the service he rendered, he was sent to Paris with the colours taken from the enemy. He took no part in the revolution of the 18th Fructidor, which occurred soon after; and already began to show that envy of Bonaparte which caused him finally to disgrace himself and well-nigh ruin his fortunes.

Being sent about this time as ambassador to Vienna, he, on his arrival, hung out the colours of the Republic before his hotel, which so enraged the populace that they tore them down, and, rushing into his house, destroyed his furniture, and endangered his life. He immediately returned to Paris in anger; and because the Directory did not resent the insult sufficiently, refused to serve it in any capacity.

While Bonaparte was fitting out his expedition to Egypt, Bernadotte was paying his addresses to Mademoiselle Désirée Clary, daughter of a Marseilles merchant. She was the sister of the wife of Joseph Bonaparte, and formerly counted on her list of suitors Napoleon himself. But the young general of artillery being then without employment, the father refused his consent to the match; saying, "that one Bonaparte was quite enough in the family." She therefore dismissed him, and accepted Bernadotte which was about as poor a compliment to her taste and judgment as she could well pay.

While Bonaparte was in Egypt, Bernadotte was intriguing at Paris. Being appointed Minister of War, his influence was thrown against the Directory, which, under the pretext of fearing that he was about to excite an insurrection, dismissed him, as before noticed, from his office. He was first apprised of it by a note declaring that his resignation was accepted. Perfectly furious at this summary way of disposing of him, he sat down and replied in bitter language, saying, "You accept a resignation which I have not given"; and demanded his half-pay.

When Bonaparte, on his return, gathered around him his young lieutenants, Bernadotte was one of the three who stood aloof Jourdan because he was a republican, Augereau because he was a Jacobin, and Bernadotte from envy and jealousy, and because he would take no part in elevating a man above himself. But no sooner was the former firmly established as First Consul, than this sturdy republican became an obsequious supplicant for office, and obtained the appointment of counsellor of state, and commander-in-chief of the Army of the West. But soon after, still filled with the idea that he was better able, and more worthy, to govern than Bonaparte, he mixed himself up with Moreau's conspiracy to overturn him. The plot being discovered, Moreau was exiled, while the former was disgraced by having his staff dissolved and his command withdrawn. English biographers, with stupid prejudice, assert that Bonaparte made the pretended conspiracy an excuse to humble a general that showed too much ability. Nothing can be more ridiculous than the endless reiteration of the charge that Napoleon was in a state of constant anxiety lest his lieutenants should be too successful, and therefore, the moment they fulfilled his commands, disgraced them.

This is the more foolish, inasmuch as these same writers never weary of charging him with rigorous severity in his judgment, and with condemning and rebuking his generals whenever they failed in executing his orders, even though insurmountable obstacles intervened. That Bernadotte *was* implicated in the conspiracy of Pichegru and Moreau is now settled, from the confessions and documents of his friends who glory in it.

Bonaparte at length became reconciled to him, through the mediation of Joseph's wife, the sister of Madame Bernadotte; and when he assumed the imperial crown, created him Marshal of the Empire, and gave him the command of the Army of Hanover, and of the eight cohort of the Legion of Honour a remarkable instance of his generosity and magnanimity. The same institution of Legion of Honour, which Bernadotte now gloried in, he had opposed in the council of state with all the declamation peculiar to his race.

In 1805 he was chosen president of the electoral college of Vaucluse, and was returned to the senate by the Lower Department of the Pyrenees and the next year, after fighting bravely at Austerlitz, was created Prince of Ponte Corvo by Napoleon. The latter seemed determined, by flattering the pride of this self-conceited and overbearing Gascon, to keep him quiet and docile. At the battle of Jena, however his pride came very near securing again his downfall. When the Emperor sent to Davoust at Auerstadt as mentioned in the description of that battle to move forward, so as to take the enemy in rear, at evening, after he himself had defeated them in front, and, if Bernadotte had not departed for Dornberg, to take his corps also, the latter had *not* departed, and it was plainly his duty to fulfil his last instructions. As it was, he took no part either in the battle of Jena or of Auerstadt, but with his splendid army marched within hearing of cannonading of both without rendering any assistance whatsoever. Napoleon's anger at his conduct, in thus leaving Davoust to maintain that unequal fight alone, was extreme. Said he, "If I should send him to a council of war nothing could save him from being shot. I will not speak to him on the subject, but I will let him see what I think of his conduct." Bernadotte, in his self-conceit, lets out the motive that prevented him from joining Davoust: "I was piqued," said he, "to be addressed in the language of authority by Davoust, but I did my duty. Let the Emperor accuse me if he pleases, I will answer him. I am a Gascon, but he is still more so." Constantly inflated with the idea of his self-importance, be struts about, boasting that he will answer the Emperor if he dares upbraid him prouder to have shown his independence than he would have been had he won a battle.

The reflection, however, that he had taken no part in either of those two great conflicts with which the world would ring, annoyed him excessively; and the opportunity furnished him a few days after, of striking a successful blow, was eagerly seized. Overtaking the Duke of Wurtemberg at Halle, he cut his army to pieces, and drove him back to Magdeburg. But failing to follow up his success as he ought, he let the greater part of the enemy slip through his fingers, when, if he had followed Napoleon's orders and pushed on, he would have captured the whole of it. This, together with his conduct at Auerstadt, brought down a torrent of indignation on him from the Emperor, and it is more than probable, that, had he not been connected with the Bonaparte family, he would have been placed where his gasconade would have been in future as harmless as it was ridiculous.

In 1808 he was sent into the neighbourhood of Hamburg with a large force; and though unsuccessful in his military operations, his administration as governor of Frionia and Jutland was so mild and conciliating that he won the esteem and good will of the inhabitants.

In 1809, with other corps of the French army, he was summoned from the banks of the Elbe with his Saxon troops, to the island of Lobau, where the forces were concentrating, previous to the battle of Wagram. But on the first day of the battle, both in his attacks on the heights of Wagram and on the village of Aderklaa, he was repulsed and on the second day he met with a still more serious discomfiture in his encounter with the Austrian centre. It was his troops that, in their confusion, overwhelmed the carriage of Massena, which so enraged the marshal that he ordered his dragoons to charge them as if they had been enemies. But, notwithstanding his defeat, Bernadotte, who never contemplated himself except with the most perfect satisfaction, and could see nothing but glory in his own actions, issued, the very day after the battle, a proclamation to his soldiers, in which he spoke in the most inflated terms of their bravery. Said he: "Saxons! on the day of the 5th of July, seven or eight thousand of you pierced the centre of the enemy's army, and reached Deutch Wagram, *despite all the efforts of forty thousand of the enemy supported by sixty pieces of cannon*; you continued the combat till midnight, and bivouacked in the middle of the Austrian lines. At daybreak on the 6th, you renewed the combat with the same perseverance, and, in the midst of the ravages of the enemy's artillery, your *living columns* have remained immovable like brass. The great Napoleon was a witness to your devotion; he has enrolled you among his bravest followers. Saxons the fortunes of a soldier consists in the performance of his duties; you have worthily performed yours." This eulogium would have applied with great pertinency to Macdonald and his iron column, or to Oudinot and his steady battalions, but, pronounced over the Saxon troops, was the most impudent falsehood ever uttered by a sane man. Napoleon immediately issued an order of the day, in which he declared, that the proclamation of the Prince of Ponte Corvo was "*contrary to truth, to policy, and to national honour,*" that "the corps of the Prince of Ponte Corvo did not remain immovable as brass, but were the first to beat a retreat." This order of the day was directed to be circulated among the marshals and ministers alone, so as not to distress the Saxon troops.

This giving the lie so direct for once, perfectly stunned Bernadotte; and his feathers dropped still more, when he found, a few days after, that his corps was dissolved, and he was disgraced from his command. He sought, again and again, a private interview with Napoleon, but the latter steadily refused to see him, and the disgraced marshal returned to Paris.

One hardly knows which to be surprised at most in this proclamation of Bernadotte the falsehood it contained, the impudence that dare publish it, or the self-conceit that would presume to distribute that praise or blame which the Emperor alone had a right to do. One cannot help from getting a supreme contempt for such a character, however much military ability he may at other times exhibit.

On his return to Paris he was appointed by the Ministry to defend Antwerp from the attacks of the English, who had just landed at Walcheren: but no sooner did Napoleon hear of the appointment, than he sent Bessieres to supersede him. Soon after, Bernadotte publishing some other folly, Bonaparte exiled him. Subsequently, however, an interview took place between them at Vienna, which allayed somewhat the anger of the Emperor, and Prince Ponte Corvo was restored to favour. He received the appointment of governor of Rome, and was preparing to depart for Italy, when the astounding news was brought him, that he was elected Crown Prince of Sweden.

A revolution had taken place in Sweden, and Gustavus IV was dethroned. The government was immediately placed under the protection of Napoleon, but he refused to involve himself with the powers of the North by accepting such a trust. Efforts were then made to conclude an alliance between Prince Augustus, the heir apparent, and some member of the Bonaparte family. But an end was suddenly put to all expectations of this kind, by the death of the prince, who fell from his horse in a fit of apoplexy, while reviewing his guards. The throne was now open to aspirants. The states of Sweden had the power to choose their king, but they wished in their election to secure themselves against the grasping power of Russia. Russia, on the other hand, was anxious to have one on the throne who would be bound to her interests Napoleon one who would act as a sort of counterpoise to the growing strength of the former. In this state of affairs, the King of Denmark put in his claim and endeavoured to induce Bonaparte to support it. But the leading men in the kingdom were opposed to his appointment, as they knew it would be displeasing to the majority of the Swedes.

In the midst of this agitation and excitement, an article appeared in the *Journal des Débats*, declaring that the election of the King of Denmark would be acceptable to the Emperor. This sent consternation through Sweden; and amid other suggestions as to the mode of relieving themselves from embarrassment, some of the chief men proposed that a French general should be elected crown prince. The public mind naturally fell on Bernadotte, who in 1807 had commanded the army on the shores of the Baltic, and, by his kindness toward some Swedish prisoners taken in Poland, endeared himself to many of the inhabitants. Besides, he was regarded in Sweden as the favourite marshal of Napoleon. How much his gasconade while on the Baltic had to do with this opinion, it is impossible to tell. He was also the nearest relative of the Emperor, of any fame, without a throne, and to elect him, therefore, seemed to secure the protection of the former, which Sweden was determined to have at all hazards, for his star was then in the ascendant, and his strong arm was sufficient to protect any ally. Still, all these reasons combined would not, probably, have secured his election, but for the timely occurrence of a single mistake. The committee of twelve, appointed to recommend a successor to the Diet, met, and at the first ballot the young prince of Augustenburg had eleven votes, and Bernadotte one. The chances of the latter, therefore, were far from being favourable; but, previous to the day of final meeting, a French agent arrived, and announced, though without any authority, that the election of Bernadotte would meet the wishes of Napoleon. This settled the question at once, and he was chosen. Whose agent this was, or by whose instigation he was sent to make such a declaration, does not appear. At all events, the trick succeeded.

When the result was announced to Bernadotte, he referred the whole matter to Napoleon as his Emperor. The latter advised him to accept, and promised him two millions of francs as an outfit. English historians say, however, that he used every effort to dissuade him from accepting, and finally submitted with as good grace as possible, and endeavoured by his generosity and kindness to bind him to his interests. The picture they draw of him in this affair makes him appear in a most unenviable light; but there is only one statement necessary to render it all plain. If Napoleon had wished to prevent Bernadotte from taking the crown, he had but to say it, and that would have ended the matter; or had he intimated to the Diet of Sweden that he never would countenance the election, it would have been put aside. The sole motive of the Diet was to secure his good will and protection while Bernadotte would as soon have laid his head on the block, as undertaken to have filled the Swedish throne contrary to his command. All powerful as the former then was, it would have been madness to have done so without his hearty co-operation; and it was only because he was so powerful, that it was permitted by Denmark and Russia. The crown of Sweden was as much the gift of Napoleon to Bernadotte as if he had himself placed it on his head. It is true he wished him still to be a subject of France, as Murat was; but finding it repugnant to his feelings, withdrew his request.

Bernadotte entered Stockholm in triumph, and was immediately adopted by the aged Charles XIV as his son, with the name of Charles John. The old king being too far advanced in life to take an active part in matters of state, the government of Sweden depended on Bernadotte as much as if he had already been crowned. But with such a man at the head of affairs, it was not to be expected that friendly relations could long exist between Sweden and France. Napoleon insisted that the former, as it had virtually put itself under his protection, should share his fortunes and as he was then at war with England, immediately close her ports against English ships.

This Bernadotte refused to do until it became a choice between a war with England and one with France, and then submitted; though the fulfilment of his contract was a piece of mockery throughout. English goods were smuggled in, and a contraband trade kept up, so that the ports were really as open to British traders as ever. This system of double dealing was to secure two things: the revenue which trade with England furnished, and peace with France at the same time. The consequence was, that England did not trouble Swedish merchantmen, but let them go and come as in time of peace. This violation of good faith, and this deception, which was to be expected from Bernadotte, exasperated Napoleon beyond bounds, and he used stern and threatening language toward the treacherous government. Finding at last that nothing was to be gained by words, he seized on Pomerania, and treated Sweden as an open enemy: this completed the estrangement, and Bernadotte waited only for a favourable opportunity to ally himself with Russia against France. He hesitated, however, to provoke the deadly blow of the man he had learned to fear; and shuffled and delayed, and expostulated and promised, till the disastrous issue of the Russian campaign gave him hopes that the hour of his rival's overthrow had come.

Soon after, when the great confederacy was formed against the falling Emperor, he was assigned a conspicuous place in the conferences of Trachenberg; yet even here, his selfish and vain heart still hesitated. With the maps illustrating the proposed operations laid out before him, and flourishing his scented white pocket-handkerchief in his hand, he harangued with his usual pomposity on the greatness of the plans, and uttered flaming declarations of his zeal for the common cause; yet still hung back from the coalition. He was afraid that the mighty genius which had shaken Europe so long and so terribly would rise superior to the disasters that environed it; and then woe to the charity-King who had dared to open his cannon on the ranks of his countrymen, and against the benefactor who had given him his crown. His unbounded vanity also stepped in; and, if he joined the confederacy at all, he wished to be appointed commander-in-chief of the allied forces.

But at length this pompous King, this half-charlatan, half-genius, struck hands with Russia and Austria the former the natural enemy of his kingdom and at the head of 30,000 troops marched into the field. A Gascon to the last, he, in order to cover his infamy and excuse his conduct wrote a hypocritical impudent, and bombastic letter to Napoleon, urging him though at the time in a death-struggle for his throne to abandon the idea of universal dominion; and ended by declaring that in fighting against him he was espousing the cause of liberty against tyranny. False-hearted and false-tongued, he seemed to be ignorant when he was committing an insult, or uttering an untruth.

Moreau, another traitor to France, landed at this time in Europe from the United States, and proceeded immediately to Stralsund, to have an interview with Bernadotte. The latter received him with thunders of artillery, and all the pomp and display becoming a triumphant hero. Cordial in their hatred of Napoleon, these two generals, nevertheless, felt a little awkward when they began to concert together to subdue their former master, and march against the troops they had so often led to battle.

While Napoleon was overthrowing the allies at Dresden, Oudinot was advancing against Bernadotte, who intercepted his route to Berlin. With a little over 70,000 men he came upon the Prince Royal at Gros Beeren with over a hundred thousand troops at his disposal. With this overwhelming force against him, Oudinot, as mentioned before, was defeated with great slaughter. Ney, who superseded him, shared the same fate. These victories, for which even the panegyrists of Bernadotte give him but partial praise, filled his mind with extravagant ideas of his greatness, and he looked forward to the overthrow of Napoleon, as paving the way to the throne of France, to which he confidently expected to be called.

When the Allies marched on Paris, he hesitated for some time to cross the Rhine, and took no part in the campaign of 1814, which ended in the capitulation of the French capital. This his friends attribute to his love for France, and repugnance to appear as an enemy on the soil of his native country. But one would think that after he had butchered the troops which once followed him joyfully into battle and helped to overturn the government that had fostered him, he would have little scruple to march on Paris.

The truth is, his supreme selfishness, vanity, and ambition lay at the bottom of his inactivity. He was afraid that, if he pushed matters to extremity, it would interfere with his future prospects, so be kept aloof and addressed an inflated proclamation to the people of France, vindicating his conduct. But neither France nor the allied powers took the same exalted views of his capacities that he himself did; and he returned to Sweden, with only the gift of Norway in his hand, as a reward for his services in the common cause, and as a remuneration for the loss of Finland which Russia had wrested from his grasp. In 1818, the old monarch dying, Bernadotte was crowned King of Sweden, with the title of Charles XIV., and a few months after King of Norway also at Drontheim; and continued to reign as a very just and equitable monarch, though completely under the thumb of Russia. He died a few years since, and left his throne to his son Oscar. To this son, born in 1799, Napoleon stood as godfather and gave him his name. He married, in 1823, Josephine Maximilienne, eldest daughter of Eugene Beaubarnois, Viceroy of Italy.

It was thought, at the death of Bernadotte, that Prince Gustavus Vasa would make an effort for the throne but Oscar seated himself quietly in the place of his father, and now rules as a wise and able king.

Bernadotte has been extravagantly eulogized by his friends, and all his stupid jealousy and vain ambition tortured into integrity of character and true patriotism. The mere fact that he occupied a throne, and was able to manage well a country that did not require as much intelligence and strength of character as to rule the State of New York; and still better, that he struck hands with the allies and turned against the author of his fortunes, and the land of his birth, have placed him in great favour with the enemies of Napoleon. But had he exhibited the same vanity and ridiculous self-conceit enacted the same follies, and yet stood as firm to his master's cause as did the other marshals, he would have been the butt and ridicule of all historians.

Still, with all his boasting, he was firm and cool in the hour of danger, and of great energy and resources on the battle-field. He is called a great general, but it is bard to show where he merited the title. He was not an inferior one, it is true, nor does his career exhibit the traits of a superior one. His vanity and sensitiveness respecting the honour due him constantly interfered with the operations of his intellect; and with his mind divided between himself and the object he was after, he necessarily committed many blunders. He was a good general, and with a little more mind would have been a distinguished one. His bravery was proverbial to the army. He has been frequently known, when his men recoiled before a deadly fire, to throw his epaulettes among the enemy and thus shame them into bravery. In this respect he resembled a fighting-cock, of which his countenance almost instantaneously reminded one. With round, sharp eyes, a small, hooked nose, feeble intellectual developments, and a brusque, confident, and pompous air, he had all the courage of this warlike bird, as well as its amazing capacities for crowing. Even the allies, with whom he made common cause, gave him the sobriquet of Charles Jean Charlatan. Querulous, bombastic, vain, declamatory, and boasting, he so tasked the patience of Napoleon, that it required all his generosity of character, backed by his relationship, and the intercessions of his brother's wife, to prevent him from putting him one side, as an impracticable general and a trustless friend. Yet the rebukes which the former sometimes administered, English biographers declare grew out of envy of Bernadotte's brilliant talents and great achievements; while the vanity, jealousy, and envy of the latter, who could appreciate nobody but himself, and was fault-finding and intractable they call patriotism and hatred of tyranny. His denunciations of Napoleon, however, sprung from any source but Republicanism. Opposing his election as First Consul, then taking appointment from his hands when elected; conspiring against his authority and life, then swearing allegiance to his throne; too Republican to help place a man in power, yet fawning upon him when there; opposing vehemently the establishment of the Legion of Honour, afterwards wearing its insignia with pride when bestowed on him; declaiming like an old Roman against the assumption of regal power by Napoleon, yet grasping eagerly the first crown placed within his reach; mourning over the fall of liberty in France at the establishment of the Empire, yet banding with tyrants to overthrow what freedom there was left in Europe, he stands before the world the most singular republican and patriot it has ever produced. Quarrelling with his king and equals alike; too vain and conceited to obey, yet too shallow to command in chief; ready to sacrifice the welfare of the entire army in order to gratify personal pride; breaking over all rules of propriety in his arrogant attempts to screen his defeats; making use of his relationship to Napoleon to be restored to favour, after he had been disgraced, yet striking at his very heart the moment he can do it with safety; receiving a crown as a gift, and then helping to uncrown the giver; uttering frothy words of patriotism to France, yet invading her territory, overturning her throne, and sending a hostile army into her capital; false to his old friends and benefactor, and cruel as the grave to the land of his birth; traitor alike to his principles and the claims of gratitude; he is about as unsymmetrical and contemptible a character as one would wish to see on a throne. His panegyrists are welcome to their subject, and the haters of Bonaparte to their ally and friend.

Still, he was not a vindictive and cruel man in his disposition. His rapacity grew out of his love of display, his unscrupulous use of the means to elevate himself out of his inordinate ambition; and nine-tenths of all his follies and quarrels, out of his boundless vanity and incurable self-conceit. He obtained the character of charlatan among his friends, from his love of declamation, and great pleasure in hearing himself harangue; in short, he was a thorough Gascon intrepid, cool in the hour of danger had some genius some talent was very lucky; and, either by mistake or trick, obtained a crown, and took a place amid the kings of the earth, which has thrown a mantle over his character and a dignity about his name.

Marshal Suchet

CHAPTER 21

Marshal Suchet

It is difficult in a single sketch to do Suchet justice, or convey any correct idea of what he accomplished in his military career. His qualities were rather solid than brilliant, and the field on which be was compelled to exhibit them the most unfavourable that could well be given him.

Never operating on a large scale as commander of a corps till he was sent to Spain, he does not shine in the reflected glory of Napoleon's genius, and the only hale around his head is that which his own actions have made. All the other marshals were allowed, during some part of their lives, to serve under the Emperor as commanders of large bodies of men, and thus to distinguish themselves on those great battlefields whose renown filled the world. To direct one of the wings of Napoleon's army in a pitched battle, or to be appointed by him to lead an immense column on the centre, with the Imperial Guard and the resistless cuirassiers in reserve, gave opportunity for a brave, determined, and skilful leader to fix his fame forever. All felt this, and constantly sought to be near the Emperor and under his immediate control. Especially those in Spain earnestly wished to be recalled from a field where success gave little renown, and victory no laurels. The bare fact that Suchet's fame is not at all eclipsed by that of the other marshals, when he was compelled to operate alone, and in most disadvantageous circumstances, is the greatest evidence of his ability that can be given, and the highest encomium that can be passed on his career.

Louis Gabriel Suchet was born at Lyons, March 2, 1770. His father was a silk manufacturer, in moderate circumstances, and young Louis, at the age of twenty, entered the army as a private. Three years after he was placed over a battalion, and at the siege of Toulon first met the young Bonaparte. He distinguished himself at this siege by his gallant behaviour, and was soon after sent to the army of Italy. He fought bravely at Loano, and, charging at the head of his battalion, carried off three Austrian standards. He served here two years before Bonaparte was appointed to the chief command of the army, and then went through the glorious campaign of 1796 as chief of the eighteenth battalion under Massena. He fought at Dego, Lodi, and Borghetto; composed part of the tired army that arrived at Rivoli barely in time to save Napoleon from defeat; charged with impetuous valour along the mountain slopes at Castiglione; fought for three days on the dikes of Arcola; and, finally, at Cerea fell severely wounded. Before he had fairly recovered, he rejoined the army, and went through the Venetian campaign. He was again wounded at Tarvis, and at the fierce conflict of Newmarket poured his battalions with such fury on the enemy that he was made chief of brigade on the spot. Here he was again wounded; and General Joubert, under whose command he fought, did not forget afterward the young officer who had behaved so nobly.

In 1798 he went through the Swiss campaign, under Menard and Brune, and for his brilliant conduct was made the bearer of twenty-three standards, taken from the enemy, to the Directory. He expected to be joined to the expedition to Egypt, but was sent to the army of Italy, and from thence to that of the Danube, and fought bravely in the Grisons. Soon after, Joubert superseded Moreau in Italy, and Suchet was appointed chief of his staff, and given the command of a division. But his office as chief of staff soon terminated for, at Novi, in his opening battle, Joubert was killed and his army defeated.

When Bonaparte returned from Egypt, and sent Massena to Genoa, Sachet was placed over that wing of the army which rested on Nice. But, being separated from the former by the Austrian forces that came pouring in overwhelming numbers through the gorges of the Apennines, he was unable to render that intrepid general any assistance in the dreadful siege he endured.

In that almost hopeless attempt, however, to restore their communication when Massena fell on the enemy in front and he in rear Suchet led his army intrepidly against the dense masses of the Austrians. But, after a long, bloody, and useless struggle on the heights of Mount Giacomo, in which he left its sides strewed with his soldiers, he was driven back, and finally entrenched himself on the Var.

Thither the Austrian general advanced in close pursuit, and vainly endeavoured to dislodge him. In the mean time Genoa surrendered; and Melas, wishing to concentrate his forces so as to meet Napoleon, already in the plains of Italy, recalled those opposed to Suchet. But no sooner did the latter see his enemy preparing to retreat, than he immediately broke from the defensive he had so long maintained into a furious offensive, and pouring his now excited columns through the gorges and over the heights of the Apennines, fell on him in flank and rear, and, chasing the broken ranks over those dreary mountains, made every cliff and valley a battlefield; so that out of the eighteen thousand with which the Austrian commander first advanced on him, not more than ten thousand ever reached the main army. At Savona he met Massena with his worn and famine-struck troops; and then they two together kept watch and ward on the crest of the Apennines, till the shout of victory from the field of Marengo came rolling over their summits, announcing the overthrow of the Austrian power in Italy.

After the treaty of Luneville he received the appointment of inspector-general of the infantry, and shortly after was named a member of the Legion of Honour, and the next year made governor of the imperial palace of Lacken.

In the campaign of Austerlitz he showed himself worthy of a higher command than the one he held, and the next year (1806) opened the battle of Jena for Napoleon. On that foggy morning, Suchet at the head of his division, and Gazan with his, stood at four o'clock in battle array, when Napoleon came riding along their lines, and thus addressed them. "Soldiers! the Russian army is turned as the Austrian was a year ago at Ulm; it no longer struggles, but to be able to retreat. The corps which should permit itself to be broken would be dishonoured. Fear not it's famed cavalry; oppose to their charges firm squares and the bayonet." Fierce shouts answered him from those two brave divisions, as they panted for the onset. But the stubborn mist that involved everything prolonged the darkness, so that Suchet was compelled to keep the shivering lines waiting for two hours, before the signal of attack was given. At six o'clock, however, the order arrived, and he led his troops steadily and swiftly forward through the defiles that opened on the Prussian lines, carrying everything before him. The enemy saw him approaching through the mist, and met the shock with a firm and serried front; the artillery opened, and a rapid and heavy fire was kept up on the head of his column, so as to prevent it from deploying into the open plain. But nothing could stay his progress; the lines bent back before his charge, and he swept with his steady battalions up to the very muzzles of the guns, and wrenched them from the artillerymen and still kept pressing forward, clearing the field, till the advancing army had time to pass the gorges, and form in battle array on fair and open ground. It was at this moment the fog lifted, and the unclouded sun flashed down on the two armies, revealing the position of each to the other. Suchet's management of his division in this engagement showed both the mettle and quality of the man, and won the highest praise from the Emperor.

Two months after, he commanded the left wing of the army at the battle of Pultusk, and, attacking the Russian advanced posts, drove them through the forest, and sustained a long and most unequal combat, till Lannes arrived and relieved him.

In 1808 the grand cordon of the Legion of Honour was conferred on him, and he was created Count of the Empire. The road to the highest summit of military fame was now open to him, and he was prepared to follow it with all the energy, and skill, and daring which characterized him. But he was taken from these brilliant campaigns, and destined to operate, for the rest of his life, in a field offering but few inducements and promising but small reward. He was sent into Spain to supersede Junot in the command of the forces in Arragon. The latter chief had been taken sick, and Napoleon was glad of an excuse to remove one whose whole course in Portugal had been marked by rashness and folly. Nothing shows the sagacity of the French Emperor more than the correct judgment be formed of his generals. Here was Suchet, who had never held a separate command, but had fought only as general of division, suddenly placed at the head of a defeated army, and expected to restore discipline, create resources, and make head against a powerful enemy. This important post was not the reward of some great act of valour or devotion, but the result of sound calculation. Napoleon, who had watched the young Suchet from the time he fought by his side at Toulon, had seen how, through all his career, bravery was tempered with prudence, impetuosity with judgment; and he knew that he was just fitted for a war where something more than brilliant charges and fierce fighting was wanted.

When Suchet took command of Junot's army, he found it in a most miserable, inefficient state, and the campaign opened with sinister omens. With little over 8000 men he issued from Saragossa, where Lannes had lately performed such prodigies; and coming up with Blake posted at Alcanitz, with an army 12,000 strong, boldly gave him battle. Repulsed, and forced back, he was compelled to order a retreat. A panic followed, and the whole army fled pell-mell over the plain. Nothing but the cowardice of the Spanish troops saved him from utter ruin. This, however, ended his defeats, and falling back to Saragossa, he strained every nerve to repair his loss. But his troops were dispirited and murmuring, and many of his generals insisted on evacuating Arragon. Things looked dark around him, but this was a good school for the young general, for it immediately brought out the immense, but hitherto hidden, resources he possessed. Becoming superior to the sympathetic influence of general discouragement, firmly withstanding the counsels of officers who had served longer in the Peninsula than himself, rising above the dangers that surrounded him, he restored confidence to his soldiers and officers, and by his moral courage and calm and noble demeanour succeeded, at length, in putting a cheerful countenance on affairs. He fortified the city, and was placing everything in preparation for a close siege, when his victorious enemy appeared before the walls.

Suchet at first hesitated whether to give battle or retreat but feeling it was of the last importance to hold Saragossa, he resolved on the latter. With only 10,000 men, and twelve cannon, he boldly marched out of the city, and drew up in battle array in presence of 17,000 victorious troops supported by a numerous artillery. He immediately advanced to the attack, and the battle soon became general; but in the midst of the conflict a fierce and blinding storm arose, which for awhile separated the combatants. A sudden darkness wrapped everything and Suchet took advantage of the concealment it afforded him to arrange another attack; and the moment the rain slackened, he was again upon the enemy in a furious charge. Nothing could resist the vigour with which he pressed the Spanish lines, and after a short but sanguinary conflict he completely routed them, taking one general as prisoner, twenty guns, and several stands of colours. Following up his success, be pursued Blake to Belchite, and attacking him, though in a strong position, utterly overthrew him, so that the army disbanded and fled in every direction. With 4000 prisoners, all the artillery, ammunition, and baggage wagons of the enemy, he returned to Saragossa, master of Arragon.

He immediately put forth great efforts to quell the separate chiefs, that still, in small parties, infested the country, now making sudden irruptions and now retiring to their fastness; for before attempting to push his victories over the border, he wished to establish himself firmly where he was, and fix a permanent basis for all future operations. He showed himself an able ruler as well as a good commander, and commenced his administration by such wise and salutary measures that he won the confidence and good-will of the inhabitants he had conquered.

In one year he put himself in a position to extend his conquests; and his army having been reinforced from time to time, and now presenting a formidable appearance, he took the field. After subduing some smaller towns, he advanced against Lerida, and sat down before it in regular siege. Amid rain and the incessant fire of the enemy, he steadily prosecuted his works, till he at length mounted his battery, and opened a fierce fire on the place. As soon as a breach was effected, be determined to make an assault. In the night, while the cannon were still playing on different parts of the walls, the assaulting companies mounted the ramparts, and carried a part of the town; the next night, the citadel also, after a dreadful carnage, fell into their hands. He here adopted the same mild and conciliatory measures he had practiced before with so much success; and while be levied taxes sufficient to pay all the expenses of the war in Arragon, the manner in which they were collected, and the tyrannical restrictions he removed, made the burdens of the people less even than they were under the established government.

Planting his feet carefully and firmly, making every step give security to the next, he advanced from place to place, consolidating while he extended his power. No sooner had Lerida fallen than he advanced on Mequinenza. After a short siege this town also fell.

By these rapid measures and skilful movements, Suchet had now a frontier well protected from invasion from Catalonia and Valencia, and a solid basis on which to commence still more extensive operations.

In Catalonia, O'Donnell, with 20,000 men, still kept the French at bay. To destroy the base of his operations it was necessary to take Taragona; and to out off all communication by land between Catalonia and Valencia he must also reduce Tortosa. It was of the utmost importance to secure both of these objects, and Napoleon ordered Suchet to undertake the reduction of the latter, while Macdonald, who commanded the army in Catalonia, was to besiege the former city.

Suchet immediately set about his task, and marched on Tortosa. Macdonald, however, was sluggish in his movements, and did not co-operate with him as he should. In the meantime, the supplies of the latter began to fail, and he was exceedingly perplexed. He had been ordered to draw all his resources from Arragon, and within six months his army had consumed 120,000 sheep and 1200 bullocks. Amid these embarrassments he showed his profound wisdom, not only in managing military affairs, but also in the administration of government. Instead of resorting to threat and violence to draw forth resources from the country, and thus both impoverish and embitter the population, he called the chief of the clergy and the principal men of Arragon to his headquarters, "and, with their assistance, reorganized the whole system of internal administration in such a manner that, giving his confidence to the natives, removing many absurd restrictions to their industry and trade, and leaving the municipal power and police entirely in their hands he drew forth the resources of the provinces in greater abundance than before. And yet with less discontent, being well served and obeyed, both in matters of administration and police, by the Arragonese, whose feelings he was careful to soothe; showing himself in all things an able governor, as well as a great commander." Indeed Suchet made the Spaniards the conductors of his convoys of provisions, and acted more as if he were their lawful and peaceful ruler than their conqueror. Had Joseph Bonaparte possessed a tithe of his military and political ability, Spain, instead of being a drag on Napoleon in the decline of his fortunes, would have been an efficient aid.

At length he sat down in regular siege before Tortosa, while Macdonald defended all the mountain passes leading to Taragona, to keep back the Spanish army that might, from that direction, advance to the relief of the besieged. The place was strongly defended, both by nature and art, and garrisoned by 9000 men. He made regular approaches toward the walls, placed his guns in battery, and, opening his fire on the ramparts, succeeded, after ten days' hard labour, in effecting a breach. When the garrison perceived this, they displayed a white flag. But as there were no other demonstrations of surrender, and the French commander had suspicion of treachery, he continued his operations, and the next morning three white flags were displayed. The guard at the gates were still uncertain what to do; and while they were hesitating whether to surrender or not, Suchet rode up to them with his staff, followed by a company of grenadiers, and asked the commanding officer to conduct him to the governor. The officer hesitated a moment, and then, advised by those about him not to obey, was about to fire, when Suchet boldly threatened them with military execution if they did not instantly submit. In the mean time, the grenadiers entered the gate, and all was over. A hundred pieces of artillery, 10,000 muskets, and immense magazines, fell into the hands of the victors.

This constant and great success so pleased Napoleon, that he immediately took 17,000 men from the army of Macdonald, and attached them to that of Suchet, thus increasing it to 42,000, and called it the army of Arragon. A part of Catalonia, however, was embraced in its operations, and the siege of Taragona committed to it. This was a wise stroke of policy, as it took out of Macdonald's hands the most important part of Catalonia, and gave it to the latter, who was better fitted, both by disposition and talent, to carry on the kind of war it was necessary to wage. Macdonald was too slow and formal in his movements, and in waiting to deliver some heavy blow, was worn out and exhausted by the small though constant efforts of the enemy.

Suchet had now been two years in Spain, and his whole career marked by uninterrupted success. Surrounded with obstacles, in the midst of a hostile country, hemmed in by a still unconquered territory, he had, by his vigour and skill as a general, fixed himself firmly in Arragon; and by his wisdom and prudence as a civil ruler subdued the hostility of the inhabitants, and secured the co-operation even of his enemies. But his labour had scarcely begun, and nowhere does the greatness of his talents shine out with more lustre than in the....

Siege of Taragona

This place, divided into an upper and lower town, with one side resting on the sea and the other standing amid inaccessible rocks, was deemed by the garrison impregnable. The lower town was down in the plain, and divided from the upper by a strong rampart; while around both stretched a massive wall, protected by a line of strong redoubts, and covered by the fire of an English fleet which occupied the harbour. On one side only could the place be approached with any hope of success, and that was in the plain around the lower town. But here were strong artificial defences, while the fort of Olivo commanded all the open space in which the besieging army must operate.

The relative strength of the forces, changed from time to time, but the average proportion was 14,000 French against 17,000 Spaniards, without counting with the latter the inhabitants of the place. This was desperate odds, but made still greater by the British fleet in the bay, as well as by a Spanish army of 14,000 men, which was making preparations to raise the siege. An ordinary man would have sunk under these difficulties and abandoned the unequal contest, but it was in such crises that Suchet exhibited his great resources. Careful, prudent, and safe in all his plans, he nevertheless determined to persist in the siege. The subjugation of the place was of the utmost importance, involving the success of all future operations, both in Catalonia and Valencia, and he resolved to effect it, or perish before the walls.

At length all things being ready, he moved his small but resolute army forward; and, on the 4th of May, invested that part of the town between Fort Olivo and the sea. In doing this, however, the guns from the fort and from the English ships played upon his troops, massed in the open field, with such precision that two hundred men fell before night. The next day the garrison made a sally, but were repulsed, and Suchet closed with a firmer coil around the walls. His ranks, however, were battered so incessantly, and his troops so severely galled by the guns from Fort Olivo, that he determined, after a fortnight of severe toil and constant exposure of his men to the enemy's fire, to concentrate all his force against it alone. Fourteen thousand men, or a number equal to his entire army, defended it, protected by heavy cannon and high walls, yet his resolution was irrevocably taken.

He broke ground before the fort on the 21st, but so great were the difficulties that opposed him in advancing his trenches, and so severe the fire to which he was subjected, that a week had been wasted before he could bring a single cannon to bear with any force on the walls. On the 28th, however, thirteen guns, which had been dragged over the rocks amid a perfect tempest of grape-shot, opened a fierce fire upon them, and, thundering all that day and night and next day, finally effected a breach, though not sufficiently low to afford much hope for success in an assault.

But Suchet's position was every day becoming more critical. His men were constantly falling before the plunging fire of the fortress, and his forces gradually weakening beneath the repeated sorties of the garrison, while an army equal to his own was daily threatening him in the rear. On the evening of the 29th, therefore, he ordered an assault to be made, and, forming two columns of attack, passed along their ranks and addressed them in words of encouragement, telling them that everything rested on their bravery and success. The night was dark, and the garrison was not expecting any serious movement, as not one of their guns had yet been silenced. Four cannon were fired as the signal for the assault, and in a moment all the drums were beat, and the whole French line, with deafening shouts, and amidst a general discharge of musketry, advanced at once from all quarters against the walls, in order to distract the attention of the besieged from the real point of attack. The Spaniards, alarmed by this general onset and unable in the darkness to see the assailants, opened a furious fire around the entire ramparts. Nothing could exceed the spectacle Taragona at that moment presented; the rocky heights in the rear stood revealed in a lurid light, the ramparts were covered with flame, and the whole town flashed up in the surrounding gloom, as if wrapped in a sudden conflagration. This wild uproar roused up the English fleet, and a fierce cannonade opened also from the ships, and blazing projectiles crossed in huge semicircles over the French army. Amid this confusion and terror, and amid the thunder of four hundred cannon on the ramparts, to which the distant English guns added their heavy accompaniment, those two columns advanced swiftly and steadily to the assault. One column stumbled in the dark against some Spanish troops advancing to succour the fort, and becoming mingled with them, a part, in the general confusion, entered the town. The principal column, which was destined for the breach, found, when they reached the ditch, that their scaling-ladders were too short, for it was fifteen feet to the bottom. In the mean time, the whole front rank went down before the plunging fire from the ramparts, and the remainder were about giving way, when Vaccani, the Italian historian, beating down the paling that blocked the entrance to an old aqueduct that passed into the town, mounted the narrow bridge, followed by the Italian grenadiers, and thus descended into the ditch, and, rushing furiously through the breach, entered the fort.

In the morning the walls and ditches presented a most melancholy spectacle. They were covered with blood; while bodies, mangled by the heavy shot, lay in confused heaps at their base, and were scattered around on the rocks as far as the eye could reach. Suchet asked for a suspension of arms, that he might bury his dead, for the ground on which they lay was too rocky to admit of graves. This humane request was denied, and he was compelled to gather the two hundred of his men who had fallen in the assault into huge piles and burn them. The smoke and stench from these burning bodies arose on the morning air, carrying heavenward a fearful testimony of the horrors of war.

Fort Olivo was taken; but this was only a stepping-stone to the reduction of the place. Suchet's labours had only commenced, the weight and terror of the struggle had yet to come, and, without any delay he continued to urge forward his works. Amid constant sorties, and under a heavy and commanding fire from the upper and lower town, which constantly carried away his men, he pressed the attack so vigorously that every day he gained some new advantage over the enemy. Under a constant shower of balls and grapeshot, that smote every moment over the spot on which the workmen were engaged, he still steadily advanced his parallels. It was one incessant roar and flash above the soldiers, yet they dug and toiled away as calmly as in the peaceful field.

Thus the siege went on for nineteen days, after Fort Olivo was taken; till at length fifty-four guns were brought to bear on the enemy's batteries. But the metal of the besieged was too heavy for them, and they gradually became silent. In the meantime the English gun-boats had become effective, and sailing up the bay, began to pour their destructive fire on the besiegers. The Spanish army, so long expected, also, now made its appearance, and dangers began to thicken still darker around the French commander. Sending off, however, for a reinforcement of 3000 men, he was able to beat off and disperse the enemy, without abandoning for a moment the siege. Twenty-three days had now elapsed since the storming of the fort, and Suchet moved to make an attempt to carry the lower town also by assault. His cannon, after the first disaster, had gradually overcome and silenced those of the besieged, and opened three narrow breaches in the bastions. Through these he ordered 1500 grenadiers to charge, seconded by a strong storming party to repel all assistance from the upper town. At seven o'clock, at the discharge of four bombs the brave grenadiers rushed forward. In a moment the walls were covered with men, and the carnage became dreadful; but after an hour's desperate fighting, the besieged were driven back, and the assailants swarmed through the town with shouts Of victory. During this breathless and sanguinary struggle, the English fleet kept up an incessant cannonading on the French, the thunder and flash of their guns through the gloom heightening inconceivably the effect of the scene, while, to crown all, the warehouses on the harbour took fire, and burned with such fierceness that "the ships in port cut their cables and stood out to sea."

But no sooner was the town carried, and the troops rallied, than the soldiers were set to work; and before the garrison in the upper town could recover their confusion were again hidden in their trenches, digging steadily forward towards the walls.

Suchet had lost over three thousand men, and still the upper town was untouched. Forty-eight days of incessant toil and fighting had passed, and now just as hope began to dawn on his efforts, nearly two thousand British soldier from Cadiz entered the bay, while the Spanish army landward again advanced to succour the city. As the besieged saw those troops step ashore they sent up a shout of joy; but fortunately for Suchet the English officers thought the town could not be held, as the walls were fast crumbling before the heavy batteries, and withdrew entirely from the contest. The Spaniards were easily repulsed, and the works again pressed with redoubled vigour. Still Suchet's position was perilous in the extreme. He had made four different assaults lost one-fifth of his entire army, and exhausted his men by the labour which the immense works demanded. But the wall which now separated the enemy from him had no ditch at its base to embarrass the columns of attack, and the cannon were playing within musket-shot of the ramparts. A hedge of aloes, however, at the base presented a strong obstacle, and came very near preventing the success of the storming party.

At length breaches being made in the walls, Suchet prepared to make a final assault on the upper town. But as the prospects grew darker around the besieged their energy seemed redoubled, and their preparations to resist this last effort were of the most formidable kind. Three battalions crowded the breaches, supported by strong reserves; while heavy barricades were stretched across every street, to arrest the enemy the moment he should enter. In the mean time such a terrible fire was kept up from the ramparts that the parapets of the French trenches were shot away, and the gunners, uncovered, stood in full view, a certain mark for the enemy's bullets. They fell one after another, in their footsteps yet still others sternly stepped in their places, while the excitement, and the wish to close in the last mortal struggle, became so intent on both sides that the soldiers shook their muskets at each other, and shouted forth defiance in the midst of the balls that smote them down.

At length the signal for assault was given, and the maddened columns rushed forward. An open space of more than twenty rods was to be crossed before the wall was reached, and as the assailants emerged on this, a plunging fire received them, crushing them to the earth with frightful rapidity. Pressing sternly on, however, they came to the aloe-trees, which stood within five rods of the walls, when they were compelled to turn one side for a passage. This, together with the destructive fire before which they stood uncovered, threw the column into confusion, and it was just beginning to break and fly, when an Italian soldier named Bianchini, who had at his own request been allowed to join the forlorn hope, coolly stepped from the ranks, and bidding his comrades follow him, began all alone to ascend the breach. Dressed in white from head to foot, he looked more like a being from the unseen world, than a living man, as he glided onward, and silently and steadily ascended the wall. Regardless of the volleys of musketry that smote his breast, apparently unconscious of the blood that was bursting in streams from every part of his body, he kept on sternly on till he reached the top, and then fell dead. The French soldiers stopped and gazed with astonishment, almost with awe, at that solitary white figure, as it fearlessly strode into the breach, and then with a shout that rent the air, rushed after him. The breach was won the Spanish troops overthrown, and amid shouts of victory, and cries of despair, and yells of execration, the French thousands went pouring in and, forming into columns of attack, dashed into the barricaded streets, and, overcoming all resistance, swept like a devastating flood through the town. Some of the inhabitants rushed through the farther gate, others streamed over the ramparts, making for the sea; others still, driven to despair, flung themselves from the rocks. Still thousands were left behind, and on these the soldiery fell in brutal ferocity, and aged men and women, the young, the beautiful, and the helpless, were butchered without mercy. The most pitiful cries and agonizing shrieks and prayers for mercy pierced the heavens on every side. But the maddened troops, hardened against every appeal, smote on the right, and on the left; and it was one incessant flash through the streets, which were literally inundated with blood. The officers put forth every effort to stay the massacre, but the passions of the soldiers had now broken over all bounds, and nothing could arrest them. For nearly two months had they been shot at and taunted by the inhabitants, and now their hour of revenge had come, and reckless alike of sleep or rest, they moved in terror through the darkness. Before morning dawned on the appalling spectacle, *six thousand* wretched beings had been butchered in cold blood.

A city sacked presents one of the most frightful scenes this stained and depraved earth of ours ever exhibits. It is the culminating act of human ferocity and pitiless cruelty.

Taragona was won, and, though Suchet mourned over the violence that had stained his triumph, he could not but rejoice at the successful termination of his long toils, and his happy deliverance from the dangers that threatened every hour to swallow him up.

Still his labours had not terminated, and in a few hours after the city fell his troops were again in motion. The army that threatened so frequently to raise the siege of Taragona was overtaken at Villa Nueva, and 1500 made prisoners. The whole country was thrown into consternation, and the Spanish troops that so long defended Catalonia were fleeing in every direction for safety. Suchet marched eagerly forward; for, added to the consciousness that he had acted worthy of the trust committed to him, he here received dispatches from Napoleon creating him Marshal of the Empire. He at length came up to Montserrat, into which some of the fugitives had cast themselves, deeming the place impregnable. Indeed, it seemed so, for the rampart on the top was one of the strongest fortresses in that part of Spain. Situated on a high mountain, surrounded by rocks, and approachable only by winding paths that were protected by batteries, it bade defiance to all attacks. There was no foothold for an army, and the irregular, rocky, and isolated height looked, as Suchet said, "like the skeleton of a mountain." Still the daring marshal poured his troops over the rocks and along the paths, and despite the fierce fire kept up by the enemy, succeeded in carrying it.

He next advanced toward Valencia, prosecuting his war of sieges with astonishing success, and in September sat down before Saguntum, and opened his batteries on the place. Finding it would be slow work to reduce the city by regular approaches, he determined to carry it by escalade. Failing in his attempt, he erected other batteries, and, after effecting a breach, made another assault and was again baffled. After these two repulses his situation became extremely perilous; for blocked in by the enemy's fortresses, his communications all cut off or interrupted, and a fortified town before him defended by a strong garrison, his destruction seemed an easy matter to accomplish. But in this painful dilemma, Blake, the commander of the Spanish army kindly came to his relief. Trusting to his superior force, the latter resolved to march from Valencia and raise the siege of Saguntum, or decide the fate of the city by a fair fight in an open field. With 25,000 men he approached the place, and Suchet, with 17,000, joyfully advanced to meet him. At eight in the morning the battle of Saguntum commenced. The Spaniards, trusting to their superior numbers, rushed boldly to the attack. Successful at first, the inhabitants and garrison of the city, who crowded the ramparts, thought the hour of their deliverance had come, and waved their caps and handkerchiefs in the air, and shouted victory in the midst of the fire of the cannon which were playing furiously on the walls. Indeed, it began to look dark around the French marshal, for his effort to arrest the first success of the enemy had only added to it, and the excited Spaniards, victorious at all points, were pressing with loud shouts over the field.

In this critical moment, when all seemed lost, Suchet showed that, with all his prudence and calculation, in an emergency, he was prompt and deadly as a thunderbolt. Galloping to his reserve cuirassiers, his now last remaining hope, he rode among them, rousing their courage by words of enthusiasm and bravery, and, putting himself at their head, sounded the charge. Just then a ball pierced his shoulder, but all heedless of the wound, he continued to ride at the head of his brave cuirassiers. "March, trot, canter," fell in quick succession from his lips, and that terrible body of horse came rushing over the field as if it knew it carried the fate of the battle in its charge. The infantry gave way before those fierce riders, or were trampled under foot; the cavalry sunk under their onset; and, amid the close volley of musketry and through the fire of the artillery, they bore steadily down on the Spanish centre. At this moment they presented a magnificent spectacle. The close-packed helmets glittered in the sun; their flashing sabres made a dazzling line of light above them, as in perfect order the black and thundering squadrons swept onward to the final shock. Suchet still rode at their head, and, pouring his own stern resolution into their hearts, broke with resistless fury through the enemy's centre, and shouted the victory.

This settled the fate of Saguntum, and gave Suchet a permanent footing in Valencia. Not thinking himself, however, sufficiently strong to besiege the city of Valencia, as Blake still had an army a third larger than his own, and the place contained a strong garrison, together with a hundred and fifty thousand inhabitants; he sent to Napoleon for reinforcements.

But, in two months after the battle of Saguntum, his army was before the town, and the governor had been summoned to surrender. Blake, with his large army, endeavoured to stimulate the garrison to a brave defence, but the courage of the soldiers was broken, for the French commander had taken every city he had attacked; fortresses, and walls, and rocky heights seemed to present no impediment to his victorious troops.

Without waiting to make regular approaches, the latter, in utter contempt of his adversary, swept with his army around the entire city, and extending his lines over a space fifteen miles in circumference, beat back all the outposts, and began to bombard the place. In the meantime Blake, at the head of 15,000 men, undertook to cut his way through the French army, but, after a short struggle was driven back within the walls. He then offered to capitulate on certain conditions. These were sternly rejected; and he was finally compelled to surrender at discretion.

By this glorious victory Suchet got possession of one of the richest cities in Spain, made 16,000 prisoners of the best troops of the army, took nearly four hundred pieces of cannon, 20,000 stand of arms, immense military stores, and laid at his feet one of the finest provinces of the Peninsula. Instead of drawing resources from abroad for his own troops, he was now able to furnish them abundantly to the other portions of the army. In reward for his great services, Napoleon created hint Duke of Albufera, with the investiture of all its rich domains.

Having fortified himself at every point, and furnished a solid basis in Catalonia and Valencia to all his future operations, he the next year resumed the offensive; but his after-career, to the downfall of Bonaparte, presents no striking features. The defeat of Marmont at Salamanca, darkened the prospects of the French cause in Spain, yet still Suchet held firm his conquered provinces: but the battle of Vittoria completed the ruin, and made all his conquests comparatively worthless. With a heavy heart he was compelled to retire behind the Ebro; and, though defeating the English in some minor combats, his army took no important part in the after-struggles. Napoleon was endeavouring to drive back the allies from France, and the great conflict in the Peninsula was between Wellington and Soult.

After the abdication of the Emperor, Suchet received King Ferdinand, and conducted him to the Spanish army; and then, handing over his authority to the Duke of Angouléme, bade farewell to the brave troops he was no longer permitted to command. Made peer of France by Louis XVIII., and governor of the fifth military division at Strasburg, he remained at the latter place till the return of Napoleon. He continued firm to the royal cause till the King left France, and then, finding the tide of public opinion too strong to be resisted, hastened to Paris, and gave in his adhesion to Bonaparte. Placed over the Army of the Alps, consisting of only 10,000 men, he defeated the Piedmontese and afterwards the Austrians. But the advance of the main Austrian army, of a hundred thousand men, compelled him to retreat to Lyons. Surrendering the city on honourable terms, he went down with the mighty genius for whom he had combated so long and so bravely.

On the second restoration be was deprived of his civil, though he was permitted to retain his military, honours. In 1822, however, he was restored to the peerage, but died, four years after, in Marseilles, at the age of fifty-six.

Suchet was one of those well-balanced characters which is known more by what it accomplishes than by any striking feature it exhibits. There was less personality in his achievements than in those of such men as Murat and Junot, because his intellect had more to do with his success than his arms.

Destined to act in a field more unfavourable to his fame than any other in Europe, he nevertheless succeeded in placing himself among the first military leaders of his time. Spain was a sort of graduated scale which tested the altitude and real strength of every general who commanded in it; and of all the marshals who, from time to time, directed the French armies there, Massena, Soult, and Suchet alone stood the test; while of the English leaders Wellington was the only one that exhibited the higher qualities of a great military chieftain.

Suchet was a noble man, both intellectually and morally. With a mind that grasped the most extensive plans, and yet lost sight of none of the details necessary to success, he also had a heart that delighted to bestow blessings the moment stern duty allowed him to sheathe the sword of war.

Cautious and prudent in his plans, he was sudden and terrible in their execution. He was impetuous without being rash, and rapid without being hasty. He calculated his blow before he made it, but it was a thunderbolt when it fell. His mind was so perfectly balanced that he never exhibits obstinacy in carrying out a favourite plan, so common to one-sided men of strong character. Graduating itself to circumstances, it was careful or headlong, tardy or swift, as the case demanded. In one respect he resembled Napoleon he knew when to abandon a minor for a greater good. This was one great secret of Bonaparte's success in his first campaign in Italy. Flinging from him one advantage to gain a better, and relinquishing one conquest to secure a greater, he kept his forces constantly so concentrated that he could at any time bring his whole power to bear on a single point. This is indispensable to success with a small force arrayed against a great one, and it was a remarkable characteristic of Suchet's career in Spain. This seems not so striking a quality at first sight, but it is one of the rarest possessed by any man.

The campaigns of Suchet in Spain will always remain among the most wonderful of military achievements. With a small force in the midst of a hostile territory, compelled to carry on a guerrilla war with separate chiefs, a regular campaign with a large army, and at the same time, reduce fortresses, assault cities, and administer the government of conquered provinces he brought to the task before him a mental resource which stamps him the great man.

Amid the most overwhelming difficulties, and pressed constantly by superior force, he did not remain on the defensive, but steadily advanced from one victory to another now fighting the enemy in the open field, and now planting cannon against strongly fortified cities, till, at length, Arragon, Catalonia, and Valencia lay at his feet, and his task in the Peninsula was nobly accomplished. Uniting the profoundest military science with the greatest personal bravery the highest practical power with the most skilful theories, he planned and executed every military movement with extraordinary precision and success. He brought the same powerful mind to the administration of civil affairs, and not only conquered the provinces, but governed them with an ability that exhibits a breadth of character and extent of knowledge possessed by few of those stern leaders whom Napoleon clustered around his throne.

Marshal Poniatowski

CHAPTER 22

Marshal Poniatowski

I introduce a short sketch of Poniatowski, for the same reason that I did one of Brune, simply to make the gallery of marshals complete. Though his life and battles would make a volume by itself, still he does not occupy a prominent part in the history of the French Empire, nor form one of the chief characters in the great Napoleonic drama.

Joseph Poniatowski was born at Warsaw in 1763 of noble parents. Eleven years after his birth, in 1774, Stanislaus, his uncle, ascended the throne of Poland, and the family received the title of Prince. He first appears on the stage of action in 1794, just before the final partition of Poland. This unhappy republic, which Providence, from some inscrutable designs of its own, has allowed to be trampled under foot, and blotted out from the map of nations by tyrants, as no other country ever before has been, was destined to see its final overthrow under the brave, noble-hearted, and patriotic Kosciusko. Divided and portioned off in 1772 by the two Imperial robbers who sat on the thrones of Russia and Austria, and re-divided in 1793 by Russia and Prussia, the cup of her suffering seemed full. The royal plunderers kept two immense armies marching over her territory, to take care of the rich booty that already began to burn in their hands; until, at length, the energy and courage of despair took the place of submission, and a devoted band of patriots, maddened by the injustice and outrage everywhere committed, resolved to save their country or perish in the effort. Kosciusko, a name which can never be spoken in an American assembly without sending a thrill of emotion through every heart, was chosen their leader. This patriot and warrior had just seen a band of freemen hurl from their necks the yoke of oppression which a tyrannical power sought to fasten there; and, side by side with their chieftains, had nobly struggled in their cause. With joy he had witnessed the triumph of freedom on these shores, and then, when his work was done, sheathed his sword, and with a sad heart turned his footsteps toward unhappy Poland. When the war-cry was shouted from the streets of Warsaw, and he was declared the leader of the patriots, he knew it was a dreadful struggle in which he was to engage. But he had learned from the success of our almost hopeless struggle to have faith in the power of Right, and firmly stepped before the little band that had nobly thrown themselves between their country and the armies of two powerful despots.

Poniatowski took command of one of the divisions in Kosciusko's army, although in 1792 the latter served as major-general under him in his expedition against the Russians; and during the short but sanguinary struggle that followed, exhibited that valour which afterwards won the highest praise from Napoleon. The Poles, though at first successful, were finally utterly routed at Maciejowice, and Kosciusko, covered with wounds, was taken prisoner. Poniatowski then fled to Warsaw, determined to defend it to the last; thither also the Russian thousands swarmed, with the pitiless Suwarrow at their head. The Poles in Praga, on the other side of the river, fortified themselves, and planted a hundred cannon so as to sweep the bridge of the Vistula; but the indomitable Russian hurled his massive columns in such strength on the patriots that in spite of their utmost endeavours they were rolled back toward the river. Forced in a confused crowd on the bridge, they crushed the yielding structure under their feet, and were precipitated headlong into the stream.

Warsaw shrieked in dismay and anguish, as she saw her brave sons cut off from her protecting walls the river ran blood, and amid the flames of the burning houses, and cries of despair, Suwarrow raged with his bloodhounds amid the defenceless multitude. Women and children fell in the indiscriminate massacre, infants were carried about on the points of Cossack lances, and over eleven thousand bodies were piled in the streets of Praga, and along the banks of the Vistula.

Warsaw fell, and Poniatowski, dejected and disheartened, went to Vienna. The Emperor and Empress, Paul and Catherine, used every endeavour to reconcile him to their sway; but his uncle was a prisoner in Petersburg, his family driven from the throne, and Poland, rent asunder, had been divided like a carcass among wild animals; and he wished no connection with the doers of all this wrong. His heart burning with indignation, and his memory still fresh with the bloody scenes he had seen at Warsaw, be rejected all their offers, and lived in retirement on his estate.

Here he remained inactive while Europe was shaking with battles, apparently indifferent to the strife going on about him, since Poland was no more; till 1807, when Napoleon overthrew the army of Russia at Friedland. In the treaty of Tilsit that followed, it was stipulated that the provinces, which before the partition in 1772 belonged to Poland, and had since been held by Prussia, should be formed into the Duchy of Warsaw, and given to the King of Saxony. This initiatory step towards wresting back from those grasping powers their ill-gotten territory aroused Poniatowski from his indifference, and he accepted the office of minister of state in the new Duchy. He now began to look on Napoleon's movements with the deepest anxiety, and gradually identified himself with his interests, till he fell in the struggle to sustain his tottering empire. He felt that the only hope of his country was in the success of the French Emperor, and he bent all his energies to secure it: he had faith in him, and knew it was the wish of his heart to re-establish the fallen throne. Many of the patriot Poles have wronged Napoleon, in condemning him or not doing more for Poland than he did, but will they lay their finger on the spot where he could, without endangering the welfare of his own country, have emancipated theirs? It required a stronger hand than even his, to wrest away the plunder the three most powerful governments of the Continent had divided among themselves. It would have been the cause of an endless quarrel; and instead of struggling for France, he would have been compelled to devote all his energies to the safety and existence of Poland. It is true the Poles poured out their blood for him like water, and, glad to scourge the nations that had trampled them under foot, and at the same time strike tyranny in any part of the world, flocked to his victorious standard, and bore him triumphantly over many a battlefield. Their great services demanded a great reward, and could Napoleon have succeeded in his invasion of Russia, they would have had no cause to complain of his want of generosity. Russia's share of Poland would certainly have been given back to her, and Poniatowski knew it. Beloved by the Emperor, he was made aware of his designs and wishes, and hence felt that in helping him to crush the powers about him he was preparing the way for the resurrection of his country. Bonaparte declared at St. Helena that he intended, if he had succeeded in Russia, to have placed him on the throne.

He continued in the Duchy of Warsaw, protected by the powerful arm of the French Emperor, till 1809, when Austria, for the sole purpose of frightening Saxony out of her friendship for France, invaded it. Russia was then the ally of the latter, and had promised to protect Warsaw, so that Napoleon had made no provisions for its defence. More than 30,000 Austrians were moving down on that dependent province, to meet which Poniatowski could bring only 12,000 men into the field. Scorning, however, to ask the co-operation of his Russian allies, whom he hated as cordially as he did the Austrians, he prepared alone to meet this formidable array. He drew up his inconsiderable force at Raszyn, and there, for four hours, withstood the whole shock of the Austrian army. But 12,000 against 30,000 was too great an inequality; and he was compelled to fall back on Warsaw. Forced, at length, to capitulate, he marched with heavy heart out of the capital, accompanied by the authorities and all the principal inhabitants of the city.

The Archduke Ferdinand supposed he would immediately abandon the Duchy and retreat to Saxony, but Poniatowski boldly resolved to dispute his territory to the last; and returned up the Vistula, towards Gallicia, whither the Russian army was slowly marching, in order to co-operate with his troops. In the mean time, however, he surprised an Austrian division and took 1500 prisoners. But, in pursuing up his advantage, he effected a more important capture, and made a discovery which showed how little reliance could be placed on the good faith of those governments with which Bonaparte was compelled to treat. A courier, on his way to the Austrian headquarters, was intercepted, and in his dispatches was found a letter from a Russian general to Archduke Ferdinand, congratulating him on his capture of Warsaw confidently predicting complete success to his efforts, and winding up with the wish that their arms might soon be united in the same cause. This certainly was a most peculiar letter to be sent from an ally to an enemy, and calculated to throw some doubts over the honesty of the Russian Emperor. Poniatowski immediately forwarded it to Bonaparte, in whom it aroused the most violent indignation. He dispatched it instantly to the Emperor Alexander, and demanded, in language that could not be misunderstood, an explanation. The Emperor declared it was written without his authority; and, as an evidence of his sincerity, immediately removed the unlucky general who was its author. Napoleon professed to be satisfied, but it was evident that the great sin of the general consisted in being found out. Conversing with Savary afterward, he said "I was perfectly in the right not to trust such allies. What worse could have happened if I had not made peace with the Russians? What have I gained by their alliance? It is more than probable that they would have declared openly against me, if a remnant of regard to the faith of treaties had not prevented them. We must not deceive ourselves; *they have all fixed a rendezvous on my tomb, but they have not the courage openly to set out thither.* That the Emperor Alexander should come to my assistance is conceivable, but that he should permit Warsaw to be taken, almost in presence of the army is, indeed, hardly credible; it is plain that I can no longer rely on an alliance in that quarter. . . . And yet, after all, they will probably say that I am wanting in my engagements, and cannot remain at peace."

Soon after Napoleon's operations on the Danube calling the attention of Ferdinand from Warsaw, he withdrew his forces, and was finally compelled to leave the Duchy. The battle of Wagram and the peace of Vienna followed, and among the stipulations of the treaty, a territory, containing about 150,000 inhabitants, was taken from Russia and added to the Duchy of Warsaw. Thus Poland seemed to be getting back by slow degrees her ancient possessions. The outcry that Russia made about this strip of land, although a piece was cut from Austria and given to her as an offset, should convince the friends of Poland how difficult it would have been for Bonaparte to have wrenched from the sordid grasp of those monarchs the entire kingdom they had dismembered. It is pitiful to see with what greediness those royal plunderers gloated over their ill-gotten gains, and how narrowly they watched every shiver of the corpse they had mutilated.

At length, all other considerations were forgotten in the contemplated invasion of Russia. Napoleon, by his wonderful genius, had at length subdued his rivals, and not only induced Austria, and Prussia, and the whole territory from the Rhine to the Niemen to allow his armies a free passage, but he had prevailed on each monarch to furnish his quota of men to march under his banners and fight for the accomplishment of his plans. Among those who opposed the expedition, yet, when resolved upon, gave soul and heart to it, was Poniatowski; bringing nearly 40,000 Poles to swell the myriad numbers of the Grand Army. He fought bravely at the head of his followers, and at Smolensko and Borodino, and throughout the desolate retreat, brought a good sword, a noble heart, and a strong intellect to the aid of the Emperor. And then was seen the just retribution of Heaven. Poniatowski had witnessed the degradation of his country by Russian power, his capital sacked by Russian barbarians, and its women and children butchered in thousands by Russian soldiers. His proud heart had been compelled to bear and to suffer all this, and now the day of vengeance had come. He poured his victorious Poles through the burning streets of Smolensko, and bade them pitch their tents amid the ruins of the capital of his haughty enemy. The fire and the sword had been carried back to the homes of the invaders, and the cup they had compelled Poland to drink pressed to their trembling lips.

In the fatal retreat the Poles suffered less than any of the others, and exhibited great bravery and endurance. The first man across the Beresina was a Pole, and Napoleon never had better or more devoted troops than the Polish soldiers.

Poniatowski still clung with his diminished army to Napoleon in his falling fortunes, and at Leipzig fought his last battle, and poured out his life-blood for him and his cause.

The defection of Bavaria previous to the battle of Leipzig, and the treachery of the Saxon troops in the heat of the engagement, determined its issue and settled the fate of the French Empire. The allies brought to the encounter nearly 300,000 men and 1300 cannon, while Bonaparte had but 175,000 and 750 cannon. The latter were drawn up around Leipzig with the city and the river Elster lying in rear awaiting the onset of the immense host that was moving to the attack. On the last fatal day, at nine o'clock, the battle opened, and nearly half a million of men engaged in mortal combat. The scene at this moment was indescribably awful the whole plain was black with the moving masses, save where the myriads of glittering helmets rose and fell in the sunlight, while 800 cannon, in one huge semi-circle, opened their united thunder on the French.

Clouds of dust filled the air and amid the roar of artillery, the strains of martial music, the shrill neighing of tens of thousands of horses moving to battle, and all the deafening clamour and solemn murmurs of a mighty army, the shock came. Nearly two thousand cannon opened with terrific explosions on the living masses, and the frightful carnage began. Poniatowski on the right, was the first engaged. Made Marshal of France the day before by the Emperor, he burned to distinguish himself; and, though at first forced back by the heavy charge, he firmly held his position against the united onsets of artillery, cavalry, and infantry, that from morning till night thundered in overwhelming numbers and power on his diminished troops. A wilder day this earth never saw, and when darkness separated the combatants both armies sank down exhausted and silence, solemn and awful, fell over the bloody field.

Napoleon was beaten, and soon gave orders to retreat. All night long the weary thousands went pouring over the bridge, and when daylight dawned the allies beheld with joy the retiring masses of the enemy. A general movement on Leipzig immediately followed, and the victorious columns went rushing with shouts to the attack. All was uproar and confusion. Artillery, infantry, cavalry, ammunition and baggage wagons, and chariots, were crowded and rolled together, and went streaming over the only remaining bridge. A rear guard under Macdonald, Lauriston, and Poniatowski, was formed to cover this disorderly retreat. As Napoleon gave his directions to each, he said to Poniatowski, "Prince, you will defend the suburbs of the south." "Sire," he replied, "I have but few followers left." (He had but 2700 men left out of all the brave Poles he led two days before into battle.) "What then," added Napoleon, "you will defend it with what you have!" "Ah, sire!" replied the exhausted but still unconquered chieftain, "we are all ready to die for your Majesty!"

I have already spoken in my sketch of Macdonald, of the heroic defence these two leaders made, and of the consternation and woe that followed the premature blowing up of the bridge. Poniatowski struggled bravely to arrest the victorious allies, until he heard the explosion that sent it into the air; and then he drew his sword, saying to the officers around him, "Gentlemen, it now behoves us to die with honour." With his little band around him, be dashed on a column of the enemy that crossed his path, and, though severely wounded, he fought his way through to the Pleisse, a small stream he must cross before he reached the Elster. Dismounting from his horse, he passed it on foot, but finding that he was fainting from fatigue and loss of blood, he attempted to mount another. With difficulty vaulting to the saddle, he spurred boldly into the Elster. His good steed bore him safely across, but as he was struggling up the opposite bank the earth gave way under his feet, and he fell back on his rider and Poniatowski disappeared in the water and never rose again. Weary, wounded, and bleeding, this last calamity was too much for his strength and he had done as he said, "died with honour."

The allies celebrated his funeral with great magnificence, and those kings who had driven his family from the throne, buried his capital in ashes, plundered and divided his country as if it were common booty, now gathered in solemn pomp around his coffin. Countless banners drooped mournfully over the fallen chief mighty armies formed his funeral procession, and elegiac strains from a thousand trumpets were breathed over his grave. But amid all this imposing mockery of woe, the noble-hearted Pole was not without some sincere mourners. His few remaining followers who had battled by his side to the last, pressed in silence around his coffin, and, with tears streaming down their faces, reached out their hands to touch the pall. There lay the Prince they had loved, the leader they had followed, the last of the royal line, and the only hope of Poland cold and stiff in death. Ah! the tears of those rough warriors were worth more than all the pomp and magnificence imperial pride had gathered round that bier, and honoured the patriot for whom they were shed more than royal eulogies or splendid pageants.

"Poniatowski," said Napoleon, "was a noble character, full of honour and bravery," a short but comprehensive eulogium. A skilful commander a bold warrior, and true friend; wise in counsel, of pure patriotism and unsullied honour, he was beloved by his friends and mourned by his enemies. He had redeemed all the follies of his weak relative Stanislaus, and proved that he was worthy to sit on the throne of Poland. Tried by misfortune, he was never found wanting: his enemies could not bribe him nor his friends allure him from that deep devotion to his country which was the great passion of his life. He left no spot on his name, and at the last preferred death to surrender, and proudly let his enemies dig his grave, conscious that when they lay his sword across his coffin none dare point to a stain on the blade.

Marshal Grouchy

CHAPTER 23

Marshal Grouchy

Grouchy's bad management at the battle of Waterloo has ruined his fame and placed him in an unenviable position before the world. In the intense excitement the final overthrow of Napoleon created, Grouchy's name became the theme of universal obloquy, and he was accused of weakness, want of energy, and, finally, of having sold France to the allies. It is true, English historians, with that liberality they always show toward those enemies who, through treachery or weakness, injured the cause of Napoleon, have endeavoured to defend him, not only against the charge of treason, but also of inefficiency. Indeed, to throw much blame on him would be to confess that the victory of Waterloo was owing more to accident than to skill.

Still Emmanuel Grouchy was a brave man, and through a long and honourable career sustained the reputation of an able commander. A count of the ancient regime, he was born at Paris in 1766, and entered the service when only fourteen years of age. At nineteen he was an officer in the King's body-guard, but threw up his commission at the breaking out of the Revolution, and joined the cause of the people, and was made colonel of a regiment of dragoons. Soon after, however, the Republican government decreed that no person of noble birth should hold any rank in the army, and he was left without employment. He retired into the country awhile, but, becoming weary of his inactive life, entered the National Guards as a private, and fought against the Vendéans. He seemed to have joined the cause of freedom sincerely, and said, "Though I am not allowed to fight at the head of the Republican phalanxes, they cannot prevent me from shedding my blood in the cause of the people." In 1792, however, he was reinstated in his former rank of commander of a regiment of dragoons, and the next year was placed at the head of all the cavalry in Savoy and the Alps. In the campaign of 1794, against the Vendéans, be distinguished himself, especially at Québeron, where he attacked and defeated the emigrants; and the next year he was made general of division.

In 1796 he was joined to the expedition under Hoche, to aid the Irish in their attempts to recover their liberty. The fleet was dispersed by a storm, and only a portion of it reached Bantry Bay, yet still Grouchy, with only 6000 men under his command, was willing to land, but was overruled by Admiral Bouvet, and the expedition abandoned. In 1798, he was sent into Piedmont as commander-in-chief of the forces there, and took possession of the country, and the next year fought gallantly at the disastrous battle of Novi.

A short time previous to this engagement, Joubert was appointed to supersede Moreau in the command of the dispirited Army of Italy, which had met with nothing but defeat since Bonaparte's departure for Egypt. Just married, he left his young wife, saying, "You will see me again either dead or victorious." With his utmost efforts he could muster but 40,000 men to resist Suwarrow, marching against him with 60,000 victorious troops. Forced to accept battle at Novi, he struggled nobly against this overwhelming force, and strained every nerve to save his army and secure a victory.

The French were formed in a semicircle on the slopes of Monte Rotondo, which commands the whole plain of Novi. Grouchy commanded a division on the left, and was the first engaged. Joubert fell at the commencement of the fight, and as the charging battalions rushed over him as he lay dying, and hesitated whether to advance, he shouted faintly forth, "Forward, my lads! forward!" The battle raged with frightful carnage during the hot August day, and the Russians were again and again repulsed; but the invincible Suwarrow, dressed in his usual costume, in his shirt down to the waist, kept pouring his strong legions into the battle, until at length Moreau, who had succeeded in the command, ordered a retreat. Grouchy had fought with the most obstinate courage during the day, and, though wounded, still led his columns again and again to the charge. Foremost in the fight he moved undauntedly through the hottest of the fire, cheering on his men by his enthusiastic appeals, and still more by his heroic example. Once, his troops reeling back from the shock, he threw himself at their head, and seizing a standard cried, "Forward!" and drove headlong on the foe. The standard being wrenched from his hand in the close and fierce struggle, he took off his helmet, and lifting it on his sabre over his head, continued to advance, when be was wounded and overthrown, and trampled under foot. Extricating himself from the dying mass amid which he lay, he again put himself at the head of his followers, and rushed to the charge.

In retreating, in obedience to the orders of Moreau, he was opposed to a succession of heavy onsets, against which his men could with difficulty bear up; and, to complete his overthrow, a Russian battalion crept around into a ravine, and poured their unexhausted fire on his exhausted troops in the rear. This threw them into disorder, and artillery, infantry, and cavalry disbanded and fled in wild confusion over the fields. Grouchy, though severely wounded, bravely attempted, with Perignon, to stem the tide; and, rallying a few followers, again charged on the overwhelming numbers that were sweeping over the broken ranks. Again overthrown, and almost cut to pieces, he was made prisoner, having received *six sabre wounds*. Nothing but the most desperate hand-to-hand fighting could have caused him to receive so many sword-cuts, and he this day proved himself worthy to command the troops that had fought under Napoleon.

His wounds would have proved mortal but for the kindness of the Grand Duke Constantine, who sent him his private physician, and made his own domestics attend upon him. After four months of suffering, he recovered his health, and in the exchanges that followed the battle of Marengo was restored to the army, and joined Moreau, then combating on the banks of the Rhine. He was present at the battle of Hohenlinden, and was one of the chief actors in that great tragedy. Struggling side by side with Ney, his actions were not eclipsed by those even of "The bravest of the brave."

Battle of Hohenlinden

The Iser and the Inn, as they flow from the Alps toward the Danube, move nearly in parallel lines, and nearly forty miles apart. As they approach the river the space between them becomes one elevated plain, covered chiefly with a sombre, dark pine forest, crossed by two roads only, while the mere country paths that wind through it here and there give no space to marching columns. Moreau had advanced across this forest to the Inn, where, on the 1st of December, he was attacked and forced to retrace his steps, and take up his position on the farther side, at the village of Hohenlinden. Here, where ore of the great roads debouched from the woods he placed Ney and Grouchy.

The Austrians, in four massive columns, plunged into this gloomy wilderness, designing to meet in the open plain of Hohenlinden the central column marching along the high road, while those on either side made their way through, amid the trees, as they best could.

It was a stormy December morning when those 70,000 men were swallowed from sight in the dark defiles of Hohenlinden. The day before it had rained heavily, and the roads were almost impassable; but now a furious snowstorm darkened the heavens and covered the ground with one white, unbroken surface. The by-paths were blotted out, and the sighing pines overhead drooped with their snowy burdens above the ranks, or shook them down on the heads of the soldiers, as the artillery wheels smote against their trunks. It was a strange spectacle, those long dark columns, out of sight of each other, stretching through the dreary forest by themselves; while the failing snow, sifting over the ranks, made the unmarked way still more solitary. The soft and yielding mass broke the tread of the advancing hosts, while the artillery and ammunition and baggage wagons gave forth a muffled sound, that seemed prophetic of some mournful catastrophe. The centre column alone had a hundred cannon in its train, while behind these were five hundred wagons the whole closed up by the slowly moving cavalry. Thus marching, it came about nine o'clock upon Hohenlinden, and attempted to debouch into the plain, when Grouchy fell upon it with such fury that it was forced back into the woods. In a moment the old forest was alive with echoes, and its gloomy recesses illumined with the blaze of artillery. Grouchy, Grandjean and Ney put forth incredible efforts to keep this immense force from deploying into the open field. The two former struggled with the energy of desperation to hold their ground, and although the soldiers could not see the enemy's lines, the storm was so thick, yet they took aim at the flashes that issued from the wood, and thus the two armies fought. The pine trees were cut in two like reeds by the artillery, and fell with a crash on the Austrian columns, while the fresh-fallen snow turned red with the flowing blood. In the mean time Richenpanse, who had been sent by a circuitous route with a single division to attack the enemy's rear, had accomplished his mission. Though his division had been cut in two, and irretrievably separated by the Austrian left wing, the brave general continued to advance, and with only 3000 men fell boldly on 40,000 Austrians. As soon as Moreau heard the sound of his cannon through the forest, and saw the alarm it spread amid the enemy's ranks, he ordered Ney and Grouchy to charge full on the Austrian centre. Checked, then overthrown, that broken column was rolled back in disorder, and utterly routed. Campbell, the poet, stood in a tower and gazed on this terrible scene, and in the midst of the fight composed, in part, that stirring ode which is known as far as the English language is spoken.

The depths of the dark forest swallowed the struggling hosts from sight; but still there issued forth from its bosom shouts and yells, mingled with the thunder of cannon and all the confused noise of battle. The Austrians were utterly routed, and the frightened cavalry went plunging through the crowds of fugitives into the wood the artillerymen cut their traces, and, leaving their guns behind, mounted their horses and galloped away and that magnificent column, as sent by some violent explosion, was hurled in shattered fragments on every side. For miles the white ground was sprinkled with dead bodies, and when the battle left the forest, and the pine-trees again stood calm and silent in the wintry night, piercing cries and groans issued out of the gloom in every direction sufferer answering sufferer as he lay and writhed on the cold snow. Twenty thousand men were scattered there amid the trees, while broken carriages and wagons, and deserted guns, spread a perfect wreck around.

Soon after this decisive battle, peace was proclaimed, and Grouchy returned to Paris, and was appointed inspector-general of cavalry. Here be remained several years, and during the trial of Moreau rather took sides with his old commander; for he had fought by his side at Novi, and in the forests of Hohenlinden, and could not bear to see him disgraced. Napoleon, however, retained him in command, though be did not honour him with those places of trust to which his long services entitled him.

But in 1807, at the battle of Friedland, he was put over the cavalry of the left wing, and charged with his accustomed impetuosity, rendering efficient aid in securing the victory. He soon after, in reward for his bravery, was named Grand Eagle of the Legion of

Honour, made Count of the Empire, and Commander of the Iron Crown. The next year he was sent with Murat into Spain, and in the insurrection in Madrid the commencement of the Spanish war he had a horse shot under him while charging on the mob. After the riot was quelled, Murat, enraged at the slaughter of his troops by the populace, ordered all the prisoners to be tried by a military commission and shot. Grouchy was president of this court, and is accused of having put forty to death after orders had been received to stop the execution; but the charge has never yet been substantiated.

In 1809 he was sent into Italy, and, after fighting bravely under Eugene, passed with him into Hungary, and helped to gain the battle of Raab. This action took place on the 1st of June, the anniversary of the battle of Marengo, and both armies were anxious to commemorate it the one to wipe out its disgrace, and the other to add to its glory. The Austrians were 45,000 strong, while the French had only 35,000. The conflict from the commencement was fierce and close; and around the centre victory for a long time wavered to and fro. One moment the Austrians would be driving the French before them with victorious shouts, and the next moment sallying back under the fierce onsets that met them. Thus the battle raged with changing success, till at length the French yielded, and the Austrians and Hungarians, carried away by the excitement of the moment, advanced rapidly, and too far, for the purpose of outflanking them. The French generals immediately took advantage of the error, and closed on them in a dense column, which rolled the disordered mass before it as a resistless current beats back the waves from the shore.

Grouchy and Montbrun commanded the right wing, the former having charge of the heavy dragoons, and were compelled to sustain the whole weight of the Hungarian cavalry, 7,000 strong. When this formidable body of horse put itself in motion, and came thundering down on the French lines, it threatened to crush everything before it. Montbrun's division was broken into fragments, and those fierce horsemen swept onward, trampling down the helpless ranks with resistless power, and sending dismay over the field. At this crisis, Grouchy ordered his terrible cuirassiers to advance, and sounded the charge. Their flashing helmets and glittering sabres were one moment seen above the dark mass below, like the foam on the crest of the wave, and the next moment driving furiously through the shattered squadrons that attempted to stay their progress.

The Austrians were routed, and Eugene hurried on his victorious troops to the Danube, where Napoleon lay with his defeated army, in the island of Lobau. In the battle of Wagram which immediately followed, Grouchy sustained his hard-earned reputation. In the attack on Neusiedel, he, with Montbrun and Arighi, commanded 10,000 horse, and made fearful havoc with the enemy's ranks. Friant and Morand, the heroes of Auerstadt, boldly mounted the heights in the face of a wasting fire, and, after a furious contest, reached the plateau. It was then the Austrian cavalry came down on the heavy-armed cuirassiers of Grouchy with their tremendous onset. Again and again did these two powerful bodies of horse meet in full career, and as often were the Austrians broken and rolled back, till at length, heavy reinforcements coming up, they rallied and charged again, and drove the now exhausted Grouchy, whose horses were blown in the long encounter, before them in confusion. Just then Montbrun rushed to the rescue, and by a gallant charge again turned the tide of success.

During this protracted and doubtful contest, Grouchy cast himself fearlessly into every danger, and rode sternly and fiercely at the head of his squadrons, and by his cheering and enthusiastic words carried his men again and again to the shock, with an impetuosity and daring worthy of Murat. He acted over again his great deeds at Novi, and seemed determined to fall on the field or win the victory.

His bravery on the plateau of Neusiedel, where Davoust struggled so bravely to redeem the day, should cover a multitude of sins.

Three years after this he was joined to the Russian expedition, and went through it with honour. He commanded the cavalry on the extreme left, at the battle of Borodino, and after Caulincourt had fallen at the head of his cuirassiers, whose charge nothing could withstand, he hurled his own cavalry in overwhelming power on the enemy, till at length, struck by a ball, he was borne wounded from the field. During the progress of the fatal retreat of the Grand Army from Moscow, the cavalry all disappeared, as well as the different corps of infantry, and Grouchy, among, a multitude of officers, was left without a command, and like a common soldier rode amid the cloud of fugitives, as they slowly swept forward through the dreary winter, toward the Beresina. He had fought, endured, and suffered, and seen with sad forebodings the mighty army lie down to die in the snow, yet still, amid the utter wreck of all things, his good steed was left him, on whose back he toiled through the wilderness. The magnificent cavalry were buried in the snow-hills and as the splendid wreck slowly drifted through the storm into the dark forest that spread away from the banks of the Beresina, Napoleon gathered around him all the mounted officers that remained, and formed them into one company, which be called "*the sacred squadron*." Over this stern band, composed of five hundred officers, Grouchy was placed as commander. Generals of division were made captains, generals of brigades and captains common dragoons, and all poorly mounted at the best. The specific duty of this *sacred squadron* was to guard the person of the Emperor and as he plunged into the gloomy forest of Minsk, already alive with the columns of the enemy, Grouchy closed around him with this devoted band. Holding the Emperor in sacred trust, it moved on toward the Beresina, and toward apparent destruction, in stern silence. It enfolded him on the banks of the river, and cleared a terrible path through the distracted crowds over the bridge that, spanning the river, formed the only hope of the army; and through the wild night that followed, kept watch around his frozen tent.

It was dissolved when Napoleon left the army for Paris, and Grouchy once more mingled in the throng that composed the Grand Army.

After this, for some cause or other, he lost the favour of the Emperor, and remained idle while the world was ringing with the deeds wrought on the fields of Bautzen, Lutzen, Dresden, and Leipzig.

In the last struggle, however, of Napoleon, on the soil of France, he was again given a command, and fought with his accustomed bravery. At Brienne be charged with the same desperate valour he did at Novi, and in the retreat of the Russians from the battle-field of Vauxchamps [sic] came near taking Blucher prisoner. While Bonaparte was pressing the retiring column in rear, he ordered Grouchy, with 3000 horse, to make a circuit round the village of Champ Aubert, and take possession of the road beyond, before the enemy could arrive. In a moment those splendid horsemen were clattering through the fields, and after an hour's hard riding found themselves two miles in advance of the Prussian army. Blucher was mowing his way through an enemy that pressed with increased vigour on his weary columns, leaving a bloody pathway behind him, and had got within a half-mile of Etoges, where his greatest danger would cease, when all at once, as he ascended a slight eminence in the road, he saw before him Grouchy's fierce horsemen drawn up in order of battle. The sun was just sinking behind the western hills, and its farewell beams fell full on the glittering helmets of the cuirassiers before him, revealing the destruction that awaited him. His fate now seemed sealed, for, blocked in front and rear, while his flanks were constantly ravaged by the enemy, he could see no way of escape. Disdaining, however, to yield, he stood for a while in front of his men waiting for a shot to strike him down; but aroused at length from his despair by the expostulations of his friends, he gave orders to march straight on that mass of cavalry. Closing up his column, and placing the cannon at its head, he moved sternly forward. Grouchy stood for a while, and let the balls mow down his riders, and then charged fiercely up to the very muzzles of the guns. Had his horse-artillery been with him he would have taken the entire army prisoners, but, impeded by the mud through which the drivers were compelled to drag their pieces, it had not yet arrived, and he had nothing but his naked horsemen with which to resist the onset. Compelled to fall back, he let the heroic column march forward; but, enraged to see his enemy thus escape his grasp, he fell on their flanks and rear with such fury that the last square gave way, and were cut to pieces. He rode like a demon through their broken ranks, and sabred down two battalions took ten entire regiments prisoners, and, following up his success, continued the work of carnage till ten o'clock at night, when he drew off his troops.

Through all this melancholy struggle in this last convulsive throe of the Empire, he exhibited his noblest qualities, and finally at Craon fell severely wounded.

On the abdication of Napoleon, Louis XVIII. allowed him to retain his titles and rank. He, however, appointed the Duke of Berri to the command of the Chasseurs in his place, which so exasperated him that his after-allegiance was but ungraciously kept. The monarch, however, made him knight, and afterward commander, of the Order of St. Louis; still, on Napoleon's return from Elba, he hastened to give in his adherence, and was immediately entrusted with the command of three military divisions, and appointed governor of Lyons. On his arrival in the city, be issued a proclamation in favour of Napoleon, calling on the National Guard to rally around their old Emperor. For his zeal and energy he was made Marshal of the Empire. This long-withheld honour was never deserved, for Grouchy, with all his bravery, did not possess the qualities belonging to a great commander.

In his new capacity, he soon after accompanied Napoleon to Belgium. He commanded the right wing at the battle of Ligny, in which Blucher was defeated, and was left with 35,000 men to watch his movements, while Napoleon should attack the English at Waterloo. Stationed at Wavres, his orders were explicit, his duty a simple one, viz., to prevent Blucher from succouring Wellington; but be failed to perform them, and Napoleon lost the battle. There has been a vast deal written about the management of Grouchy on this day, and more uncertainty than really exists thrown over the whole affair by English writers, in endeavouring to prove that Wellington did not owe his success to an accident. The French, on the other hand, have accused him of treachery: but the truth is, he designed to do his duty for, fighting as he did, with a rope round his neck, he was not likely to put it purposely in the hands of his enemies. Still he failed egregiously: he was to keep watch of Blucher, and yet Blucher marched on Waterloo without his knowledge. The latter was a defeated general, and yet he carried heavy reinforcements to Wellington, while Grouchy did not send a man to Napoleon. Both heard the tremendous cannonading that told where the great struggle was going on, and one hastened to turn the scale of victory, while the other remained at his post. Even if Blucher had not stirred, if Grouchy had been an able general he would have dispatched some divisions to the field of battle, while with the remainder he kept the Prussians at bay. The Prussian general did this, and in it showed his ability as a commander. But if he had failed in this stroke of policy, he should never have allowed the very army he was appointed to watch, to march away from him unmolested. The only excuse for him is, he obeyed orders. But he did *not* obey orders. It is a miserable shuffling to declare he obeyed implicitly the directions given him, because he continued his manoeuvres at Wavres, when the only person they were designed to affect had departed for Waterloo.

English writers would have us believe Grouchy acted the part of a faithful officer, simply because he stayed where he was told to. A thousand changes are rung on the words, "he obeyed orders." By this mode of construction, he would have been an equally faithful officer performed his duty just as faithfully, had he quietly bivouacked his army at Wavres, while the Prussian columns, one and all, were marching to join Wellington. He should not have stirred though he had been left without an enemy to oppose him, unless he had received *orders* to move. It would be just as reasonable to say that he performed his duty if he had stayed at Wavres when the hostile army had *all* gone, as to declare he performed it in remaining, when forty or fifty thousand had left. He was not wanted there if he could not keep Blucher from forming a junction with Wellington; and to remain was simply to carry out the *letter* of his orders, and neglect entirely their *spirit*. The generals under him knew their duty better, and besought him to let them march their divisions to the spot where the heavy and incessant thunder of cannon told that the decisive battle was passing; but he refused his permission. *They* did not wish for orders, for they knew if Bonaparte was acquainted with the state of affairs, they would be given soon enough. There is one thing, however, which needs clearing up. Napoleon declared, when a prisoner at St. Helena, that he dispatched an order to Grouchy the night before the battle, to occupy a defile which would have obstructed the march of Blucher on Waterloo, which order Grouchy asserts he never received. In speaking of it, Napoleon remarked that he must have had some traitor in his staff, and it is very probable this was the case, and Blucher, and not Grouchy, received the important tidings he had sent. But even if this were so, still he showed great weakness of character in the course he adopted. The truth is, he was not an able officer. A brave fighter and a good general when acting under immediate orders, he was not equal to a separate command, and never would have been entrusted with the great interests he was had the marshals who had grown up around Napoleon been with him in this last struggle.

    Nothing can show the imbecility of Grouchy more than a remark he once made at a dinner-table in New York city, in company with several exiled French generals. In speaking of their old campaigns, one of the generals turned to Grouchy and said: "How is it Marshal Grouchy, that you did not, when you heard the heavy cannonading at Waterloo, leave Blucher and march thither?" "Why," replied the other, "you see if I had, Blucher *might have marched on Paris*." The idea of Blucher's marching on Paris, with Napoleon at his back, was too ludicrous even for the politeness of Grouchy's friends, and they could not refrain a smile at the reply. General Vandamme, who was present at the table, immediately said, "I wanted to go with my division, but Grouchy would not let me, and when I insisted, he threatened to treat me as an insubordinate officer."

Grouchy wanted the energy and self-reliance of a strong character there was a lightness and frivolity about him, incompatible with a vigorous mind. He lacked judgment entirely, and though his charge was brilliant, his comprehension was anything but clear. He failed miserably, fatally failed at Waterloo, but he was not guilty of treachery. The only charge that can be brought against him is that of incapacity. He failed through weakness, not from design but what a failure it was. The destiny of Europe hung on the feeble intellect of a single man, and his sluggish arm in its tardy movements swept crowns and thrones before it overturned one of the mightiest spirits the world ever nurtured, and set back the day of Europe's final emancipation half a century. It is painful to see how the plans of the loftiest mind, its best combinations, and the hopes of an entire nation are sometimes, from circumstances, made to hinge on the determination of a weak or careless man.

After the defeat at Waterloo, Grouchy retreated to Laon, where he arrived with 32,000 men and over a hundred cannon. On the second abdication of Napoleon he came to the United States and remained here several years. Being at length allowed to return, he was restored to his rank, and given a seat in the Chamber of Peers. He is still living, though at the advanced age of eighty.

It is a little singular, that the two generals who inflicted the greatest disasters on Napoleon were both of noble parentage. Nearly every marshal was born of poor parents, and rose from the ranks, except Marmont and Grouchy and the former hurled him from his throne at Paris and the latter at Waterloo.

Marshal Ney

Chapter 26
Marshal Ney

Michael Ney was born in 1770, in the town of Sarre Louis. He was the son of a cooper, and at the age of thirteen became notary of the village. But the stirring events passing around him inflamed his youthful imagination, and four years after he entered the army as a hussar, and commenced his military career.

I do not design to follow him through all his history, but select out those acts which illustrate the great and striking qualities he possessed. His air and bearing stamped him, at an early age, as a soldier, and made him from the first a great favourite in his corps. Being selected by his regiment to challenge the fencing-master of another, for some real or supposed insult, he gladly undertook the commission. The day was appointed to settle the difficulty, and the combatants met; but just as they had crossed their sabres, they were arrested by their respective officers and thrown into prison. As soon, however, as young Ney was released, he renewed the quarrel, and having met his antagonist in a secret place, where they would not be disturbed, fought and wounded him in the hand, so that he was unable to practice his profession, and was consequently reduced to poverty. But Ney did not forget him in the day of his greatness, and settled on the poor fencing-master a pension for life. In 1793 he was promoted for his bravery and skill, and the next year, being then twenty-four years of age, was presented with a company. General Kleber, having noticed his admirable qualities, placed him at the head of a corps composed of five hundred partisans, who received no pay and lived on plunder. It was their duty to reconnoitre the enemy's position, and cut off their convoys, which exposed them to many hair breadth escapes and fierce encounters. Young Ney, being resolved on promotion, brought to this perilous service all his mental and physical powers. His iron will seemed to compensate for the loss of sleep and food and rest. Daunted by no danger, exhausted by no toil, caught by no stratagem, he acquired at the head of this bold band of warriors the title of the "Indefatigable." Three years after he found occasion to distinguish himself in the engagements of Dierdorf, Altenkirchen, and Montabaur. With 100 cavalry be took 2000 prisoners and obtained possession of Wurtsburg. He led two columns straight into the river, and forcing the opposite banks, though lined with cannon, made himself master of Forsheim.

For these exploits be was appointed general of a brigade. At the battle of Neuwied he had command of the cavalry, and in a furious charge passed entirely through the Austrian lines; but being surrounded by a superior force he was compelled to retreat. The enemy, however, closed on him with such numbers and impetuosity that his ranks were broken through, and he and his steed overthrown together. While he lay entangled under his horse, six dragoons made at him, against whom he defended himself with his usual daring, and finally sprang to his feet and laid about with his sabre till it snapped in two, leaving but the stump in his hand. With this he continued to keep his astonished antagonists at bay, till a company of thirty horsemen coming up they succeeded in capturing him. Taken to headquarters, he was one day strolling through the camp, when he saw several officers standing round his good battle-steed admiring his fine proportions and high spirit, yet utterly unable to manage him. The moment one undertook to mount his back, he reared and plunged so wildly, that the venturesome rider was glad to find himself safe on the ground again. Ney stepped up, and remarking that they did not know how to manage his horse, politely asked permission to mount him. It being given, he vaulted to the saddle, when the noble animal, conscious of bearing his master, stepped proudly away. After making one or two sweeps, he darted off in a straight line, and stretched across the plain in a gallop that outstripped the wind. As he continued to flee on in that headlong speed, they began to fear he would attempt to escape, and immediately mounted in pursuit, when Ney wheeled, and with a smile rode back to his captors.

Having been liberated by exchange, he was raised to the rank of general of division. For a while, after the peace of Leoben, he remained in Paris, but the commencement of hostilities in 1799 found him again in the field of battle, struggling with the allied forces on the banks of the Rhine. Here occurred one of those adventures that belong rather to the period of romance than to the practical history of our times. The Rhine flowed between him and the city of Manheim, which was strongly garrisoned and filled with stores of every kind. It was a matter of much discussion how this key of Germany should be captured, and the generals of the army met in frequent consultation on the proper mode of attacking it. Ney, in the meantime, thinking it could be better taken by surprise, resolved to visit it in disguise and ascertain its weak points; so, one evening assuming the garb of a peasant, he entered the city, and, after satisfying himself as to the best plan of attack, returned. Selecting a hundred and fifty brave men, be recrossed the river at eight in the evening, and at eleven made a furious assault on the outposts. A portion of the garrison having made a sally, he repulsed them, and following hard after the fugitives entered the town with them, and after a short but desperate engagement captured it. This fixed his rising fame; while at Worms, and at Frankenthal, and Frankfort, and Stuttgard, and Zurich, he maintained the character he had gained.

In 1802 he returned to Paris, as inspector-general of cavalry, and there married Mademoiselle Augné, an intimate friend of Hortense Beauharnais. Bonaparte presented him at the nuptials with a magnificent Egyptian sabre, which eventually cost the bold marshal his life. In 1803, he was sent as Minister Plenipotentiary into Switzerland, where he exhibited those higher qualities of justice and kindness so uniformly, that the Swiss Cantons presented him with a medal on his departure. The next year Bonaparte made him a marshal. The year following this, he was created Duke of Elchingen, in honour of the battle he there fought. In this engagement be exposed himself so recklessly that Jomini says of him, "he seemed to court death." Dressed in full uniform, he marched at the head of his divisions along streets completely swept by grape-shot; and though constantly surrounded by fire and enveloped in the blaze of batteries, he unaccountably escaped death. In the campaigns of 1806-7, he reached the height of his fame and power, and ever after Bonaparte regarded him as one of the strongest pillars of his throne. In 1808 he joined the army in Spain, where he remained till called to take part in the expedition to Russia. After the failure of this, he fought at Bautzen, Dresden, and Leipzig, and on the soil of France, in almost every great battle with his accustomed bravery, nobly struggling to the last to save his country from the feet of invaders and at Waterloo delivered his last stroke for the Empire.

The three distinguishing characteristics of Ney were great personal bravery, almost unparalleled coolness in the hour of peril, and an excellent judgment. In the first two, all writers are agreed, while the last is not generally conceded to him. No man can deny he was brave, for there can be no appeal from the decision of an army of heroes, who named him "bravest of the brave." Such a distinction, among the men and in the times he lived, was not won by ordinary actions. In an army where Davoust, Junot, Macdonald, Murat, and Lannes commanded, to be crowned "bravest of the brave," was the highest honour a military chieftain could desire. Napoleon when at St. Helena said, "Ney was the bravest man I ever saw." But his courage was not the rashness of headlong excitement, like that of Junot and Murat. The enthusiasm born in the hour of battle amid the tossing of plumes, the tramping of the host, the shout of trumpets and roar of cannon, has always been found sufficient to hurl man into any scene of horror or of peril. Junot could coolly sit and write to Bonaparte's dictation, while the shot whistled around him, and laughingly shake the paper as a cannon-ball ploughing past him threw the dirt over it, with the exclamation, "This is lucky, I shall have no need of sand." Murat could ride on his magnificent steed up to a whole company of Cossacks, and disperse them by a single wave of the hand. Lannes could forage like a lion 'mid the foe at Montibello, while the cannon-shot wasted so awfully around him that he himself said afterwards, "I could hear the bones crash in my division like hail-stones against a window." Yet each of these was but one among a thousand heroic acts, and gained for their authors no such title as that given to Ney. There was a reason for this. Theirs was a heroism called forth by sudden energies, such as the commonest soldier often exhibits in the heat of battle. Ney's courage was something more and greater: it dared just as much without the least apparent excitement. His thoughts were just as clear and his eye as quiet amid the falling ranks, as if he were standing on some far observatory and looking over the scene of slaughter. He would sit almost within the blaze of two hundred cannon, and while his horses were sinking under him, and whole companies melting like frost-work before his eyes, give orders as calmly as though manoeuvring at a grand review. It was his wonderful, almost *marble calmness* in the most sudden and extremest danger, that struck even heroes with astonishment. He would stand within musket-shot of a most terrific and hotly worked battery, and while the storm of bullets swept where he stood, eye all its operations and scan its assailable points with imperturbable quietness. The fierce shock of cavalry, and the steady charge of bayonets, could not for one moment divert his gaze, or disturb the clear and natural operations of his mind. The alarming cry through his own rank, "*Sauve qui peut!*" or the full belief that all was lost, could not shake his steadiness. One would have thought him an iron man, and strung with no ordinary nerves, had they not seen him in a desperate charge. Then his eye glanced like an eagle's, and with his form towering amid the smoke of battle and flash of sabres, he seemed an embodied hurricane sweeping over the field. Much of this doubtless was constitutional, and much was owing to the wonderful power of mental concentration. He could literally shut up his mind to the one object he had in view. The overthrow of the enemy absorbed every thought within him, and he had none to give to danger or to death. Where he placed his mind he held it, and not all the uproar and confusion of battle could divert it. He would not *allow* himself to see anything else, and hence he was almost as insensible to the danger around him, as a deaf and dumb and blind man would have been. He himself once expressed the true secret of his calmness, when, after one of those exhibitions of composure, amid the most horrid carnage, one of his officers asking him if he never had fear, he replied, "*I never had time.*" This was another way of saying that fear and danger had nothing to do with the object before him, and therefore he would not suffer his thoughts to rest on them for a single moment. It would not require much "time," one would think, to see the danger of marching straight into the flash of a hundred cannon, or to feel a thrill of terror as the last discharge left him almost alone amid his dead and dying guard. But he had trained his mind not to see these things for the time being. This devotion and concentration of all his powers to a single object gave him great advantage in moments of peril, and when the fate of a battle was turning on a single thought. Where other men would become confused in the confusion around them, he, remaining clear as ever, was able frequently to redeem everything when everything seemed lost.

His tenacity of will was equal to his bravery. *He would not be beat*, and in the last extremity, rallied like a dying man for a final blow, then planted it where the clearest practical wisdom would have done. He disputed every inch he yielded, as if it were his last hope, and fought on the threshold of the next as if that were but the commencement of the struggle. So, in encountering obstacles in the execution of any plan he had formed, he would scarcely admit their existence, and seemed to think he could wring the decree against him out of the iron hand of fate itself. These qualities rendered him an invaluable ally to Bonaparte in his great battles. Standing in his observatory, and looking over the conflict, Napoleon often saw where the whole issue turned on a single point. Such a column *must* be shaken, such a place in the lines broken or a certain battery carried, or the day was lost. On such missions he would send Ney, knowing if human skill and valour could avail, it would be done; and when he saw him start with his column and move down toward the spot where the fate of the battle was vibrating, his countenance always wore a complacent look. Again and again did he fling his crown and France into his keeping, and that of his legions, and almost without fear see them borne on into the smoke of the battle. The bold marshal never disappointed him, and it was for this reason Bonaparte placed his throne and empire into his hands, and saw them both go down in the last charge of the Old Guard at Waterloo. Even here Ney would have saved his master if bravery and devotion could have done it.

During the whole campaign of 1806-7, Ney moves before us as some hero of former ages. At Jena, borne on by his impetuous courage, he charged and took a battery, and the next instant found himself surrounded by an army that no other man would have thought of resisting. But though hemmed in, and apparently overwhelmed, instead of yielding, as prudence itself seemed to dictate, he immediately formed his men into squares, and kept up such a rolling, devouring fire on every side, that the headlong masses fell by hundreds at every discharge. Bonaparte, seeing the imminent peril of his brave marshal, detached Bertrand with several regiments of horse to his relief. No sooner was he extricated, than he unrolled his men again into column, and with a firm and rapid step ascended the hill on which Vierzhen Heiligen stood, and, after a fierce conflict took it. This was the centre of the enemy's position, and Napoleon saw from a distance with delight his favourite marshal in the very heart of the Prussian lines. Repulsing for a while with prodigious slaughter every attempt of the enemy to regain it, he again unrolled his squares into column, and marched through a most scourging fire, straight on the Prussians' right. The tempest of musketry and grape through which he advanced drove like a storm of sleet in the face of his men; but nothing could resist the impetuous charge, and the right line of the allies was swept away. Around the wall of Erfurt and Magdeburg crossing the Vistula at the terrible battle of Soldau annihilating a Russian corps at Deppen, at Gustadt and Amskerdorff he is the same calm, determined, and terrible man.

In the picture the imagination draws of the battle of Friedland, Ney always occupies the foreground. There, the tried veteran was appointed to commence the action. The engagements with detached corps had ceased, and both armies were drawn up in battle array. For several hours there had been no firing, and, it being now four o'clock, the Russian general supposed there would be no engagement until morning. But at five o'clock the sudden discharge of twenty cannon from the French centre, the signal of attack, announced to the Russian army that the day was to end in blood. The troops were ordered to stand to their arms, and the next moment the head of Ney's mighty column was seen to emerge from a wood behind Posthenen and stretch itself, in a huge black line into the open field. In close array and quick time it moved straight upon Friedland. The sun was stooping to the western horizon, as if hasting from the scene of carnage about to open yet his departing light gave new splendour to the magnificent array. A forest of glittering steel seemed moving over the field, while from the steeples and towers of Friedland the countless thousands of those that still remained in the wood were visible. But all eyes were directed on Ney and his magnificent column, that, crossing the field at a rapid step, scattered like a whirlwind everything that opposed their progress. Whole regiments of cavalry and Cossacks, the chasseurs of the guard, militia and all, went down, or were driven before its tide-like movement. On every side were seen flying horsemen and scattered infantry. The other divisions now advanced to the attack, but the victory seemed about to be won by Ney alone, for he was close upon Friedland, and about rolling along the whole column, and heard above the roar of the battle, announced that the town was about to be carried by assault. But just at this crisis the Russian Imperial Guard was ordered to advance. With fixed bayonets, this mass of living valour hurled itself upon its adversary. The head of Ney's column went down before the charge, and the whole body was rolled back over the field. But falling on Victor's corps rapidly advancing to sustain him, he rallied his broken ranks and again pressed to the assault. Friedland was carried after an obstinate resistance and immense slaughter, and soon the bridges in the rear over the Alle were in flames. The smoke rolled over the field of battle like that of a burning forest the sun went down in gloom, and the dead were piled over the ground, and Ney had made Bonaparte again conqueror by his indomitable valour.

Napoleon's confidence in him was almost unbounded, During the battle of Bautzen he lay on the ground, sheltered by a height in front of the town, at his breakfast, when suddenly he heard the sound of Ney's guns thundering on the left. At the same instant a bomb burst over his head. Without noticing the bursting shell, he sat down and wrote to Marie Louise that the victory was gained. He waited only to learn that Ney was where the crisis turned, to be sure of victory.

Yet the latter has often been accused of wanting generalship. Mr. Alison makes him a brave man and no more. This decision is based on a single declaration of Bonaparte; speaking once of Ney, he said "he was the bravest of men; there terminated all his faculties." But this disparagement of Ney was doubtless made after contemplating some failure in which the marshal was implicated. Besides, Bonaparte was the last man to estimate the character of his own officers. He rated all military leaders low but himself. The whole history of Bonaparte's career the confidence he everywhere reposed in Ney's skill as well as bravery, pronounce this declaration false; while the manner in which he managed the rear guard in that unparalleled retreat of the Grand Army from Russia, shows the injustice of the declaration in every way. Something more than bravery was needed to cover the retreat of the French there, and Bonaparte knew it. He never placed Ney at the head of the army in invading Russia, and in the rear when retreating from it, simply because he was a *brave* man. His actions and statements here contradict each other, and the former is more likely to be honest than the latter.

The two great and ruinous errors of Bonaparte's ambitious career would have been prevented had be listened to Ney's counsel. The conquest of Spain brought nothing but disaster, and the invasion of Russia overturned his throne. Against both these Ney urged his strenuous remonstrance as long as it seemed of any avail, and then did his utmost to prevent the ruin he knew must follow. One day at Madrid Napoleon entered the room where Ney and several officers were standing, and said in great glee: "Everything goes on well; Romana will be reduced in a fortnight; the English are defeated and will be unable to advance; in three months the war will be finished." The officers to whom this was addressed made no reply; but Ney, shaking his head, said with his characteristic bluntness: "Sire, this war has lasted long already, and our affairs are not improved. These people are obstinate, even their women and children fight; they massacre our men in detail. To-day we cut the enemy in pieces, to-morrow we have to oppose another twice as numerous. It is not an army we have to fight, it is a whole nation. I see no end to this business." Bonaparte followed his own inclinations and was eventually defeated. Ney saw the difference between conquering an army and a people. Though engaged in no general battle while in Spain, he exhibited his wonted skill and bravery in Asturia.

But it is in the Russian campaign that he displayed his greatest qualities as a commander. The history of the Grand Army, in its invasion of Russia and retreat from it, combines more of glory and of gloom than anything of its kind in the annals of man. The contrast between that army of nearly half a million of men, crossing the Niemen in the presence of Napoleon, as he sat in his tower and saw those glorious legions move in beautiful order and high spirits before him; and the remnant of that scattered army in rags, wan and ghastly, staggering like a band of spectres over that same river, always fills one with the profoundest melancholy. At Smolensko, Ney made a last effort to dissuade the Emperor from passing into Russia so late in the season. But neither he nor the other generals that formed his councils could divert his purpose. The battles of Valentina and Krasnoi soon followed, and last of all came Borodino, in which Ney outdid himself, and earned the title Napoleon gave him on the spot of "Prince of Moskwa."

At the commencement of that action Bonaparte kept Ney close beside him, and would not for a long time allow him to take part in the conflict. There they stood within hailing distance of each other, and gazed on the battle that raged on the right. At length the former called Ney to him and gave his last orders. The trumpets sounded, the drums beat their hurried charge, and Ney with his three divisions hurled himself on the foe. The enemy's artillery swept within a certain limit every inch of ground, and it seemed impossible that a body of men could stand there a single moment. But with a firm and rapid step that unflinching column moved forward, till it at length entered the storm of grape-shot, when the head of it sunk down and disappeared like snow when it meets the river. Yet Ney still moved unhurt at its head, and, without faltering a moment, led the remnant straight through the destructive fire, up to the very entrenchments, and carried them.

Then commenced that terrific struggle for the heights of Denienowskoie. Davoust and Ney strove together with more than human valour to gain the eminence. After four hours of steady, unparalleled effort against superior force, and in the midst of incessant discharges of artillery, Ney sent to Bonaparte for help. The Young Guard and the reserve cavalry were ordered down, though they still, at the command of Napoleon, remained idle spectators of the fight, while he directed four hundred cannon on the redoubt. Under cover of this terrible fire, the intrepid columns moved to the assault. The Russian artillery from the batteries stretched whole battalions on the field at every discharge. But it was all in vain. The rent columns closed again as before, "each treading where his comrade stood," and pressed on like the in-rolling wave of the sea. Finding the French were gaining ground, the Russian commander ordered his whole left wing to leave the entrenchments and meet the French in the plain below. The shock was awful. Eighty thousand men were crowded into a small space, and for more than an hour raged against each other in all the ferocity of war, while seven hundred pieces of cannon played incessantly upon the dense masses of living, flesh. Ney moved amid this wild storm calm and collected, though heated by the battle, like some terrible spirit of the fight. His uniform riddled with balls, and his face begrimed with powder and smoke, he still, with his clear clarion voice, cheered on his troops, and with his cool bravery held his exhausted men to the encounter with a tenacity that could not be overcome, and which saved Bonaparte that day from a ruinous defeat.

Napoleon often gazed with astonishment on the movements of his favourite marshal. The quiet determination with which he set out to execute the most hopeless order, the progress he would make against the most desperate odds, and the victory he would wring from defeat itself, brought even from him bursts of admiration.

THE RETREAT FROM MOSCOW

The blazing towers of Moscow, the turning-point of Napoleon's invasion and his fortune, have scarcely crumbled to ashes before the fated army turn their faces homeward. One would like to be made acquainted with the conversations of Ney and the other marshals as they sat together in the Kremlin, and talked over the disastrous issue they had met, and the only way of escape from total annihilation. The fiery and impetuous harangues of some, and the blunt characteristic replies of others, while the crackling of the flames and the falling of columns and walls without were borne to their cars, must have been in the highest degree dramatic. From the heap of ruins and from the solitude which was more prophetic than the uproar of the storm, the Grand Army commenced its retreat. A hundred and fifty thousand men, with nearly six hundred pieces of cannon, marched in separate columns over the open country, while behind in three separate files stretching away till they were lost in the distance followed forty thousand stragglers, with an endless train of carriages and wagons, loaded with the rich booty of the capital, and surmounted by countless standards, and the cross of Ivan the Great. Multitudes of women were mingled in this confused throng, and among them Russian girls, who were willing captives, Thus the mighty caravan dragged its slow length along, gradually diminishing day after day, under the fatiguing march and increasing cold, strewing the roads with the costliest furs and stuffs of the East, together with wagons and carriages.

At length, fighting its way, the army approached the field of Borodino, on which, nearly two months before, that "Battle of Giants" had been fought. As the column slowly toiled on, they came upon heaps of human skeletons, and corpses half devoured. Thirty thousand mutilated forms covered the plain, and amid them deserted drums, broken helmets, shattered wagons, gun-stocks, and fragments of uniforms, and torn and bloody standards sweeping the ground over which they lately floated in pride. The earth was all furrowed up, and desolation and gloom reigned over the scene. The height, on which stood the great redoubt, where the heat of the conflict had been, was white with skeletons that lay unburied where they fell. The field seemed a great cemetery which an earthquake had suddenly rent asunder, emptying all its inmates upon the surface. Oh! it was a melancholy spectacle that sad and dispirited throng treading amid the wreck and skeletons of a dead army.

At Wiazma Ney was appointed to relieve Davoust, and with his corps cover the retreat. In this act Napoleon utters more distinctly his opinion of that Marshal's generalship than language *can* do. The whole history of Ney's conduct during that memorable retreat seems to belong rather to some hero of romance than an actual man. The wonderful details appear incredible, and would not be believed if the evidence was not incontestable. With a mere handful of men he placed himself between the French and Russian armies, and by his marvellous exertion, desperate valour, and exhaustless ingenuity, saved a portion of that host which would otherwise have been totally annihilated. The retreat alone would make him immortal. With all the fault found with his generalship, there was not a commander among either the French or allied forces during the whole war, that ever did or ever could accomplish what Ney performed in that memorable flight. Had he fallen Bonaparte would have probably fallen also, and the former *really* saved the army, which the latter never could have alone. Without provisions, almost without arms, he battled the well-tried and countless legions of Russia back from his Emperor; and over the wintry fields of snow and amid the driving storm, with a heart untamed and a will unsubdued, he hovered like a protecting spirit around the divided and flying ranks of his countrymen. The soldiers, exhausted and despairing, threw their muskets from them into the snow-drifts, and lay down by thousands to die. Cold, benumbed, and famine-struck, this ghost of an army straggled on through the deep snow, with nothing, but the tall pines swaying and roaring mournfully in the blast for landmarks to the glazing eye, while an enraged and well-disciplined army was pressing in the rear. Clouds of ravens, whose dusky forms glanced like spirits through the snow-filled air croaked over the falling columns, while troops of dogs, that had followed the army from Moscow, fell on the prostrate forms before life was wholly extinct. The storm howled by as the soldiers sunk at night in the snow to rest, many to rise no more, while the morning sun, if it shone at all, looked cold and dimly down through the flying clouds of a northern sky. There were long intervals when not a drum or trumpet-note broke the muffled tread of the staggering legions.

On the rear of such an army, and in sight of such horrors did Ney combat. Nothing but a spirit unconquerable as fate itself could have sustained him, or kept alive the flagging courage of his troops. Stumbling every moment over the dead bodies of their comrades who had marched but a few hours in advance of them, thousands threw away their arms in despair, and wandered off into the wilderness to die with cold, or be slain by the Cossacks. Yet Ney kept a firm band around him that all the power of Russia could not conquer. Now ordering his march with the skill of a general, and now with musket in hand fighting like a common soldier, the moral force of his example accomplished what authority alone never could have done. At length the brave and heroic commander seemed to have reached the crisis of his fate, and there appeared no escape from the doom that hung over him. The Russians had finally placed themselves between the French army and that rear guard, now dwindled to a few thousand. Ignorant of his danger, Ney was leading his columns through a dense fog to the banks of the Lossmina, on which were strewed the dead bodies of his countrymen, when a battery of forty cannon suddenly poured a destructive storm of grape-shot into the very heart of his ranks. The next moment the heights before him and on either side appeared lined with dense masses of infantry and artillery. Ney had done all that man could do, and here his career seemed about to close. He was ordered to capitulate. He replied, "A Marshal of France never surrenders," and closing his column marched straight upon the batteries. Vain valour. His noble and devoted followers proved themselves worthy of their heroic leader, but after a loss of half their number they were compelled to retire. Finding the army gradually extending itself on every side to hem him in, he returned back toward Smolensk.

He had left this city on the 17th of November, supposing that Davoust was to sustain him; but he soon found that he must fight his way alone to the army. Despair then seized every heart, and a fathomless abyss yawned beneath that lone rear guard; and all discipline would have been lost, but for the sway which the lofty mind, rather than outward command, of Ney held over his troops.

His kindness to the sufferers, and his care for the wounded, and the great generosity and self-denial he exhibited, were more potent than discipline to bind his devoted band to him. As they left the gates of Smolensko, a French mother, finding she had not room in her sledge for her infant child, cast it from her into the snow in spite of its piercing cries and pleading tones. Ney, touched by the spectacle, lifted up the infant himself, and replaced it on the mother's breast, bidding her cherish and protect it. Again did she cast it away, and again did he carry it in his own brave arms back to her; and though the mother was finally left to die on the frozen ground, that tender infant survived all the horrors of the retreat and lived to see France. What an eulogy on this man of steel was this single act! With destruction staring him and his army in the face, he, though hardened in a hundred battles, and called "the bravest of the brave," could forget his own dangers and duties in the efforts to save the life of a single infant. Countless acts of this kind, showing that in that fearless heart dwelt the kindliest sympathies of our nature, created a bond of affection between him and the meanest soldier, and enhanced ten-fold their awe of him when he moved in such terrible strength through the carnage of battle.

Pressing eagerly on, Ney and his six thousand men came upon Krasnoi, where Napoleon had struggled so nobly to save Davoust. Ignorant of the battle that had been fought there, the soldiers still knew its whole history; for by the caps lying amid the corpses, and the uniforms scattered here and there over the frosty ground, they could pick out even the regiments that had suffered most. Hurrying over this sad field, where they stumbled every moment over their unburied comrades, and horses lying still alive in their harness, amid broken muskets, and helmets, and dismounted cannon kicking up, along every ravine where the snow had drifted, the horrid relies as they marched forward, they came at length to the Lossmina.

It was back over such a road that Ney, after his repulse, ordered his soldiers to march. They stood and gazed in amazement at him, as if they could not have heard aright, and then, wondering, as they afterwards said, at their own submission, quietly obeyed him. It was a dark and cold, night a night of sixteen hours in length, when the shattered and bleeding column began its retreat, and retrod the battlefield over which it had marched with shuddering only a short time before. At length coming to a ravine, Ney halted and ordered the snow to be cleared away, thinking there must be a stream beneath leading to the Dneiper. The men soon came to ice, when the marshal, taking out his map and looking at it for a moment, ordered the army to keep along the ravine. After proceeding a short distance, he directed the fires to be kindled as if he intended to bivouac for the night, in order to deceive the enemy. As the lights blazed upon the darkness, the Russians fired off their cannon in joy, for their foes now seemed within their grasp. Ney listened a moment to the sullen echo, thinking at first that Davoust had come; but the next moment, understanding the language it spoke, "he swore he would give the lie to their joy," and immediately recommenced his march. In the hurry and darkness, many, who from wounds and exhaustion lagged behind, wandered out of the way, as the column, without the sound of a drum or trumpet, swept silently and swiftly across the fields; so that, when he reached the Dneiper, Ney saw that but a part of his followers had arrived.

As good fortune, or rather a kind Heaven above, ordained it, the river where they struck it was frozen across, while above and below the ice was all afloat. Still this narrow bridge was weak, and would bear only one at a time, and the position of Ney was perilous in the extreme.

To save himself and his army no time was to be lost, for not only were forty thousand men in his rear, but the ice was gradually giving way. But here he again exhibited that greatness of heart which honours him more than his bravery, and our love for him exceeds even our admiration for, having arranged his fragment of an army so as to march over the ice at a moment's warning, he waited *three hours* before crossing to allow the weak and wounded stragglers to come in. Pressed by the most appalling dangers, he still yielded to the dictates of mercy; and there on the banks of the frozen river, and during this time of intense anxiety, with the ice melting before him, did this strange, indomitable man, lie down with his cloak about him, and sleep.

Bonaparte, far in advance, struggling forward on foot with a birch stick in his hand to keep him from falling on the ice, surrounded by his few exhausted yet faithful followers, was pressed with anxiety for the fate of Ney his now last remaining hope. As he strode on over the desolate track, he was heard continually murmuring to himself, and "Ney, Ney," almost momentarily escaped from his lips, accompanied with passionate exclamations of grief.

But the marshal, of whom he had heard nothing for so long a time, had crossed the Dnieper with his three thousand men, although he had left in its frozen current scores under whose feet the treacherous ice had given way. Still there was a wilderness between him and his Emperor, and that wilderness was filled with Cossacks. For sixty miles he struggled on with his weary columns amid six thousand of these wild warriors standing in order of battle by day, and marching through the deep snow by night. At one time they got in advance of him, and fell unexpectedly upon his advanced posts, which were immediately driven in, and all was given up as lost. But Ney ordered the trumpets to sound the charge, and with the cheering words, "Comrades, now is the moment; forward, they are ours," rallied their courage to the assault, and the Cossacks fled. Thinking their general saw what they did not see, and that the enemy were cut off, the soldiers pressed forward where otherwise they would have yielded and fled. At length with only *fifteen hundred* men out of the forty thousand with which he had started, he approached Orcha, and sent forward fifty horsemen to ask for help. Davoust, Eugene, and Mortier were there, and had just got their soldiers nicely quartered for the night the first night the poor fellows had had a house to shelter them, or sufficient food to eat when these horsemen galloped into the village. But as soon as it was known that Ney was near, asking assistance, the brave men turned cheerfully out into the cold, while Eugene and Mortier disputed the honour of going to his relief. Eugene carried it on the ground of superior rank, and at the head of four thousand men plunged into the deep snow, and marched six miles without getting any tidings of the fugitives. He then ordered a halt and directed some cannon to be fired. Their thunder rolled away through the gloom, and when silence again fell on the illimitable snow-fields, there came the dull report of musketry on the air. Ney had no cannon with which to answer those of Eugene, and his reply was like his army, weak and languishing. Eugene, however, heard it, and marching swiftly up, saw the black column of the brave marshal moving over the snow. Rushing up he clasped him in his arms and wept like a child on his neck. Ney strained him to his manly bosom, and then began sternly to upbraid Davoust for thus endangering him, and through him the French army. The soldiers also threw themselves into each other's arms with the most enthusiastic exclamations, and with joy retraced their steps to Orcha. Arrived there, the provisions and fire and beds were cheerfully shared, and the tired armies, after recounting their toils and dangers, lay down to sleep in each other's embrace. Still Ney could not forgive Davoust, and when the latter attempted to make some explanation of his conduct, he only replied in a stern voice, "Monsieur le Maréchal, I have no reproaches to make to you; God is our witness and your judge."

When Bonaparte heard of his arrival, he exclaimed, "I have three hundred millions in my coffers in the Tuileries; I would willingly have given them to save Marshal Ney." Well he might, and half his empire with it, for without him he had been a throneless Emperor. The meeting of Bonaparte and this brave man shows the profound impression the conduct of the latter had made on him. As his eyes fell on the worn, yet still proud, unconquerable veteran, he exclaimed, "What a man, what a soldier!" But words failed to express his admiration, and he clasped the stern warrior to his bosom and embraced him with all the rapture one hero embraces another.

But Ney's exhausting efforts were not yet over; Bonaparte dare not relieve him from the important and dangerous post he had filled with such honour, and another rear guard was put under his command. At the awful passage of the Beresina he again stood between the army and destruction, and while Victor on one side of the river, he on the other side after Oudinot's wound kept back with a mere handful of men the Russian thousands. From this time on his duty became still more painful. At every step he came upon corpses the whole country was covered with hillocks formed by the snow drifting over fallen soldiers, while the piercing cold and gnawing hunger and fatigue, thinned his ranks with frightful rapidity. Even when the enemy kept at a distance, the work of mortality went on; and all along the edges of the column men were staggering from the line of march, and with a groan pitching into snow-drifts. Others, unable to proceed, would sit down, and, resting their chills on their clenched hands, gaze with a look of unutterable despair on their retiring comrades. Others still would drop upon their knees, and tears of real blood streaming from their inflamed eyes, rest a moment in that pleading attitude, and then fall on their hands, while the most pitiful sobs and moans would escape their breasts. Struggling still for life they remained a short time in this position, and then their heads would begin to sway backward and forward, and the next moment they lay stretched stark and stiff amid the snow, while the blinding storm rapidly wove their winding-sheet. When the weather cleared up it was so cold the very air seemed frozen, and the birds dropped dead from the trees, and then the benumbed and stiffened column would go staggering over the frosty fields in dead silence the crackling of the snow-crust and flakes of ice under their feet the only sounds that disturbed the solitude that surrounded them. At night the poor creatures would sit in circles all doubled up to retain the warmth of their bodies, and in the morning were still seen in that attitude frozen stiff, and left thus by their retreating companions. The bivouacs could be traced through the wilderness by the circles that marked their locality. Some became delirious, and roamed about, howling and gnashing their teeth, or making the clear, cold air ring with their demoniacal laughter. These, when the fire was built, would cast themselves frantically into the flames, and perish in horrible convulsions. Piteous moans and prayers and cries arose on every side, as the frozen, bleeding column dragged its weary length over the icy plains; and hunger and madness and pain filled every heart. At the head of such an army, and in the midst of such difficulties, was Ney compelled to struggle, and with such soldiers was he compelled to fight. But undaunted by the dangers that surrounded him unsubdued by the despair that rested on every face gnawed himself by the pangs of hunger, and his limbs stiffened with the frost, he still endeavoured to keep alive the courage of his men; and with his noble heart bleeding at the sights and the sounds he saw and heard, still spoke encouraging words of France and of safety. Now helping a poor wretch to his feet, and now fighting with his musket beside the dispirited soldiers, he shamed even despair, and made the dying give another effort, then bless him as they fell. None but a man of wonderful intellect could have held the moral power he did over such soldiers in such calamities. There was a grandeur and nobleness in that character, which secured obedience, long after bravery and authority were forgotten.

At length the scattered remnants of the French legions reached the Niemen, the boundary of the Russian territory. Ney arrived destitute of troops the rear guard had again melted away. Collecting in haste a few hundred men be found in the town (Wilna), he planted seventy-four cannon on the redoubts, and kept back the enemy all day, while the army was retiring. The next morning he continued his defence, but the soldiers, seeing their comrades bending their footsteps toward France, and away from the bullets of the Russians, began to follow after till he was left almost alone, Still, true to his duty, he continued to cover the retreat of the army he had so often saved. All had not yet passed the Niemen, and, by dint of persuasion and threats and promises, he collected *thirty men* around him, and with his musket in hand defended with this handful the gate of Wilna. These too finally deserted him; and then he fought alone, slowly retiring through the streets with his face to the enemy, and crossing the river, *"was the last of the Grand Army who left the Russian territory."*

Gumbinnen was the first place in Germany, after passing the river, at which rest could be obtained. General Dumas, who was sick, had just entered the house of a French physician in this town, when a man accosted him whom he took to be a perfect stranger. His powerful form was wrapped in a large military cloak his beard was long and untrimmed his countenance begrimed with powder, and his whiskers half burned off, while his emaciated face spoke of toils and privations of no common magnitude. But his eye still burned with that lustre no one ever forgot who once saw it in battle. "What," said the stranger, "General Dumas, do you not know me?" "No," replied Dumas, "who are you?" "I am the rear guard of the Grand Army Marshal Ney. I have fired the last musket shot on the bridge of Kowno; I have thrown into the Niemen the last of our arms; and I have walked hither as you see me, across the forests." He had done all that man could do fought till his army was annihilated, then formed another created means where they did not exist sustained the sinking courage of his followers when all before him was blank and hopeless struggled at last with a few hundred, and then thirty, and then alone, as rear guard of the army, and finally on foot and unattended, crossed the forests to join his companions.

After the abdication of Napoleon he lived in Paris in almost entire seclusion. Too rough for the polished society of the French capital, and too stern and grave to be dissipated, he dwelt by himself. His palace was elegantly furnished; and his wife, fond of gayety and luxury, entertained her friends there, while he would be dining by himself, musing over the stormy and adventurous life he had led. Sick of the inactive monotonous life of the city, be retired to his country-seat, where in the sports of the field he could find some relief to his restlessness. It was here he received his unexpected order to join the sixth military division. On arriving at Paris he learned to his astonishment that Bonaparte had left Elba and was on his way to the capital.

Here occurs the only dark passage in his whole history. Bonaparte's star had apparently set forever at his exile, and Ney did perfectly right to sustain the government of France; but he had no right to betray the trust his monarch reposed in him and go over with his army to the side of the invader. He, by this act, became a traitor; but his treason had more excuses than the like crime ever had before. At first he regarded the descent of Napoleon on the shores of France as the most extravagant rashness, and designed, as he declared, to bring him a prisoner to Paris. But he had hardly set out on his expedition, before Bonaparte began to ply him with those arts he knew so well how to use. He had made Ney what he was, and he appealed to the gratitude of the noble-hearted veteran. He had stood by his side in the smoke and thunder of battle, and he recalled those scenes to his imagination. They had been warriors together in danger, and Bonaparte excited him with those recollections, so calculated to move a heart like his. He kept his emissaries constantly about him, representing to him the utter feebleness and imbecility of the Bourbon throne he called him again the "Bravest of the Brave," and entreated him not to fight against his old companion in arms. At the same time he promised peace to France, and all that Ney could desire. A plain, blunt soldier, with a heart full of great affections for heroes like himself, what wonder is it that his constancy shook! Added to all this, the emissaries of Bonaparte had at length affected the fidelity of the army, and while Ney was wavering his soldiers had already determined for Napoleon. He felt that he could not resist the tide if he would, while he evidently had lost all desire to do so. His act of treason has many palliations: still it was unworthy of him. If his old affection and gratitude were too strong to allow him to fight against his *former* monarch, his honour should have prevented him from fighting against his *new* one. He should have returned and resigned his command, and retired from the contest. He himself afterwards felt so. The excitement and enthusiasm under which he had acted had passed away, and he saw the transaction in a clear and just light. It weighed on his heart, and he grew melancholy and spiritless. He had lost his self-respect; and his honour, which he hitherto had kept bright as his sword, was tarnished. Kindly feeling had conquered him whom no enemy could subdue and now the eye no danger could daunt or hardship dim, became dull and lustreless. That glorious forehead that had been the terror of so many hundred battles, had a spot upon it, and Ney felt feebler than in the hour of extremest peril. Remorse gnawed at his heart, and the feeling of personal dignity was gone forever. He became morose and restless, and not until ordered by Bonaparte to Lille, "if he would see the first battle," did he evince any of his old fire.

This single fact is the best excuse that could be offered for him. It shows that, whatever his act may be, his *heart* was right. It was not deliberate treason, but the sudden impulse of a man too frequently governed by his feelings. He afterwards doubtless hoped, in the excitement of battle, to rid himself of remorse, and perhaps by his valour to wipe out the disgrace he had brought on his name.

BATTLE OF WATERLOO

After the hundred days' preparation, Napoleon advanced to the Low Countries, to meet the allies, again banded together for his overthrow. He attacked Blucher at Ligny, and defeated him; and so hard pressed was this old veteran that he was overthrown, and lay entangled under his horse in the darkness, while the French cavalry passed twice over his body without observing him: he then extricated himself, and joining his troops retreated to Wavres. Ney had been less successful at Quatre Bras in his attack on Wellington, but he had retired in good order, and effected a junction with Napoleon, and the two together moved down on Waterloo where the Duke had taken up his position entirely separated from the Prussian army.

To understand the field of battle, imagine two slightly elevated semi-circular ridges, or rather slopes, a half-mile apart, curving gently forward, somewhat in the form of a parenthesis, and you have the positions of the two armies. On the summit of one of these slopes was drawn up the French army, and on the other that of the English and the allies. The night of the 17th of June was dark and stormy the rain fell in torrents, and the two armies lay down in the tall rye drenched with rain, to wait the morning that was to decide the fate of Europe and of Napoleon. From the ball-room at Brussels many English officers had been summoned in haste to the field, and shivering and cold were compelled to pass the night in mud and rain, in their elegant attire. The artillery had cut up the ground, so that the mud was ankle-deep, while the tall rye lay crushed and matted beneath the feet of the soldiers. The morning of the 18th opened with a drizzling rain, and the two armies, benumbed with cold and soaking wet, arose from their damp beds to the contest. Eighty thousand French soldiers were seen moving in close, massive columns on the crest of the height, as they took up their several positions for the day. After all was completed Bonaparte rode along the lines in the highest spirits, confident of success, and exclaiming, "Now to breakfast," galloped away, while the shout "*Vive l'Empereur!*" that rolled after him shook the field on which they stood, and fell with ominous tones on the allied army. Two hundred and sixty-two cannon lined the ridge like a wall of death, ready to open their fire on the enemy. At eleven o'clock the signal of attack was given, and the columns moved in beautiful order down the slope. Wellington's lines occupied two miles in extent, with the right resting on Chateau Hougomont, which from the defences it furnished was equal to a redoubt. The centre was protected by a farmhouse, La Haye Sainte, while the left stretched out into the open field. First, Jerome Bonaparte led a column of 6000 men down on Hougomont, who in the face of a most destructive fire pushed up to the very walls of the chateau, and thrust their bayonets through the door. But the Coldstream Guards held the court-yard with invincible obstinacy, and he was compelled at length to retire, after leaving 1400 men in a little orchard beside the walls, where it does not seem so many men could be laid. In a short time the battle became general along the whole line, and heroic deeds were performed on every rod of the contested field. The heavy French cavalry came thundering down on the steady English squares, that had already been wasted by the heavy artillery, and strove with almost superhuman energy to break them. Driven to desperation by their repeatedly foiled attempts, they at length stopped their horses and coolly walked them round and round the squares, and whenever a man fell dashed in, in vain valour. Whole ranks went down like smitten grass before the headlong charges of cavalry and infantry. In the centre the conflict at length became awful, for there the crisis of the battle was fixed. Wellington stood under a tree while the boughs were crashing with the cannon-shot overhead, and nearly his whole guard smitten down by his side, anxiously watching the progress of the fight. His brave squares torn into fragments by bombs and ricochet shot, still refused to yield one foot of ground. Napoleon rode through his ranks, cheering on the exhausted columns of infantry and cavalry, that rent the heavens with the shout of "*Vive l'Empereur!*" and dashed with unparalleled recklessness on the bayonets of the English.

The hero of Wagram, and Borodino, and Austerlitz, and Marengo, and Jena, enraged at the stubborn obstinacy of the British, rode over the field, and was still sure of victory. Wellington, seeing that he could not much longer sustain the desperate charges of the French battalions, wiped the sweat from his anxious forehead, and exclaimed, "Oh, that Blucher or night would come!" Thus from eleven till four did the battle rage with sanguinary ferocity, and still around the centre it grew more awful every moment. The mangled cavalry staggered up to the exhausted British squares, which, though diminished and bleeding in every part, seemed rooted to the ground they stood upon. The heroic Picton had fallen at the head of his brigade, while his sword was flashing over his head. Ponsonby had gone down on the hard-fought field, and terror and slaughter were on every side; still the charge of the French cavalry on the centre was terrific. Disregarding the close and murderous fire of the British batteries, they rode steadily forward till they came to the bayonet's point, and then firmly urged their horses heads against the barrier, but in vain pierced through, and broken, they were rolled back over the field, but rallied again and again to the charge, and prodigies of valour were wrought, and heroes fell at every discharge. The rent and trodden field ran blood, yet through the deep mud the determined foemen pressed on, while out of the smoke of every volley arose from the French lines the shout of "*Vive l'Empereur!*"

THE CHARGE OF THE OLD GUARD

At length a dark object was seen to emerge from the distant wood, and soon an army of 30,000 men deployed into the field, and began to march straight for the scene of conflict. Blucher and his Prussians had come, but no Grouchy, who had been left to hold them in check, followed after. In a moment Napoleon saw that he could not sustain the attack of so many fresh troops, if once allowed to form a junction with the allied forces, and so he determined to stake his fate on one bold cast, and endeavour to pierce the allied centre with a grand charge of the Old Guard and, thus throwing himself between the two armies, fight them separately. For this purpose the Imperial Guard was called up, which had remained inactive during the whole day, and divided into two immense columns, which were to meet at the British centre. That under Reille no sooner entered the fire than it disappeared. The other was placed under Ney, the "bravest of the brave," and the order to advance given. Napoleon accompanied them part way down the slope, and halting for a moment in a hollow, addressed them in his fiery, impetuous manner. He told them the battle rested with them, and that he relied on their valour. *"Vive l'Empereur!"* answered him with a shout that was heard all over the field of battle.

He then left them to Ney, who ordered the charge. Bonaparte has been blamed for not heading this charge himself; but he knew he could not carry that guard so far, nor hold them so long before the artillery, as Ney. The moral power the latter carried with him, from the reputation he bad gained of being the "bravest of the brave," was worth a whole division. Whenever a column saw him at their head, they knew that it was to be victory or annihilation. With the exception of Macdonald, I do not know a general in the two armies who could hold his soldiers so long in the very face of destruction, as he.

The whole Continental struggle exhibited no sublimer spectacle than this last effort of Napoleon to save his sinking empire. Europe had been put upon the plains of Waterloo to be battled for. The greatest military energy and skill the world possessed had been tasked to the utmost during the day. Thrones were tottering on the ensanguined field, and the shadows of fugitive kings flitted through the smoke of battle. Bonaparte's star trembled in the zenith now blazing out in its ancient splendour, now suddenly paling before his anxious eye. At length, when the Prussians appeared on the field, he resolved to stake Europe on one bold throw. He committed himself and France to Ney, and saw his empire rest on a single charge. The intense anxiety with which he watched the advance of that column, and the terrible suspense he suffered when the smoke of battle wrapped it from sight, and the utter despair of his great heart when the curtain lifted over a fugitive army, and the despairing shriek rung on every side, "*La garde recule, La garde recule,*" make us for the moment forget all the carnage in sympathy with his distress.

Ney felt the pressure of the immense responsibility on his brave heart, and resolved not to prove unworthy of the great trust committed to his care. Nothing could be more imposing than the movement of that grand column to the assault. That guard had never yet recoiled before a human foe, and the allied forces beheld with awe its firm and terrible advance to the final charge. For a moment the batteries stopped playing, and the firing ceased along the British lines, as without the beating of a drum, or the blast of a bugle, to cheer their steady courage, they moved in dead silence over the plain. The next moment the artillery opened, and the head of that gallant column seemed to sink into the earth. Rank after rank went down, yet they neither stopped nor faltered. Dissolving squadrons and whole battalions disappearing one after another in the destructive fire, affected not their steady courage. The ranks closed up as before, and, each treading over his fallen comrade, pressed firmly on. The horse which Ney rode fell under him, and he had scarcely mounted another before it also sank to the earth. Again and again did that unflinching man feel his steed sink down, till five had been shot under him. Then, with his uniform riddled with bullets, and his face singed and blackened with powder, he marched on foot with drawn sabre at the head of his men. In vain did the artillery hurl its storm of fire and lead into that living mass. Up to the very muzzles they pressed, and driving the artillerymen from their own pieces, pushed on through the English lines. But at that moment a file of soldiers who had lain flat on the ground, behind a low ridge of earth, suddenly rose and poured a volley in their very faces. Another and another followed till one broad sheet of flame rolled on their bosoms, and in such a fierce and unexpected flow that human courage could not withstand it. They reeled, shook, staggered back, then turned and fled. Ney was borne back in the refluent tide, and hurried over the field. But for the crowd of fugitives that forced him on, he would have stood alone, and fallen on his footsteps. As it was, disdaining to fly, though the whole army was flying, he formed his men into two immense squares, and endeavoured to stem the terrific current, and would have done so had it not been for the 30,000 fresh Prussians that pressed on his exhausted ranks. For a long time these squares stood and let the artillery plough through them. But the fate of Napoleon was writ, and though Ney doubtless did what no other man in the army could have done, the decree could not be reversed. The star that had blazed so brightly over the world went down in blood, and the "bravest of the brave" had fought his last battle. It was worthy of his great name, and the charge of the Old Guard at Waterloo, with him at their head, will be pointed to by remotest generations with a shudder.

We now come to the expiation of his treason by a public execution. The allies, after they assembled in Paris, demanded some victims to appease their anger. Many were selected, but better counsel prevailed, and they were saved. Ney was a prominent example; he had routed their armies too frequently, and too nearly wrested their crowns from them at Waterloo, to be forgiven. It was intended at first to try him by martial law, but the Marshals of France refused to sit in judgment on so brave, generous, and heroic a warrior. By a royal ordinance, the Chamber of Peers was then directed to try him. Scorning to take advantage of any technicalities of the law, he was speedily found guilty and condemned to death, by a majority of a hundred and fifty-two. Seventeen only were found to vote in his favour. That he was guilty of treason in the letter of the charge is evident, but not to that extent which demanded his death. No man had done more for France than he, or loved her honour and glory with a higher affection; and his ignominious death is a lasting disgrace to the French nation. Justice was the excuse, not the ground, of his condemnation. To have carried out the principle on which his sentence was based would have ended in a public massacre. Ney and Labedoyère were the only victims offered up to appease an unjust hatred. Besides, Ney's person was sacred under a solemn treaty that Wellington had himself made. One of the articles of that treaty expressly declared that "no person should be molested for his political conduct or opinions during the hundred days." On such conditions was Paris surrendered, and there never was a more flagrant violation of national honour than the trial of Ney. The whole affair, from beginning to end, was a deliberate murder, committed from feelings of revenge alone. Napoleon never did so base an act in his life and on Wellington's forehead is a spot that shall grow darker with time, and cause many a curse to be muttered over his grave. He should have interfered to have saved so gallant an enemy at the hazard of his life, but be let his honour go down before the clamour of vindictive enemies, and become a *murderer* in the sight of the world. *Ney was publicly shot as a traitor.*

His last moments did not disgrace his life. He was called from his bed and a tranquil sleep to hear his sentence read. As the preamble went on enumerating his many titles he hastily broke in, "Why cannot you simply call me Michael Ney, now a French soldier and soon a heap of dust?" The last interview with his wife and children shook his stern heart more than all the battles he had passed through, or his approaching death. This over he resumed his wonted calmness. In reply to one of his sentinels, who said, "Marshal, you should now think of death," he replied, "Do you suppose any one should teach me to die?" But recollecting himself, he said in a milder tone, "Comrade, you are right, send for the curate of St. Sulpice; I will die as becomes a Christian!" As he alighted from the coach, he advanced toward the file of soldiers drawn up as executioners, with the same calm mien he was wont to exhibit on the field of battle. An officer stepping forward to bandage his eyes, he stopped him with the proud interrogation, "Are you ignorant that for twenty-five years I have been accustomed to face both ball and bullets?" He then took off his hat, and with his eagle eye, now subdued and solemn, turned toward heaven, and with the same calm and decided voice that had turned the tide of so many battles, "I declare before God and man, that I have never betrayed my country; may my death render her happy! *Vive la France!*" He then turned to the soldiers, and gazing on them a moment, struck one hand upon his heart and said, "My comrades, fire on me." Ten balls entered him, and he fell dead. Shame upon his judges that for a single act could condemn one braver and nobler than they all to a base death. A sterner warrior never trod a battlefield a kinder heart never beat in a human bosom, and a truer patriot never shed his blood for his country. If France never has a worse traitor, the days of her betrayal will be far distant, and if she has no worse defender, disgrace will never visit her armies. Says Colonel Napier, in speaking of his death, "thus he who had fought *five hundred battles* for France not *one* against her was shot as a traitor."

His wife was on her knees before the King praying for his pardon when the fatal news was brought her, and immediately fainted away, then went into convulsions, which well-nigh added another victim to this base murder. His father, who loved him tenderly as the son of his pride and the glory of his name, was never told of his ignominious death. He was at this time eighty-eight years of age, and lived to be a hundred years old. He saw by the mourning weeds of his family that some catastrophe had happened, and his father's heart told him too well where the bolt had struck; but he made no inquiries, and though he lived for twelve years after, never mentioned his son's name, and was never told of his fate. He knew he was dead, but he asked not how or where he died.

The great fault in Ney's character was indolence. Unless his energies were summoned from their repose by some pressing danger, he was inclined to inactivity. Yet this tendency, which has so often been severely censured, is almost necessarily associated with the prodigious power and resolution he possessed. The Lion is not easily roused and strength is always immobile till there is a call equal to its capacity. The heavy English squares can never be converted into light troops without losing their invincible tenacity.

He was also plain and direct even to bluntness, and often offended his friends by the freedom with which he spoke of their errors. He never lost sight of his low origin and was never ashamed of it. To some young officers boasting of their rank, titles, etc., he said, "Gentlemen, I was less fortunate than you. I got nothing from my family, and I esteemed myself rich at Metz, when I had two loaves of bread on my table." Simple and austere in his habits, he reminds one of an old Greek or Roman hero. The vacillation of feeling which caused him to commit the great error of his life adds to our sympathy with him, while it injures the perfection of his character. It led him to be a humane soldier, and when second in command frequently to disobey orders for the execution of criminals. He died in debt, having saved nothing from all his toils. His last words were for France, and his last injunction to his children not to treasure any feelings of animosity towards those who had slain him.

A small monument still stands in the garden of the Luxembourg, on the spot where he fell, but his noblest monument is in the hearts of men, who will take care that his fame survives that of his destroyers.

The Empire of Napoleon had departed forever; the infamous coalitions had finally triumphed, and despotism slowly settled back to its ancient places, but not to its ancient strength. The putrid mass still heaves on the subdued but not chained billows, and its doom on the continent is writ. Said Robert Hall, that great as well as good man, "When I heard of the result of the battle of Waterloo, I felt as if the clock of the world had gone back six ages." Let those who so readily adopt English authorities respecting Napoleon's wars, ask themselves why this Christian divine and Englishman uttered such a sentiment.

Let all who regard Napoleon as a scourge of his race go and ask Italy and Prussia, and Sweden and Poland the Waldenses of Piedmont the Caucasians of Asia the Jews of Paris, and all the people of France how much they think they have gained by his overthrow. Let them ask Italy, groaning under Austrian and Papal tyranny till one fruitless conspiracy follows another in quick succession, ending only in the death and banishment of patriots, and the despair of noble hearts. Let them ask the people of Prussia, who, when his fearless hand was ringing with such rapid strokes the death-knell of feudalism on the continent, demanded from their king a constitution and congress, and obtained the royal promise they should be given aye, ask them now, when after long years that promise has not been fulfilled, and the bold man who dare publish the *fier fragen* (four questions) demanding why it had not been fulfilled, has been condemned to two years' imprisonment for his presumption. Let them ask Poland, the last symbol of whose nationality disappeared forever in the carnage of Waterloo. Let them ask Sweden what she gained by the victory of Dennewitz and the disasters of Leipzig, as she now sits and trembles under the frown of Russia, daring only to throw in her childish complaint as that haughty power threatens momentarily to make of her merely a dependent province in name as she is in fact. Let them ask the brave and unconquerable tribes that still struggle for their ancient rights amid the forests and mountain gorges of Caucasus, what they think of the success which has emboldened despots to carry out those aggressions which have so long made the world mourn. Let them ask the Waldenses, who, under the sword of Napoleon, for the first time saw light beaming on their darkness, and in spite of Papal complaints, and the astonishment of Catholic kings, stood up amid their countrymen, freemen endowed with all the rights of citizenship, and free to worship God as their consciences dictated how *they* feel when they think of Waterloo. The shout that despotism sent up from that fatal field was the knell of their hopes and the end of their joy. From its bloody margin, the wave of oppression surged slowly back, till it covered once more their mountain homes and the altars of their sacred religion. To them the name of Bonaparte is that of a deliverer, under his sway they sat down in peace and freedom; at his fall they fell in tears, and have wept ever since. Let them ask the thousands of the Jews in Paris, who, for the first time under any Christian or infidel king, heard themselves with astonishment called to assemble like freeborn subjects, and addressed as men, with promises of future protection how they regard the Christian thanksgiving that followed the downfall of him on whom his enemies have fixed the brand of "Scourge of God." Let them ask the people of France, and the lovers of human progress the world over, what man and liberty gained by the disappearance of that power which shed such terror and dismay on the hearts of oppressors. Let silent Italy, and rent Poland and the starving millions of Europe, have a voice in the general outcry, before the unjust decision is ratified.

The prejudice and falsehood that have loaded France with crime begin already to be detected, and every year will see the woes and suffering of the wars she carried on rolled from her shoulders, and laid at the door of England and Russia, and Austria and Prussia.

I have never endeavoured to justify Napoleon's wrong acts by offsetting them with similar outrages committed by his foes, nor to defend an unjust war of France because other nations exhibited equal recklessness and want of honesty. The comparisons of this kind have all been made for one single purpose to prove that Napoleon and France do not deserve the exclusive condemnation which has been meted out to them. I have designed to place Napoleon above the monarchs that surrounded him, both in virtue and genius not to make him a model for the conduct of others.

ALSO FROM LEONAUR
AVAILABLE IN SOFTCOVER OR HARDCOVER WITH DUST JACKET

SEPOYS, SIEGE & STORM by *Charles John Griffiths*—The Experiences of a young officer of H.M.'s 61st Regiment at Ferozepore, Delhi ridge and at the fall of Delhi during the Indian mutiny 1857.

CAMPAIGNING IN ZULULAND by *W. E. Montague*—Experiences on campaign during the Zulu war of 1879 with the 94th Regiment.

THE STORY OF THE GUIDES by *G. J. Younghusband*—The Exploits of the Soldiers of the famous Indian Army Regiment from the northwest frontier 1847 - 1900..

ZULU: 1879 by *D.C.F. Moodie & the Leonaur Editors*—The Anglo-Zulu War of 1879 from contemporary sources: First Hand Accounts, Interviews, Dispatches, Official Documents & Newspaper Reports.

THE RECOLLECTIONS OF SKINNER OF SKINNER'S HORSE by *James Skinner*—James Skinner and his 'Yellow Boys' Irregular cavalry in the wars of India between the British, Mahratta, Rajput, Mogul, Sikh & Pindarree Forces.

TOMMY ATKINS' WAR STORIES 14 FIRST HAND ACCOUNTS—Fourteen first hand accounts from the ranks of the British Army during Queen Victoria's Empire Original & True Battle Stories Recollections of the Indian Mutiny With the 49th in the Crimea With the Guards in Egypt The Charge of the Six Hundred With Wolseley in Ashanti Alma, Inkermann and Magdala With the Gunners at Tel-el-Kebir Russian Guns and Indian Rebels Rough Work in the Crimea In the Maori Rising Facing the Zulus From Sebastopol to Lucknow Sent to Save Gordon On the March to Chitral Tommy by Rudyard Kipling

CHASSEUR OF 1914 by *Marcel Dupont*—Experiences of the twilight of the French Light Cavalry by a young officer during the early battles of the great war in Europe.

TROOP HORSE & TRENCH by *R. A. Lloyd*—The experiences of a British Lifeguardsman of the household cavalry fighting on the western front during the First World War 1914-18.

THE EAST AFRICAN MOUNTED RIFLES by *C. J. Wilson*—Experiences of the campaign in the East African bush during the First World War.

THE FIGHTING CAMELIERS by *Frank Reid*—The exploits of the Imperial Camel Corps in the desert and Palestine campaigns of the First World War.

AVAILABLE ONLINE AT
www.leonaur.com
AND OTHER GOOD BOOK STORES

ALSO FROM LEONAUR
AVAILABLE IN SOFTCOVER OR HARDCOVER WITH DUST JACKET

THE COMPLEAT RIFLEMAN HARRIS by Benjamin Harris as told to & transcribed by Captain Henry Curling—The adventures of a soldier of the 95th (Rifles) during the Peninsular Campaign of the Napoleonic Wars

WITH WELLINGTON'S LIGHT CAVALRY by William Tomkinson—The Experiences of an officer of the 16th Light Dragoons in the Peninsular and Waterloo campaigns of the Napoleonic Wars.

SERGEANT BOURGOGNE by Adrien Bourgogne—With Napoleon's Imperial Guard in the Russian Campaign and on the Retreat from Moscow 1812 - 13.

SWORDS OF HONOUR by Henry Newbolt & Stanley L. Wood—The Careers of Six Outstanding Officers from the Napoleonic Wars, the Wars for India and the American Civil War, with dozens of illustrations by Stanley L. Wood.

SURTEES OF THE RIFLES by William Surtees—A Soldier of the 95th (Rifles) in the Peninsular campaign of the Napoleonic Wars.

ENSIGN BELL IN THE PENINSULAR WAR by George Bell—The Experiences of a young British Soldier of the 34th Regiment 'The Cumberland Gentlemen' in the Napoleonic wars.

HUSSAR IN WINTER by Alexander Gordon—A British Cavalry Officer during the retreat to Corunna in the Peninsular campaign of the Napoleonic Wars.

NAPOLEONIC WAR STORIES by Sir Arthur Quiller-Couch—Tales of soldiers, spies, battles & sieges from the Peninsular & Waterloo campaingns.

JOURNALS OF ROBERT ROGERS OF THE RANGERS by Robert Rogers—The exploits of Rogers & the Rangers in his own words during 1755-1761 in the French & Indian War.

KERSHAW'S BRIGADE VOLUME 1 by D. Augustus Dickert—Manassas, Seven Pines, Sharpsburg (Antietam), Fredricksburg, Chancellorsville, Gettysburg, Chickamauga, Chattanooga, Fort Sanders & Bean Station..

KERSHAW'S BRIGADE VOLUME 2 by D. Augustus Dickert—At the wilderness, Cold Harbour, Petersburg, The Shenandoah Valley and Cedar Creek.

A TIGER ON HORSEBACK by L. March Phillips—The Experiences of a Trooper & Officer of Rimington's Guides - The Tigers - during the Anglo-Boer war 1899 - 1902.

AVAILABLE ONLINE AT
www.leonaur.com
AND OTHER GOOD BOOK STORES

ALSO FROM LEONAUR
AVAILABLE IN SOFTCOVER OR HARDCOVER WITH DUST JACKET

CAPTAIN OF THE 95th (Rifles) *by Jonathan Leach*—An officer of Wellington's Sharpshooters during the Peninsular, South of France and Waterloo Campaigns of the Napoleonic Wars.

THE KHAKEE RESSALAH *by Robert Henry Wallace Dunlop*—Service & adventure with the Meerut volunteer horse during the Indian mutiny 1857-1858

BUGLER AND OFFICER OF THE RIFLES *by William Green & Harry Smith* With the 95th (Rifles) during the Peninsular & Waterloo Campaigns of the Napoleonic Wars

BAYONETS, BUGLES AND BONNETS *by James 'Thomas' Todd*—Experiences of hard soldiering with the 71st Foot - the Highland Light Infantry - through many battles of the Napoleonic wars including the Peninsular & Waterloo Campaigns

A NORFOLK SOLDIER IN THE FIRST SIKH WAR *by J W Baldwin*—Experiences of a private of H.M. 9th Regiment of Foot in the battles for the Punjab, India 1845-46

A CAVALRY OFFICER DURING THE SEPOY REVOLT *by A.R.D. Mackenzie*—Experiences with the 3rd Bengal Light Cavalry, the Guides and Sikh Irregular Cavalry from the outbreak to Delhi and Lucknow

THE ADVENTURES OF A LIGHT DRAGOON *by George Farmer & G.R. Gleig*—A cavalryman during the Peninsular & Waterloo Campaigns, in captivity & at the siege of Bhurtpore, India

THE COMPLEAT RIFLEMAN HARRIS *by Benjamin Harris as told to & transcribed by Captain Henry Curling*—The adventures of a soldier of the 95th (Rifles) during the Peninsular Campaign of the Napoleonic Wars

THE RED DRAGOON *by W.J. Adams*—With the 7th Dragoon Guards in the Cape of Good Hope against the Boers & the Kaffir tribes during the 'war of the axe' 1843-48

THE LIFE OF THE REAL BRIGADIER GERARD - Volume 1 - THE YOUNG HUSSAR 1782 - 1807 *by Jean-Baptiste De Marbot*—A French Cavalryman Of the Napoleonic Wars at Marengo, Austerlitz, Jena, Eylau & Friedland

THE LIFE OF THE REAL BRIGADIER GERARD Volume 2 IMPERIAL AIDE-DE-CAMP 1807 - 1811 *by Jean-Baptiste De Marbot*—A French Cavalryman of the Napoleonic Wars at Saragossa, Landshut, Eckmuhl, Ratisbon, Aspern-Essling, Wagram, Busaco & Torres Vedras

AVAILABLE ONLINE AT
www.leonaur.com
AND OTHER GOOD BOOK STORES

ALSO FROM LEONAUR
AVAILABLE IN SOFTCOVER OR HARDCOVER WITH DUST JACKET

EW2 EYEWITNESS TO WAR SERIES
CAPTAIN OF THE 95th (Rifles) *by Jonathan Leach*

An officer of Wellington's Sharpshooters during the Peninsular, South of France and Waterloo Campaigns of the Napoleonic Wars.

SOFTCOVER : **ISBN 1-84677-001-7**
HARDCOVER : **ISBN 1-84677-016-5**

WF1 THE WARFARE FICTION SERIES
NAPOLEONIC WAR STORIES
by Sir Arthur Quiller-Couch

Tales of soldiers, spies, battles & Sieges from the Peninsular & Waterloo campaigns

SOFTCOVER : **ISBN 1-84677-003-3**
HARDCOVER : **ISBN 1-84677-014-9**

EW1 EYEWITNESS TO WAR SERIES
RIFLEMAN COSTELLO *by Edward Costello*

The adventures of a soldier of the 95th (Rifles) in the Peninsular & Waterloo Campaigns of the Napoleonic wars.

SOFTCOVER : **ISBN 1-84677-000-9**
HARDCOVER : **ISBN 1-84677-018-1**

MC1 THE MILITARY COMMANDERS SERIES
JOURNALS OF ROBERT ROGERS OF THE RANGERS *by Robert Rogers*

The exploits of Rogers & the Rangers in his own words during 1755-1761 in the French & Indian War.

SOFTCOVER : **ISBN 1-84677-002-5**
HARDCOVER : **ISBN 1-84677-010-6**

AVAILABLE ONLINE AT
www.leonaur.com
AND OTHER GOOD BOOK STORES

www.ingramcontent.com/pod-product-compliance
Lightning Source LLC
Chambersburg PA
CBHW020938230426
43666CB00005B/74